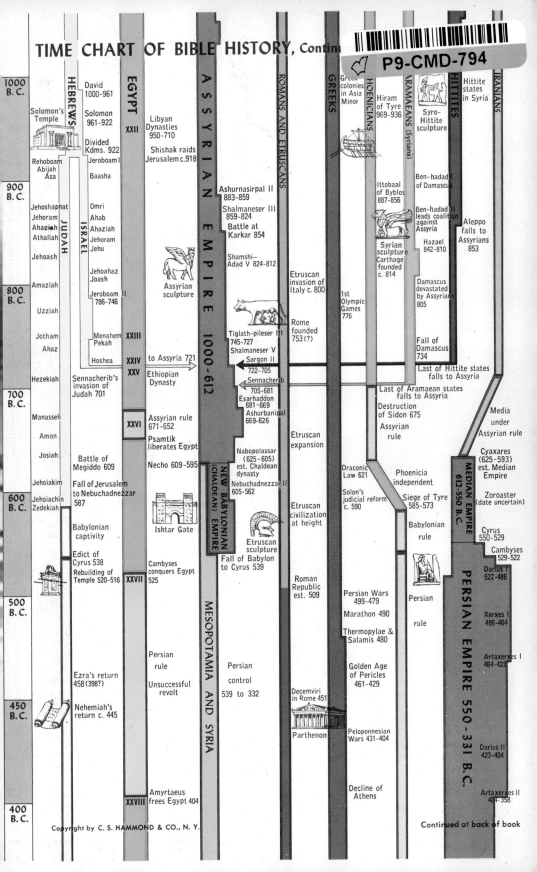

TIME CHART OF BIBLE HISTORY, Continued

GOD'S KINGDOM
IN THE
OLD TESTAMENT

GOD'S KINGDOM
IN THE
OLD TESTAMENT

by

Rev. Martin K. Hopkins, O.P.

HENRY REGNERY COMPANY

Chicago   1964

Nihil Obstat:

Very Rev. J. S. Considine, O.P., S.T.M.
Rev. S. J. Oatis, O.P.

Imprimi Potest:

Very Rev. J. E. Marr, O.P., S.T.M., Provincial

Imprimatur:

†Most Rev. Edward A. Fitzgerald, D.D.
Bishop of Winona
April 3, 1963

1st Printing — 1964

2nd Printing — 1965

Foreword

Ours is a golden age of Bible interest, equal — as Pope Pius XII did not hesitate to say — to the most productive periods of the past. The contemporary biblical revival makes the twentieth century rank with the early days of the Fathers of the Church and with the energetic days following the Council of Trent. Just as it would be flying in the face of all scholarly procedure to ignore the Bible when attempting a study of the early Middle Ages, or even a small segment of Medieval life like the miracle play, likewise, would a student be guilty of sloth or bigotry to overlook the present biblical revival and yet pretend to evaluate the present state of religion or the forces behind the Second Vatican Council.

Religion, however, is more than an historical movement. Its effect upon the human race exceeds the impact, for instance, of the eighteenth and nineteenth century industrial revolution and the twentieth century probe of outer space. More than any other element of life, religion lies at the heart of human existence, where men and women form attitudes and ideals, confront problems and seek their solution, imbibe strength for heroic endeavors and make decisions of lifelong consequence. Religion is as relevant to life as God is, for religion is the attitude taken by man and society before God. Some people use names other than "God" and "religion," but all seek some ultimate goal and all have laid down a way to get there. The quest for the supreme, the desire for a practical plan of achievement — these hopes are imbedded deeply in each man. We call the way "religion" and the goal "Almighty God."

The source of religious truth is the Bible; the heart of religion is God. Whatever affects man's understanding of the Bible, therefore, will sway all the rest of his life. During the last sixty years a great transformation has swept through biblical studies which we cannot ignore.

Not only does Scripture regulate religion, and religion direct life, but the reverse is also true. What happens in life reacts upon religion and the study of the Bible. Modern influences touch almost every segment of biblical knowledge. This interaction is not at all regrettable but highly appreciated, for it makes religion relevant to anyone interested in life at this moment of history.

vii

In the contemporary study of the Bible, we detect, for instance: *historical interests,* to disentangle later additions from the original accounts of Abraham, Moses and other great leaders, and thus to reconstruct the social and cultural background of their age; *literary interests,* to distinguish various types of myth, folklore, genealogy, satire, sagas, songs, aphorisms, etc.; *liturgical interests,* to associate various sections of the Bible with sanctuary worship and temple festivals; *comparative religion interests,* to understand biblical theology from the ritual, songs and practices of neighboring peoples; *scientific or philosophic interests,* to differentiate the Hebrew approach towards creation, the universe, the nature of man and the process of knowledge, from our modern approach; *theological interests,* to isolate the functional or existential presentation of doctrine in the Bible, from the more theoretical or essential presentation of modern theology books.

The impact of modern scientific method is not only shaking dust off the ancient Bible; it is also making the college student wake up to all kinds of questions about religion.

College students are asking serious questions which profoundly affect their faith in the Christian God, their appreciation of organized religion, their trust in tradition, their respect for religious authority. Changes have admittedly taken place in Catholic biblical scholarship. Has doctrine changed? Exactly what has taken place?

The college student is challenging the theology professor. He wants frank, clear answers, not age-old platitudes. If one hundred per cent certitude is impossible, then, he is willing to accept provisional answers. But at the same time, particularly in matters of religion, he wants to know: "Why can't you give me a final answer?" This attitude is not disrespect but honesty.

Professor and students, in any case, can reach no answer without careful, mature study. Too much is at stake to hazard quick, unscholarly replies. If the Bible is to be subjected to the exacting procedure of modern scholarship, then the same scientific energy must regulate the quest for a solution.

More than scientific integrity, however, is expected of a Bible student. Because the scriptures are so intimately associated with life and touch man at the heart of his existence, the scriptures must not be approached with the cold aloofness of a chemical analysis but with the personal involvement of psychoanalysis. The Bible, in fact, demands even more. A psychologist never becomes a member of a family in order to grasp the problems of that family, but the Bible student must belong to the family of God's people to fully appreciate what is happening in the Word of God. In the case of Scripture, a student must live in order to know; he is obliged to experience the redemptive acts of God before he can summarize his conclusions about them.

St. Paul advises us:

Wisdom, however, we speak among those who are mature, yet not a wisdom of this world nor of the rulers of this world, who are passing away. But we speak the wisdom of God, mysterious, hidden, which God foreordained before the world unto our glory, a wisdom which none of the rulers of this world has known; for had they known it, they would never have crucified the Lord of glory. But, as it is written, 'Eye has not seen nor ear heard, nor has it entered into the heart of man, what things God has prepared for those who love him.' But to us God has revealed them through his Spirit. For the Spirit searches all things, even the deep things of God. . . . Now we have received not the spirit of the world, but the spirit that is from God, that we may know the things that have been given us by God.

Faith is a participation in the life of God, a sharing in His Knowledge. Faith alone, however, is not sufficient, at least not sufficient for the college student who would exert a control upon his knowledge and possess a power to communicate it to others. Modern, scientific methodology in the study of the Bible helps him to distinguish God's genuine idea from his own pious reactions. It also prepares him to present biblical knowledge in a style congenial to the contemporary world.

Fr. Martin Hopkins, O.P., combines the deep faith of our forefathers with the scientific method of today, and in so doing has prepared an excellent college text in the Old Testament. He doesn't give quick, catechism answers; often, he simply points the way to a solution by indicating the trends of modern biblical research. He remains, however, the practical, experienced teacher. He usually cites not books but pages, so that the busy student will lose no time. He includes charts, maps and outlines. He realizes that the religion course, like most areas of modern life, is limited by an inadequate budget of time.

He provides professor and student with a working schema of thirty chapters, each one normally representing a single class assignment. The text fits excellently into a two-credit course, and at the end the student will have a mature grasp not only of the onward sweep of salvation history, moving forward to the fullness of time in Christ Jesus, but also of each Old Testament book which appears along the way from Genesis to Second Machabees.

This textbook, it has already been said, challenges the college student. If it asks serious questions about the Bible, then it presumes that the student is anxious to work intellectually for a satisfying answer. In this scientific search to understand *God's Kingdom in the Old Testament*, Fr. Hopkins never lets the student forget that the Bible above all else is salvation-history, involving faith, obedience, humility and compunction.

No textbook on the Bible can give answers of such luminous clarity as to remove all further questioning. The Bible, treating of God and man in the existential level of human history, is involved in the greatest of mysteries. The Bible student is seeking *some* intellectual grasp of a matter far beyond the limits of his intellectual ability. God is not to be contained within the area of any man's mind. God comes to the student's and professor's assistance with the gift of faith, a humble willingness to accept the message of the Bible simply because God has spoken and acted. This message places demands, however, not only upon the intellect but also upon every area of student and adult life. God's word is not always easy, but once we know that *God* has spoken, we have only the alternatives of obedience, leading to life in the family of God; or disobedience, plunging one to eventual destruction. Compunction will frequently bring a sinful Bible reader to his knees, begging forgiveness as he puts himself next to the image of what he should be in Christ Jesus.

The biblical message, most of all, is *spirit and life,* for God is the Word, mysteriously spoken in the Bible and still more mysteriously heard in the soul of the reader. Heard obediently with faith, the word of God becomes the life of Jesus within the Christian.

Students will be grateful for this guide to God's kingdom, for to know Christ in the scriptures is to live eternally. *This is everlasting life, that they may know thee, the only true God, and him whom thou has sent, Jesus Christ.*

CARROLL STUHLMUELLER, C. P.
Passionist Fathers Seminary
Louisville, Kentucky

May 4, 1963

Preface

Basically, this book represents a college text in the Old Testament. It includes in the first four and the last chapters what is ordinarily covered under the title of "Introduction to the Bible." In addition, it contains a thorough reading guide to all of the inspired books from Genesis to II Machabees. Designed for a two-hour, one-semester course, the material is divided into 30 chapters, each one normally representing a single class assignment. Thus, the knotty problem of which chapters of the individual books should be read and which may be skipped is provided for. Key passages, both historical and messianic, are noted at the beginning of each chapter along with the assigned reading.

Particular emphasis is given to the concept of salvation history and the key ideas associated with it: Original Justice and the Fall; the Covenant; the Ark and the Temple; the Theocracy, Kingdom, and Davidic Dynasty; Prophecy; Exile, the Remnant and the Anawim. Because Sacred Scripture uses the historical dimension so extensively, considerable background material in this area is included in the form of dates, genealogical charts, etc. Students will perhaps find this feature one of the most valuable contributions of this text, making the purchase of three or four supplementary books unnecessary. The aim has been to bring together in one text all of the data, from the latest solid biblical research, needed to understand the Old Testament. Outside reading suggestions are also provided with each chapter.

Special treatment is accorded to Semitic literary genres, together with the literary history of the Old Testament. Moden scholarship has proven this to be an indispensable key to understanding the biblical message. The important contribution of the Wisdom Literature is not overlooked. Because of their peculiar significance, the Psalms are spread throughout the whole text and studied one at a time. By taking at least one Psalm with each chapter beginning with Chapter 5, this text considers in detail nearly forty key poems of the Psalter.

Last but not least, this book is designed to clarify the Old Testament origins of the "Kingdom of God" concept which finds fulfillment only in the New Testament. For this reason the author has produced a companion volume, *God's Kingdom in the New Testament*. The thread running through the whole work is the Kingdom of God in its various stages of development. In pursuit of this theme up to the birth of Christ, all of the significant religious, cultural, and political forces which accompanied and influenced its growth are treated in their natural context. Such religious bodies as the Pharisees and the Essenes, for example, are seen as divisions of the Hasidim of the Machabean era. Besides providing a profound, stimulating theology of history, such an approach also furnishes the only adequate introduction to the New Testament.

Acknowledgement is due of the use of the biblical text published by the Confraternity of Christian Doctrine; this translation has been used for all quotations except those from the later historical books and from Tobias, Judith, and Esther. Gratitude is hereby expressed to the Newman Press for permission to quote from Charlier, *The Christian Approach to the Bible,* and from Dyson and Jones, *The Kingdom of Promise;* also to Prentice-Hall, Inc. for permission to quote from Anderson, *Understanding the Old Testament,* and to Desclee Company for permission to quote from Brillet, *Meditations on the Old Testament,* Vol. I; *The Narratives.*

Maps on pages xxi, 83, 188, 203 and quotations from *The Hebrew Scriptures,* c.1963 by Samuel Sandmel, reproduced through the courtesty of Alfred A. Knopf, Inc.

Note For The Instructor

Some chapters in this text will require more than one class. In particular, I have in mind Chapters 4, 28, and 30. On the other hand, you may find that certain pairs of chapters can be handled in a single class period, e.g., 6-7, 12-13. Usually not more than twenty chapters of Bible reading are assigned with any one chapter, though this procedure has been violated toward the end of the text. Constant reference is made throughout the New Testament in an attempt to let one inspired text interpret another wherever possible. Each instructor will have his or her own special emphases, and may wish to present a different interpretation of certain episodes. With this the author has no quarrel; what is set down here is not the last word in exegesis! The author only hopes that the text will provide a basic guide for a college Scripture course worthy of the title.

Table of Contents

Foreword vii

Preface xi

Table of Charts and Maps xvii

List of Principal Messianic Texts xix

Selected Bibliography xxiii

Chapter	TITLE	BASIC ASSIGNMENT	ADDITIONAL ASSIGNMENT*	
1.	THE WORKS OF GOD VS. THE WORKS OF MAN.	Text	(Vawter, Intro.) (Charlier, 15–27)	1
2.	THE WORK OF GOD: BIBLICAL INSPIRATION.	Text	(Bouyer, Chap. 1) (Charlier, 206– 220)	11
3.	THE WORK OF MAN: SEMITIC LITERARY GENRES.	Text	(Vann, Chap. 1) (Charlier, Chap. 5–8)	21
4.	A THEANDRIC WORK: THE "SENSES" OF SCRIPTURE.	Text	(Benoit, *Theology Digest* IX:1, 3–8)	30
5.	PRIESTLY AC-COUNT OF CRE-ATION: ALL THINGS COME FROM GOD!	Genesis 1; Ps. 103.	Eccles. 1:5–7 Job. 26:5–11	46
6.	THE GARDEN AND THE TREE OF LIFE: MAN'S HAPPINESS IN GOD'S IMAGE.	Genesis 2; Ps. 8.	*Summa Theologia,* Ia Qq. 95, 96, 100	57

*Consult bibliography for titles. Readings in parentheses are optional. All biblical texts in this column should be studied unless specifically excluded by the instructor for lack of time.

Chapter	TITLE	BASIC ASSIGNMENT	ADDITIONAL ASSIGNMENT*	
7.	THE TREE OF KNOWLEDGE: EXISTENCE WITHOUT GOD.	Genesis 3; Ps. 129.	*Beginnings,* Chap. 5	67
8.	SEMITIC GENE-ALOGIES: THE SPREAD OF SIN.	Genesis 4–11; Ps. 1.	Hasseveldt, 65–74	74
9.	ABRAHAM'S JUS-TIFICATION: THE NATURE OF FAITH.	Genesis 12–24; Ps. 22.	Romans 4, James 2, Hebrews 7, 11	82
10.	ISAAC, JACOB, JUDA: THE MES-SIANIC LINE.	Genesis 25–36; 38; Ps. 77.	Deuteronomy 25: 5–10	90
11.	JOSEPH IN EGYPT: PROVI-DENCE AND "PROPHECY".	Genesis 37; 39–50; Ps. 104, 105.	Wisdom 10	96
12.	THE CALL OF MOSES: A NEW REVELATION.	Exodus 1–6; Ps. 46.	Acts 7:17–43	101
13.	YAHWEH VS. PHARAO: THE "PASSOVER".	Exodus 7–13; Ps. 113.	Ez. 16:1–14; Rom. 9, Hasse-veldt, 75–83	107
14.	THEOPHANY AND THE-OCRACY: THE DECALOGUE.	Exodus 14–20; Ps. 135.	Numbers 11: 31–34; Wisdom 11; 13–19	113
15.	THE MOSAIC COVENANT: THE ARK AND THE PRESENCE.	Exodus 20–25; 32–34; 40; Ps. 18.	Galatians 3, 4	121
16.	THE LAW OF HOLINESS: LEVITICUS AND LITURGY.	Lev. 1–4, 8, 10–13:8, 17, 19, 23; Ps. 19, 20.	I Corinthians 10, Hebrews 9	127

Chapter	TITLE	BASIC ASSIGNMENT	ADDITIONAL ASSIGNMENT*	
17.	THE WILDERNESS: TEMPTATION AND THE TEST.	Numbers 6, 10–14, 16, 17, 20–25. Ps. 94.	Hebrews 3, 4	132
18.	THE DEUTERONOMIC TRADITION: A THEOLOGY OF HISTORY.	Deuteronomy 1–12, 17–19, 34; Ps. 90.		137
19.	JOSUE AND RUTH: "HEREM" AND THE ROLE OF THE GENTILES.	Josue 1–3, 6–8, 22, 24; Ruth 1–4; Ps. 86, 108.	Wisdom 12	145
20.	PERIOD OF THE JUDGES: FROM DELIVERER TO PROPHET.	Judges 2–8, 11–13, 16; I Kings 1–4, 8, 9.	Canticle of Anna	153
21.	SAUL VS. DAVID: KINGSHIP IN ISRAEL.	I Kings 10, 12, 15, 16, 18, 28, 31; II Kings 3, 6, 7, 11, 12, 15, 22.	Psalms 15, 23, 50, 100, 109, 131	160
22.	SOLOMON'S FALL FROM WISDOM INTO IDOLATRY: ISRAEL VS. JUDA.	III Kings 1, 3, 6, 9, 11, 12, 15; Ps. 44, 126.	Wis. 6-9; Prov. 1, 3, 4, 6, 10, 22, 25, 31	170
23.	ELIAS, AMOS, OSEE: A NEW THEOPHANY AND THE GOLDEN AGE OF PROPHECY.	III Kings 17–19 IV Kings 1, 2, 5 Amos, 3, 5, 7–9 Osee 1–4, 6, 8, 11 Ps. 49, 102	Canticles 2, 6	180
24.	FIRST ISAIA: GOD'S TRANSCENDENCE AND THE DAVIDIC DYNASTY.	IV Kings 16–20; Isaia 1–12; Psalm 138.	Michea 6; Nahum 3; Soph. 1; Habacuc 1	189

Chapter	TITLE	BASIC ASSIGNMENT	ADDITIONAL ASSIGNMENT*	
25.	JEREMIA: EXILE AND THE INTIMACY OF GOD.	IV Kings 21–25; Jeremia 1, 16, 20, 25, 27, 31, 36, 43; Ps. 136.	Lamentations 1, 3; Baruch 3; Abdia; Hebrews 8	196
26.	EZECHIEL AND SECOND ISAIA: THE NEW ISRAEL AND SUFFERING SERVANT.	Ezechiel 10, 11, 18, 20, 37, 43, 44; Isaia 40–45, 53, 58, 65; Ps. 21.	Jona 1–4, Hebrews 7	204
27.	ESDRAS AND NEHEMIA: THE CANONICAL TORAH AND SHAPING OF JUDAISM.	I Esdras 1, 5–6; II Esdras 2, 4, 8, 9, 13; Psalms 146–147.	Zach. 3, 4, 6, 9, 12, 13. Joel 1–4; Malachia 1–3	211
28.	FROM PERSIAN TO GREEK DOMINATION: WISDOM CIRCUMCISED.	Eccles. 1–3; Job 1–3, 8–10, 28, 38, 40, 42; Sirach 1–3, 6, 7, 24, 34, 35, 39–41; 44–51; Ps. 118.	Esther 3, 9; I Machabees 1	217
29.	TOBIAS AND MACHABEES: HASIDIM TO PHARISEES.	I Mach. 2; II Mach, 2, 6, 7, 10, 12; Ps. 41–42.	Tobias 1–14	224
30.	DANEL, JUDITH, WISDOM: THE EVERLASTING KINGDOM AND IMMORTALITY.	Daniel 1–3, 5, 7, 9, 12, 14; Wis. 1–5; Ps. 71, 72.	Judith 1, 5, 7, 8, 10–13	231

Appendix

On the Canon of the Old Testament 241

Myth in Genesis 243

Indexes

General Index 248

Index of Psalms 256

Table of Charts and Maps

List of Principal Messianic Texts xix

The Exodus and Wanderings in the Desert xxi

Bibliography xxiii

History of Divine Communication, and Genealogy of Christ ... 9

Semitic Literary Genres 27

Senses of Sacred Scripture 36

Deposits of Faith 39

Introductory Theses 43

Semitic Cosmogony 48

Literary History of the Old Testament 53

Original Justice 61

Evolutionism 64

Genealogies in Genesis, Chapters 4, 5, 10, 11 77

Duplicate Accounts of the Deluge Story 78

Source Readings for Genesis, Chapters 4–11 (For More Intensive
Study) 81

Peoples of the Ancient Near East 83

The Messianic Line 90

The Ten Plagues 108

The Development of Languages 116

Midrashic Account of the Plagues in the Book of Wisdom 119

Classification of Laws (Including the Decalogue) 123

Tabernacle, Ark, Altar of Sacrifice, Bronze Laver, Enclosure ... 125

Types of Hebrew Sacrifice 128

The Three Jewish Pilgrimage Feasts 130

Biblical Numerology 133

Formation of the Pentateuch 139

Division of Precepts in the Pentateuch 140

The Politico–Cultural Situation and the Development of Biblical
Literature 141

Table of Biblical Types, Antitypes, and Christian Symbols 142

Editorial Groupings of Old Testament Historical Books 146

Division of the Hebrew Bible 158

Correlation of the Four Books of Kings with I–II Paralipomenon 163

Classification of the Psalms (Genres) 169

Locations of the Ark and the Tabernacle 171

Kings of Israel and Juda 178

Yahweh–Israel compared with Osee–Gomer 185

Assyrian and Babylonian Empires 188

Tree, Trunk, Stump, Shoot 191

Persian and Greek Empires 203
The Books of Machabees 226
Syrian and Jewish Leaders of Machabean Era 228
Messianic Symbolism in Daniel 233
Division of the Book of Wisdom 238
Evolution of the Notion of Retribution 239
Catholic, Jewish, and Protestant Canons of the Old Testament .. 242

List of Principal Messianic Texts

1. GENESIS 3:15 (Cf. also Gen. 9:26, p. 79) 69–71
2. GENESIS 12:3 84
3. GENESIS 49:10 99
4. NUMBERS 24:17 136
5. DEUTERONOMY 18:15 141
6. II KINGS 7:11–13 (Cf. Psalm 131:11–12) 165
7. PSALM 109 165
8. PSALM 15:10–11 167
10. MICHEA 5:1 194
11. JEREMIA 22:30—23:6; 31:31–34 200–201
12. ISAIA 53 208–209
13. PSALM 21 210
14. MALACHIA 1:11, 3:23 216
15. DANIEL 7:13, 14, 18; 9:24–27 233–234
16. PSALM 71 257

In presenting this summary of messianic texts, the author has no intention of giving the impression that they constitute a series of thumb-nail sketches of Jesus Christ. On the contrary, this presentation is intended more as a cautionary measure against engaging in the bogus apologetical procedure which would see the texts as so many "clues" offered to the Jews to enable them to "solve" the mystery of the Messia as they would a detective story. One of the main lessons of a course in the Old Testament is the true nature of messianism. This term designated primarily an ERA to be characterized by the practical reign of God over the earth. The Israelites gradually developed the expectation that their nation would be the medium whereby this era would be established. Although it had universal implications, the messianic era would be especially beneficial to them. The historical origin of this conviction dates back to the promise made to Abraham and his descendants about 1850 B.C. Messianism, then, was a corporate concept.

Gradually the dimensions of messianic expectancy were narrowed down: first to the Tribe of Juda, then to the House of David. It seems that only with the waning of the Davidic dynasty did any clear notion of a personal (as opposed to a corporate, dynastic) Messia take shape.

And even with this development the concept of one individual saving the nation was not at all obvious as one king after another proved to be a miserable failure. It was the prophet Jeremia who finally broke with the dynasty as he envisaged a Davidic (but non-royal) "shoot" rising to the rescue (Jer. 23:5). Yet, for the most part the messianic hopes of Israel continued to be lodged with the remnant rather than with an individual champion (cf. Dan. 7:13,14,18). It was the unique genius of Christ that He alone recapitulated in His Person the totality of biblical messianism in a manner which transcended their wildest dreams.

At the very outset of the course, then, we desire to illustrate this point emphatically lest the unwary student stumble on the block hewn out by the traditional "biographical" apologetics. To offset this tendency, we have tried to present the Old Testament books largely from an historico-literary viewpoint — that is, by distinguishing the message from its envelope. This approach presupposes a working knowledge of Semitic mentality and literary types, as well as Jewish history. This information is supplied in the first four chapters and includes a literary "timetable" of the books of the Old Testament. If the student keeps these facts in mind he will not be greatly disillusioned as he notes that not one of the messianic texts treated is applied to Christ in its immediate, literal sense. Rather than focusing directly on the person of Christ, our interpretation suggests the *contemporary* person, place, or thing to which the sacred author seemed to be referring. In proceding thus we are not denying the messianic implications intended by the Holy Spirit; in most cases, we are merely shifting them from the literal to the typical sense. In fact, we are doing more: we are bearing witness to the fact that God chose to dramatize His divine economy of salvation in seemingly disconnected skits rather than content Himself with predicting them comprehensively in words. The human authors had never seen the whole play and they didn't understand the plot. For them, each skit had to be appreciated in the light of its own significance and those universal insights God chose to reveal to them. Today we realize that such insights were much more meager than previous generations were willing to admit.

One example will help to understand this method of interpretation. Let us take the first messianic text, Genesis 3:15: "I will put enmity between you and the woman, between your seed and her seed; he shall crush your head, and you shall lie in wait for his heel." Granting the messianic character of this passage in the broad sense outlined in the first paragraph, modern exegetes have greatly added to our knowledge of its meaning in tracing its *literary* origin to the Jewish scribe known as the "Yahwist" editor. This man (or men) probably lived in southern Palestine during the reign of Solomon (c.950 B.C.). At this

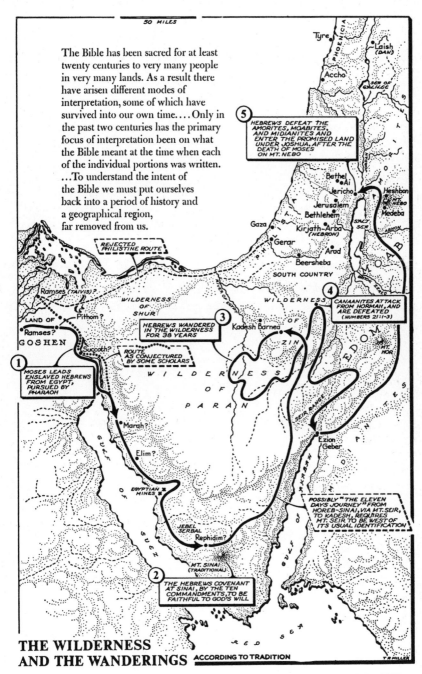

The Bible has been sacred for at least twenty centuries to very many people in very many lands. As a result there have arisen different modes of interpretation, some of which have survived into our own time.... Only in the past two centuries has the primary focus of interpretation been on what the Bible meant at the time when each of the individual portions was written. ...To understand the intent of the Bible we must put ourselves back into a period of history and a geographical region, far removed from us.

50 MILES

Tyre
Laish (DAN)
PHOENICIA
Accho
SEA OF GALILEE

⑤ HEBREWS DEFEAT THE AMORITES, MOABITES, AND MIDIANITES AND ENTER THE PROMISED LAND UNDER JOSHUA, AFTER THE DEATH OF MOSES ON MT. NEBO

Bethel
•Ai
Jericho
Jerusalem
Bethlehem
Gaza
Kirjath-Arba (HEBRON)
Gerar
•Arad
Beersheba
SOUTH COUNTRY
Heshbon
MT. NEBO
Medeba
MT. SEIR

REJECTED PHILISTINE ROUTE

WILDERNESS OF SHUR

Ramses (TAIVIS)?
Pithom?
LAND OF
Ramses?
GOSHEN
Succoth?

③ HEBREWS WANDERED IN THE WILDERNESS FOR 38 YEARS
Kadesh Barnea
ZIN
WILDERNESS OF

④ CANAANITES ATTACK FROM HORMAH, AND ARE DEFEATED (NUMBERS 21:1-3)

EDOM
MT. HOR.

ROUTE, AS CONJECTURED BY SOME SCHOLARS

① MOSES LEADS ENSLAVED HEBREWS FROM EGYPT, PURSUED BY PHARAOH

WILDERNESS OF PARAN

SEIR RANGE

•Marah?

•Elim?

EGYPTIAN MINES

Ezion Geber

POSSIBLY "THE ELEVEN DAYS JOURNEY" FROM HOREB-SINAI, VIA MT. SEIR, TO KADESH, REQUIRES MT. SEIR TO BE WEST OF ITS USUAL IDENTIFICATION

GULF OF SUEZ

JEBEL SERBAL
Rephidim?

GULF OF AKABAH

MT. SINAI (TRADITIONAL)

② THE HEBREWS COVENANT AT SINAI, BY THE TEN COMMANDMENTS, TO BE FAITHFUL TO GOD'S WILL

RED SEA

THE WILDERNESS
AND THE WANDERINGS   ACCORDING TO TRADITION

T.R.MILLER

"HE BROUGHT US OUT OF EGYPT WITH HIS STRONG HAND AND OUTSTRETCHED ARM" — ISRAEL'S CREED (Deut. 26:8)

period of Jewish history the great threat to the religious and national existence of the community was the surrounding pagan (Chanaanite) cult and culture. Solomon would have succumbed (or been in the process of succumbing) to the idolatrous worship of Baal through his polygamous unions with that god's devotees. The nature and fertility cults of Chanaan thus became proximate occasions of sin for the Chosen People. Inspired by the Holy Spirit to recall to their minds the primitive oracles of human redemption, the Yahwist editor couched his message in terms meaningful to his contemporaries. And so he deliberately chose as a symbol of the power of evil whereby the First Man and First Woman had been seduced one which would simultaneously reprobate the heinous Chanaanite cult: the serpent, symbol of the deification of nature and fertility, the abuse of sex, and the oppression of woman. (Cf. Chapter VII; also *The Catholic Biblical Quarterly*, XIX:1 [January 1957], especially the first three articles by Fathers Roland Murphy, Eamonn O'Doherty, and John L. McKenzie, pp. 5-52. Fr. Ellis gives a fine summary of messianism in Chapter 10 of his *The Men and Message of the Old Testament*.)

Selected Bibliography

During the past twenty years an unprecedented number of works on the Bible by Catholic authors have been published in the wake of Pope Pius XII's encouraging encyclical, *Divino Afflante Spiritu* of 1943. The following titles are recommended; those starred with an asterisk are particularly valuable for this course.

I. BY CATHOLIC AUTHORS

Texts of The Bible

It is desirable and necessary that each student possess the Confraternity text of all books which have appeared thus far — including the prophets. Benziger Brothers *New American Catholic Edition* of 1961 is satisfactory.

The introductions and footnotes of *LA SAINTE BIBLE* (L'Ecole Biblique de Jerusalem, 1956), are very helpful for those who read French. An English translation is in preparation.

Commentaries

BARROSSE, THOMAS, C.S.C. *God Exists: The Biblical Record of God's Self-Revelation.* Notre Dame, Ind.: University of Notre Dame Press, 1963, 79 pp. (Paperback)

*BOUYER, LOUIS *The Meaning of Sacred Scripture.* Notre Dame, Ind.: University of Notre Dame Press, 1958, 258 pp. Important themes running through Old and New Testaments.

CALLAN, C. J., O. P. *The New Psalter* (J. P. Wagner, 1949), 532 pp. Treats each Psalm individually.

*CHARLIER, CLESTIN, O.S.B. *The Christian Approach to the Bible.* Westminster, Md.: Newman Press, 1958, 298 pp. One of the finest introductions to the Bible yet published for the layman.

DOUGHERTY, J. J. *Searching the Scriptures.* Garden City, N. Y.: Doubleday & Co., Inc. A readable introduction to the Bible and to the individual books of Old and New Testaments.

*DYSON, R. A., S.J. and JONES, ALEXANDER *The Kingdom of Promise.* Westminster, Md.: Newman Press, 1957, 222 pp. (Paperback) Splendid development of the Kingdom of God in Scripture.

*ELLIS, PETER, C.SS.R. *The Men and Message of the Old Testament.* Collegeville, Minn.: Liturgical Press, 1963, 559 pp. Chapter 10 on "Messianism" especially fine. Contains color outline of the four sources of the Pentateuch, p. 57ff.

FICHTNER, JOSEPH, O.S.C. *Theological Anthropology: The Science of Man in his Relations to God.* Notre Dame, Ind.: University of Notre Dame Press, 1963, 100 pp. (Paperback)

GELIN, ALBERT. *Key Concepts of the Old Testament.* New York: Sheed and Ward, 1955, 94 pp. Especially good for the Jewish notion of retribution and future life.

——————————————*The Religion of Israel.* (*Twentieth Century Encyclopedia of Catholicism,* Vol. 65) New York: Hawthorn Books, Inc., 111 pp. Fine treatise on the Psalms included in Chapter 4, "A Praying People."

GIBLET, J., et.al. *The God of Israel, the God of Christians.* New York: Desclee Company, 1961, 261 pp. Vocation and related themes in the Old Testament.

GROLLENBERG, L. H., O.P. *Atlas of the Bible.* New York: Thomas Nelson and Sons, Ltd., 1956, 166 pp. Also, *Shorter Atlas of the Bible,* 1959, by the same author.

GUILLET, JACQUES. *Themes of the Bible.* Notre Dame, Ind.: Fides, 1961, 279 pp. More abstract than Bouyer.

*HARTMAN, LOUIS F., C.SS.R., (trans.) *Encyclopedic Dictionary of the Bible.* New York: McGraw-Hill Book Company, Inc., 1963, 1334 pp. Up to date and thoroughly scholarly.

*HASSEVELDT, ROGER. *The Church, A Divine Mystery.* Notre Dame, Ind.; Fides, 1954. A treatise on the Mystical Body in a Biblical context.

HAURET, CHARLES. *Beginnings: Genesis and Modern Science.* Dubuque, Iowa: Priory Press, 1955, 305 pp. A detailed commentary on the first three chapters of Genesis.

HUNT, IGNATIUS, O.S.B. *Understanding the Bible.* New York: Sheed and Ward, 1962, 207 pp. A brief introduction to the books of the Bible reflecting latest scholarship.

LEVIE, JEAN, S.J. *The Bible, Word of God in Words of Men.* New York: P. J. Kenedy & Sons, 1961, 323 pp.

MCKENZIE, JOHN L., S.J. *The Two-Edged Sword.* Milwaukee, Wis.: Bruce, 1956, 253 pp. This work represents a refreshingly liberal Catholic interpretation of the Old Testament.

——————————*The Bible in Current Catholic Thought.* New York: Herder and Herder, 1962, 247 pp. An anthology of recent critical biblical research.

MONKS OF MAREDSOUS. *Guide to the Bible.* Springfield, Ill.: Templegate, 1953, 95 pp. (Paperback)

MONTJUVIN, JACQUES. *Panorama of Biblical History.* Notre Dame, Ind.: Fides. Historical chart of Old Testament events. (Included in the book by Fr. Ellis).

MORIARTY, F. L., S.J. *Foreword to the Old Testament Books* (Weston College, 1954), 118 pp.

——————————*Introducing the Old Testament.* Milwaukee, Wis.: Bruce, 1960, 253 pp. Principal characters of the Old Testament are treated in historical context.

MURPHY, ROLAND E., O. Carm. *The Seven Books of Wisdom.* Milwaukee, Wis.: Bruce, 1960, 163 pp. Treats Proverbs, Psalms, Job, Canticles, Ecclesiastes, Sirach, and Wisdom.

Old Testament Study Guide, by Members of the Boston College Theology Department. Boston, Mass.: Boston College Press, 1961, 209 pp. Leading questions for students.

*ORCHARD, SUTCLIFFE, et.al. *A Catholic Commentary on Holy Scripture.* Thomas Nelson and Sons, Ltd., 1953, 1312 pp. Comments on each verse of Bible; somewhat outdated.

*PAGANO, SEBASTIANO. *Chronological Table of the Books of the Old Testament.* Ottawa, Ontario, Canada: University Seminary, 1959. An eleven-page folio depicting the literary history of the Old Testament.

Pamphlet Bible Series. Glen Rock, N.J.: Paulist Press, 1960. Confraternity text of the Bible with a commentary on each book. Most of the Old Testament has now appeared.

PARSCH, PIUS. *The Church's Year of Grace,* 5 vols. Collegeville, Minn.: Liturgical Press, 1959. A fine liturgical commentary steeped in Old Testament lore.

ROBERT, A. and TRICOT, A. *Guide to the Bible,* 2 vols. New York: Desclee & Co., 1955. A scholarly work, useful for particular topics. A new edition is in preparation.

SCHOKEL, LUIS ALONSO, S. J. *Understanding Biblical Research.* New York: Herder and Herder, 1963, 130 pp. A readable, competent treatise on how to read the Bible.

SULLIVAN, KATHRYN, R.S.C.J. *God's Word and Work.* Collegeville, Minn.: Liturgical Press, 1958, 164 pp. Helpful background material for some Old Testament books.

SYNAVE, PAUL, O.P. and BENOIT, PIERRE, O.P. *Prophecy and Inspiration.* New York: Desclee Company, 1961, 186 pp. Second part on inspiration particularly applicable.

*TOS, ALDO J. *Approaches to The Bible: The Old Testament.* Englewood Cliffs, N. J.: Prentice-Hall, Inc., 1963, 286 pp. A complete textbook. Chapter 23 explains Dead Sea Scrolls.

VANN, GERALD, O.P. *The Paradise Tree.* New York: Sheed and Ward, 1959, 320 pp. Excellent treatment of biblical symbols.

VAUX, ROLAND DE, O. P. *Ancient Israel.* New York: McGraw-Hill, 1961, 592 pp. Best in its field.

*VAWTER, BRUCE. *A Path Through Genesis.* New York: Bruce, 1956, 308 pp. An excellent commentary on the whole of Genesis.

————————*The Conscience of Israel.* New York: Sheed and Ward, 1961, 308 pp. An analysis of prophecy and a treatise on the pre-Exilic prophets.

II. BY PROTESTANT AUTHORS

The following two editions of the Bible by Protestant scholars are reasonably accurate translations and would seem to be permitted to Catholic students of Sacred Scripture in accordance with Canon 1400 of the Code of Canon Law: (1) *The Revised Standard Version* (1946-1952) which replaces the King James version, and was published by the National Council of Churches; (2) *The Bible: An American Translation* (1931) by Smith-Goodspeed, published by the University of Chicago Press.

Commentaries

Protestant scholars got a head-start on Catholic scholars at the turn of the century and, until 1940, were more productive. Hence it is important to take note of the valuable insights furnished by these sincere experts. A word of caution is necessary, however. Although the books recommended below do not contain anything contrary to Catholic faith — and therefore may be read by Catholics in accordance with Canon 1399, #4—their authors tend to put more emphasis on secondary causes in recounting biblical events than do Catholic authors. While acknowledging the intervention of God in the big stages of salvation history and the presence of miracles, they nevertheless give greater play to fictional literary elements than Catholics are willing to admit, at least at the present time. Similarly, in explaining divine revelation, Protestant writers generally place greater stress on the subjective element of the interpretation of events by the human author than do Catholic writers.

ALBRIGHT, W. F. *The Biblical Period.* Pittsburgh: Biblical Colloquium, 1950, 66 pp.

Atlas of the Bible Lands. Maplewood, N.J.: C. S. Hammond and Company, 1959, 32 pp. Contains excellent historical charts and maps of ancient empires.

*ANDERSON, BERNHARD W. *Understanding the Old Testament.* Englewood Cliffs, N. J.: Prentice Hall, 1957, 551 pp. This comes very close to being an ideal college text.

DODD, C. H. *The Bible To-day.* Cambridge, Eng.: Cambridge University Press, 1961, 168 pp. (Paperback). Fine statement of the contemporary relevance of the Bible.

KELLER, WERNER. *The Bible As History.* New York: William Morrow, 1956, 453 pp. Popular archeology. This journalist occasionally overstates his case.

KRAELING, EMIL G. *Bible Atlas.* Chicago, Ill.: Rand McNally, 1962, 487 pp. Penetrating historical and archeological sidelights on Old and New Testament themes.

OESTERLY, W. O. E., and ROBINSON, THEODORE H. *An Introduction to the Books of the Old Testament.* Cleveland, Ohio: Meridian Books: Living Age Book 23, 1958, 454 pp. A classic work.

SANDMEL, SAMUEL. *The Hebrew Scriptures.* New York: Alfred A. Knopf, 1963, 552 pp. A Jewish scholar's insights into the Old Testament and its relation to the New Testament.

THOMAS, D. WINTON, ed. *Documents from Old Testament Times.* New York: Harper and Brothers, Torchbook 85, 1961, 302 pp. Valuable selection of pagan myths.

*WRIGHT, G. E., and FULLER, R. H. *The Book of the Acts of God.* Garden City, N.Y.: Doubleday, Anchor Book A222, 1960, 420 pp. A work of profound insight and scholarship on Old and New Testaments.

GOD'S KINGDOM
IN THE
OLD TESTAMENT

Chapter I

The Works of God Versus the Works of Man: The Biblical Crisis of the 1800's

Introduction

The greatest insult that one can pay God is to remove Him from the world of man — even on the pretext that human affairs are too petty to be of concern to Him. If there really is a God, then the whole of creation must lie in the palm of His hand. Creatures cannot be merely remote show pieces, independent of their Maker. Either God is running this world and continually intervening in the affairs of men, or else there is no God. A distant, aloof deity is a product of wishful thinking. Conversely, to admit the existence of God is tantamount to denying that the world and its activities are primarily the work of man.

There have been tribes of men who have overemphasized the miraculous, it is true. Certain primitive peoples, terrorized by storms and earthquakes, have in times past tended to deify natural forces of which they were ignorant. By and large, however, the more typical tendency in human nature is to underestimate the influence of the divine. Man likes to pride himself with the thought that he is running the show, with perhaps an occasional assist from above. This position, so rampant during the nineteenth century, is known as deism. By setting God apart from the physical universe, it makes man the complete master of his destiny. As William Ernest Henley phrased it, "It matters not how strait the gate, how charged with punishments the scroll, I am the master of my fate: I am the captain of my soul!" *(Invictus)*

It would be hard to find any truth which emerges more clearly from the Bible than the decisive role of God in the world. While usually recognizing the delicate intermingling of human and divine causality, the biblical authors consistently accord God an emphatic priority: "He spreads snow like wool; frost He strews like ashes. He scatters His hail like crumbs. . . . He lets His breeze blow and the waters run" (Psalm 147). Not only does Sacred Scripture reveal God everywhere in nature, but its pages are themselves the work of God in a very special way. It

1

is a divine book, written by the hand of God using the fingers of men. Along with the Redemption and the Church, it is one of the three great works of God in history.

The Debunking of The Bible

Yet the rationalists of the last century attempted to strip even the Word of God of its divine character and reduce it to the level of mere human activity. The new "scientific" approach assumed that the Bible had "evolved," together with the religious development of mankind, from primitive polytheistic notions into an elaborate moral code. Three rationalistic "schools" of thought can be roughly distinguished in the process of removing God from the Bible:

The Philosophical Approach: This was the beginning of the attempt to apply the evolutionism of the German philosopher, Hegel, to the study of the origin of the Bible. It represented an extremely subjective method based on the axiom, "The supernatural is impossible." Such men as Strauss and Bauer ended up by making the Old Testament an amalgamation of myths and the New Testament a product of pious hallucinations.

The Era of Higher Criticism: As the "philosophical" approach began to lose its following, a new avenue of criticism was explored—internal literary analysis of the Sacred Books. Sparked by the findings of Graff and Wellhausen, this effort resulted in the "discovery" that the Pentateuch was NOT the work of Moses (to whom both Jewish and Christian tradition had consistently attributed its authorship); rather, it was composed from at least four different documents designated by the letters J, E, P and D. As the falsity of two of the basic assumptions of this school became evident (that writing was unknown to the Israelites of Moses' time, and that Jewish historians were unreliable), the so-called "Documentary Hypothesis" was partly discredited. However, the theory does have definite merits when purged of its rationalistic, anti-Mosaic tendencies. It will be considered in greater detail later.

The School of Comparative Religions: The trend at the turn of the century was an attempt to prove that the source of divine revelation to be found in Scripture lay in non-Christian religions. The Jewish heritage was seen as borrowings from Babylonian and other Semitic sources; Christianity was traced to a combination of Greek and Jewish elements. This endeavor degenerated, in effect, to the mythical explanations of the Philosophical Period.

The final blow came in the wake of the publication of Charles Darwin's *The Descent of Man* in 1871. In this book, the father of biological evolution extended his theory to explain the origin of man. Though admitting that man's beginning is mysterious, and that there are gaps in the evolutionary process, Darwin was not very careful to distinguish between body and soul. Later evolutionists reduced man's ancestors to the plant kingdom. The tremendous discovery of continuity among higher and lower biological species appeared to have profound theological implications. Unfortunately, it caught the great majority of Christian exegetes unprepared. It seemed that a choice had to be made between the Book of Genesis and evolution, and once again the whole concept of revealed religion was called into question. The kingdom of man seemed to be triumphing over the kingdom of God, because it appeared that the kingdom of man was the only kingdom.

What finally emerged in the twentieth century was the viewpoint termed "Liberal Protestantism." This mentality sees Christ as a great and holy man, a peerless moral teacher, indeed, but ONLY A MAN. Lives of Christ by rationalists such as Renan and Strauss, which wrecked the faith of many Christians in France and Germany, reflect this rejection of the divinity of Christ. The Bible had become a prime battle ground in the contest between the natural and the supernatural and the former seemed to be getting the upper hand. For many of our grandparents' generation, not only the hand of Moses but God's as well, had been removed effectively from the composition of Sacred Scripture.

The Renaissance of Catholic Criticism

Yet, it must not be concluded that faith in the supernatural character of the Bible had been universally undermined. The conviction of the majority of believers had remained unshaken. But what were "loyalist" biblical scholars doing during this attack on their Sacred Book? For the most part, both Catholic and Protestant fundamentalists had been hiding their heads in the sand. They met the challenge of nineteenth century scientism by attempting to ignore it. Instead of engaging in independent literary criticism and examining each new scientific theory to see what light it could throw on a broader interpretation of the Bible, these men took refuge in the strict, literal (and often narrow) exegesis of the text, and insisted on trying to defend positions which were no longer tenable. Even where there was an attempt to meet the scientists part way, the effort was frequently pathetic. The Period Theory is one example. In the face of advances in the geological and biological sciences, biblical scholars tried to "harmonize" these findings with the six days of the creation account by matching up the latter with the four geological agres of the earth. To establish this harmony (also known as "Concordism"), they were obliged to interpret the Hebrew word *Yom* (day) in the sense of *era*. The rug was pulled out from under this position when linguistic studies demonstrated that the term *Yom* was never used in the Bible in this sense. Besides, to match four items with six is not good mathematics!

This and other efforts to put new wine into old skins proved conclusively that a die-hard reactionary rests on as perilous a footing as does a reckless radical. The keen mind of Pope Leo XIII clearly recognized the nature of the issues at stake and wisely intervened with the famous encyclical, *Providentissimus Deus* in 1893. In it he encouraged biblical scholars to defend Sacred Scripture by an authentic biblical criticism backed by a study of Oriental languages and the natural sciences. His advice was taken up quickly by Catholic exegetes. In fact, three years before the Encyclical appeared, the now famous Ecole Biblique in Jerusalem had been founded for just such research by the Dominican scholar, Father M. J. Lagrange.

But the atmosphere was not purged of its conservatism — or its radicalism — overnight. Soon Catholics themselves split into liberal and conservative factions. A number of liberals got out of hand, as in the case of Alfred Loisy. Pope Leo's successor, St. Pius X, was compelled to condemn the subsequent wave of modernism in his encyclical *Pascendi* of 1907. Unfortunately, even some moderate liberals such as Father Lagrange were temporarily silenced. After the publication in 1903 of his now classic work, *La Methode Historique*, this great pioneer was forced to interrupt his Old Testament research for at least a year. Here was a man whose only crime consisted in being about thirty years ahead of his time! From instances like this, one can gain some understanding of how far Scriptural studies had been lagging behind progress in the secular sciences.

The Key to Twentieth Century Criticism

What finally developed from this renaissance of orthodox biblical criticism was a vital reunderstanding of the sacred text, based on a pivotal principle worth its weight in gold: The Bible is a book of religious truth, NOT a scientific textbook! Galileo had pointed out this truth centuries before, but only giants among the scholars had been able to appreciate his statement. He phrased it thus: "The Bible does not tell us how the heavens go, but how to go to heaven." Many sincere exegetes had failed to grasp this principle simply because, in overemphasizing God's causality, they had neglected to take sufficient cognizance of the human element. At last a happy balance was being struck. In the wake of this reorientation following the First World War, the Scriptures began to yield a fresh harvest which surprised even the experts.

Slowly the realization dawned that, whereas God could have enlightened the ancient Semitic authors of the Bible to enable them to

4

convey His message in an advanced scientific vein, the fact is that He did not. He took them as they were, with all their glaring cultural limitations and unscientific methodology, and contented Himself with stopping at what has so aptly been termed "salvation history." Hence the all-important key to interpretation lies in a faithful reconstruction of Semitic mentality and a mastery of Oriental literary genres, which will be treated in Chapter III. Especially is it necessary to understand the Semites' use of history. As a prominent Jewish scholar puts it,

> History as the mere record of events is of limited importance in the present quest. In one sense, it is valuable primarily for enabling the reader to acquire a tolerably good orientation to those ideas that events called forth. But in quite another sense, history tends to become the most acute problem to the student of the Tanak [Old Testament]. He often falls into the error of many modern readers of telling himself that events are true only if they are correct as history. He asks, Did Moses really get the Ten Commandments on Mount Sinai? Did Abraham really beget Isaac long after Sarah had lost her fertility? Did God really create the world in seven days? Did Jonah really spend three days in the belly of the whale?
>
> The extraordinary conclusion of many readers, and of college students especially, is that if these matters are not historically accurate the Tanak is false and therefore worthless. . . . The reader must begin to understand that the biblical authors were not research historians who frequented archives and libraries. He must not shrink from concluding that they could be, and were, wrong on many points in history. Quibbles about these matters of "history" are analogous to the situation in which a man begins to relate a funny incident that occurred on his way downtown the previous Thursday. His wife promptly intervenes to insist that it happened on Wednesday. The usual outcome is that the anecdote is never told, and the assembly is titillated, if at all, only by the Thursday-Wednesday exchange.[1]

As biblical exegesis began to fill in the gap which had held it in bondage for over a century, allied secular sciences suddenly took on a remarkable twist. This was especially noticeable in the fields of archeology and histoy. Many of the new discoveries made during the two World Wars, instead of seeming to contradict the historicity of Sacred Scripture, actually corroborated the traditional positions in an uncanny degree! Almost in spite of themselves, anthropologists, geologists, linguists, — many of whom had dismissed the biblical stories as pious legends — found that their researches were lending historical credence to the inspired Word of God. And this at the very

---

[1] Samuel Sandmel, *The Hebrew Scriptures* (New York: Alfred Knopf, 1963) p. 9.

moment when even Fundamentalists were agreeing that Scripture is not supposed to be a history book or a science text!

Names which are unmistakably biblical began to appear on newly discovered cuneiform tablets dug up at the ancient sites of Mari and Ugarit. Rummaging among buried ruins in the area of the Fertile Crescent, archeologists found themselves confronted with Hittite warriors like those described in the Pentateuch, tall Philistines, and Canaanite chiefs with their iron chariots. One group of scholars claimed they had reconstructed the Tower of Babel, while excavations in the Nile Delta yielded the treasure cities of Rameses and Phithon built by Jewish slave labor at the time of the Exodus. Not even the magnificent stables of King Solomon could any longer be passed off as legend: at least 450 stalls for horses and sheds for 150 chariots were unearthed at Megiddo alone by archeologists Gordon Loud and P. L. O. Guy.[2] Other archeologists, digging in Mesopotamia in 1929 under the direction of Sir Leonard Woolley, came upon a vast layer of mud which testifies to the occurrence of a widespread inundation of the area about 4,000 B.C. Leaders of the expedition flashed back the startling news, which made the headlines: "We have found the Flood! "[3]

The Israeli government has had remarkable results in rehabilitating much of the 8,000 square miles which make up their section of Palestine by returning to biblical patterns. Following the advice of Genesis 21:33, they have been successful in making large numbers of tamarisk trees grow in the southern region, where few other species will flourish. Copper mines are paying off by the Red Sea on the same site on which Solomon's miners had their encampments. An Israeli business man, Xiel Federmann, concluded from the story of the destruction of Sodom and Gomorra that there must be oil deposits at the south end of the Dead Sea. His reasoning was that the violence of the conflagration described in Genesis 19:28 pointed to the presence of escaping gas, and where there is gas, there is oil. His conclusion was vindicated with the drilling of the first Israeli oil well in 1953. In 1947, a Bedouin shepherd discovered in a cave at Qumran on the western shore of the Dead Sea (by coincidence, not far from the ancient site of Sodom and Gomorra and the modern oil well) a twenty-three-foot-long scroll containing the whole of the Book of Isaia in Hebrew, and dating before Christ!

---

[2] Cf. III Kings 4:26 and 10:26-29. These discoveries are described in Werner Keller's intriguing book, *The Bible As History* (New York: William Morrow and Company, 1956).

[3] *Ibid.*, pp. 25-32. This conclusion was later proven to be unfounded, however.

The Meaning of Sacred Scripture

But we have no intention of exploring the Bible simply for its historical or scientific dimensions, for it is primarily a religious book — as modern biblical criticism insists. Insofar as it records history, we must say that it is history with a vengeance: salvation history. It is this theme which unifies the two Testaments so neatly, by showing the marvelous way in which

> . . . the historical acts of God continue to live in each generation by means of oral or liturgical recital. . . . No merely natural evolutionary development can be detected here. Almighty God was the workman tending the vineyard (Is. 5:1-7); He was the potter working with the clay of human stuff (Is. 29:16; Jer. 18:1-13). The Bible is the record of God's loving and personal intervention in the lives of His children, in order to achieve 'a kingdom of priests, a holy nation' (Ex. 19:6). . . . These redemptive acts of God could not be confined to the past, but were thought to happen repeatedly in each generation; therefore, the sacred words which narrated the stirring events of the past contained in themselves the power to make that past once again a present reality. For these words, like the marvelous deeds of old, come from God and contain within their syllables the mystery of God's living presence. Did not Isaia cry out to the discouraged exiles: 'As the rain and snow come down from the heavens, and never return without watering the earth and making it bring forth and sprout. . . . So is my word which goes out of my mouth — it does not return to me fruitless, without doing the work which I desired, and accomplishing the purpose for which I sent it' (Is. 55:10 f.).[4]

The Church of Christ is the final stage in this divine evolution of the Word of God as it spells out the economy of human salvation: here is the basic truth, the golden thread uniting the Old and New Testaments, which we hope to illustrate convincingly in this course. For too many generations now the kingdom of Christ has been divorced in Christian mentality from the kingdom of Israel. Old Testament events were looked upon as little more than historical metaphors arbitrarily linked up with theological truths by dint of the fertile imaginations of textbook writers. And so, without forcing any text, and scrupulously trying to avoid any preconceived conclusions, we shall let the Sacred Books speak for themselves the inspired message for which mankind has yearned since the dawn of time. Our ultimate hope and prayer is that each reader of these pages will come to experience, through his study of the Bible, a new and vital appreciation

---

[4] Carroll Stuhlmueller, "Catholic Biblical Scholarship and College Theology," *The Thomist,* XIII (October, 1960), pp. 553-554.

of the Church as Christ's Body, and what it means to belong to the People of God.

But before we leave off these introductory remarks on the Word of God it would be well to fill out the picture with a brief consideration of the notion of Tradition.

Divine Tradition

Sacred scripture was not the first communication between God and man; the Bible is part of a much larger picture. Man had been on intimate terms with God in the Garden of Eden, in a situation equivalent to infused contemplation. When Adam and Eve broke the line of divine communication by their disobedience, it was God who took the initiative in restoring it through the first promise of a Redeemer, recorded in Genesis 3:15. The unwritten message of God to man, then, goes back to the latter's creation, and first existed in that form which we call Divine Tradition. The substance of primitive revelation began to be committed to writing centuries later at the time of Moses and subsequently.

In the meantime, the Word of God had not been idle. From the moment of the Fall, it had been engaged in bringing back the golden era of divine intimacy through a series of long-range stages. The passage quoted from the prophet Isaia on the previous page is typical of the many Old Testament texts which illustrate God's activity in the world. This activity centered itself in a very special manner in Israel, as the Book of Sirach declares:

> From the mouth of the Most High I came forth, and mistlike covered the earth. In the highest heavens did I dwell, my throne on a pillar of cloud. The vault of heaven I compassed alone, through the deep abyss I wandered. Over waves of the sea, over all the land, over every people and nation I held sway. Among all these I sought a resting place; in whose inheritance should I abide? Then the Creator of all gave me his command, and he who formed me chose the spot for my tent, saying, 'In Jacob make your dwelling, in Israel your inheritance.' (Sir. 24:3-8. Note also Prov. 8:22-31 and Wisd. 7:24-26 for striking parallels.)

It was on the thundering heights of Mt. Sinai that the Word finally became legible — twelve centuries before it became incarnate. Choosing the Jews as the special object of His election, God entered history in a dynamic, visible manner; His Word took on geographical proportions as it became associated with the Land of Promise. Divine Wisdom was beginning to manifest its special pattern, its true direction, in the midst of human affairs. The Kingdom of Heaven had established

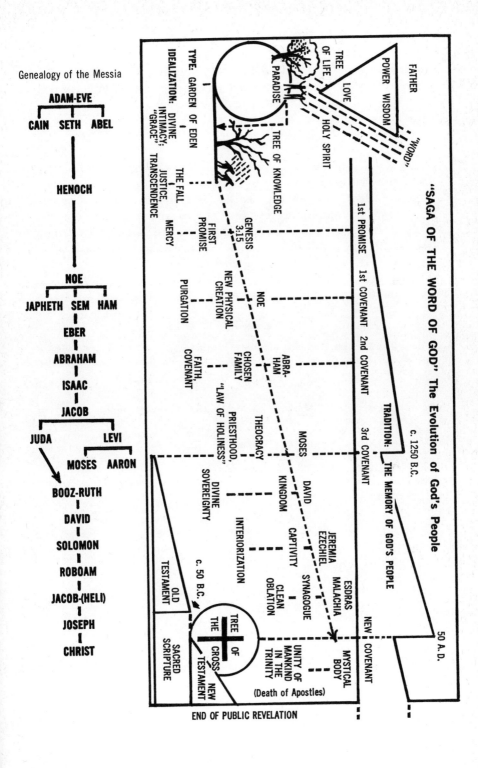

Genealogy of the Messia

ADAM-EVE
CAIN SETH ABEL

HENOCH

NOE
JAPHETH SEM HAM

EBER

ABRAHAM

ISAAC

JACOB

JUDA LEVI

MOSES AARON

BOOZ-RUTH

DAVID

SOLOMON

ROBOAM

JACOB-(HELI)

JOSEPH

CHRIST

"SAGA OF THE WORD OF GOD" The Evolution of God's People

FATHER

POWER WISDOM

"WORD"

TREE OF LIFE LOVE HOLY SPIRIT

PARADISE

TREE OF KNOWLEDGE

TYPE: GARDEN OF EDEN
IDEALIZATION: DIVINE INTIMACY; "GRACE"; TRANSCENDENCE

THE FALL — JUSTICE, MERCY

FIRST PROMISE — GENESIS 3:15

1st PROMISE

1st COVENANT 2nd COVENANT

PURGATION — NEW PHYSICAL CREATION — NOE

c. 1250 B.C.

TRADITION: THE MEMORY OF GOD'S PEOPLE

FAITH, COVENANT — CHOSEN FAMILY — ABRA-HAM

3rd COVENANT

"LAW OF HOLINESS" — PRIESTHOOD, THEOCRACY — MOSES

DIVINE SOVEREIGNTY — KINGDOM — DAVID

INTERIORIZATION — CAPTIVITY

JEREMIA EZECHIEL

ESDRAS MALACHIA

NEW COVENANT

50 A.D.

CLEAN OBLATION

SYNAGOGUE

c. 50 B.C.

OLD TESTAMENT

SACRED SCRIPTURE

NEW TESTAMENT

TREE OF THE CROSS

UNITY OF MANKIND IN THE TRINITY

MYSTICAL BODY

(Death of Apostles)

END OF PUBLIC REVELATION

a fresh beach-head on earth; it would undertake to transform the Kingdom of Israel into the Kingdom of God.[5]

Just how the Word of God found its way onto parchment in this pre-incarnate fashion is the burden of Chapter Two. Our task is to explain how a series of books could have at one and the same time both a divine and a human author. But first it will be helpful to see in a single panoramic view the various stages of God's plan as it unfolded.

The chart "Saga of the Word of God" gives a brief survey of the milestones in the progress of divine communication, enshrined in the history of His Chosen Ones. The line of communication reached its climax with the appearance of the Word in human form at the time of the Incarnation. The Savior's credentials are given in the family tree on the left, paralleling the historical events in the main body of the chart. At the same time, the chart brings out the close relationship between the two forms which divine communication took: Tradition, the oral form; and Sacred Scripture, the written form.

Suggested Readings

Bouyer, *The Meaning of Sacred Scripture,* Chapter 1.

Catholic Commentary on Holy Scripture, col. 43–46. Brief history of biblical criticism.

Charlier, *The Christian Approach to the Bible,* pp. 15–27. Brief history of biblical criticism.

Duncker, Peter G., "Biblical Criticism," *The Catholic Biblical Quarterly,* XXV:1 (January, 1963) pp. 22–33.

Keller, *The Bible as History,* Introduction and last three chapters.

Moriarty, *Foreword to the Old Testament Books,* pp. 1–11. Literary forms and the "Documentary Hypothesis."

Schokel, *Understanding Biblical Research.*

Steinmann, Jean, *Biblical Criticism,* Vol. 63, *Twentieth Century Encyclopedia of Religion.*

Stuhlmueller, "Catholic Biblical Scholarship and College Theology," *Thomist* (October, 1960) pp. 533–563. Brief history of biblical criticism.

Vawter, *Path Through Genesis,* Introduction. Stresses relevance of the Old Testament.

---

[5] There is an interesting passage in Baruch, formerly used as one of the lessons of the Easter Vigil service, which underscores this concept of wisdom: "(God) has traced out all the way of understanding, and has given her to Jacob, his servant, to Israel, his beloved son. Since then she has appeared on earth, and moved among men" (3:37-38).

Chapter II

The Work of God: Biblical Inspiration

From what has been said thus far, the answers to two basic questions about the Bible have emerged: 1) WHAT is it — i.e., what *form or shape* did it take? and 2) FROM WHAT was it formed — i.e., what *literary medium* was used by the authors? In other words, we have given two of the *causes* which brought Sacred Scripture into being. Borrowing our terminology from philosophy, the *formal cause* of Scripture (in answer to the first question, WHAT is the Bible?) has been shown to be the *pattern or rules of human salvation*. Its material *cause* (in answer to the second question, FROM WHAT is Scripture?) is the *history of the Jewish people* — and, if we are to include the New Testament — *the biography of Christ and early apostolic writings*. This second question will be treated in greater detail in the next two chapters. In this chapter, we are interested in yet a third question about Sacred Scripture: HOW did God form the Bible?

For a human being to be able to capture the ineffable with pen and ink required the special assistance of the Divine Author. We call this assistance biblical inspiration. Two extremes must be avoided in conceiving this phenomenon: to imagine, on the one hand, that the Second Person of the Trinity somehow was converted into parchment, as bread is converted into His Sacred Body in the Eucharist; and, on the other hand, to conclude that biblical inspiration belongs to the same category as such everyday "inspirations" as the urge to say a prayer, give an alms, etc. Somewhere between these extremes lies the true notion. While insisting on the reality of the divine authorship, we must in no way minimize the created author's instrumentality.

The best explanation of this phenomenon, we believe, lies in having recourse once again to the philosophical concept of causality. This will provide us with a third element in the production of Scripture, *the efficient cause*. Answering the question of HOW the Bible came to be written, this philosophical framework enables us to retain an activity of God and an activity of the human author in such a way that both may be called authors in the full sense of the word. Both, each in his own way, must be the source of the thoughts and of their expression as they are found in the books of the Bible.

The Concept of Efficient Causality as Applied
To Biblical Inspiration

An efficient cause is that which explains the actual production of an effect; it points out the agent which brought it about. It may be twofold: the principal efficient cause, which furnishes the impetus for the activity producing the effect; or the instrumental cause, which acts under the power and stimulation of the principal cause to channel its activity along particular lines. An example is the use of a piano by a man in order to play a piece of music. The man is the principal efficient cause of the playing; the piano is the instrumental efficient cause. In the case of biblical inspiration, God was the principal cause; the human author was the instrumental cause.

Under the principal causal action of God, the human author — who was at the same time God's living instrument, acted upon and moved to act precisely as a human being — produced the sacred book. And since the human instrument was used by God in complete conformity with his nature as a man, he must have responded especially by his intellect and his will: knowingly, deliberately, voluntarily. All of this demands that authorship be attributed to him also. Here is the way Pope Leo XIII put it in his monumental encyclical, *Providentissimus Deus:*

> For, by supernatural power, He so moved and impelled them [the human authors] to write . . . He so assisted them when writing . . . that the things which He ordered, and those only, they first rightly understood, then willed faithfully to write down, and finally expressed in apt words and with infallible truth.[6]

Definition of Biblical Inspiration

From this pontifical statement we can formulate the following definition of biblical inspiration: that divine action whereby God excited the intellect and moved the will of the sacred authors so that they wrote only what He wanted without error. Dom Celestin Charlier explains admirably why it is a divine action:

> The Bible is the Word of God. This means that it is the living Word, energized by the Spirit of God. When God speaks, it is the Breath of His mouth that renders His word audible. At the very center of the mystery of the incarnation lies the eternal mystery of the procession of the Spirit in the generation of the Son.

---

[6] *Providentissimus Deus*, Catholic Biblical Association edition, 1943, p. 24.

. . . Just as in eternity the Father's revelation of Himself (which is the Son) gives to the Son, in His Father, that vital inspiration which is the Spirit: so in time the revelation of the Word is achieved in Scripture, and in the womb of the Virgin, in the Eucharist and in the Mystical Body, by the efficacious inspiration of the same Spirit. As the incarnation of the Word in the Bible is prolonged in Christ, so Christ is prolonged in the Church and in the humblest of her children, and the same fertile love of the Spirit prevails throughout.[7]

Although it is a divine gift and partakes of the nature of grace in the wide sense, biblical inspiration is not sanctifying to the individual who possesses it. That is to say, it is given for the sake of the Church, not for the sake of the author. Moreover, it is a transitory grace, possessed only in the act of composing the sacred books. We can delineate a fourfold effect of inspiration on the human author:

Excitement of the intellect. Although the whole man was involved — his imagination, memory, sight, hearing, etc., as well as his bodily members — inspiration exercised its influence predominantly on the sacred author's intellect and will. This is clear from the fact that writing is fundamentally an intellectual activity, and the main intellectual act involved is judgment. After evaluating his sources and rightly conceiving the truth contained in them, the human author had to make a judgment as to not only what portion God wanted written down, but also how God wanted it written. This meant a decision as to the opportuneness of a given item, choice of literary form, vocabulary, etc.

It is important to note here that inspiration does not necessarily involve *revelation*. The process we have just described is entirely verified in the conception of *already* known truths, insofar as it is ordered to writing them down. Now, if any of the material to be incorporated into the account represented *new truth* (i.e., not previously communicated by God — and usually otherwise unknowable), then a special additional divine help would have been necessary, namely, revelation. From this it follows that, although all of Scripture is inspired (including any revelations which it contains), not all of Scripture is revealed; indeed, only a very small percentage of the Bible is revelation.

Moved the will. Now we are at the heart of inspiration. The excitement of the intellect just described would be utterly fruitless unless God moved the will of the sacred author actually to *write down* what he so conceived. All of the executive faculties were affected: will, brain, nerves, muscles, fingers. Yet, as in the case of His ordinary motion of the will through divine Providence, inspiration did not do

---

[7] Charlier, *The Christian Approach to the Bible*, pp. 206-207.

the slightest violence to the human mechanism. Many factors were involved: the personality of the writer, the atmosphere and tradition surrounding him, local conditions such as political crises, etc. By means of some of these factors, and in spite of others, God simply brought it about that the human author spontaneously willed to write what the divine judgment ordered. Dom Charlier sums up this aspect of inspiration thus:

> We saw first of all that the inspiration of the Bible was a particularized form of Israel's general religious inspiration. We saw that it was not confined to writers properly so called, but extended to all those who contributed in some way to the slow and complex formation of the Book. The Bible is the expression of a living tradition, moulded into the life of the people by God's delegates, but developing in the community as such. . . . As the life of the early Church was dominated by the Spirit of Christ, so was the life of the people of Israel dominated by the Spirit of Yahweh. . . .
> Biblical inspiration thus falls under the general category of divine Providence. In both, God works through secondary causes, and does not replace them with his own activity, as he does in miracles. . . . There is no obvious intervention by God. Biblical writers wrote as other men do, and left the imprint of their personality on their work. For the most part they were not even conscious that they were inspired. Inspiration must not therefore be thought of as a *substitution* of God's action for the normal activity of the writer. There is no question of an artificial insemination of ready-made concepts into the author's mind, nor of any arbitrary interference with his imagination or feelings. Normally God acts here with a delicacy of touch that shows his respect for his own creation and his intimate knowledge of its mechanism.[8]

To write only what He wanted. The important word here is "only." Lest the sacred author include superfluous details, the Holy Spirit exercised a preventive action in the composition of the sacred books. The essence of Scripture is *religious* truth; all else must be excluded which does not in some way contribute to the imparting of the blueprint of human salvation. Even such obiter dicta as the fact that the dog of Tobias wagged its tail and fawned (Tob. 11:9) can be explained as enrichment of the religious significance of the story through local color, etc.

Without error. Like the previous element, this last work of the Spirit is negative. It guarantees that whatever is found in Scripture is free from even the minutest error. If the Holy Spirit were to permit the human author to deviate from the truth in no matter how small a measure, the resulting error would be imputable to Him, the Principal Author, as well. *Inerrancy*, then, is one of the properties of the Bible. Leo XIII was most emphatic on this score in *Providentissimus Deus*:

---

[8] *Ibid.*, pp. 209-210.

It follows that those who maintain that an error is possible in any genuine passage of the sacred writings either pervert the Catholic notion of inspiration or make God the author of such error. And so emphatically were all the Fathers and Doctors agreed that the divine writings, as left by the *hagiographers,* are free from all error, that they labored earnestly, with no less skill than reverence, to reconcile with each other those numerous passages which seem at variance — the very passages which in great measure have been taken up by the 'higher criticism'; for they were unanimous in laying down that those writings, in their entirety and in all their parts were equally from the 'afflatus' of Almighty God, and that God, speaking by the sacred writers, could not set down anything but what was true. The words of St. Augustine to St. Jerome may sum up what they taught:

'On my own part I confess to your charity that it is only to those books of Scripture which are now called canonical that I have learned to pay such honor and reverence as to believe most firmly that none of their writers had fallen into any error. And if in these books I meet anything which seems contrary to truth, I shall not hesitate to conclude either *that the text is faulty,* or that *the translator has not expressed the meaning* of the passage, or *that I myself do not understand*' (Ep. lxxxii, i, and elsewhere).[9]

Extent of Inspiration

It is clear from the Pope's words that only the original manuscripts as they came from the hands of the sacred authors were inspired, and therefore possessed the property of inerrancy. All of these "autographs" have perished; hence, the texts which we use today are only copies, and may well contain some errors. That St. Augustine took this possibility into consideration is indicated by the italicized portion of the quotation above. This matter will receive further consideration in the discussions of texts and versions of Scripture, where the unique position of the Vulgate will be pointed out, viz., the quality of being substantially in agreement with the autographs.

Assuming, then, that our own text is a reasonably accurate translation, the question arises: just how far did the influence of God in the writing of the sacred books extend? He is the main Author; therefore, He is responsible for the contents of the books. Must we say, then, that biblical inspiration applied to all of the truths in Scripture: not only the moral and dogmatic truths therein, but also the profane matters treated — science, history, politics, etc.? Can we maintain that inspiration affected equally the fundamental truths of salvation and likewise the more unimportant truths, such as the obiter dicta referred to on the previous page? Finally, are we to say that inspira-

---

[9] Catholic Biblical Association ed., *Providentissimus Deus,* p. 25. (Italics added.)

tion extends not only to the ideas presented, but also to the very words in which the ideas are clothed?

The answer is clear: we must hold that every single book of Sacred Scripture, together with every part of these books, is inspired. And inspiration must be applied to the total content of all the books, whether religious or profane. Here is the testimony of St. Paul:

> For *whatsoever things have been written* have been written for our instruction, that through the patience and the consolation afforded by the Scriptures we may have hope (Rom. 15:4).
> *All* Scripture is inspired by God and useful for teaching, for reproving, for correcting, for instructing in justice (2 Tim. 3:16).

In both quotations, we see that St. Paul was including all of the Old Testament as falling under divine inspiration. Similar teaching is found in the dogmatic decrees of the councils of Trent and Vatican. We quote Pope Leo XIII on this subject:

> But it is absolutely wrong and forbidden to narrow inspiration to certain parts only of Holy Scripture. . . . As to the system of those who, in order to rid themselves of these difficulties, do not hesitate to concede that divine inspiration regards the things of faith and morals, and nothing beyond . . . this system cannot be tolerated.[10]

The same conclusion follows from the rational explanation already given for the mechanism of inspiration: the doctrine of efficient causality. When a principal efficient cause uses an instrumental cause in the production of an effect, the effect belongs to both entirely. Therefore, the whole of the Bible belongs to God, and the whole of it belongs to the sacred writers. Inspiration is not an instance of collaboration, where each collaborator contributes a determined part. Each part of the Bible is both human and divine. At the same time, we may admit that God's intervention in the scribal activities of the human authors was of varying degrees. It was, for example, more pronounced when they wrote under the influence of a vision, or reported a revelation, and especially when they only vaguely understood the import of what they were writing. Yet, the least degree of inspiration involved all four elements of the definition which we have elaborated.

From what has been stated, we must conclude likewise that inspiration reached to the very words used by the sacred authors. It was not enough for the human authors merely to conceive rightly what to put down; they had to express "in apt words" their inspired thoughts. Respecting their freedom, and without dictating the words, the Holy

---

[10] *Ibid.*, pp. 23-24.

Spirit extended His influence to their choice of words. Even words quoted from profane sources verbatim are to be considered inspired as quotations. This means that, though they were originally written by uninspired authors, the judgment of the biblical authors concerning these quotations and the use they made of them in the sacred text was inspired.

For example, when the author of Psalm 13 wrote, "The fool says in his heart, 'There is no God,'" he is enunciating the fact that the fool makes such statements, and only to this extent is the passage inspired; the sacred author is not affirming that there is no God. Again, in II Machabees 2:24 we learn that the sacred author is giving us an abridgment of the "five books of Jason of Cyrene." Since Jason was not, so far as we know, an inspired writer, we must conclude that the abridgment was inspired only to the extent that Jason's words were accurately *condensed and reported* (but the information contained not infallibly guaranteed); and that only such things were included as were in accordance with the will of the Holy Spirit.[11]

Two basic principles emerge from these clarifications: 1) When a biblical passage is clear, and the meaning certain, scientific and other profane statements must be made to conform with it. For example, when the sacred author states in Genesis 1:1, "In the beginning God created the heavens and the earth," he intended to teach that the whole visible universe comes from God; hence, we must reject any cosmological system which maintains its spontaneous origin. The Author of nature cannot contradict Himself in the sacred text. 2) When the biblical passage is not clear, or its meaning is not certain, it may be interpreted tentatively in the light of solid scientific, historical, etc., conclusions. The genealogical tables in the fourth chapter of Genesis, for example, are very vague; hence, the data of archeology, anthropology, etc., may be employed to explain the text.

General Rules of Interpretation

What we have just said clearly illustrates that the reader of the Bible has not only the problem of securing an accurate text, but also the *psychological* problem of penetrating the mentality of the human author. The following rules summarize the conditions which must be fulfilled before the would-be interpreter is obliged to make an act of faith in the contents of a given biblical passage:

1. **The original text of the sacred books must be reconstructed** insofar as possible, since only the autographs were inspired.

---

[11] Cf. Orchard, *A Catholic Commentary on Holy Scripture,* col. 574c.

2. **The meaning of the sacred author must be perfectly clear.** Besides determining the precise meaning of each word and phrase in their grammatical and logical context by consulting parallel passages, we must know:

   a) **The exact (formal) aspect** under which the author is treating his subject. This demands that we be able to distinguish his direct affirmations or **message** from secondary considerations (e.g., its medium).

   b) **The degree of assertion** contained in each statement; e.g., Is the author proposing this as certain or doubtful? A total or partial view?

   c) **The degree of intellectual adherence** demanded of the reader through an evaluation of the importance which the author attaches to his message. For example, are we to take Josue 6:17 at face value, where God orders the extermination of every single Chanaanite?

3. The reader must have an over-all view of the Bible as a whole; that is, he must be familiar with: a) its **literary history,** including the order of composition of the various books and the origin of the oral tradition behind them; and b) its main lines of **dogmatic and moral development.**

False Theories of Inspiration

The doctrine outlined above becomes clearer when we contrast it with some of the unorthodox theories which have been proposed through the centuries to explain biblical inspiration. The first three of the theories presented here were offered by sincere, believing scholars who veered somewhat in the direction of the rationalists by slighting God's activity.

1. *Theory of subsequent approbation.* The human authors wrote the sacred books independently; they were afterwards approved by divine authority, and thus given the status of "inspired" books. This theory is rejected in *Providentissimus Deus:*

> And the Church holds them as sacred and canonical not because, having been composed by human industry, they were afterwards approved by her authority; nor only because they contain revelation without errors, but because, having been written under the inspiration of the Holy Spirit, they have God for their Author.[12]

2. *Mere inerrancy.* In the quotation above, His Holiness likewise rejects the theory which would *limit* biblical inspiration to only *one*

---

[12] *Ibid.,* p. 24.

of the four effects which it actually had on the sacred authors, viz., the prevention of error.

3. *External moral impulse.* According to this theory, God chose certain men to be authors of the sacred books, then prevailed upon them by means of counseling, urging, commanding, etc., to undertake the task. This was God's only contribution: in every other way, the books were but human products. Like the two previous theories, this one denies God any genuine role in the actual composition; His influence is external rather than internal.

The two remaining theories overemphasize God's role; at the same time, they fail to give the human author his full due. They are products of the fundamentalist mentality which tended to forget that the Bible is also the work of man.

4. *Dictation.* God, according to the proponents of this theory, dictated the contents of the various books to the human authors. In other words, their contribution in the order of instrumental causality was that of stenographers. But, just as in the business world we do not hold the typist responsible for the contents of a dictated letter, neither can we attribute true authorship to one who merely transcribes God's own words onto parchment. Furthermore, the vast differences of style, language, culture, literary forms, etc., from author to author betray the absurdity of this contention. When we run across the term "dictated by the Holy Spirit" in the works of the Fathers — or even in the encyclical of Pope Leo XIII — we must not understand it literally, but rather in the sense of a free instrumental cause. Nor does it help the situation by claiming that they wrote the books after having been elevated to a state of ecstasy. This is an extrasensory condition; the sacred authors would not have been aware of what their pens were putting down on the parchment; hence, they would not have been fully responsible for what was written, and authorship could not be claimed for them in any genuine sense.

5. *Theory of revelation.* This false theory declares that the Bible is an inspired book because some (or all) of it is revealed by God. Basically, it fails to distinguish revelation from inspiration. When it is remembered that inspiration is simply the *transmission* of truth under divine guidance, whereas revelation involves *arriving at new truth,* the error becomes obvious. All of the divine mysteries in Sacred Scripture had, of course, to be revealed to the human authors before they could be recorded. But a very small percentage of the content of Scripture represents divine mysteries; the vast majority of the material was known naturally by the men who wrote it down, either *directly* (through personal experience), or *indirectly* (through eye witnesses, documents, etc.).

✿   ✿   ✿   ✿

We have attempted in this chapter to do justice to the role of God in the composition of the Bible. We shall turn our attention in the following chapter to the human element.

❋   ❋   ❋   ❋

Suggested Readings

Charlier, *The Christian Approach to the Bible,* pp. 206-220.
Dougherty, *Searching the Scriptures,* pp. 19-33.
Orchard, *A Catholic Commentary on Holy Scripture,* cols. 34-38.

Chapter III

The Work of Man: Semitic Literary Genres

From the great variety of interpretations which various Christian and non-Christian sources have placed upon the sacred text, it is clear that merely possessing an accurate copy of the Bible is not enough. The serious reader needs special guidance in determining the meaning of God's inspired communication. The science which provides him with the necessary rules is known as hermeneutics, which is derived from the Greek verb meaning "to explain" or "to interpret." This science assumes that the sacred authors had a message to deliver, and that they expressed this message in language which they felt would accomplish that end. Consequently, the authors must have expressed themselves according to the conventions of communication prevalent among the people for whom they were writing. They must have used words in their accepted meaning; they must have employed literary figures familiar to their audience. If the sacred authors intended to express themselves in prose, they must have adhered quite closely to the dictionary or idiomatic sense of the phrases they used. And if they wished to express themselves poetically, it is assumed that they used such literary images as the common people would have quickly grasped.

Thus, scientific facts would be described in popular, non-technical language. The sun, for example, is said to rise in the east and to set in the west. Although this description is not scientifically correct (the effect results from the earth turning on its axis), it cannot be branded as erroneous, since it accounts for what seems to be taking place in adequate fashion. Not even the most exacting scientist hesitates to express himself in this way. So we must not condemn the biblical authors for using this and similar phrases. Again, a truth may be expressed with some exaggeration of details. In the ancient monuments of Egypt and Babylonia this was a standard convention; in describing victories, for example, the number of individuals killed and conquered was almost invariably increased in the report in order to bring out the importance of the battle and the glory of the victor. And in our own civilization, hyperbole has its place — from exaggerating the size of

21

the bully overcome by the little boy to romanticizing the length of the fish caught by his father.

All of these considerations we take very much for granted. In our contemporary society, the thoughtful person—especially one who has received at least a high school training — does not have too much difficulty in making allowance for idiomatic language, nor in recognizing familiar figures of speech. In other words, he is able to pull the message out of the envelope of language in which it is delivered. We all realize that many statements—such as many news editorials— may be taken only at a considerable discount. Yet, we have been very slow to apply these principles regarding the use of conventional and figurative language to the understanding of Sacred Scripture. Somehow — especially during the Victorian era — the inviolability of the biblical message had rubbed off onto the literary garb in which the human authors had clothed it. And it is from this confusion of the package with the product that most of the modern problems of interpretation rise. It has been the genius of the twentieth century to disentangle these two elements definitively, it seems — at least in broad outline. To state the matter philosophically, we have finally distinguished clearly the material cause (literary medium: history, etc.) from the formal cause (message: the pattern or rules of salvation).

The Historico-Literary Method

In coming to grips with the human element in Sacred Scripture, our procedure will be along the lines of historico-literary exegesis. We call it *historico-* because we recognize that the biblical message, coming from the Author of truth, can be nothing but the truth. The Bible is based upon historical realities which God Himself had a hand in fashioning. But since the vehicle or "envelope" through which these realities are conveyed was proportioned to the limitations and characteristics of the human instruments whom God used in the writing of the various books and to the unschooled audience for whom they were writing, we must take cognizance also of the literary devices which they employed.

It was quite a blow to the Fundamentalists to have to admit that there was such a genuine human element in Scripture. As we saw in the previous chapter, the theories of inspiration which explained that phenomenon as merely *revelation* or outright dictation were products of this mentality. In their eagerness to safeguard the inerrancy of the text, die-hard conservatives of the nineteenth century had actually compromised the faith by their negative efforts to protect it. Confronted with the facts, they finally had to capitulate and to take cognizance of the laws of human psychology as well as of the divine omni-

potence. The psychology involved was that of a civilization almost
3000 years old, separated from our world by vast differences of history,
environment and technology — not to mention literary style. Moreover, the world into which the Bible was born was not the Western
Hemisphere of Greek logic and preciseness, but the Eastern Hemisphere of sapiential intuition.

The error of previous centuries—even among the more "scientific"
of the believing scholars — was the propensity for trying to fit a piece
of Eastern (Semitic) literature into the mould of Western (Greek)
philosophy. And just as the mentalities of East and West are poles
apart, so are the languages in which their enduring ideas have been
enshrined. If we of the twentieth century are to recapture the genuine
thought of the biblical authors, it is imperative that we first reconstruct their mentality and their literary forms. In fact, this constitutes
the principal point of the late Pope Pius XII's encyclical, *Divino
Afflante Spiritu,* of 1943. After reviewing the directives of his immediate predecessors in regard to biblical studies — especially *Providentissimus Deus,* issued exactly fifty years previously—the Pope
noted the changed conditions of biblical scholarship resulting from
Palestinian excavations, scientific progress, and the discovery of papyri
and manuscripts. After urging a more intensive effort in the fields of
textual criticism and linguistic studies (in which, he notes, the Scholastics were lacking), he turned his attention to the literary forms of
the ancient East. Because of the timeliness of his remarks, the encyclical deserves to be quoted at length.

> *Literary forms of the ancient East* — But frequently the literal
> sense is not so obvious in the words and writings of the ancient
> oriental authors as it is with the writers of today. For what they
> intended to signify by their words is not determined only by the
> laws of grammar or philology, nor merely by the context; it is
> absolutely necessary for the interpreter to go back in spirit to
> those remote centuries of the East, and make proper use of the
> aids afforded by history, archaeology, ethnology, and other sci-
> ences, in order to discover what literary forms the writers of that
> early age intended to use, and did in fact employ. *For to express
> what they had in mind the ancients of the East did not always
> use the same forms and expressions as we use to-day; they used
> those which were current among the people of their own time
> and place; and what these were the exegete cannot determine
> a priori, but only from a careful study of ancient oriental literature.*
> This study has been pursued during the past few decades with
> greater care and industry than formerly, and has made us better
> acquainted with the literary forms used in those ancient times,
> whether in poetical descriptions, or in the formulation of rules
> and laws of conduct, or in the narration of historical facts and
> events. It has now also clearly demonstrated the unique pre-
> eminence among all the ancient nations of the East which the

people of Israel enjoyed in historical writing, both in regard to the antiquity of the events recorded and to the accuracy with which they are related — a circumstance, of course, which is explained by the charisma of divine inspiration and by the special purpose, the religious purpose, of biblical history.

Divine words in human language — At the same time, no one who has a just conception of biblical inspiration will be surprised to find that the sacred writers, like the other ancients, employ certain arts of exposition and narrative, certain idioms especially characteristic of the semitic languages (known as "approximations"), and certain hyperbolical and even paradoxical expressions designed for the sake of emphasis. The Sacred Books need not exclude any of the forms of expressions which were commonly used in human speech by the ancient peoples, especially of the East, to convey their meaning, so long as they are in no way incompatible with God's sanctity and truth. 'In the divine Scripture,' observes St. Thomas, with characteristic shrewdness, 'divine things are conveyed to us in the manner to which men are accustomed.' *For just as the substantial Word of God became like to men in all things, 'without sin,' so the words of God, expressed in human language, became in all things like to human speech, except error.* This is that 'condescension' of divine Providence which St. John Chrysostom so highly extolled and which he repeatedly asserted to be found in the Sacred Books.

The importance of this branch of study — Consequently, if the Catholic exegete is to meet fully the requirements of modern biblical study he must, in expounding Sacred Scripture and vindicating its immunity from all error, make prudent use also of this further aid: he must, that is, ask himself how far the form of expression or literary idiom employed by the sacred writer may contribute to the true and genuine interpretation; and he may be sure that this part of his task cannot be neglected without great detriment to Catholic exegesis. *For — to mention only this example — in many cases in which the sacred authors are accused of some historical inaccuracy or of the inexact recording of some events, it is found to be a question of nothing more than those customary and characteristic forms of expression or styles of narrative which were current in human intercourse among the ancients, and which were in fact quite legitimately and commonly employed.* A just impartiality therefore demands that when these are found in the word of God, which is expressed in human language for men's sake, they should be no more stigmatized as error than when similar expressions are employed in daily usage. *Thus a knowledge and careful appreciation of ancient modes of expression and literary forms and styles will provide a solution to many of the objections made against the truth and historical accuracy of Holy Writ; and the same study will contribute with equal profit to a fuller and clearer perception of the mind of the Sacred Author.*

The research of lay scholars — To this matter also, then, our biblical scholars must pay due attention, neglecting no new information which archaeology, ancient history, or the study of ancient literature may provide, and which may serve to throw further light upon the mentality of ancient writers, their processes of thought, and their historical and literary methods, forms, and devices. And the Catholic laity should here observe that, by devoting themselves with active zeal to antiquarian study and research, and by assisting in the measure of their power towards the elucidation of cognate questions hitherto not fully solved, they will be not only making a contribution to the advancement of profane knowledge, but also rendering a very great service to the Christian cause. For all human knowledge, even other than sacred knowledge, has an intrinsic worth and excellence of its own, because it is a finite sharing of the infinite knowledge of God; and it receives an added and nobler dignity, a consecration as it were, when it is used to shed a brighter light upon divine things.

Many problems already solved — The progress in the investigation of oriental antiquities which we mentioned above, and the more careful study of the original text, as well as the wider and more exact knowledge of biblical languages and of oriental languages generally, have with God's help borne fruit in the final solution of many of the objections which, in the days of Our Predecessor of immortal memory Leo XIII, were being raised by non-Catholic or even anti-Catholic critics against the authenticity, antiquity, integrity, and historical authority of the Sacred Books. Catholic exegetes, using aright those very weapons of learning which their opponents were frequently abusing, have propounded interpretations which, while being in accordance with Catholic teaching and true traditional thought, appear at the same time to have met the difficulties which have either arisen from recent research and recent discoveries or had been left for our solution as a legacy from ancient times.

The credit of the Bible vindicated — The result has been that confidence in the authority and historical truth of the Bible, which, in the face of so many attacks, had in some minds been partially shaken, has now among Catholics been wholly restored: indeed, even among non-Catholic writers there are some who have been led by a serious and impartial examination to abandon the views of the moderns and to return, in some cases at least, to the older opinions. This change is due in great part to the untiring labour of Catholic scriptural exegetes who, undeterred by difficulties and obstacles of every sort, have devoted all their efforts to making a proper use of the contributions made by the research of modern scholars, whether in archaeology, history, or philology, towards the solution of new problems.[1]

Eastern Mentality

From what has been said, it would seem to be of the utmost importance to make some attempt at understanding the mentality of the Orient, which is the ultimate key to an appreciation of Semitic literary forms. The first characteristic which arrests our attention about the

---

[1] Catholic Truth Society, *Biblical Studies* (London, 1943), paragraphs 39-45. This whole encyclical makes profitable reading.

Oriental is his *concrete* conception of reality, as opposed to the Western or Greek *abstract* view. Identifying himself with his surroundings, the Semite tends to be very subjective in his evaluations; the Greek mind, on the other hand, deliberately isolates itself from the situation and strains to get an objective viewpoint. The Semite will be found to be intuitive, reflective, synthetic in his approach to life; the Greek is rather logical, perceptive, analytical. Where the Semite prefers to use symbols to represent reality, the Western mind prefers to use signs and syllogisms. A good way to characterize the two outlooks is to designate the Jew as "sapiential," the Greek as "scientific." Modern "impressionist" writers and painters remind one of the Orient; they represent an anomaly in the Western world.

Without looking too far, we can find three basic characteristics in Semitic literature: parallelism, juxtaposition and antithesis. To emphasize a point, a Jew will repeat the idea over and over again by the use of synonyms (parallelism), rather than give a succinct definition. He has an aversion for subordinate clauses: hence, he will use a string of phrases and clauses connected by *"and"* to bring out his meaning (juxtaposition). Finally, the repetition will be modified somewhat by the employment of vivid contrasts of words and phrases (antithesis). The over-all difference in the two mentalities is well illustrated by the difference between a *parable* (peculiar to Hebrew style) and an *allegory* (proper to Greek style). The parable is a fictitious story which, when taken as a whole, conveys a lesson. It paints a picture, betrays a mood: it is anything but a schematic analogy. An allegory, on the other hand, correlates the details of the story with the corresponding elements of reality. The former is imaginative, the latter is a product of abstraction.[2]

A forceful illustration of this point is concordism. This was the attempt, referred to in Chapter I, to harmonize the Bible with the positive sciences: biology, anthropology, geology, etc. Especially noteworthy was the attempt — ultimately abandoned — to match up the six days of creation with the geological periods of physical evolution. As long as biblical scholars insisted on interpreting the work of the six days as an allegory, they were bound to run into difficulties. But after they had become more familiar with Semitic literary genres and treated the six days as an historical parable, the first chapter of Genesis yielded for them a rich content of religious truth without challenging the conclusions of modern science in the least.

Here is a list of the more common literary genres in use among the Jewish people in biblical times. The three forms preceded by an asterisk are unique: they have no counterpart in Western literature.

---

2 Cf. Charlier, *Op. cit.,* pp. 45-46; 133-146.

Semitic Literary Genres

I. *History.* This is the principal thread or medium used by the Sacred Authors to convey their inspired messages; it is the "material cause" of Scripture. In the classical tradition, history has been classed under rhetoric; this certainly fits in with the Hebrew notion. For the Semitic mind, history was never merely an enumeration of dates and events; it was a tool to be used to convey some dogmatic or moral truth. Hence, they nearly always "slanted" the facts in the direction of the message they offered, so that the Bible is really a *theology of history.*

   *A. *Primitive History* (Popular traditions). The first eleven chapters of Genesis are unique; the Sacred Author has filled in the gap before recorded history from the traditions of his people with the help of divine revelation. A prominent feature of this folk history is the *historical parable,* exemplified in the six days of creation. These chapters are not to be confused with myths.

   B. *Ancient History.* From the eleventh chapter of Genesis to the Book of Ruth we have history more in our Western mould; yet, the author takes many liberties, and his work lacks critical sources and technical preciseness. With Kings begins history proper (detailed accounts). The Gospels and Acts of the Apostles belong here. *None of these books exactly equals our idea of history.*

   *C. *Genealogies.* Here is another example of a literary genre proper to the Oriental mind—artificial, skeletal and often symbolic lists of ancestors with an historical background. (See Chapter XVII for Hebrew numerology.)

   D. *Dramatic Dialogue.* Conversations reported in the Old Testament (e.g., between Eve and the serpent, God and Abraham) are not to be taken as the stenographic account of a court reporter, but rather as a literary device to convey truth.

   E. *Edifying History.* Bordering on poetry, this literary form uses history (especially biography) as a dressing for some truth or lesson. Usually the hero is an historical personage (Job, Tobias, Judith, Esther were all probably real persons; Jona probably was not: here we have a satire) embellished with fictional details. This form is comparable to morality plays.

II. *Legal Literature.* Taking rise from the fact of God's Covenant with His Chosen People and its consequent obligations, this genre envelops the precepts of the Pentateuch in an historical atmosphere. These five books emphasize the legal tenor of the whole Old Testament.

III. *Poetry.* Whether written in prose or verse, the essence of poetry is to focus on the beautiful and thereby to create a contemplative mood. This genre makes extensive use of *imaginative* (fictional) and *emotional* elements.

    A. *Lyric Poetry.* Usually in rhyme, this form is an expression of the author's personal viewpoint. It appeals to the emotions and is adaptable to song. The Psalms are classical examples of lyric poetry, making God the center of lofty sentiments.

    B. *Dramatic Poetry.* The poem is enhanced by the invention of characters and episodes in order to cast the theme in a beautiful mould (e.g., the Canticle of Canticles).

    C. *Epic (Narrative) Poetry.* Grandiose details are inserted in the story to embellish the picture (e.g., Psalm 105; Wisdom 16 and 17).

IV. *Wisdom Literature.* This consists in collections of moral truths adorned with striking figures of speech, homely examples, satire, wit and enigma. Books of this class teach the way to happiness through keeping the law of God.

    A. *Sapiential Books.* Best examples are Wisdom, Proverbs, Sirach, Ecclesiastes.

    B. *Epistles* of the New Testament may be classed here: instruction through essays.

V. *Prophecy.* The primary role of the prophet was to "speak for" God, to interpret His mind and will for the people at a specific moment in history. The foretelling of events was incidental to his mission, though the prophet often did predict the future. Prophecy often includes statements of God's judgments on men, embodied in penetrating and sweeping analyses of history. There are four major (plus Baruch) and twelve minor prophets in the Old Testament.

    A. *Prophetic Books Proper.* These are manifestations of God's will to a given segment of individuals, often by means of arresting metaphors and symbols (the "envelope" of the message). Though both the message and envelope are inspired, the envelope is sometimes conditional, and hence not necessarily fulfilled; e.g., the predicted political restoration of the Jews contained in some prophecies did not materialize; it was the "envelope" of a spiritual restoration.

    *B. *Apocalyse.* Another unique oriental form—the word means "unveiling." The apocalyptic genre consists in a series of startling "revelations" referring to the eschatological era when God will intervene decisively in history. Events are clothed in dramatic, symbolic—and sometimes coded—language. Often they are pre-dated and authorship is attributed to a famous deceased person, such as Moses or Daniel. The purpose is to console and strengthen faithful souls who are under some trial. (Cf. Deuteronomy 28, Daniel, Apocalypse.)

C. *Utopian Model.* A description of a traditional Jewish institution (e.g., the Temple in Ezechiel 44, ff.) in idealistic terms, foreshadowing a later *replacement* by its New Testament counterpart: the Temple was replaced by the (Mystical) Body of Christ.

Suggested Readings

Charlier, *The Christian Approach to the Bible,* Chap. 5 and 8.
McKenzie, *The Two-Edged Sword,* Chap. 1, 2, 4.
Orchard, *A Catholic Commentary on Holy Scripture,* cols. 32-33.
Vann, *The Paradise Tree,* Chap. 1. Discusses man's basic need of symbols.

Chapter IV

A Theandric Work: The "Senses" of Sacred Scripture

The fact of inspiration entails that each book of the Bible have at least two authors: God and one or more human beings. As one would expect, this gives a unique character to the sacred text. In what does this uniqueness consist? To answer the question completely would demand infused knowledge: we are dealing here with a mystery, since inspiration involves God's own divine action. At the very least, we can say that the pages of Scripture will surely be richer in meaning than a merely human book. Indeed, it is clear that in many cases not even the human author himself understood fully the whole import of what he, as God's instrument, was writing. To say, then, that the Bible is a book of double meanings is a masterpiece of understatement, not blasphemy. Often the second meanings come to light only in a later book of the Bible, or through the insight that God has given to His Church; undoubtedly some meanings will come to light only in the next life.

As a consequence, standard literary classifications are inadequate when applied to Scripture. We can begin to appreciate this once we examine the customary division studied in English literature. The meaning of a literary work is divided into two basic categories: *literal* and *figurative* (or metaphorical). These divisions are opposed to each other as a complete dichotomy. The *literal* meaning is taken to be the ordinary, dictionary meaning proper to exposition; the *figurative* meaning is understood to be the improper, metaphorical meaning found in imaginative works (poetry, fiction). This division is insufficient for biblical use since it makes no provision for the hidden "double" meaning intended by the Holy Spirit.

Following the example of Fr. Pierre Benoit, O.P., we shall designate the meaning intended by the human author as the *primary sense*. The further meaning intended by the Holy Spirit can thus conveniently be designated the *secondary sense*. The following schema brings out the distinction between the two:[1]

---

[1] Paul Synave, O.P., and Pierre Benoit, O.P., *Prophecy and Inspiration* (New York: Desclee Co., 1961) pp. 147 ff.

I. *The primary or literal sense* is that meaning clearly seen and intended by the human author. This division will include both the *proper* and *improper* (figurative) usages of words.

II. *The secondary or spiritual sense* is that meaning not clearly seen by the human author, but intended by the Principal Author (God) through the words which He inspired the instrumental author to employ. This sense emerges only later (and especially in the New Testament) as salvation history progresses. As we shall see, this division includes both the *fuller* and the *typical* (or mystical) senses.

Historical Background

The basic division noted above has been recognized since the days of St. Paul, who speaks of Old Testament characters and events as "types" of New Testament realities (I Cor. 10). In the third century two schools of biblical interpretation sprang up within the Church. At Antioch a group of scholars flourished under the direction of St. Lucian and, later, under St. John Chrysostom. Devoted to Aristotelian philosophy, these exegetes emphasized the *literal* (primary) meaning of the text — sometimes perhaps a bit too rigidly (e.g., in explaining creation, they interpreted the story of the six days in Genesis as a blow-by-blow account of how God did it). However, they by no means excluded secondary meanings from their exegesis, and their concept of *theoria* can be seen as a forerunner of the modern notion of the fuller sense.[2]

Across the Mediterranean at Alexandria in Egypt, another school arose under the leadership of St. Clement and the great Platonist scholar, Origen. Intent on capturing what they considered the all-important "spiritual" sense of the Scriptures, these men tended to by-pass the primary sense in favor of the secondary. The result was that a good deal of their exegesis turned out to be accommodations (artificial applications). They taught, for example, that the word *heaven* in Genesis 1 means the abode of the spirits, whereas the *abyss* is hell. This tendency, known as allegorism, was not extensive enough to vitiate the main core of Alexandrian exegesis, and their method had great influence on later scholars.

Though St. Augustine's (d. 430) Platonist leaning inclined him toward the Alexandrian school, he managed to hit a happy medium in his exegesis. Thus, though he taught that the divine act of creation was instantaneous, he saw in the account of the six days a metaphor representing the evolution of the various species of life. After the genuine Dark Ages of 800-1100, the Scholastics took up biblical exegesis

---

[2] Cf. Brown, *The Sensus Plenior of Sacred Scripture*, pp. 108-112.

where St. Augustine had left off. Until the popularization of the *Summa Theologica* of St. Thomas, all theological training was imparted by way of commentaries on Sacred Scripture. Though it is a monument of systematic theology, the *Summa* clearly presupposes a thorough knowledge of the Bible on the part of the reader—a fact which was tragically forgotten by later ages.[3] Systematic theology gradually displaced positive (biblical) theology. For a short time after the Council of Trent (1545-1563) there were a few great commentators on Scripture[4] followed by a notable decline during the period 1650-1800. In the wake of Protestant emphasis on the Bible alone, Catholics became timid about reading the Scriptures.

In 1753 a Frenchman, Jean Astruc, dared to propose a "documentary" approach to the Pentateuch, but the effort received little notice at the time; he was a century ahead of his age. The spirit of rationalism following upon the French Revolution precipitated the biblical crisis described in the first chapter. The tremendous progress of the past fifty years has produced a vigorous new springtime in scriptural studies, with positive theology once again coming into its own. One of the many fruits of this revival is mirrored in the rapidly developing notion of the *fuller sense* of Scripture which will be treated below.

The Primary or Literal Sense of Scripture

Every passage in Scripture must have a literal sense — that is, a meaning intended by the human author. God did not dictate the sacred text; rather, He used the human agent to conceive the truth He wished to be transmitted, then enabled him to put it down in apt words. For unless the man who wrote it had some idea in mind which he intended to convey, the text would be a senseless babbling from the human viewpoint or, at best, just an arbitrary cipher for the divine communication. The human author would have been acting simply as a stenographer, not as an author. Biblical scholars are generally agreed, moreover, that there can be only one literal sense in a given passage; otherwise, the text would be ambiguous. Finally, the author expressed himself either in the proper meaning of the words (i.e., prosaically) or else he expressed himself in an improper, figurative mode (i.e., poetically) in any given passage; the one excludes the other.

But it must not be forgotten that words are signs used to express concepts. Concepts, in turn, are either concrete or abstract. To state this another way, concepts and words may be used to designate either

---

[3] Cf. J. R. Sheets, S.J., "The Scriptural Dimensions of St. Thomas," *The American Ecclesiastical Review*, CXLIV (1961), pp. 154-173.

[4] Notably Richard Simon in the 17th century. Had this "Father of Biblical Criticism" been permitted to continue his research without episcopal interference, the 19th century biblical crisis might never have been precipitated.

individuals or classes. Thus, in logic we divide concepts into particular and universal, remembering of course that the intellect works in conjunction with the senses in forming particular concepts. In the case of abstract, universal concepts (man, life, goodness), the concept rises completely above concrete individual things, and words used to express such concepts share in their universality. In the case of particular concepts (Adam, Jerusalem), the concept is rooted in some thing or event which may be either *historical* (Moses, the Exodus) or *literary* (Jona). Over a long period of time, things and events may acquire a new meaning through subsequent historical developments, and the concepts and words which represent these things likewise are enriched. For example, the term "Adam" certainly took on a tremendous new depth of meaning when Christ became identified as the "New Adam." But this consideration projects our treatise into the secondary sense of Scripture.

The Secondary or Spiritual Sense of Scripture

We say, then, that the term "Adam" as it designates the First Adam represents the primary, literal sense of the word; inasmuch as it designates Christ, the same term is being used in its secondary or spiritual sense, intended all along by the Holy Spirit. Because we are dealing with concrete, individual entities, the first Adam is said to be the "type"; the Second Adam (Christ) is the "antitype." This "typology" (relationship between *type* — usually found in the Old Testament — and *antitype* — usually found in the New Testament) has always been recognized by Christian exegetes. The development and enrichment of particular terms which it represents stems fundamentally from the fact that no part of Scripture can be understood adequately except in the light of the whole Bible. Scripture's organic unity is guaranteed, moreover, by the divine Author Who is giving us therein an accurate (if miniature) blueprint of salvation history. Only from the top of the mountain can one gain a panoramic view of what lies below.[5]

But in the case of abstract concepts and terms, the general run of scholars has been slow to admit—or at least to recognize clearly— any legitimate development apart from parallel typology and theological deductions. Yet it seems obvious that such development does exist and demands attention and classification. For example, does not the very limited term "life" envisaged by the author of Genesis as denoting

---

[5] The reader will note that many types contain definite prophetic overtones. However, because of the limited insight and unfocused view of the sacred author, he fused all his details into a composite picture, being unable to differentiate those which pertained to the type from those which overflowed into the antitype (for example: Ps. 15, 21, 109; Isa. 7:14, 53). Such "overreaching" is known as "compenetration," and is usually present in a utopian model.

"longevity" assume an enormously profounder meaning when enriched by the New Testament notion of *divine* life actually shared by Christians? We know now that the Patriarchs did share in this divine life by reason of their faith — even if they and the biblical author were evidently unaware of it.

It seems that the first exegete to call this development of abstract terms in Scripture the "fuller" sense was Fr. A. Fernandez, S.J., about 1925, though the notion is much older. This topic has been the subject of heated debate among scholars in recent years, with a number of first-rate exegetes still refusing to admit the division. The principal objection seems to be this: the fuller sense represents a "reading back" into the Old Testament (usually) meanings which can be validly attached only to the New Testament. In the case of the typical sense, there is no difficulty; the new meaning is rooted in the *type* even though the human author was unaware of it. But in the case of the fuller sense, since the author presumably did not perceive the new meaning — at least not clearly — it cannot be attached in any way to the literal sense; hence, it is not a sense of Scripture.

In answer we reply that the primary as well as the secondary sense has God as its author; since He is the *Principal* Author, the effect is basically proportioned to His knowledge and may exceed the competence of the instrument. From all eternity God willed and perceived a hidden meaning to exist not only under concrete types, but also behind abstract terms and concepts. But how do we know that He intended this fuller meaning in the earlier text? In general we can say that the very pattern of salvation history gives a higher meaning to the whole text as manifested through the analogy of faith. For specific interpretations, we depend upon Scripture itself (especially the New Testament) and upon the Church's magisterium as contained in the sources noted on page 39 in the column marked "Deposits of Faith." St. Paul cites the instance of *wisdom:*

> But we speak the wisdom of God, mysterious, hidden, which God foreordained before the world unto our glory, a wisdom which none of the rulers of this world has known. . . . Even so, the things of God no one knows but the Spirit of God. Now we have received not the spirit of the world, but the spirit that is from God, that we may know the things that have been given us by God. (I Cor. 1:7-8, 11-12)

This example has been chosen because it furnishes us with a case — quite common, as we would expect — where we can see a distinct parallel between the fuller and the corresponding typical senses of Scripture. The notion of wisdom (as we shall see in Chapter XXII) was a pagan concept borrowed by the Jews. It consisted largely in pragmatic formulae designed to influence people and, ideally, to govern men. The Egyptian Pharao of the Exodus exemplified human wisdom before it was taken over by Jewish sages into their wisdom literature. The following diagram illustrates the unfolding of the fuller meaning parallel with significant types:

Development of the FULLER MEANING of wisdom (abstract)	I. Pagan pragmatism becomes obedience to God via Torah (Prov.)	II. Wisdom is personified as an attribute of God only	III. True wisdom is obedience to Christ and His law (I Cor.)
Parallel development of TYPOLOGY of the wise man (concrete)	Solomon in early life is the model sage: his fall from wisdom	Suffering teaches Job: God alone can right injustice	Christ, Second Person of the Trinity = Wisdom incarnate

In his recent book, Fr. Benoit classifies the fuller sense as a secondary meaning. Fr. Brown states: "[The fuller sense] is a distinct sense from either the literal or the typical, holding a position between the two, but closer to the literal. Like the literal sense, it is a meaning of the text; unlike it, it is not within the clear purview of the hagiographer. . . it is not a sense of 'things' but of words."[6] Nevertheless, in the first of his alternate divisions, Fr. Brown places the fuller meaning under the *spiritual* (secondary) sense.

Finally, it should be noted that the **accommodated sense** is *not* a sense of Scripture, but rather the use of a passage or type from the Bible by a writer, preacher, etc., to illustrate a point. Thus, I might call a strong boy "a real Samson" because of his strength. My statement does not make Samson a type of this boy; the comparison is mine, not the Holy Spirit's. Many liturgical texts represent accommodations, e.g., Sirach 24 is applied to the Blessed Virgin Mary in many of her feasts.

Particular Rules of Interpretation, Proper to Sacred Scripture As a Divine Book

In the last chapter we gave a set of norms whereby any human literary production should be interpreted. The rules which follow apply to the Bible precisely as an inspired book whose principal author is the Holy Spirit.

1) *The books of the Bible must be read with the submissiveness due to a divine pronouncement.* A rationalistic approach to Scripture

---

[6] Synave and Benoit, *Op. cit.*, p. 151, and Brown, *Op. cit.*, p. 122. In an earlier article condensed in *Theology Digest*, IX:1 (Winter 1961), p. 8, Fr. Benoit treats the fuller sense as a division of the literal.

THE SENSES OF SACRED SCRIPTURE*

LITERAL SENSE:	SPIRITUAL SENSE:		CONSEQUENT (THEOLOGICAL) SENSE:
The meaning clearly understood and expressed by the human author through the words he used, whether in their proper (dictionary) or improper (metaphorical) sense. This meaning of the words is known as the LITERAL SENSE, which may be in:	The meaning intended by the Holy Spirit, usually beyond that of the human author, and only gradually unfolded in the light of subsequent revelation and historical developments. We divide it as follows:		Meanings not evidently intended either by the human author or the Holy Spirit —hence, strictly NOT senses of Scripture unless contained elsewhere in the Bible at least implicitly.
	FULLER SENSE: (of abstract terms)	TYPICAL SENSE: (of concrete terms)	
I. ABSTRACT (or categorical) terms			
1. Life as applied to Patriarchs (=longevity).	Participation in the divine life; eternal life of heaven.		Grace as a kind of created quality in the soul constituting its supernatural life.
2. Redemption in terms of physical deliverance.	Spiritual deliverance through the remission of sins.		Redemption as a sharing in the capital grace of Christ; Mary as cooperator and mediatrix.
II. CONCRETE (individual) things, events ("TYPES")		ANTITYPES	
1. Isaac, offered by his father.		Christ sacrificed on Calvary by His Father.	Christ's Passion = the efficient cause of human salvation.
2. Jews crossing the Red Sea.		Reception of baptism by Christians.	Baptism produces its effects in the soul "ex opere operato."

*ACCOMMODATED SENSE—The Accommodated Sense is not a sense of scripture, but of the user. It is useful for preaching and sometimes found in the Liturgy.

THEOLOGICAL CLASSIFICATION

Establishing the literal meaning of the words—i.e., exposing what was in the mind of the human author insofar as his words reveal his meaning.	Establishing the spiritual meaning of the words—i.e., "that enrichment in objective meaning which the words of the Old Testament receive when used again in the New Testament."	Establishing theological meaning of texts by exploring what is only virtually revealed, using reason plus revelation.

Title: EXEGESIS   BIBLICAL THEOLOGY

DOGMATIC THEOLOGY
—God One and Three
—Christ, Sacraments

MORAL THEOLOGY
—Christian Life.

Division:

II. POSITIVE THEOLOGY

III. SYSTEMATIC THEOLOGY

Function: EXPLANATION OF REVELATION. Positive theology deals with formally revealed truths; hence, no true reasoning process is employed. The process is explicative rather than discursive or illative.

Function: DRAWING CONCLUSIONS "illatively" by a true syllogism (effect in cause and vice versa; property in essence, etc.).

I. FUNDAMENTAL THEOLOGY (APOLOGETICS) or the DEFENSE OF REVELATION AND THE CHURCH by reason under guidance of faith is presupposed to Positive Theology.

is doomed to fail from the very start, as the bitter controversies and abandoned hypotheses stemming from the "biblical crisis" amply illustrate. Supernatural faith is a prerequisite to that sympathetic study necessary in arriving at its authentic message. But this does not exclude a genuinely critical attitude which will penetrate beneath the superficial meaning and sound the depths of hidden truths. Mindful of the divine authorship, then, the reader will be *uncriticizing without being uncritical.*

2) *We must reject any interpretation which accuses the sacred author of the least formal error.* This is simply a corollary of the quality of inerrancy, discussed in Chapter II. *There can be no conflict between the Bible and any profane source of knowledge,* regardless of how insistently and sophisticatedly the latter's conclusions are urged. Students of Holy Scripture need not proceed in fear and trembling lest they stumble onto some insurmountable scientific or historical objection. As Saint Augustine said,

> Whatever they (physical scientists) can really demonstrate to be true of physical nature we must show to be capable of reconciliation with our Scriptures; and whatever they assert in their treatises, which is contrary to these Scriptures of ours, that is, to Catholic faith, we must either prove it as well as we can to be entirely false, or at all events we must, without the smallest hesitation, believe it to be so.[7]

As we have already seen, modern advances in scientific biblical criticism are vying with the absolute guarantee of faith in supporting the inerrancy of God's Word. Nineteenth century rationalism concluded that the Bible simply could not stand up under the sweeping long-range view of the "new science"; today, it is more clear than ever that it is Sacred Scripture which has the long-range view, which the limited outlook of science cannot but corroborate as it puts its house in order.

3) *The various texts of Scripture must always be interpreted in the sense in which the Church interprets them.* Any written document — even though inspired — demands a living authority for its authentic interpretation. For the Catholic, this authority has always been the magisterium of his Church. Although very few texts of the Bible have been explicitly interpreted by the Church, when she does propose a definite meaning as the correct sense of a specific text, this meaning must be held. How does the Church promulgate her decisions in this matter? Sometimes she does so solemnly, through the pronouncements of ecumenical councils or of the Pope, through creeds and professions of faith, or through the teaching of the Fathers of the Church. Other

---

[7] *De Genesi ad Litteram,* quoted in the encyclical, *Providentissimus Deus.*

decisions are manifested less solemnly through a Roman congregation, the teaching of her bishops and theologians, and also through the liturgy. An important step in biblical criticism was taken in 1902 when Pope Leo XIII set up the Pontifical Biblical Commission with head-quarters in Rome to explain and defend the Church's interpretation of the Scriptures and to supervise biblical studies and the granting of degrees in this area. The decisions of this Commission are binding in conscience when they are connected mediately or immediately with matters of faith and morals. In the light of modern research, we now realize that a number of issues formerly thought to be at least mediately so connected actually are not — viz., the authorship, date, and even the integrity of an inspired book. On such non-connected matters, biblical experts are free to pursue their investigations. Moreover, many of the Biblical Commission's decrees, true at the moment they were issued, have now yielded to more recent discoveries in the field. For example, the lack of sufficient evidence for postulating "Deutero-Isaia" at the turn of the century has been filled in; hence, the plurality of authorship of this book is now generally taught in Catholic as well as Protestant circles.[8]

4) *The unanimous teaching of the Fathers of the Church must be followed.* Those learned and saintly writers of the first eight centuries of the Church who enjoy the title of "father of the Church" hold special place as authoritative teachers. Hence when they manifest a moral unanimity of opinion with regard to the interpretation of a biblical passage — whether in its primary or secondary sense — such an opinion is to be considered as reflecting the mind of the Church.

5) *We must reject any interpretation which violates the "analogy of faith."* By this is meant that no passage of Scripture may be inter-

	DEPOSITS OF FAITH		DEPOSITS OF REASON
RULE 5 STATES THAT THERE CANNOT BE ANY DISAGREE-MENT AMONG THESE SOURCES	1. Tradition. 2. The Old Testament, and all of its parts. 3. The New Testament, and all of its parts. 4. Creeds and professions of faith. 5. Conciliar decisions. 6. Teaching of the Fathers and Doctors. 7. The Pontifical Biblical Commission, etc.	RULE 2 STATES THAT THERE CANNOT BE ANY DIS-AGREEMENT BETWEEN THE BIBLE AND ANY OF THE ITEMS ON THE RIGHT.	1. Philosophy 2. History 3. Biology 4. Physics 5. Chemistry 6. Paleontology 7. Anthropology 8. Geology 9. Archeology 10. Geography 11. Linguistics, etc.

[8] See Orchard, *A Catholic Commentary on Holy Scripture*, col. 47; also E. F. Siegman, C.PP.S., "The Decrees of the Pontifical Biblical Commission" in *The Catholic Biblical Quarterly*, 18 (1956), pp. 23–29.

preted so as to come in conflict with any other scriptural passage or with any other teaching of the Church. In Rule 2 above, it was a question of *external* agreement between the sources of faith and the sources of reason; here it is a question of *internal* agreement among the various sources of faith. These two relationships are shown in the diagram on the preceding page.

A few applications of these rules will help the student to grasp their importance.

The Bible and Science

The general principle with regard to all of the natural sciences is that the Bible was written to teach religious and moral truths, not scientific knowledge. We must not expect to find scientific accuracy in a religious textbook whose sacred authors simply used the language and conventions of their own day in referring to the universe. God could have revealed to these men the secrets of science, but the fact is that He did not. Such revelations in a religious book would have distracted men's minds from the principal message. The Divine Author has made it a point to adapt His truths to the level and atmosphere of the people to whom the communication was being made — in the case of the Old Testament (and the New Testament also) — to an unscientific generation. Hence, the story of creation is unfolded according to the external appearances of the world, not according to its internal structure. The Jewish people were not aware of atoms, molecules, gravity, etc.; to speak in these terms would have been foolish.[9] This explains why, for example, the sacred author has God create the light before the sun and planets. In his mind and that of his contemporaries, light was independent of the heavenly bodies; does it not stream from the horizon long before the sun rises, and endure for some time after the sun sets?

The Bible and History

Generally speaking, ancient people (including the Greeks and Romans, as well as the Orientals) did not consider history a science as modern historians do, but rather a kind of literary art. This is notably true of the biblical authors; their "historical method" was quite different from ours. For them, recounting data in a precise and orderly fashion was relatively unimportant. The religious meaning of the facts, particularly the moral lessons contained in them, was their primary concern. They "used" history without the least qualms of conscience to illustrate the divine economy of salvation. What they have left us is really a theology of history. The exaggerated ages of the patriarchs,

---

[9] See, for example, the description in Eccles. 1:5–7.

together with the dearth of names, is a prime example; even their genealogies were geared to the over-all religious message. Anachronisms are common; Cain founded a "city" (Gen. 4:17); iron is mentioned before the Flood (Gen. 4:22); the languages of men were differentiated in a day (Gen. 11:9).

Yet, whenever the sacred authors set out to recount history in the more strict sense of the word, there cannot be any inaccuracies in their statements. In this case, we may not "take too ready refuge in such notions as 'implicit quotations' or 'pseudo-historical narratives', or in 'kinds of literature' in the Bible such as cannot be reconciled with the entire and perfect truth of God's word," as Pope Benedict XV laid down in his encyclical, *Spiritus Paraclitus*.[10] This same Pope also warned against making too close an analogy between science and history in the interpretation of the Scriptures:

> Those, too, who hold that the historical portions of Scripture do not rest on the absolute truth of the facts but merely upon what they are pleased to term their relative truth, namely, what people then commonly thought . . . on the ground that he [Pope Leo XIII] allowed that the principles he had laid down touching the things of nature could be applied to historical things as well . . . are out of harmony with the Church's teaching.[11]

True biblical methodology demands that the serious reader, when confronted with a difficult passage, pause and ask himself: "Is this section meant to be historical? If it is, then which of the three 'species' of history are we dealing with: primitive history, ancient history, or strict history? Did the sacred author wish to convey some fact of history here, or is his purpose primarily the religious truth?" In arriving at a solution to the difficulty, the student will avoid two extremes. On the one hand, he will avoid a rigid literalism which is content to find only the superficial meaning of the words in a given text. On the other hand, he will not slough off genuine textual problems connected with the obvious meaning by having recourse to pagan myths and fables, "implicit quotations" (i.e., the claim that the sacred writer was quoting a profane document without indicating this fact), or explaining away the literal meaning as pure symbolism or allegory.

The Bible and Theology and Philosophy

Sacred Scripture abounds with both theological and philosophical truth; it was written to impart to mankind the fundamental facts of human existence. In interpreting these truths, four points should be kept in mind:

---

10 Cf. *Rome and the Study of Scripture* (1958 edition), p. 54.
11 *Ibid.*, p. 52.

41

1) The Jews were not of an abstract, philosophical bent of mind; their thought was concrete, poetical; we must not expect philosophical formulae nor theological precision.

2) There is a certain development of dogma in the Bible; truths are unfolded gradually, according to the capacity of the recipients. Thus, the doctrine of future life is very vague in the earlier books of the Old Testament, and becomes explicit only in a few books written after the Babylonian Captivity.

3) The fact that the sacred author recounts immoral acts sometimes rather casually, e.g., Jacob's deception of Isaac, does not mean that either he or God approves them.

4) Although the natural law is fundamentally immutable, God did not demand the same degree of moral purity at every age: there is a notable moral progression among the Jews, e.g., the gradual elimination of polygamy.

The Theandric Nature of Sacred Scripture

In explaining the nature of the Bible through its causes, we have cast our ideas in the mold most familiar to our readers — that of Scholastic philosophy. But, as one would expect from what has been pointed out regarding Semitic mentality, this Western framework fails to do full justice to the concepts involved. It tends to betray the unity of Scripture by its analytical approach. Therefore, to safeguard both the unity of the two authorships and the unity which exists between the Bible and Tradition, we must supplement our explanation with a few words about the "theandric" (from the Greek *Theos*, God, and *andros*, man) character of Scripture. By dint of His extremely delicate influence on the sacred authors, God was able to produce a divine-human document. As we have seen, the Bible represents a climax in the history of divine communication, the moment when the Word of God became legible. And it was through the inspiration of the Holy Spirit that this new penetration of the Word into the world of man was effected. But we shall not forget that Sacred Scripture is not the only — nor even the primary — manifestation of the Word. Always presupposed to the inspired text is the "inspired" Tradition which it mirrors. For the same Spirit Who moved the sacred authors to write without error infallibly guaranteed the errorless transmission of the unwritten Word of God. Listen to the eloquent words of Dom Charlier:

> We have tried to show the Bible's place in the economy of this divine plan. We saw how it was a pre-incarnation of the Son of God in words, designed to support His incarnation in the flesh. This double incarnation in time could take place only once, but its eternal repercussions continue through all time. The mystery of Christ is continued in His Church; the mystery of the Bible is con-

tinued in tradition. We saw how the Church's living Tradition is the leaven which ensures that the Bible continues to give life, and to reveal the same incarnate Word under the inspiration of the same Spirit. . . .

There is therefore an analogy in the Christian economy between the Eucharist and the Bible, both of which have similar functions. Neither is the source of Christian life but both watch over its development. They assure not the birth of Christian life but its growth. They are not its seed but its food. . . . The Eucharist is a sacrament in the proper sense of the word. The Bible is a sacrament only by analogy. That does not mean that its part in the economy of salvation is any less important. A sacrament is an *action* stemming from the divine energy by which we share in the vitality of the Spirit of Christ. But Christianity offers man not only the means of supernatural action; it offers him also the means of supernatural *thought*. It is here that the function of the Bible lies. Christian life is founded on Christian knowledge; charity is founded on faith. The Spirit of God cannot move the will until the Word of God has enlightened the mind. If the sacraments are the channels through which we are given the Spirit of Christ, Christian instruction in all its forms is the doorway through which the Spirit ushers the Word. If we are to be saved we need both 'to believe and to be baptized' (Mark 16:16); and if our Christian life is to grow we must eat the bread of the Word by our faith in its teachings no less than by our reception of His risen body. . . .

Both are a living memorial of the past, the Eucharist of the Word humbled in the flesh and glorified in the Spirit, the Bible of the Word humbled in the flesh of human language.[13]

We are now in a position to fill in the answer to a fourth basic question about the Bible: WHY did God cause it to be written? (the FINAL CAUSE or purpose in terms of Scholastic philosophy). In its broadest implications, the answer to this question is, of course, for the salvation of men. But the precise purpose God had in mind was to insure obedience to the rules laid down — not just by the Jews, but for their spiritual descendants to the end of time. This explains why the Holy Spirit has left a legible, permanent blueprint of salvation-history valid both before and after Christ; and it explains why He continues to guarantee the integrity and interpretation of this document within the bosom of Church.

And now a final summary of these introductory chapters to provide a skeleton of the pivotal points which have been covered.

Introductory Theses

I. *Communication* is the manifestation of any truth; revelation is the manifestation of a previously unknown truth, either knowable in itself, or unknowable (mystery). Although all of Scripture is inspired,

---

[13] Charlier, *The Christian Approach to the Bible,* pp. 295-297.

only a fraction is revealed in the strict sense. Catholics must believe all of God's public communication at least *implicity*, by accepting *in globo* every truth contained in Scripture and Tradition (their remote rule of faith); they must believe *explicitly* whatever is proposed to them by the Church (their proximate rule of faith).

II. The two sources of public communication are:

Tradition—those divinely communicated truths handed down outside of the Bible.

Sacred Scripture—that *collection* of sacred, legal books which, written under the inspiration of the Holy Spirit, have God as their principal author. (The *canon* of Sacred Scripture will be considered in Chapter XXX.)

III. The Bible contains a part of God's communication with man, enshrined in the history of the Jews, the "biographies" of Christ, and early apostolic writings. This communication began as Tradition with Adam, found its way partially into writing beginning with Moses about 1250 B.C., and was completed with the death of the last of the apostles about 100 A.D. (We are concerned here only with public divine communication, not with private revelations.)

IV. *Inspiration* is that divine action whereby God excited the intellect and moved the will of the biblical authors so that they wrote only what He wanted without error. Each book thus has two authors: God, the Principal Cause; man, the instrumental cause.

V. The only sufficient evidence for the inspiration of the various books of the Bible is the authority of God Himself as proposed by the Catholic Church. Hence, the following criteria of inspiration are *not* sufficient: (a) The contents of the books—miraculous events, lofty truths, sublime style, etc.—because many profane books have nobler themes than some parts of the Bible, and have an equally exhilarating effect on the reader. b) Illumination of the reader by the Holy Spirit to detect the book's inspired nature—because many sincere readers disagree as to the inspiration of certain books; moreover, this creates as many popes as there are readers! c) The testimony of the writer (e.g., II Tim. 3:16)—because we accept the authority of St Paul, etc., only because we have already accepted their books as inspired from some other source. d) The apostolic character of the writer (the fact that he was a prophet, apostle or disciple)—because we do not know, in fact, who the author of certain books were (Job, Jona, etc.).

VI. While only the autographs of Sacred Scripture were inspired, the Council of Trent declared that the Latin Vulgate of St. Jerome is substantially identical with the original manuscripts. (All modern Catholic versions have been diligently compared with the Vulgate.)

VII. Biblical hermeneutics, the science which develops the rules of interpretation, demands a clear knowledge of the senses of Sacred Scripture. The two basic meanings are the PRIMARY (literal) sense and the SECONDARY (spiritual) sense. The literal sense is the immediate meaning of the words as intended by the human author, whether he was using words in their proper or improper sense. The spiritual or secondary sense is that additional, deeper meaning, intended by God but not clearly intended by the human author, in the light of further revelation or in the context of the whole Bible. If the spiritual meaning is perceived in the words of a biblical text (or group of texts), we call this the fuller meaning of the text; if it is seen to exist in things (persons, places, events in the text which serve as *types* of later realities), we call this the typical sense (sometimes referred to also as the mystical sense).

VIII. Every passage in the Bible has one, and only one, primary (literal) meaning. It is this meaning which is to be used for deducing or proving dogmatic and moral truths. The fuller and typical senses may be used for this purpose only if they have been established by the Church's magisterium. Students should be familiar with the rules on pages 35–40.

IX. We follow the historico-literary method of interpretation which, recognizing the key significance of Hebrew literary genres, distinguishes between the truth or message of Scripture and its medium.

Suggested Readings

Benoit, Pierre, O.P., "The Fuller Meaning of Scripture," *Theology Digest,* IX:1 (Winter, 1961) pp. 3-8, and the subsequent issue, IX:2 (Spring, 1961) pp. 66, 126.

Brown, Raymond, S.S., *The Sensus Plenior of Sacred Scripture* (Baltimore: St. Mary's University, 1955), 161 pp. Very thorough and helpful.

——————, "The Sensus Plenior in the Last Ten Years," *Catholic Biblical Quarterly,* XXV:3 (July 1963) pp. 262-285.

Charlier, *The Christian Approach to the Bible,* Chap. 9 and 10.

Orchard, *A Catholic Commentary on Holy Scripture,* cols. 39-42.

Chapter V

The Priestly Account of Creation: All Things Come From God

READINGS: *Genesis 1; Ecclesiastes 1:5–7; Job 26:5–11; 38; Psalm 103.*

Having paused just long enough to grasp the divine nature of the Bible as God's word, and the key to understanding it—Semitic literary genres—we shall plunge into the Book of Genesis. A careful examination of the first eleven chapters of this book should convince any student that this section is different—in fact, unique. Actually, the events narrated in these chapters represent pre-history, or "primitive history"; there was, of course, no human eye-witness account of the origins of man, the Fall, or the Deluge. The account given in Genesis of these events is "folk history"—popular traditions brought by their ancestors from Mesopotamia, plus a generous mixture of revelation.[1] But it is not the purpose of Genesis to teach history; the point is to convey to man the fundamental truths of religion. A reply of the Pontifical Biblical Commission dated January 16, 1948 clarifies this:

> The question of the literary forms of the first eleven chapters of Genesis is far more obscure and complex. These literary forms do not correspond to any of our classical categories and cannot be judged in the light of the Greco–Latin or modern literary types. It is therefore impossible to deny or to affirm their historicity as a whole without unduly applying to them norms of a literary type under which they cannot be classed. If it is agreed not to see in these chapters history in the classical and modern sense, it must be admitted also that known scientific facts do not allow a *positive* solution of all the problems which they present. . . To declare *a priori* that these narratives do not contain history in the modern sense of the word might easily be understood to mean that they do not contain history in any sense, whereas they relate in simple and figurative language, adapted to the understanding of mankind at a lower stage of development, the funda-

---

[1] The opinion of modern commentators leans heavily towards the improbability of the survival of a continuous human tradition from the time of Adam; in view of recent estimates of the age of man, the transmission in substantially ungarbled form of any such tradition would seem nothing short of miraculous. Cf. Orchard, *A Catholic Commentary on Holy Scripture*, col. 138c; also, Hauret, *Beginnings*, pp. 146–147.

mental truths underlying the divine scheme of salvation, as well as a popular description of the origins of the human race and of the chosen people.[2]

Another important consideration is that Genesis is the introduction to a legal document, the Pentateuch. In fact, it is in these terms that we defined the Bible as a whole, but they are especially applicable to the first five books. Taking its nature from the material to which it is the introduction, Genesis itself is legal in character. It contains the beginnings of the pattern of human salvation and the first laws binding on mankind. We shall gain an increasingly clearer insight into its nature as we progress; what we want to avoid is — in the words of the Biblical Commission — any a priori judgment of its true message.

We shall proceed, then, along the lines of the method we have resolved upon: historico-literary exegesis. While recognizing the factual basis of the narrative, we shall also recognize that the manner in which the events are proposed is to be referred to the sacred (human) author. To grasp his frame of reference, we must understand something of the primitive cosmology to which Hebrew mentality was heir. To this end, parallel passages selected from Ecclesiastes and Job are included in the assignment. The chart given on page 48 should be studied in conjunction with these texts.

Hebraic Concept of the Universe

(Semitic cosmogony)

In the minds of the Semites, the earth was a flat, floating solid mass supported by huge columns fixed in the rock portion of the Abyss, i.e., the waters below the earth. Here and there arose mountains; some particularly high ones at the ends of the earth supported the firmament (sky). The sky or firmament was conceived as an inverted bowl set over the earth. Its purpose was twofold: to sustain the sun, moon and stars; and to keep the upper waters from flooding the earth. They thought that there was water all around the firmament, i.e., above and under and on all sides of the earth. Periodically, God opens the floodgates (apertures) fixed on the firmament, thus causing it to rain. The water below the earth, on the other hand, forces its way to the surface through subterranean apertures to form springs, rivers, lakes and oceans. Eventually, these waters return to the Abyss. Deep down under the earth is located Sheol, the dwelling place of all the dead.

---

[2] The whole doctrinal portion of the reply is reproduced in Orchard, *A Catholic Commentary on Holy Scripture*, cols. 53i–m.

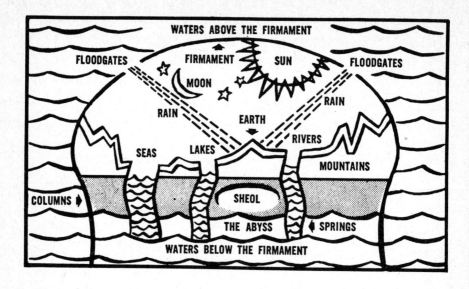

Exegesis of the Priestly Account of Creation

Genesis 1

Semetic

v. 1: We might paraphrase the first five words thus: "When God began to create . . . " The Hebrew word for "create" (*bara*) is
used exclusively of God's activity. It shows that God is not dependent upon matter, but vice versa. Creation in time is implied, though it cannot be demonstrated from this text. The
"heavens and the earth" are a circumlocution for the (visible)
universe; the Hebrews had no word for it. The sacred writer
is not concerned with the world of spirits.

2: The "abyss" (not chaos) is disorganized because: a) there is
no light; b) it is covered with water; and c) it is without vegetation of any kind. This is the "raw material" on which God is
about to go to work. The "spirit of God" is not the Holy Spirit;
it shows that the Jews recognized God's transcendence.

3-5: Light is a most important entity to man; without it, he would
be helpless. God is portrayed as "separating" light from darkness on the first day. It is created before the heavenly bodies
(fourth day) because it was considered to be — along with
darkness — a positive entity independent of them. Notice that
the Hebrew day runs from sunset to sunset. In calling the light
"good," the sacred author is clearly teaching monotheism: there
is no other (evil) god. As we shall learn in Chapter Three, evil
is the result of man's disobedience.

48

6-8: The "firmament" is to provide a dry area for living creatures by sealing off the mass of "upper" waters. The firmament will likewise serve as a framework for the stars, planets, etc.

9-10: The final "separation" is the draining off of certain areas on the surface of the earth (we call them continents) to provide a place for living things. This is accomplished by God's "assembling" of all of the surface waters into seas and rivers, which are fed from the waters of the Abyss below.

11-13: The third day does double duty: plant life makes its appearance on the earth, with provision for the future via reproduction. The sacred author thus stresses divine providence to stimulate feelings of gratitude in his readers.

14-19: Now begins the "decoration" of the universe with appropriate furniture. The firmament is studded with stars and planets, to "rule" the night and the day. The sacred author pictures the already-created light as now gathered together and assigned to accompany the particular heavenly body with which men associate daylight, moonlight, starlight, etc. Again providence is insinuated; it is as if the sacred author had said, "How could we ever tell the different seasons of the year if God had not made these celestial calendars? How good He is!"

20-23: The decoration of the sky with birds and the sea with fish is the work of the fifth day, corresponding to the creation of the firmament on the second day. Note that these are the first creatures to be "blessed" by God; perhaps this is to explain the mysterious way in which these creatures reproduce themselves.

24-25: The final work of decoration takes place on the surface of the earth, now to be stocked with animals and men, corresponding to the third day of creation. Notice the specific mention of cattle: worshipped by pagans, but "clean" meat for the Jew.

26: God seems to be taking counsel with Himself (the plural of majesty, not the Holy Trinity!) before the important step of creating man, for whom all the other things have been provided in advance. "In our image and likeness" designates: a) that man is higher than brutes; and b) he has some quality which makes him resemble God — epitomized by his power to govern the animal kingdom: we would say "intellect and will," but the Hebrew author was content with this concrete example of intelligent action.

27-28: Emphasis by repetition — with the added knowledge that man, like the higher forms of brutes, is given the role of filling the earth with his offspring by sexual ("male and female") conjugation. This may be considered the first step in the institution of marriage, the general vocation of the human race.

49

29-31: This allotment by God of vegetables to men and beasts as their food should not be interpreted as a prohibition of the eating of meat; indeed, man has already been given (v. 26) dominion over animals, and this dominion would presumably carry with it the power to kill them. This symbolic act of God seems rather to manifest the *harmony* which characterized primitive creation; no creature's survival depended upon its killing of its fellow creatures for food. His work finished, God sees that everything is very good; no defect exists in it.

Genesis 2, vv. 1-4a.

1-4: These first three and one-half verses belong to the events narrated in Chapter One; they provide the climax to the story of creation. God is pictured, anthropomorphically, as "resting" on the seventh day and blessing it. The distinct implication is that man, too, should rest in imitation of God — as an act of grateful homage.

The Religious Message: Conclusions From Genesis 1

What is the sacred author trying to convey to his readers by this simple, yet beautiful story? Fidelity to our hermeneutical principles demands that we see here the symbolism of the Orient, not the fixed terminology of the Western mentality. What we have here is a parable, not an allegory. The writer is presenting us with a homely figure of speech to set forth "the fundamental truths underlying the divine plan of salvation, as well as a popular description of the origin of the human race and of the chosen people." The oriental mind would respond to this symbolism, and would in no way be disturbed by the use of a schematic rather than chronological ordering. The sacred author has, moreover, succeeded in bringing into his list those things which the pagans most frequently worshipped showing that they are, after all, only creatures. Hence, we may draw the following conclusions:

All things come from the one true God, Yahweh, Who alone is deserving of worship; He has no rival, e.g., no evil god fighting against Him. The deliberate omission of secondary (created) causes — even when the sacred author is aware of their existence — enhances this lesson.

The seventh day is to be dedicated in a very special manner to Yahweh as the *Sabbath*, or day of rest, in thanksgiving for the act of creation and for His continued providence. This became, as we know, the heart of the Mosaic Law — though its institution probably antedated Moses by a considerable period of time. God's wonderful acts in providing for His creatures — especially man — are spelled out to furnish a solid motive for the observance of this basic "law."

The Priestly Account of Creation: All Things Come From God

The Source of This Account

(Cf. Chapter XII)

Where did this story of creation in six days originate? We are certain that it must have been a part of the Mosaic tradition. Yet, on closer examination, it bears the unmistakable stamp of a late, *liturgical* orientation, reflecting years of usage in the Temple. The solemn, measured language, the repeated refrains ("and God saw that it was good," etc.) all bespeak a prayerful, poetic setting, and the fruit of long meditation. This means that the account must have received its final form in writing much later than Moses—indeed, not earlier than the building of the first Temple under Solomon (c. 960 B.C.). In fact, modern scholars are fairly well agreed that the date of composition, in its final form, should be placed after the Babylonian Captivity (i.e., after 538 B.C.) and during the period of the second Temple. This account, say the scholars, is part of the so-called "Priestly Tradition," recorded by the Jewish priests in Jerusalem. It is commonly designated by the letter "P."

But is this the only account of the cosmic origins of mankind to be found in Scripture? By no means; there is an even more primitive story — undoubtedly of pre-Mosaic origin, in view of its similarity to pagan myths — which has been incorporated into the sacred text. It is known as the "Yahwist Tradition," abbreviated "J" because during the Middle Ages *Yahweh* had been corrupted to *Jehovah*. This story represents the special concerns of southern Palestine and will be treated in the next chapter. These two strands do not, however, exhaust the Mosaic corpus: there remain the "Elohist" or "E" Tradition (first appearing in Gen. 15) and the "Deuteronomic" or "D" Tradition (making up the bulk of the fifth book of the Pentateuch).

The Literary History of the Pentateuch

(Cf. Chapter XXVII)

Although neither of these last-mentioned traditions describe man's beginnings, they do — in common with "J" and "P" — contain vivid and extensive accounts of the events on Mt. Sinai and the Exodus. We should raise the question, then, Why this emphasis on the Covenant events? *It is because the Mosaic Covenant is the one fact above all others which stands at the center of the Israelites' theology of history.* It is the Exodus and the Covenant which alone explain adequately the peculiar status of the Jews as the People of God before Christ. For this reason a number of modern Old Testament texts begin with the Exodus and related literature rather than with Genesis. Moreover, it can be shown that the Book of Deuteronomy (focused exclusively on

51

the Mosaic Covenant) and its sequels,—Josue, Judges, I-IV Kings,—appeared in written form prior to the appearance of Genesis. In other words, the creation narrative is a latecomer on the scene: a flashback, as it were, to provide a world background for Abraham and (especially) for the events connected with Mt. Sinai. Here is how the author of one of these modern textbooks sums it up:

The Yahwist wrote his epic backward, as it were, looking through the historical experiences that had brought the community of Israel into being. Accordingly, the first step (A) was the expansion of the themes of the Mosaic tradition. This involved a full narration of the Exodus story, the wandering in the wilderness and the people's murmuring and rebellion, and the march toward Canaan. The next step (B), reading the story backward, was the unification of the traditions of the patriarchal period, with the result that the stories concerning Abraham, Isaac, and Jacob are now governed by the theme of the promise given to Abraham (Gen. 12:1-4). In the Yahwist's account, the patriarchal period is one of anticipation — a movement toward the inheritance of the Promised Land and Israel's full participation in the divine plan that embraces all nations. The final extension (C) was the prefixing of the stories of primeval history — stories that deal not with Israel alone, but with the potential glory and the actual tragedy of human history.

ORDER OF EVENTS:	A Genesis 2–11	B Genesis 12–50	C Exodus to Josue
	Creation, Garden of Eden, other narratives of primeval history which include all mankind.	The patriarchal period. Israel's early history represented by Abraham, Isaac, Jacob and Joseph.	Israel's life story from the Exodus to the Conquest. The Mosaic Tradition.
	C	B	A

EDITOR'S VIEWPOINT

We see, then, that the Yahwist accomplished an extraordinary feat of literary creativity. In the very period when the Mosaic Tradition was threatened by the collapse of the old Confederacy and the syncretistic tendencies of Solomon's reign, he gave new expression to the faith of his fathers. . . . With the Exodus as the fulcrum of his historical interpretation, he reworked the traditions now found in the book of Genesis. To the Yahwist the meaning of the Exodus was the meaning of all history, right back to the Creation. And to substantiate his conviction that Yahweh is Lord of all history, he insisted that men began to worship Yahweh in the earliest times (the grandson of Adam, Gen. 4:26).[3]

---

[3] Cf. Bernhard Anderson, *Understanding the Old Testament* (Englewood Cliffs, N. J.: Prentice-Hall, 1957) pp. 162-64. See also C. H. Dodd, *The Bible To-Day* (New York: Cambridge University Press, 1961) pp. 30-32.

Admittedly the temptation to postpone Genesis until after the Exile and to plunge immediately into Exodus is a strong one. The student would then be in a much better position to understand Genesis as a legal document introducing the Torah (Pentateuch). A great many puzzling anachronisms would be cleared up, for one thing. The Sabbath, for example, comes as a strange interlude in Eden, since it was instituted much later. Its insertion into the creation account is probably explained by the fact that the "P" editors who put it in performed their literary task at a time when Sabbath observance needed bolstering up (i.e., at the return from the Babylonian Captivity). At any rate, I have not succumbed to the temptation — though I might have done so had I been writing for a Jewish audience primarily. As it is, Genesis 1-3 with its sweeping universalism represents a Gentile manifesto. The situation is somewhat analogous to that of the evangelists Luke and Matthew: the latter, in a section intended for Jewish Christians, traces Christ's genealogy back to Abraham, their remote ancestor. Luke, on the other hand, begins with Adam and carries the line down to Christ for his Gentile readers. Though our approach in general will follow the literary provenance of the books as illustrated in the chart below, the Pentateuch will provide the exception which proves the rule:

THE LITERARY HISTORY OF THE OLD TESTAMENT

PROPHETS WRITINGS	LAW - HISTORY MOSES			DATE	HEBREW	PERIOD
				1200		Egyptian
Canticle of Moses	Y A H W I S T	E L O H I S T	P R I E S T L Y	Josue Judges		
Canticle of Debora						Confederacy
Canticle of Anna				DAVID		
			DEUTERONOMIC	1000 Solomon	ISRAELITE	Independent Kingdom
Court				Achab		
chronicles (Elias)				800		
(Amos, Osee, Isaia, Michea)				Ezechia		
						Assyrian Babyl'n.
	Job			600		
Editions of: Amos, Osee, Isaia, Michea, Jer., Ezechiel	2. PENTATEUCH			(Exile) Esdras	JEWISH	Persian
Minor Proph.	Proverbs, Canticles			400		
WISDOM LITERATURE	Ruth,	3. CHR. - ESDRAS - NEHEMIA				Greek
	Esther, Tobias, Ecclesiastes			200 Machabees		Syrian
	4. PSALTER					
APOCALYPSE	Sirach, Daniel, Judith, Wisdom			63		Roman

1. JOSUE - JUDGES - KINGS

An Introduction to the Psalms

The one hundred and fifty psalms of the Old Testament make up a complete book in themselves. They come at the beginning of the third part, or "Writings," of the Hebrew Bible; in our Bible, they are placed between Job and Proverbs — i.e., with the sapiential books. Although a number of psalms are undoubtedly of ancient origin, the Book of Psalms (or Psalter, as it is called) was not put together until after the Babylonian Captivity. It is sometimes called the "hymnbook of the second (i.e., post-Exilic) Temple." This means that the psalms were collected for liturgical use in the Temple at Jerusalem after 515 B.C. They were used in sacrificial rites, processions, thanksgivings, etc., both by the community and by individuals. They are peerless masterpieces, both as poetry and as prayers.

But the Psalms are not only prayers. We find in them all of the themes which appear in the other books of the Bible: history, biography, natural science (such as it was), law, philosophy, theology, etc., as well as adoration, petition, thanksgiving, etc. They are truly a cross-section of Sacred Scripture. Reflecting the tradition and teachings of the sacred historians: altar, Ark, covenant, Levitical priesthood, Temple, Davidic dynasty — they show us Israel at its best, a worshipping community. Indeed, the Psalms give us a new dimension on the Jewish people, unique and indispensable to understanding the biblical message. Best of all, they show us the universalism that sparked the true spirit of the Old Testament: that Yahweh is a God above all other "gods," to be worshipped by Gentile as well as by Jew. Likewise, they portray salvation as attainable not only by the "Sons of the Covenant," but by all nations — if they but call on Yahweh.

Finally, we must not fail to point out at the very beginning that the Psalms have a very special interest for Christians because they form the core of our liturgical worship. The first Christians did not find it necessary to write a new Psalter to express the worship of the Mystical Body; they took over bodily the Hebrew Psalms as capable of nourishing the lofty sentiments of the new and eternal covenant bequeathed them by Christ—Who Himself relied on the Psalter as His official prayer book. The Mass, and especially the Divine Office, are built around these one hundred and fifty religious poems. *No Christian can live fully the prayer life of the Church unless he has an understanding of the Psalms.* For this reason we shall begin immediately to intersperse key Psalms of the Psalter in either their schematic or historical context as we proceed with our exegesis of the Old Testament. Thus, these precious texts can be absorbed gradually by the student in an atmosphere that will lend itself to a fuller penetration of their profound significance. And he will find, with the early Christians, that the Psalms are capable of nourishing the deepest form of Christian piety.

Praise of God The Creator

Psalm 103

To understand this sacred poem fully, one must be aware of the class of Psalms to which it belongs (cf. Chapter XXI). Since the basic theme here is that of *praise*, Psalm 103 is a *hymn* in the technical biblical sense of "the lyrical expression of the feeling of God's transcendence . . . inclining the mind to prostration, wonder, praise, thanks and love."[4] The hymn was a perfect accompaniment of the sacrifice designated "holocaust" in which the victim was entirely burned. The following structure—detectable in Psalm 103—characterizes the hymn: 1) By way of introduction, an *invitation* to praise Yahweh (v.1; "Bless . . ."). 2) The *motive* or *occasion* for the hymn: the divine attributes (God's might, or His dwelling in heaven, etc.), manifestations of His presence in nature, His providence, the act of creation, etc. Psalm 103 glorifies the last theme. 3) Usually the original words of invitation are repeated at the end (v.35). Other hymns similar in structure to this one are Psalms 8, 28, 99, 104, 113.

This Psalm is "unsurpassed in grandeur and magnificence."[5] Following, in general, the narrative of the first chapter of Genesis, it portrays the universe as a vast, open book revealing the divine attributes. It was almost certainly composed after the Exile, yet it reflects a cosmology virtually identical with that of Genesis 1. This fact lends additional evidence to the conclusion that what we have described as the "Priestly" account of creation (not the *figure*, which goes back at least to the time of Moses, but the *phrasing*) dates from the liturgical outlook of the second Temple. Here is a brief explanation of this hymn of praise:

vv. 1-4: A stirring picture of the majesty of Yahweh, seated in heaven with light as His garment, clouds His chariot, the winds His messenger, fire His servant.

5-9: A poetic description of creation, with special attention to the third day.

10-18: God's providence takes care of every creature; note that the description pre-supposes the cosmology depicted in the diagram which appeared earlier in this chapter.

19-23: The work of the fourth day: all nature obeys God's heavenly timetable.

---

[4] See Gelin, *The Religion of Israel*, pp. 46-50.
[5] Cf. Charles J. Callan, O.P., *The New Psalter* (New York, 1948), pp. 358-364.

24-26: The fifth day: it is Yahweh Who furnished the ocean with sea monsters. The pagan monster, Leviathan, who fought with the gods, is here pictured as one of Yahweh's creatures.

27-30: A detailed appreciation of Yahweh's providence; surely this passage is the product of intense meditation.

31-35: A typical hymn ending: a heartfelt petition that Yahweh be praised forever, and that those who disturb His harmony (sinners) be "removed" from the scene. In its concreteness, the Hebrew mind did not distinguish (as we are taught to do) between sin and the sinner; the sacred author's sole preoccupation was to vindicate Yahweh and His interests. Verse 31 comes as a kind of corollary to Genesis 1:31, "God saw that all He had made was very good."

Suggested Readings

Callan, *The New Psalter of Pius XII in Latin and English, with Introductions, Notes and Spiritual Reflections*, pp. 358-364.

Hauret, *Beginnings: Genesis and Modern Science*, Introduction and Chap. 2.

Hunt, *The Book of Genesis*, Part 1 (No. 2 of the Pamphlet Bible Series of the Paulist Press), pp. 5-11.

Orchard, *A Catholic Commentary on Holy Scripture*, cols. 136-142.

Vawter, *A Path Through Genesis*, Chap. 1.

Chapter VI

The Garden and the Tree of Life: Man's Happiness In God's Image

READINGS: *Genesis 2; Psalm 8; (Summa Theologica Ia, qq. 95, 96 and 100)*

We have noted the two special points of doctrine contained in the first chapter of Genesis: ALL things come from God (a reaction against idolatry); and an insistence on the Sabbath observance (through special treatment of the seventh day at the beginning of Chapter Two). These points reflect the priestly editors' concern for divine worship. In the fourth verse of the second chapter, the sacred editors go back over the story of creation and reproduce another ancient tradition because of the additional basic truths which it contains. Whereas the Priestly editors had used the term "Elohim" ("spirits") for God, the present editors use His proper name, "Yahweh" ("He Who Is"); for this reason, the tradition from which this second account of creation comes is known as the "Yahwist Tradition." It presents us with a whole series of imaginative, anthropomorphic symbols: Yahweh fashions a man "out of the dust of the ground" and then "breathed into his nostrils the breath of life": He plants a garden with a good tree and an evil tree in it, then "put there the man He had formed"; next, He parades all of the animals before him so that he can name them; finally, He puts the man to sleep and forms the first woman from one of his ribs.

This account is a far cry from the orderly enumeration of the first chapter; indeed, the story of the six days (which we have classified as an historical parable) possesses a certain theological precision when compared to the primitiveness of the second account. In view of the manner in which these two stories are put together, this second account seems to serve as an elaboration of Genesis 1:27: "God created man in His image. In the image of God He created him. Male and female He created them." This single verse from the first chapter summarizes the special teaching of the second chapter of Genesis, as we shall see.

The "theological" priestly account defines man as a creature made in the image of God, and records the creation of woman rather tersely as the female member of the species. The primitive Yahwist account, on the other hand, gives a description instead of a definition: it calls man breathing dust, and woman is denoted as Adam's rib. It is something like the difference between defining man as a rational animal, and calling him a featherless biped. But again, we wish the sacred author to speak for himself.

Exegesis of The Yahwist Account of Creation
(Genesis 2:4–25)

v. 5-6: God is an intelligent, provident Workman; He makes provision for a very important item: water.

7: The imagery is that of the potter and his clay. God is pictured as producing man from moistened earth. For the Semite, life was mysterious — so it is described as the breath of God. Here the sacred author is teaching the special intervention of God in the production of the first man. Only in retrospect, in what we have termed the fuller sense of Scripture, can we read into the text our concept of the human soul: the Jews had no such clear idea of the soul as a separate, spiritual substance until about three centuries before Christ. Not even Adam's superiority over the lower animals is apodictically taught here, as all living things are referred to in Genesis 6:17 as having the "breath of life." Although the sacred author thus indicates that there is an element in man which cannot evolve, he completely by-passes the question of the evolution of his body. Finally, we should note that the Hebrew word *Adam* means both "Adam" and "man," depending on whether or not it has the definite article in front of it. In this chapter, it always carries the article; hence, it is correctly translated "the man" (in the sense of "everyman" or "mankind"). It is also interesting to note that the similar Hebrew word, *Adamah,* means "the ground."

8: "The man" was evidently created outside of the garden; God now transfers him into it. Eden was a place on this earth, it is certain; but this is not the important lesson here. The main teaching is the fact that man was elevated to a state above his nature at the time of his creation; that is, he possessed special privileges or gifts not due to human nature as such. (Theologians call this state with all of its privileges original justice.) The Douay-Rheims Version translates the word "Eden" as "paradise of pleasure"; reading between the lines, we can see here also the gift of impassibility, or freedom from suffering and disease. All was to be pleasurable in paradise, without any pain, sorrow or accident.

9: The sacred author singles out two trees in paradise for special attention; in this verse, he mentions the tree of life, from which Adam was to eat in order to maintain the gift of *immortality.* In verse 17, he will refer to the tree of knowledge.

10-14: Only the Tigris and the Euphrates can be located today with certainty. The sacred author did not know where the garden of Eden was located; so he places it off "to the east," the area from which the patriarch Abraham came, and the land of mystery.

15-17: Again the man is placed in the garden to take care of it, and is given the first command: Do not eat of the tree of knowledge! The sacred author did not know the nature of the first sin; the forbidden fruit is a symbol which the average Jew would clearly understand. Genesis is part of a legal document. Immortality is portrayed as the chief gift, since it has held a special appeal to mankind from time immemorial (cf. Ponce de Leon and the Fountain of Youth).

18-20: That man and woman complement each other is gracefully pointed out: he needs a "helper." Note the emphasis which the sacred author places on the equality of the sexes: a) the helper is to be "like himself," and b) man examines the animals one by one, and does not find his helper at that lower level. His naming of the animals does double symbolic duty: a) it indicates his *dominion* over them (the imposition of a name always had this significance for the Semites); b) it may indicate a special knowledge of nature, although current biblical scholarship tends to frown upon any appeal to infused knowledge.

21-22: The rib is yet another way of inculcating the notion of male-female equality: God did not take the bone from the head (= superiority of woman), nor from the big toe (= superiority of man), but from his torso. This is to be seen as a symbolic, not a scientific, account of the origin of woman.

23: The man recognizes the identity of nature in his helper, as indicated by the generic name he gives her, "woman." The same play on words is found in Hebrew as in the English: man is *ish,* woman is *ishshah.*

24: The sacred author is careful to point out the original divine blueprint for marriage: it is intended to be a *monogamous* union, permanent and indissoluble.

25: In this final verse, still another privilege is symbolized: the gift of *integrity,* or perfect control over the lower appetites (passions).

The special teaching contained in this chapter can be summarized under the two captions we have borrowed from Genesis 1:27 — "in the image of God", and "male and female" and their counterparts in Chapter Two, the *garden* and the *rib*.

The Garden of Eden: In the Image of God

It is unmistakably clear from these first two chapters that our first parents were brought into being in a world far different from the "vale of tears" familiar to us. They enjoyed, above all, a child-like intimacy with God. They lived in His presence, they were on speaking terms with Him; they were contemplatives. The whole account depicts a certain continuity between God and His creation, with man serving as the middle or connecting link at the summit of creatures. This intimacy we know to have been the fruit of sanctifying grace and the grace of the infused virtues and gifts. But the image of the garden is as close as the mentality of His Semitic audience would permit the sacred author to approach the supernatural.

Grace alone is supernatural; all of the other privileges of our first parents were preternatural. Whereas *supernatural* means proper to God — i.e., divine; *preternatural* signifies something which is normally beyond the endowments of a particular order of creation, but not divine. We can illustrate this distinction with an outline:

I. <u>PROPER TO CREATURES</u>

NATURAL: Something due to a being as part of its ordinary endowment (body, soul, hands in regard to man).

PRETERNATURAL: Something above the nature of a particular creature, given to it by privilege, but not divine. (Hands on a dog, legs on a cabbage, etc.)

II. <u>PROPER TO GOD ALONE</u>: SUPERNATURAL, divine: omniscience, eternity, and (in the created order), habitual grace, which is a share in God's own life by a creature.

Thus, immortality, infused knowledge and impassibility are all *natural* to the angels, but *preternatural* to man. Whereas the sacred author emphasizes the *continuity between the natural and the supernatural* by his symbolism, we tend to emphasize the great distinction between the two orders. With our Western mentality, we can interpret the theological conclusions behind these texts in the light of the threefold subjection which existed in Eden as follows:

Original Justice

(Cf. Ecclesiastes 7:29; also, Summa Theologica I, Q. 95, art. 1)

The whole ensemble of gifts possessed by Adam and Eve in the Garden of Eden is known as original justice. Only one of these gifts was supernatural: sanctifying grace: the other five — which depended upon sanctifying grace — were preternatural. By these gifts, the naturally "incompatible" elements of spirit and matter were harmonized in man.

SUBJECTION	GIFT	PERTINENT TEXTS IN GENESIS	CATEGORY
I. MAN SUBJECT TO GOD. (He was God's gardener)	1) Sanctifying grace	II:8–" . . . and He put there (in Eden) the man He had formed." III:8–" . . . the Lord God walking in the garden . . ." (=intimacy)	SUPERNATURAL —proper to God; divine.
	2) Brutes subject to man	I:28–"Have dominion over the fish . . . birds . . . cattle . . . and all the animals. (Cf. II:20)	P —beyond R the power E of one T particular
II. MAN'S BODY TO HIS SOUL	3) Impassibility	II:8–"The Lord God planted a garden in Eden ('paradise of pleasure')" (Cf. III:16–19)	E class of R creatures, N not A beyond all
	4) Immortality	II:9–"tree of life" (Cf. III:22)	T created U possibility.
III. MAN'S ANIMAL NATURE TO REASON	5) Infused knowledge(?)	II:20–"The man named all the cattle . . ." (Cf. Wisdom 9:15–17)	R A L
	6) Integrity	II:25–"Both the man and his wife were naked, but they felt no shame." (Cf. III:7).	

God's goodness to mankind is manifest in the realization that not one of these gifts is natural to man. Death, suffering, inordinate passions, etc. all flow quite normally from one or another of the various components in man's constitution: mineral, plant or animal. He was to understand his limitations after his disobedience had reduced him to the body-soul conflict so natural to him.

The Rib: Male and Female

The primary reason for the diversity of sexes, as we learn from Genesis 1:28, is the propagation of the human race. The second account of creation adds to this cryptic phrase; in fact, we can derive a rather complete theology of woman from it:

1) *Woman is equal to man in nature:* both belong to the same species of humanity. (Gen. 2:18) "I will make him a helper like himself"; (Gen. 2:20) " . . . but he [the man] found no helper like himself [among the animals]"; (Gen. 2:22) " . . . and the rib He made into a woman" (rib symbolizes equality). Even the dominion which man acquired over his wife after the Fall did not destroy this equality.

2) *There is a diversity of roles between man and woman based on differences in their constitutions, and especially applicable in family life.*

   a) Man is meant to be the head of the family, to take the initiative (Gen. 2:15, 2:18, 2:20, 2:23). And Genesis 3:17 gives as the reason for man's punishment (by way of corroboration): "Because you have listened to your wife . . ."; in other words, man had sinned in reversing his role as head.

   b) Woman is meant to be the heart of the family, to help man (Gen. 2:18) "I will make him a helper like himself."

   c) In family life, woman is dependent on man, just as she was in her origin from his rib (cf. Gen. 3:16).

   d) Just as man is fitted for his role by excelling woman in speculative reason (he is the planner, the discoverer), so is woman fitted for her role by excelling in practical reasoning (she is the executor, expert in following).

3) *In reality, man and woman admirably complement each other;* they are called by a general vocation to the married state: "It is not good that the man is alone" (Gen. 2:18); The unity and indissolubility of his state are indicated in ". . . and the two become one flesh" (Gen. 2:24).

Genesis and Evolution

When God formed man from the dust of the ground, did He take pure dust (inorganic matter), or did He take already formed dust (organic matter)? Most evolutionists today hold that the great variety of living species, including the human body, developed over many centuries from one or several primitive species.[1] In support of this contention, scientists have produced a number of ancient skulls which, they claim, represent homo sapiens. On July 17, 1959 a man and wife team of archeologists, Dr. and Mrs. L. S. B. Leakey, discovered what the National Geographic Society claimed to be the skull of the oldest

---

[1] Pius XII maintained that scientific evolution has *not* been demonstrated (*Humani Generis,* paragraph 5).

known human being. Named Zinjanthropus because it was discovered in Tanganyika, East Africa, the "man" whose skull was painstakingly pieced together is said to date back 600,000 years. This makes the creature centuries older than either the Peking or Java man.[2]

Actually Genesis does not solve the problem one way or the other. It simply teaches on this score:

1) That man was created by a special act of God; in other words, God intervened, as it were, in the production of at least the finished product, Adam. From this we conclude that man has a unique feature (which we call the soul) that owes its origin directly to God. This part could not have evolved.

2) As for man's body, this could have evolved from an animal until the moment that God "touched it up" by infusing a human soul into it; in this case, however, it must be presupposed that He had given the primitive species the potency to evolve as it did. This excludes from the realm of possibility any spontaneous origin or development. Pages 64–65 give a typical "timetable" of scientific evolution.

The Three-Dimensional World of Man

But we must not let scientific problems distract us from the important religious picture which Genesis 2 has painted. It presents for our consideration a precious blueprint of God's original plan for mankind: a contemplative union with Him in a "paradise of pleasure"; a brief testing, after which Adam and Eve presumably would have been confirmed in grace; finally, bodily transferral into uninterrupted contemplation of God in heaven without the necessity of dying. Great emphasis is laid on the family, which was created ready-made, as it were, in Adam and Eve, who were to bring forth children enjoying the same divine intimacy. Adam's infused knowledge (if he had such a gift) would have rendered the education of his offspring easy and painless, no doubt.

At the same time, Genesis makes clear the foundation of all of these preternatural gifts: they depended absolutely on man's complete subjection to his Maker. His friendship with God was the key to the harmony that existed within his person as well as the external harmony in the universe. Adam and Eve were, indeed, at the summit of creation, but they were not to seek their main happiness in creatures. There is no evidence of any "sacraments" in Eden: they would have been super-

---

[2] "Finding the World's Earliest Man," *National Geographic Magazine,* Vol. 118 (June, 1960) pp. 420–435. But *Science Digest* (October, 1961, p. 34) dates skull at 1,750,000 B. C. and denies that "it" was a "true man."

EVOLUTIONISM

A Tentative Outline of Life on Earth

GEOLOGIC PERIODS		BIOLOGIC MANIFESTATIONS	YEARS AGO 5-2 billion 2½ billion
PRECAMBRIAN (Archeozoic) (Proterozoic)		No life Non-fossilized first life?	Years in Millions 600
Cambrian	Lower Upper	Algae (?): Seaweed Many of the invertebra—Trilobites dominant—Algae etc.	
ORDOVICIAN		Graptolites dominant—rise of Cephalopods	500
SILURIAN		Crinoids—armored fish—some say 1st amphibians	425
DEVONIAN		Corals—rise of Goniatites—Fish—oldest known land plants	405
Pennsylvanian (Carboniferous) Mississippian " PERMIAN		Amphibians—sharks Coal plants—primitive reptiles—insects Rise of land vertebrates—Conifers	345
TRIASSIC		Dinosaurs—Ammonites—last Othocaras first mammals (?)	230
JURASSIC		Dinosaur climax—flying reptiles—toothed birds—first feather—frogs—salamander (Solnhofen Kalk)	181
CRETACEOUS	Lower	First placental mammals—rise of flowering plants	135
	Upper	Gigantinism—Dinosaurs extinction; Ammonites extinction—Angiosperms	
EOCENE		Rise of mammals—a few reptiles—first horse.	58
OLIGOCENE		Modern mammals—Nummilites—Orbitoids— Early apes—early Camels, etc.	36
MIOCENE		Mammals—many akin to those of today—same with flowering plants—few reptiles like turtles—crocodiles	25
PLIOCENE		Continuation of Miocene—MAN (??)	13

PALEOZOIC — 600-230 million yrs. ago

MESOZOIC — 230-63 million

CENOZOIC — TERTIARY 63-1 million

CENOZOIC
QUATERNARY
1,000,000 years ago—to date

PLEISTOCENE	Mans' Associates	Cultural Divisions	Human Types
I. Glacial (Gunz) (U.S.—Nebraskan)	Sabre toothed cats	PRECHELLEAN	AUSTRALOPITHECINES [660,000 yrs.]
1. Interglacial	Hippopotamus So. Elephant	CHELLEAN	Homo Heidelberg
II. Glacial (Mindel) (U.S.—Kansan)		ACHEULIAN	PITHECANTHROPUS [500,000 yrs.]
2. Interglacial	Straight tusk elephant—Merck's rhinoceros		SINANTHROPUS
III. Glacial (Riss) (U.S.—Illinoisan)	Cave bear—Woolly rhinoceros	MOUSTERIAN	NEANDERTHAL La Chappelle Le Moustier, et al. [150,000 yrs.]
3. Interglacial			
IV. Glacial (Wurm) (U.S.—Wisconsin)	Mastodon—Mammoth—Reindeer, et al.—Musk Ox.	AURIGNACIAN	Cro-Magnon, et al —Modern man type Man in U. S. (?) [35,000 yrs.]
4. Post Glacial (Early) (Late)	Modern Animals	SOLUTREAN MAGDALENIAN AZILIAN NEOLITHIC Age of Metals	Lake Dwellers, et al.

fluous. All nature was "sacramental" in that creatures, perfectly subject to man, served as an aid to his union with the Creator. Man himself recapitulated the three principal orders of being:

He possessed in himself the *divine* world:
"God created man in His image."

He possessed in himself the *angelic* world:
"In the image of *Elohim* (this title of God actually means "spirits")[3] He created him."

He possessed in himself the *animal* world:
"Male and female He created them." (Gen. 1:27)

Psalm 8: A Hymn of Praise

This psalm belongs to a large general class designated as hymns, the theme of which is the praise of God for one of His attributes, or for some act of goodness. As in the case of Psalm 103 (also a hymn), this psalm praises God for creation—especially the dignity which He has heaped upon man. With the exception of verse 3, it reflects perfectly the sentiments which Adam and Eve must have felt in Eden as they meditated on the glory of God and their own dignity as His favored children. This psalm may well have been composed by David, to whom the inscription (not inspired) attributes it.

v.2-5: God is exalted; all creation—including man—is puny in comparison with Him.

6-9: The dignity of man, thanks to God's infinite goodness. Verse 6 lends encouragement to the interpretation of Genesis 1:27 referred to in the footnote.

10: The opening verse of the Psalm, repeated as a refrain at the end.

Suggested Readings

Anderson, *Understanding the Old Testament*, pp. 160-169. Discusses Yahwist tradition, Paradise.
Callan, *The New Psalter*, pp. 35-37. Although this book is highly recommended for the study of each psalm, it will not be specifically mentioned henceforth in the bibliography.
Hauret, *Beginnings*, pp. 75-174.
Hunt, *The Book of Genesis*, Part 1, pp. 10-14.
Murphy, "And Adam Ate of the Fruit," in *The Living Christ*, Chap. 5 (1956 ed.).
Orchard, *A Catholic Commentary on Holy Scripture*, col. 143.
Vawter, *A Path Through Genesis*, Chap. 2.

---

[3] " . . . the sphere of spiritual and moral beings to whom man belongs": Hauret, *Beginnings*, p. 128; see also pp. 85-87; and *Job* 1:6.

Chapter VII

The Tree of Knowledge: Existence Without God

READINGS: *Genesis 3; Psalms 28, 129; Hauret, Beginnings, Chapter 5. (Know Genesis 3:15)*

Salvation history reaches a climax in this chapter as we witness the marring of God's work by His creature, man. The sacred author continues his account in the same symbolic vein from the Yahwist tradition. In addition to having to fight the tendency to interpret his symbols in the light of subsequent knowledge, we find them growing more and more obscure. A new character enters the scene. Who is this outsider who masquerades under the disguise of a serpent? Christian tradition has consistently seen the hand of the devil behind this "more cunning" beast; but did the sacred author understand the symbolism in the same way?

If we agree with the experts that the Yahwist tradition (the oldest of the four) took its distinctive literary form roughly during the reign of King Solomon (about 950 B.C.), then we shall have to answer "no" to this question. There is ample evidence, beginning with the Book of Genesis, that the Jews knew of the existence of good angels at that time: Genesis 18; 24:7; Exodus 14:19 and 23:20; Psalm 90:11, etc. But they seem to have arrived at a notion of the fall of some of the angels and the consequent existence of devils only much later—after the Babylonian Captivity. Taken for granted by the authors of the New Testament (cf. Matt. 12:24 and Apoc. 12:9), revealed demonology makes its appearance clearly in Wisdom 2:24, where the serpent is identified with the devil.

However, we need not conclude that Genesis 3 in no way has reference to Satan. Both typology and the fuller sense of Scripture may be invoked in support of the Church's long-standing tradition in this regard. Even though the sacred author does not employ the term "devil" and probably did not himself understand that Satan was the power behind the symbol, the reading of Satan into the text by the later author of the Book of Wisdom gives us adequate reason to see the serpent as a type of Satan here.[1] To do otherwise would seem to be going against the overwhelming teaching of the Fathers of the Church. We have here a concrete example of the distinction made by Father Hauret in the chapter included in the assignment above, between "historico-critical" exegesis (based on what is explicit in the literal sense) and "theological" exegesis (based on the implicit content of the words in the light of their fulfillment and of later texts). We can proceed now to give this first type of exegesis for the third chapter:

Exegesis of the Story of Original Sin

v. 1: Probably the sacred author selected the serpent as his symbol of the instigator of the first sin in order to lash out against the Chanaanite practice of nature worship. This symbol is appropriate, as it indicates a) that the sin came from the outside (this is logical, in view of the close friendship between Adam and God) and b) that it was a sly, underhanded thing—not the result of unruly passion. Note the vicious suggestion in the serpent's rhetorical question: "God is up to no good; He is afraid to trust you too far."

2-3: Neither Adam nor Eve could later plead ignorance; they had memorized the command. (Note how the sacred author uses immortality as the key gift.)

4-5: The serpent insinuates that God has deceived them; the real purpose of the command is to prevent them from acquiring equality with Him through the esoteric knowledge attached to the eating of the fruit.

6: Eve's second mistake (after the first of listening to the serpent) was to toy with the possibilities of the temptation. But it was NOT a sin of gluttony; they had no inordinate appetites. Note how Adam, the "head" of the family, snatches at the fruit without any reflection; his crime was failure to make this important decision, letting his wife lead him by the nose. In the first showdown, the man and his wife have reversed their true roles. (Do you suppose they said grace before partaking of this fateful meal?)

7: Original sin is here described in terms of *loss of integrity* (concupiscence); their shame indicates the first pangs of disorderly passions.

---

[1] Adhering to what he considers to be the full extent of the literal sense, Fr. John L. McKenzie denies any reference to Satan here, and sees the sin as that of deifying nature, especially the forces of fertility. Cf. *The Two-edged Sword* (Milwaukee, 1956), Chap. 6, esp. pp. 100 and 104. Cf. also Orchard, *A Catholic Commentary on Holy Scripture*, cols. 592d-593a and col. 48g for a reply of the Biblical Commission bearing on this topic.

8: God is pictured as still their intimate friend, "walking in the garden," as the crime has not been proven. This intimacy is a symbol of grace.

9: Note God's disappointment at not being met by His friends.

10-11: There is only one explanation possible for the shame they feel; they have disobeyed the commandment, they have failed the test!

12-13: The man passes the blame onto his wife, who in turn blames the serpent, claiming that she was deceived.

14: The serpent's punishment is symbolic, indicating a curtailment of malicious activity. To conclude that snakes once had legs is unwarranted.

15: This divine promise represents a second chance for mankind. Taking the initiative, God will establish hostility—a state of warfare—between the woman and her Tempter. This state will continue between her "seed" (the human race) and the powers of evil until finally the former wins out. According to one possible translation, the serpent will bruise the heel that crushes it. This is as far as historico-critical exegesis will take us.

16: Note the punishment of the woman; the loss of impassibility will include, for her, pain in childbirth. And she is made dependent upon her husband and subject to him!

17: Man's sweat becomes the price at which he will have to eke out a living from the soil. There would have been work in paradise, but it would have consisted of a pleasant display of energy in the development of bodily and mental powers.

18-19: Elated by his brief dominion over lower creatures, Adam had lost sight of his own creaturehood. Now his continuity with the vegetable and even mineral worlds is vividly forced upon his attention. No longer will nature be his faithful slave and gallant ally; from this point forward, creatures will get in his way, thwart him, and provide the instruments of his punishment. Like Lucifer, who snatched at divinity and lost completely the divine spark he had possessed, so also is Adam stripped of grace and all of the preternatural gifts because of a similar gamble. He who was lord of creation has now become subject to thistles and thorns in a most humiliating manner. And *immortality* is lost—here the author returns to his key concept.

20: Adam immediately asserts his dominion by imposing the proper name, Eve.

21: The sacred author does not avert to the loss of God's friendship directly; in fact, He portrays God as still the kind provider, making clothes for His disobedient children.

22: Irony—continuing the tree of life symbolism. He has actually *lost* the divine likeness of grace, as well as immortality.

23-24: Expulsion from garden symbolizes loss of the Original Justice; the cherubim guarding the place indicate that it is a sacred spot, now forbidden to the human race. (For a clue to Adam's fate, cf. Wisd. 10:1.)

Theological Conclusions Regarding the Fall

The Sin. It is interesting but futile to speculate on the species of sin committed by our first parents. About all that we can say is that basically it was a sin of pride: a blind assertion of human freedom in violation of the will of God. In seeking happiness according to the method suggested by Satan—eating of the forbidden fruit—Adam and Eve were at least implicitly rebelling against God. In daring to snatch at some parity with Him, they struck out on their own and declared their independence. Disobedience, ingratitude, envy—these spiritual vices were all involved; we must avoid putting the sin in their lower nature. Possessing integrity, they were not victims of gluttony or impurity. Those exegetes who do hold for a sin against sex must maintain that this was merely the *matter* of the crime; the *motive* had to be in the intellectual order (e. g., an insubordinate curiosity).[2] Perhaps we should dismiss the topic at this point with the borrowed observation, "Adam sinned when he fell from contemplation"—which is even more significant than saying that he fell from contemplation after he had sinned.

The Punishment. We have already noted that the penalty for original sin consisted in a reduction to the purely natural level, symbolized by expulsion from the garden. Sanctifying grace and the preternatural gifts were lost for themselves and their posterity, but human nature was not totally corrupted. The intellect was "darkened" and the will weakened: human nature universally experiences this travail. The woman received her penalty for starting the mischief: though retaining equality of nature with man, she is made subordinate to him in the marital union. He is no longer merely the coordinator in a happy partnership where each party instinctively would recognize the role assigned; now he is the boss. Still this dominion of the husband over his wife was not meant to be tyranny—as the sacred author well knew in spite of all the contrary pagan customs. The man, too, is punished; he must leave his gardening and take up farming.

What seems most impressive about the whole story is the sweeping, universal realities behind the concrete symbolism of the Semitic author. It is not just Eve who succumbs to the devil; it is human nature. It is

---

[2] Cf. McKenzie, *Op. cit.*, 93-100.

not only Adam who loses his precious privileges; it is mankind that suffers. Here is a strange singular-collective paradox: Adam and Eve are individual, historical personages; at the same time, they are mankind—whole and entire! In Adam, each and every human being was there in the garden, confronted with the fateful decision; in him, each of us failed the test and forfeited the joys of Eden—just as each of us would have prospered in his success had he surrendered to the indirect light of faith instead of to the woman.[3]

The Promise. If mankind has shared collectively in the punishment of its progenitors, it has also shared in the promise of salvation—in a way that Adam and Eve probably did not even dream of sharing. The pattern was fixed in Eden: if sin and punishment were to have singular-collective repercussions, salvation would likewise be a singular-collective affair. Genesis 3:15 is couched in future tenses; to say that its full impact was not realized in the Eve-serpent combination would be a masterpiece of understatement. The opposition *begins* with Eve and Satan; then it expands to include the whole human race and all the powers of evil; finally, it narrows down again to individuals: *the* seed and *the* serpent. Just as the defeat was suffered by one pair whose fate was passed on to humanity, so is the victory to be won by a single pair in the name of the human race: the "woman" in the promise cannot be Eve alone, since the enmity was to continue in her posterity and climax only much later in the crushing of the serpent's head. The "seed" who was to do this could not be Eve's seed immediately: she would have long since died; it had to be the seed of some future heroine, mother of Him who was to win the definitive victory over the devil, Christ. And the mother's name was Mary, the "New Eve" gradually unveiled by the Fathers of the Church.

The Unity of the Human Race

The lines of thought elaborated in the previous section all revolve about a single postulate: the human race is ONE. Sin, punishment and promise: all three demand that we limit the number of "first" parents to a single couple. Polygenism seems to be contrary to the revealed message of Sacred Scripture, and, specifically, to these first three chapters of Genesis. This is how Pope Pius XII stated it in *Humani Generis:*

> For the faithful cannot embrace that opinion which maintains either that after Adam there existed on this earth true men who did not take their origin from him as from the first parent of all,

---

[3] Again the reader is referred to the *Summa Theologica*, Ia, q. 100, art. 2, where St. Thomas argues that each descendant of an obedient Adam would have had a personal testing before being confirmed in grace in Eden.

or that Adam represents a certain number of first parents. Now it is in no way apparent how such an opinion can be reconciled with that which the sources of revealed truth and the documents of the teaching authority of the Church propose with regard to original sin, which proceeds from a sin actually committed by an individual, Adam, and which through generation is passed on to all and is in everyone as his own.[4]

Hence, monophyleticism is not enough to satisfy the demands of revelation. Maintaining as certain the evolution of the human body from lower animal forms, this hypothesis admits that all men are descended from a single pair of brutes. But it makes the further claim that this primitive pair gave birth to several pairs of human beings of diverse characteristics from whom the human race sprang. This hypothesis, offered to explain the plurality of racial types among men, postulates several sets of first human parents and destroys monogenism. As for the existence of men on Mars, it seems a bit premature to plan a planetary missionary expedition. Some theologians maintain that there could be rational animals who are not members of the human race. Their salvific status could embrace a number of possible combinations: fallen or not fallen, redeemed or unredeemed, or even not elevated to the supernatural order. Genesis considered, this hypothesis seems unlikely; the burden of proof rests on those scientists and theologians who maintain the affirmative.

Conclusions drawn from the first three chapters of Genesis may be summed up thus:

1) All things were created by God in terms strongly suggesting a beginning in time. (The Fourth General Council of the Lateran in 1215 defined creation in time.)

2) Man is not a part of the divine substance, but a creature of God (no pantheism.)

3) The creation of man's soul requires a special act of God, Whose image it bears through intelligence and a capacity for grace (soul does not evolve).

4) The first woman was created from the first man somehow, to be his helper in the propagation of children in a permanent marital state.

5) The human race is one, having a single set of first parents (no polygenism).

6) Adam and Eve were created in a state of happiness above their nature, known as "original justice," in which they were destined to enjoy the friendship of God forever.

7) Our first parents fell from this state through disobedience at the instigation of the devil, thereby forfeiting original justice for the whole race.

---

[4] Paragraph 64. See also Acts 17:26 and Romans 5:12.

8) God promised them a redeemer who would conquer evil and restore mankind to His friendship.

De Profundis: Psalm 129

Perhaps no psalm is more widely used in the liturgy than this moving plea of a sinner for pardon. It is daily recited for the dead in monasteries and convents of religious women, and is used frequently in the missal and breviary. One of the seven "penitential psalms," it is classified with *psalms of lament*. This is the largest literary type found in the Psalter, embracing approximately one third of the psalms. The usual formula for this type is: 1) a vivid appeal to God for help; 2) a specific request—for pardon, rescue from enemies, etc.; and 3) a complaint, outlining the reason for the psalmist's predicament. In Psalm 129, the complaint is lacking (i. e., the specific nature of the sin(s) which he wants forgiven); consequently, we are not in a position to give a detailed notion of its historical setting. It may have been composed (or adapted) "as a prayer for the day of public repentance appointed by Esdras after the return of the exiles from Babylon."[5]

In presenting this psalm in conjunction with the story of the Fall, we have no intention of implying that the poem was composed by Adam and Eve or recited by them. For the most part, our selection of psalms will represent an accommodation: the shoe seems to fit, so we put it on. But I believe the reader will agree that if we change the word "Israel" in verses 7 and 8 to "mankind," this psalm seems to express admirably the repentant hope which our first parents must have felt after God promised them redemption.

vv. 1-4: Steeped in grievous sin, the psalmist cries out to God from his wretched plight. Not daring to ask for forgiveness directly, he cites the divine reputation for mercy.

5-6: Confident that his plea will be heard, the sinner begins his vigil of petition.

7-8: His great confidence leads him to extend his petition for forgiveness on a national scale.

See Appendix, "Myth in Genesis," p. 243, for additional material.

Suggested Readings

Hunt, *The Book of Genesis*, Part I, pp. 14-17.
McKenzie, *The Two-Edged Sword*, Chap. 6.
Orchard, *A Catholic Commentary on Holy Scripture*, col. 144-145.
Thomas, D. Winton, ed., *Documents from Old Testament Times*, pp. 3-26.
Vann, Gerald, *Myth, Symbol and Revelation* (Washington, D. C.: The Thomist Press, 1962) 28 pp.
Vawter, *A Path Through Genesis*, Chap. 3.

[5] C. J. Callan, O.P., *The New Psalter* (J. P. Wagner, 1949) p. 464.

Chapter VIII

Semitic Genealogies:
The Spread of Sin

READINGS: *Genesis 4-11; Psalm 1.*

By now it should be clear that the Jews tended to think and to write thematically; that is, they shied away from scientific accounts, preferring to subordinate all details to an over-all portrayal of a specific theme. This is the way in which their minds worked, and we have no right to criticize them for being "inaccurate." They approached reality through symbols and their symbols are rich in meaning. These next eight chapters continue in the same vein (mostly Yahwist). One of the principal symbols is the genealogies in Genesis 4, 5, 10 and 11; these sweeping family trees teach more lessons than an atomic weight chart.

What is the main teaching of this section of Genesis? We do not wish to anticipate the sacred author; however, it will not be out of place to point out that we have here what seems to be an extended commentary on the third chapter, viz., the Fall and its effects. The insinuation is constant and insistent: Adam and Eve were not merely individual sinners; they were the human race at sin. Three episodes give unity to the many details and spell out the implications of our first parents' cosmic rebellion: 1) the story of Cain and Abel, where we see sin spread through the family; 2) the Deluge, representing sin as a disease of society at large; 3) the Tower of Babel, showing sin as an international institution.

The Story of Cain and Abel
(Genesis 4)

We are still in the "primitive history" genre. Just as Adam is "the man," so is Cain "the murderer" and Abel "the just one." Many popular but unscientific etymologies occur, as we shall see. The importance of the fourth chapter demands that we give a detailed analysis of the text, as we have done for each of the first three chapters.

v. 1-2: "Cain" (similar to other Hebrew words meaning *to beget* and *blacksmith*) is described as the firstborn of Adam and Eve. The name of his brother, "Abel," is like the Hebrew word for *breath*

74

—perhaps because his life was cut short. The sacred author reveals the relative dispositions of the two boys through their occupations: shepherding was a noble profession, whereas original sin had turned gardening into the less desirable task of farming.

3-5: By noting the parallel passage in I John 3:12 we learn more details of this primitive tradition: Cain had a record of sin, but Abel was a good boy. Their sacrifices reflect their inner sentiments: Cain offered non-descript fruits; Abel took the firstlings of his flock, which won divine favor.

6-7: God is pictured as appearing to Cain, reminding him that he is free to resist the proneness to sin which he has inherited.

8-9: Resisting the voice of conscience, Cain falls into deeper sin: fratricide. Note the anti-social implications of his reply to God's question regarding Abel's whereabouts. This is the beginning of the disintegration of the community.

10-16: God's disfavor is shown in vivid, concrete terms; Cain is not to be killed (by whom?), but is to be a social outcast, symbolic of an evil progeny.

17-18: Cain's descendants are given in broad outline, as the sacred author wishes to complete his story so that he can leave him out of the picture (strategic elimination) and pass on to the Sethites. This first of the family trees is extremely skeletal: the Yahwist tradition possessed only a handful of proper names, so they have to be stretched out. The evil character of this segment of the human race is emphasized by their founding of a city; among the Jews, urban life was not the ideal.

19-20: It is not left up to the reader's imagination to ferret out the vicious character of Lamech. He is the first of the patriarchs to practice bigamy. Jabel, the shepherd, and Jubal, the harp and flute artist, have names that resemble the Hebrew words for flocks and horn, respectively. Thubalcain is the evil genius who becomes the first industrialist ("forerunner of those who forge vessels of bronze and iron"). Note the anachronism: historians assure us that the Bronze Age yielded to the Iron Age only about 1200 B.C. — *after* the Deluge! The sacred author was certainly aware of the incongruity, but reproduced the tradition as he received it for the sake of its religious message.

23-24: Lamech practices the law of unmitigated blood vengeance against which the Mosaic Law will strike out. His statement in v. 24 is a blasphemous paraphrase of God's declaration in v. 15.

25-26: The sacred author now introduces the line with which he is actually concerned, that of Seth. The word "Adam" is here used as a proper name for the first time. The good character of the Sethites is indicated by their engaging in some type of formal worship of Yahweh.

All of these bits of popular tradition are put together with one purpose in view: to illustrate the wickedness of the Cainites. Not a single good deed is told of them. They are described as victims of crass materialism which results in bigamy, violence and blasphemy.

The Virtuous Sethites
(Genesis 5)

Here the priestly editors have inserted a genealogy from their tradition. In giving us the line of Seth, they have used a number of names which overlap with those in Chapter 4: Henoch occurs in each list; Mahujael resembles Malaleel; Mathusael is like Mathusale; each list has a Lamech. We must conclude, then, that the two lists are from a common source, and each one is used for a particular purpose. There are exactly ten generations from Adam to Noe, inclusive; ten was a "round" number for the Semites as well as for us. That this list is an artificial, symbolic device becomes unmistakably clear when we lay it out and analyze it.

The real significance of the Sethites appears from a study of their life spans. Although some of the original figures have been altered in transmission, the pattern is still recognizable: the lives of the patriarchs are seen to *decrease* in length. What is the lesson that is being taught? It is the same as that taught by the Cainites: sin is on the rampage — even among these "good" people. For the Hebrews, longevity was a sign of innocence, whereas a short life was to be expected by sinners. Henoch is no exception; the conventional number 365 is assigned to him because he never did die, but "walked with God."[1] In order to appreciate the symbolism, all four genealogies in this section are given in the chart, "Adam-Eve."

The Deluge
(Genesis 6–9)

It is still controverted whether "the sons of God" in Genesis 6:2 represent angelic creatures, or simply Sethites (and the "daughters of men" Cainites).[2] The 120-year lifespan also presents a difficulty —

---

[1] In Hebrew 11:5, the author explains this as being "taken up" by God (but not into the Beatific Vision!).

[2] See the end of this chapter, For More Intensive Study, for references.

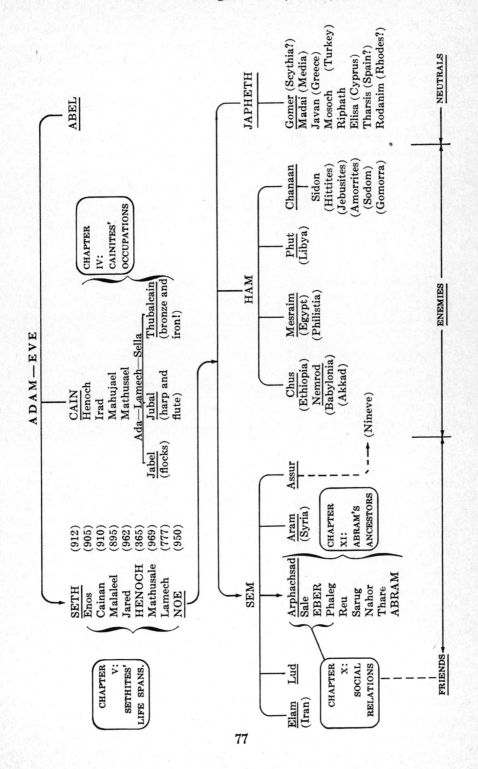

unless it merely means the assignation of a period of repentance for sinful man before the Deluge. What is certain is that mankind was wicked, and a Deluge did take place. As to this latter point, no one today who has studied the matter thinks that it covered the whole earth; the Deluge was a local inundation, probably in the vicinity of Mesopotamia. Yet it would be useless to challenge the sacred author's claim that "All flesh that moved on the earth died: birds, cattle, wild animals, all creatures that creep on the earth, and all men" (Gen. 7:21). If he were writing as a modern historian, he would be guilty of at least material error. However, since he is merely using the Flood tradition as a vehicle of religious truth, we cannot expect him to produce a scientific research paper on the subject. Indeed, the concept of a universal cataclysm adds immensely to the moral truth being conveyed, and we have already noted that he makes the Cainites survive the Deluge.

One of the disconcerting features (to the modern reader) is the duplication of details. Here are several instances of the repetition:

DETAIL	TEXT #1	TEXT #2
God observes the malice of men	6:5	6:11–12
God predicts the Flood	6:13, 17	7:4
God orders Noe to enter the Ark	6:18	7:1
God commands Noe to take animals into the Ark	6:19–20	7:2–3
Noe obeys God	6:22	7:5
Noe enters the Ark	7:7	7:13
The animals enter the Ark	7:8–9	7:14–15
The Deluge begins	7:10	7:11
The waters increase and raise the Ark	7:17	7:18
All living creatures perish	7:21	7:22
The waters abate	8:1–b	8:3–a
The length of the Deluge	7:24	8:3–b
The earth dries up	8:13	8:14

Two explanations are offered for this duplication. One is that the account represents an amalgamation of two traditions (*Yahwist* and *Priestly*).[3] Another explanation attributes the repetition of the style of the sacred author: he is "going back on the story to add new information." Very likely the true reason is a combination of the two explanations: the sacred author may have combined the two traditions deliberately in order to heighten the moral truth which he wished to convey by repetition.

---

[3] Most of Text #1 is from "P," and most of Text #2 is from "J."

There are several lessons being taught by the story of the Deluge which lend a transcendence to the biblical account over pagan sources of a similar catastrophe: the ugliness of sin in God's eyes; the ever-increasing evil of mankind: God's justice in the wake of human malice and His mercy towards the righteous. God on this occasion makes His first "covenant" with man: the Covenant of the Rainbow. In this covenant, which is a preparation for the two later ones, God rescues Noe from the mire of human debasement — just as He will rescue Abraham from his polytheistic ancestors, and the Jews under Moses from the pagan, devil-worshipping Egyptians. The story of Noe proves (against pagan myths) that it is possible for a single man to hold out against his evil surroundings and to be faithful to his conscience. It shows, likewise, that God is implacably on the side of holiness and morality, not a capricious, pleasure-seeking being like man: that He is ready and able to intervene in human affairs on the side of justice. Note the reference here to II Peter 2:5.

Two powerful symbols emerge from the Flood story. The first is the Ark, symbol of God's protection and salvation. The Fathers saw here a type of the Church; St. Peter explicitly links up the Ark with the sacrament of Baptism (I Pet. 3:20). The other symbol is water, exposed in its mysterious ambivalence. The dual character of its typology is unmistakable: water symbolizes both *death* (in the destruction of sinners) and *life* (in the salvation of Noe and the others in the Ark).[4]

As his response to God's kindness, Noe is asked to observe two laws: 1) Don't murder; and 2) Don't drink blood (this would be equivalent to murdering symbolically since blood represents life). Capital punishment is recognized in verse 6. This whole ninth chapter breathes forth the atmosphere of a new creation in the form of a reorientation between God and man. God now formally takes into account the weakness of fallen human nature (8:21: "the inclination of man's heart is evil from his youth"), and the disharmony in nature wrought by original sin. Hence, accepting man as he is, God permits him explicitly to eat the flesh of animals and promises never to destroy the earth again by water. The rainbow acquires a new significance.

The Genealogy in Genesis 10: Friends Versus Enemies

The blessing of Sem in Genesis 9:26 is messianic in tone. Japheth is to share in his blessing, but Ham is cursed—apparently for the sin of his son, Chanaan, after whom the hated Chanaanites were designated. The genealogical table in Chapter Ten of this text expands upon this

---

[4] The same Hebrew word for *Ark* is again used in Exodus for the basket in which the infant Moses was placed in the Nile River.

situation in uniquely Semitic fashion, now that the key has been revealed: the descendants of Sem are the Jews and all of their *friends* among the nations of the earth; the descendants of the accursed Ham are their traditional *enemies;* and the descendants of Japheth (the more remote Gentiles) are "neutrals"[5] The word *Hebrew* seems to be related to *Eber*, one of Sem's descendants.

The Tower of Babel: Sin Marches On

Genesis 10:5 and 10:20 presuppose the differentiation of languages throughout the world. When we come to the statement in 11:1, then, that "The whole earth used the same language," we must take it in the same vein as the Deluge story — i.e., as another case of "limited universality." In the Tower of Babel we have the Tree of Knowledge all over again: man attempting to live independently of God. Originally, among the Babylonians, this story may have been used to teach children how it happens that there are so many different languages on the earth; here it is used to illustrate the puniness of man and the folly of human pride. Dr. Anderson's summary of the first eleven chapters of Genesis is worth noting:

> Primeval history, then, had a sad outcome, for man had failed to find the fullness of life—life in communion with God and in community with his neighbor. From Adam to the Tower of Babel the human tragedy increased, despite the advances in the arts and sciences. History was urged on by an evil impulse that spoiled God's creation, leaving man estranged from his Creator and at odds with his fellow men. Taken by itself, the story would be extremely pessimistic. But the primeval history is part of the larger epic of the Yahwist. It is a prologue to what follows: the call of Abraham.[6]

The Genealogy in Genesis 11: Abraham's Ancestors

The main line of Sem's descendants in the genealogy in Chapter Ten extended only as far as Phaleg, in whose time "the world was divided" (v. 25). It is not certain whether or not this phrase refers to the Tower of Babel episode. At any rate, the genealogy in Chapter Eleven continues this branch of Noe's family down to the descendant in whom the sacred author is vitally interested: Abraham. Again we see that the arrangement (exactly ten generations) and the ages are notably artificial. Taken literally, the recorded lifespans (now decreasing rapidly as we approach historical times) would have Sem outlive Abraham! Beginning with Genesis 11:27 we have a new genre of history: "ancient" rather than "primitive," for we are no longer in the pre-historic era.

---

[5] Cf. "Prophecy" on page 77.

[6] Bernhard W. Anderson, *Understanding the Old Testament* (Englewood Cliffs, N.J.: Prentice-Hall, 1957) p. 173.

Psalm 1: The Way of the Just vs. the Way of the Sinner

Serving as the introduction to the Psalter, this short, majestic psalm belongs to much the same genre as the sapiential or wisdom literature; hence, we may call it a "Wisdom Psalm." Such psalms are didactic in tenor and often glorify the Law, as does this one in verse 2. The author is unknown; the psalm has no title. Internal evidence would suggest a late (Post-Exilic) composition. This poem would fit well in the mouth of either of the two just men described in these chapters of Genesis: Abel and Noe — if we abstract from the fact that they ante-date the Mosaic Law. (See also Psalms 13 and 52.)

---

vv. 1-3: The just man is praised and compared to a fruitful, irrigated tree.

4-6: In contrast, the sinner is like chaff, scattered by the wind. Just how the just shall prosper or the sinner perish beyond this life is not clarified — except that "the Lord cares for the way of the just" (v. 6).

Suggested Readings

Hasseveldt, *The Church A Divine Mystery*, pp. 65-74.
Hunt, *The Book of Genesis, Part I*, pp. 17-25.

FOR MORE INTENSIVE STUDY: Look up one or more of the following topics, comparing the treatment given each one by the two different sources indicated:[7]

TOPIC	Vawter, PATH THROUGH GENESIS	Orchard, A CATHOLIC COMMENTARY
1. The meaning of the story of the Cainites and the genealogy in Chapter 4	pp. 72–77	col. 146a–e
2. The meaning of the genealogy in Chapter 5	pp. 78–83	col. 140b–e
3. The "sons of God" vs. the "daughters of men"	pp. 84–86	col. 146f–k
4. The extent and meaning of the Deluge	{ pp. 87–89 } pp. 95–97	col. 147c–148a col. 149a, b
5. Duplications in the Deluge story, and its Babylonian counterpart	pp. 90–94	col. 148b–d
6. Meaning of the curse of Chanaan, and of the genealogies in Chapter 10	pp. 98–105	col. 149c–k
7. Meaning of the Tower of Babel, and of the genealogy in Chapter 11	pp. 105–110	col. 149 l–q

[7] See also Emil S. Kraeling, *Bible Atlas* (Chicago, Ill.: Rand-McNally, 1962) Chap. 3.

Chapter IX

Abraham's Justification: The Nature of Faith

READINGS: *Genesis 12–24; Romans 4; Hebrews 7, 11; James 2; Psalm 22. (Note: Genesis 12:3; 17:8–10; Josue 24:2)*

Abraham held a unique position in the religious tradition of the Jews. They were wont to cite their blood relationship with him as their peculiar title to being the "Chosen People"—although *de facto* it was Jacob who was their specific ancestor. At any rate, it was Abraham who emerged from the confusion of the Tower of Babel episode as God's choice in the fulfillment of His special plans for mankind. The final editors of these chapters of Genesis have woven together a variety of traditions and legends into a coherent story illustrating their understanding of the divine pattern in history. Basically, it is their own history which has served as the warp and woof of the mosaic; but the blessings of which they were the depositories were clearly earmarked for the world at large, as we shall see.

With the patriarch Abraham we are firmly anchored in documented history. We can now begin to correlate biblical history with world history, even though the correlation is imperfect. The same is much more true of biblical geography, especially in the light of modern archeological excavations. The map on the next page is an attempt to reproduce the Middle East of Abraham's era and to show the path of his migration along the Fertile Crescent to the Land of Promise.

Election and Promise
(Genesis 12–14)

At the end of Chapter Eleven we were introduced to Abraham's relatives. His father, Thare, took Abram (this was the original form of his name) and his wife, Sarai, and his grandson (Abram's nephew), Lot, from their homeland, Ur of the Chaldees, some 600 miles to the northwestern Mesopotamian city of Haran. Very likely this move was part of the Amorrite migration of the period.[1] Both cities wor-

---

[1] Cf. B. W. Anderson, *Understanding the Old Testament* (Englewood Cliffs, N. J.: Prentice-Hall, Inc., 1957) pp. 16-24. Written by a Protestant dean, this book contains many brilliant insights.

PEOPLES OF THE ANCIENT NEAR EAST, 2000–1400 B.C.

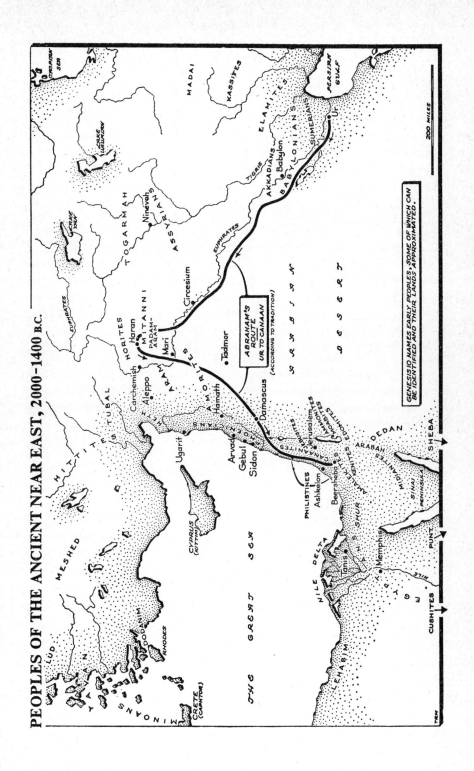

ABRAHAM'S ROUTE
UR TO CANAAN
(ACCORDING TO TRADITION)

GENESIS 10 NAMES EARLY PEOPLES, SOME OF WHICH CAN
BE IDENTIFIED AND THEIR LANDS APPROXIMATED.

200 MILES

shipped pagan deities; the Book of Josue tells us (24:2) that they were polytheists. But out of a clear sky, God summoned Abram to leave Haran and to migrate into the land occupied by the Chanaanites. We are not told why Abram was chosen, nor why Lot accompanied him. The sacred author simply takes it for granted that Yahweh is the free master of His own counsel, choosing some and rejecting others. He makes no attempt to solve the mystery of the divine choice, but is content to select carefully from his oral materials those threads which, woven together, will best illustrate the salvation history he is trying to convey.

Genesis 12:2-3 represents the second messianic promise. Like Genesis 3:15, it is universal in scope: "In you shall all the nations of the earth be blessed." These two verses contain the promise of a blessing, which is a characteristic feature of God's act of election. The next step, the covenant, will follow in Chapters 15-17. In the meantime, Abram's character is revealed in three episodes. In the first, he appears quite shabby in the way he treats Sarai in Egypt: passing her off as his sister rather than his wife, thereby releasing her into the Pharao's harem in order to save his own skin. Although Abram's moral awareness was quite different from ours, this action cannot be entirely condoned: it was a weakness on his part. In fact, a similar (or the same?) episode will be related of him in Chapter 20, and of Isaac in Chapter 26. Nevertheless, Yahweh does not repent of His choice; rather, His provident hand reaches out and saves Sarai from this dire threat which otherwise could well have thwarted God's promise of a numerous posterity.

In Genesis 13, a noble deed is recounted about Abram: he lets his nephew have his choice of land when circumstances force them to part. Again divine Providence is watching over Abram, for it is the southern area of Lot's choice which is exposed to the predatory excursion of the four kings. With 318 men, Abram rescues his nephew from their clutches. Then a mysterious event occurs: on the return trip, a man designated simply as "the king of Salem" and "a priest of the Most High God," blesses Abram and makes a sacrifice of bread and wine. Abram, in turn, gives him tithes from his booty. Many modern Scripture scholars believe that Melchisedec was a pagan priest of the Canaanite God, El-Elyon ("most high god").[2] However, in view of the fact that he has found his way into a messianic psalm, 109:4: "The Lord has sworn and he will not repent: 'Thou are a priest forever

---

[2] For example, Ignatius Hunt, *The Book of Genesis*, Part I (Glen Rock, N. J.: Paulist Press, 1960) p. 28. Father Hunt also maintains that the comparison between Christ and Melchisedec in the Epistle to the Hebrews is an accommodation. It is true that Melchisedec does not seem to have been recognized as a priestly "type" of the Messia in Old Testament times.

according to the order of Melchisedec,'" may we not conclude with Hebrew 7 that Melchisedec is a true type of Christ. In every Mass we ask God to accept our gifts as "You were pleased to accept the offering of Your just servant Abel, and the sacrifice of Abraham, our patriarch, and that which Melchisedec, *Your* high priest, offered up to You: a holy sacrifice, and a spotless Victim." The whole seventh chapter of the Epistle to the Hebrews should be read by the student as a commentary on Genesis 14.

The Covenant of Circumcision
(Genesis 15–17)

"Abram believed the Lord, who credited the act to him as justice." Here is the key to the Hebrew religion: justification through faith. Faith in what? Faith in God's word, His promise of a numerous posterity through whom the earth would be somehow blessed. Rather vague, we must admit. But where Adam and Eve had doubted, and the contemporaries of Noe had scorned God's word, the Patriarch Abram was willing to go along on blind trust. Salvation, then, was possible under the Old Testament by such faith, which restored a man to divine intimacy.[3] Nor should we interpret verse 8 as a doubt; Abram is simply asking God for more information, and God consents to give him a sign. Using the symbolism to which Abram would be accustomed, the Lord causes fire and smoke to pass between the halves of animals prepared by Abram as a seal of the new covenant. The "prophecy" in verses 13-16 is really more of an explanation in retrospect.

Although monogamy is held up as the ideal even in the Old Testament, Abram was not guilty of sin in his relationship with Agar. Another truth is being exemplified here: the tremendous importance which Semites, along with other Orientals, attached to offspring — especially a male heir. Sarai's desperation is turned to envy when Agar provides Abram with a son, so she reduces the maid to her former position of a slave. Verse 13 shows that these primitive people had already formed some notion of God's transcendence; it also furnishes an example of the occasional marked difference between the Douay and Confraternity Versions. In Genesis 17 the covenant is made bilateral. Abram is told by God to "be perfect" (v. 1) and is commanded to circumcise all male offspring. At the same time, his name is changed to Abraham ("father of a multitude"), and Sarai's name is simplified to "Sara." This is, indeed, a solemn occasion: a person's name was thought to be intimately connected with his personality

---

[3] It is certain that this justification included sanctifying grace and the remission of original sin. This was in anticipation of the merits of Christ.

85

and his destiny. Verses 17-18, and verse 12 in the next chapter, show that their faith was still not entirely perfect, though God was satisfied with it.

God's Plan Begins to Unfold

(Genesis 18–21)

Abraham's meticulous hospitality to the three strangers (Yahweh and two angels in human garb) illustrates the great emphasis which Orientals placed on this virtue. His intimacy with the Lord is shown by his bargaining power in the Sodom-Gomorra affair. The peculiar vice of the inhabitants of these two cities has left its mark in the naming of this unnatural sin, "sodomy." Although not even ten just men could be found in Sodom, God agreed to spare Lot and his family at Abraham's request. Lot's two daughters (whose virginity he had been willing to sacrifice on the altar of hospitality) played an unwholesome but understandable trick on him. In evaluating this story, we should remember that the Ammonites and Moabites were among the standing enemies of the Jews. Genesis 19 is another monument to the delicate blending of justice and mercy by Yahweh.

The episode described in Genesis 20 may well be the same event recounted in Genesis 12, but from a different source.[4] Verse 12 indicates that Abraham and Sara were blood relatives. In Genesis 21 the first stage of the promise is finally realized: a son is born to Abraham (100 years old) and Sara (90 years old). There is probably exaggeration in these ages to enhance the reader's appreciation of the miraculous intervention of Providence. One who has followed the story thus far can well appreciate the scene that ensues: the expulsion of Ismael and his mother. In his Epistle to the Galatians, 4:21-31 (the lesson for the fourth Sunday of Lent), St. Paul gives us the spiritual meaning. Agar and Ismael represent the Old Testament, which ceased to bind after the promulgation of the New Testament represented by Sara and Isaac.

Abraham's Response

(Genesis 22–24)

Seldom in the Old Testament do we find a heroism which measures up to that of Abraham as he prepares to offer Isaac at the command of Yahweh. Note carefully the details which the sacred author has left us: 1) Abraham is asked to sacrifice his *only-begotten* son; 2) Isaac is *innocent* and no protest is recorded on the part of either father or

---

[4] The Elohist tradition makes its first appearance with the story of Abraham.

son; 3) It is described as basically an act of *obedience*. Only in the light of Isaac's antitype, Christ, can we appreciate the fuller sense of this vibrant story in the Book of Genesis. We may be sure that Abraham had been living his faith, and that sacrifice was the pattern of his daily existence: his brand of heroism does not suddenly emerge out of a clear sky. Some exegetes would have the initiative for the deed come from Abraham rather than Yahweh, on the grounds that the patriarch was unwilling to be outdone by the "generosity" of the Chanaanites in their child-sacrifices.[5] Whatever may be the case, it is certain that Abraham did what he believed God wanted him to do, and that Yahweh accepted his sublime act as a sign of his faith. At this point the biblical analysis of the role played by faith in the lives of the patriarchs in Hebrews 11:1-19 should be studied.

The death of Sara furnishes Abraham an occasion to get a solid foothold in Chanaan by buying a field from one of the Hethites (Hittites?) as a burial ground. All of God's promises regarding the gift of the Promised Land are couched in the future tense; the Jews will not obtain definitive possession of it until after their sojourn in Egypt. The "blow-by-blow" description of the manner in which a wife was obtained for Isaac among Abraham's relatives near Haran accurately reflects the marriage customs of the period.

The Meaning of the Story of Abraham

We have already seen the central role played by faith in Abraham's justification and in his relationship with God. The story of his life manifests the dynamic quality of his faith. It was more than an assent of the intellect for him; it was the reorientation of the whole man. The early Christians exemplified the same spirit in deeming the martyr the man of faith par excellence. As noted above, Abraham's willingness to sacrifice Isaac was a corollary of his faith. The patriarch did not only believe God; he believed IN God. Centuries later, when certain of Abraham's descendants had lost the initial fervor of their patriarch and were allowing the external observance of the Mosaic Law to substitute for the total commitment of faith, St. Paul severely chided them. "For not through the Law but through the justice of faith was the promise made to Abraham and to his posterity" (Rom. 4:13). The Apostle is not here denying that good works and the observance of the Mosaic Law had any part in the salvation of the Jews; he is declaring that works which are not rooted in faith are inefficacious.

In the sixteenth century when certain Christians became alarmed at the abuses which had crept into the preaching of indulgences and

---

[5] Hunt, *Op cit.*, p. 31.

the use of the sacraments and attempted to recapture the dynamism of faith, they harked back to the words of Saint Paul. The Protestant Reformation developed out of an unfortunate misunderstanding of the Apostle's statements, which were used as a basis for the doctrine of justification by faith alone under the New Testament. Thus, we find in the "Augsburg Confession," drawn up in 1530 by Luther's friend, Melanchthon: "Also they [the Reformers] teach that men can not be justified by their own powers, merits, or works; but they are justified freely for Christ's sake through faith, when they believe that they are received into favor, and their sins forgiven for Christ's sake, who by his death hath satisfied for our sins. This faith doth God impute for righteousness before him" (Art. IV).

This statement contains a profound truth, viz., that salvation is basically the work of God in man, and that faith is the first vital factor in the process and cannot be merited; as St. Thomas says, "belief itself is the first act of justice which God works in him [the believer]."[6] However, it is evident that they confused salvation with justification — which is only the first step toward salvation — from Article XV, in which "vows and traditions concerning foods, days, and such like" are branded as "useless and contrary to the Gospel." St. James balances out the picture for us when he affirms the meritorious value of works along with faith in conjunction with his discussion of Abraham's offering of Isaac:

> Was not Abraham our father justified by works, when he offered up Isaac? Dost thou see that faith worked along with his works, and by the works of faith was made perfect? And the Scripture was fulfilled which says, 'Abraham believed God, and it was reckoned to him as justice, and he was called the friend of God.' You see that by works a man is justified, and not by faith only.
> (2:21-22)

Psalm 22: "The Lord is My Shepherd"

This well-known literary masterpiece, which introduces a new class of "Psalms of Confidence," does not require much explanation. Picturing Yahweh as the Good Shepherd, it describes His intimacy with His Chosen Ones in terms of pastoral life. Undoubtedly Abraham was a shepherd; we can easily imagine this psalm on the lips of the "man of faith" even though it was composed centuries after he received the Covenant of Circumcision. The climax comes in portraying Yahweh as receiving the psalmist into His own house as a permanent dweller. Typical of the Psalter as a whole, this sacred poem transcends the distinction between Old and New Testaments and fits perfectly into the spirit of Christianity.

---

[6] In his *Commentary on the Epistle to the Romans*, 4:5.

Suggested Readings

Dyson and Jones, *The Kingdom of Promise*, pp. 1-15. These pages provide an excellent survey of the formation of the Kingdom of God in its patriarchal beginnings.

Hunt, *The Book of Genesis, Part 1*, pp. 25-33.

Orchard, *A Catholic Commentary on Holy Scripture*, cols. 150-153e.

Vawter, Bruce, "The Biblical Idea of Faith," *Worship*, XXXIV (August-September, 1960) pp. 443-450.

—————, *A Path Through Genesis*, pp. 113-181.

Chapter X

Isaac, Jacob, Juda:
The Messianic Line

READINGS: *Genesis 25–36; Deuteronomy 25:5–10; Psalm 77:1–9; 32–39; 65–72. (Note: Genesis 35:10; 38:8–10)*

Before finishing the story of Abraham, the sacred author completes the record with another genealogy. We learn at the beginning of Genesis 25 that Abraham had a third wife, Cetura, who gave him six boys. Among them is Madian, father of the Madianites, who later were to provide a home for Moses. Since family relationships play a very important part in the events of these chapters, it will help to start out with a master genealogy, continuing the one given on page 77:

THE MESSIANIC LINE

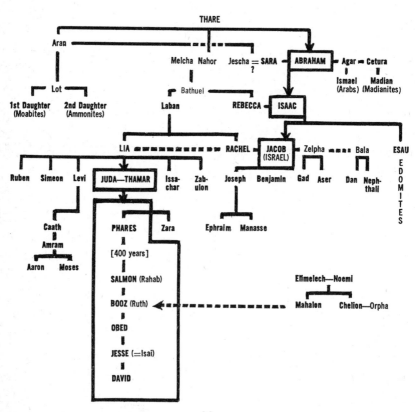

Jacob's Eternal Election

(Genesis 25–27)

After Abraham died at the moderate age of 175, both Ismael and Isaac are depicted at his side to bury him. Then begins the story of Isaac, who plays little more than the role of a link between Abraham and Jacob. Isaac's wife, Rebecca — like Sara — 1) is sterile until Isaac's prayer for offspring is heard; 2) sees her "younger" son supplant his firstborn twin brother; 3) is involved in a sister-wife deception. At what shrine she prays to learn the meaning of her difficult pregnancy (Gen. 25:23), we are not informed. Whatever the source of the oracle, the sacred author uses it to convey to his readers that the future supplanting of Esau by Jacob was strictly by the design of Yahweh. We are also prepared for this deed by the episode of the sale of the birthright for a meal: Jacob is predestined![1]

The story in Chapter 26 has become a bit monotonous. Whether or not it is the same event already twice described of Abraham, or a similar event, we are given to understand by it that Isaac is no more perfect than his father. In verse 30 the meal is ceremonial, sealing the covenant between Isaac and Abimelech. Among Orientals, eating together is a mark of friendship: enemies simply do not sit down at the same table. At the end of the chapter, Esau's reprobation is insinuated by his polygamy — and his wives are Chanaanite women at that. In Chapter 27 we are presented with what St. Augustine calls a "mystery" rather than a lie. We are not so kind to Jacob and Rebecca; it was a lie and a deception, and therefore a sin — at least objectively. Note that it is the mother who plays the leading role in this episode: she was an Aramean, like the rest of Abraham's pagan relatives. Her fault was a refusal to wait for God to work out His plans for Jacob's future; she insisted on taking matters into her own hands. It appears from Genesis 27:39-40 that a father's blessing was considered to be irrevocable — even when it fell upon the wrong person.

The Seed of Jacob: Jewish Beginnings

(Genesis 28–33)

Forced to flee because of Esau's great wrath, Jacob finds another reason for the departure in his mother's insistence that he choose a wife from among her kinsfolk. On the way to Phaddan-Aram, Jacob has a vision at Luza (which he renames Bethel, "House of God": cf. 35:6-7). The ladder between heaven and earth indicates God's

---

[1] Cf. Malachia 1:2-3 and Romans 9:13. Although they were twins, Esau was born first.

closeness to this chosen line of Abraham's descendants. The original promise of Genesis 12:3 is renewed to him, and his faith is strengthened. The opening lines of the Mass for the dedication of a church, "Terribile," are taken from Genesis 28:17.

Chapter 29 records a story of success: Jacob finds not one, but two, wives among his first cousins. However, in the process he has to undergo something of the treatment which he himself had administered to his rustic brother, Esau. His uncle Laban proves to be a good match for his cleverness, and these chapters read like a game of chess between two seasoned masters. Jacob suffers the first attack. It had been love at first sight in his meeting with Rachel, Laban's younger daughter.[2] After working seven years for his uncle on the understanding that he would receive Rachel in marriage as his wages, Jacob discovers on his wedding night that the crafty Laban has foisted off his older daughter, the ugly Lia, on him. As women kept themselves veiled in the presence of the opposite sex before marriage, this substitution would not be too difficult. The reader will note that there was not much formality in the marriage ceremony itself; after the nuptial feast, the man and woman simply consummated the union. Jacob did gain one consolation, viz., he got Rachel before the second set of seven years; in other words, he acquired two wives within a space of eight days and worked fourteen years for the pair. But as a kind of divine retribution for his cheating of Esau, it turns out that Rachel is barren.

Immediately after the weddings there follows what Fr. Hunt describes as an apparent "rapid-fire birth race."[3] Lia gets off to a head start because of Rachel's sterility and gives Jacob four sons. At the beginning of Chapter 30 Rachel plays her last card: like Sara, she offers her handmaid, Bala, to her husband to secure substitute motherhood. Dan and Nephthali are the products of this union, and Rachel is consoled. Not to be outdone, Lia — temporarily sterile after the birth of Juda — turns her handmaid, Zelpha, over to Jacob, and two more boys are born: Gad and Aser. In the scene that follows it is hard to discern whether Lia's fertility (resulting in the births of Isaachar, Zabulon and a girl, Dina) are the effect of prayer, of eating the mandrakes ("love-apples"), or of both. Rachel, too, is finally relieved of her barrenness and gives birth to her first son, Joseph.

The manner in which Jacob increases his flocks at the expense of Laban is mysterious and further complicated by a faulty Hebrew text. Somehow he manages to bring it about that his agreed share, the off-colored black sheep and spotted goats, are able to breed hardier offspring in greater numbers than Laban's flocks. When Laban observes

---

[2] Hence, the Nuptial blessing in the Mass describes her as "dear to her husband."

[3] *The Book of Genesis, Part 2,* p. 11.

that Jacob's wealth is increasing while his is decreasing, his cunning turns into hostility and envy. Advised by God in Chapter 31 to return home, Jacob prepares to flee secretly. But he has a problem: where will the loyalty of his wives be — with their father or with their husband? In the ancient Orient, ties of blood were often stronger than marital ties, as we shall note later in the case of Michol, Saul's daughter. After he has briefed them regarding his plans, however, the matter turns out well; they take his part and agree to leave their father.

Whatever the meaning of the household gods which Rachel took, the episode illustrates the pagan background of Laban and his daughters, and it is underscored in verse 53. Laban's vain search for the gods provides Jacob with an occasion for an outburst of righteous indignation ending with a flourish in verse 42. The wealth and power of both parties make it clear that some peaceful settlement is the only practical solution and a covenant is made on their mutual oaths invoking their respective deities.

The next two chapters describe Jacob's reconciliation with his twin, Esau, of whom he is mortally afraid. Still operating more by brains than brawn, Jacob divides his possessions into two camps and is prepared to sacrifice one of them to Esau's wrath. The story is interrupted by an account of Jacob's struggle with a mysterious heavenly visitor — commonly assumed to be an angel. Jacob proves to be a good match in the wrestling bout which follows, and the angel predicts that his name will be changed to Israel ("may God show Himself strong").[4] This event portends Jacob's successful outcome with Esau, and in general, his future protection by God. Genesis 32:31 repeats the theme of God's transcendence (cf. 16:13). Esau is placated on the following day, and the two brothers part on ostensibly friendly terms.

Early History of the Jacobites

(Genesis 34–36; 38)

Jacob finally settles his family in the city of Sichem. Note that the town is named after its leading citizen (or vice versa?). The sordid story of the rape of Dina by Sichem in Chapter 34 will explain the rejection of Simeon and Levi (second and third in line) from the birthright forfeited by Ruben. They were blood brothers (having Lia as their mother in common with Dina) — hence their zeal in avenging her disgrace. Although Jacob condemns their violence, which put the whole family in jeopardy of the Sichemites, the author of the Book of Judith will later praise the zeal of Simeon (Jdt. 9:2-3).

---

[4] See the parallel passage in Osee 12:3-4.

Chapter 35 ties together many loose ends. At God's command, Jacob makes a pilgrimage to the sacred place, Bethel, where Yahweh had appeared to him on his way to Phaddan-Aram. His zeal in purging his household of idolatry before their departure is commendable. In verse 10, his name is changed to Israel as the angel had predicted in Genesis 32:29. This explains why the Jews, who trace their ancestry to him, are known as "Israelites." On this occasion, the messianic promise is renewed. Rachel dies on the journey homeward in giving birth to her husband's twelfth son, Benjamin, and is buried near Bethlehem (only later known as Ephratha). Ruben's crime of incest, for which he will be excluded from his rights as firstborn of Jacob, is mentioned in verse 22. The Priestly editors carefully classify the twelve sons according to their respective mothers in the verses which follow. The chapter ends peacefully with the burial of Isaac by the erstwhile enemies, Esau and Jacob (cf. Gen. 27:41). For an inspired evaluation of Jacob, see Wisdom 10:10-12.

The genealogy of Esau, father of the Edomites, recorded in Chapter 36, does not interest us, and we shall hold Chapter 37 for the rest of the story of Joseph in the following section. Chapter 38 furnishes us with vital information about the key figure of Juda. This fourth son of Israel started out unpromisingly; he separated from his brethren and married a Chanaanite woman. He pays for his waywardness through the wickedness of his oldest sons, Her and Onan. We don't know exactly what Her's sin was, but it evinced drastic punishment from God. According to primitive custom (later incorporated into the Mosaic Code and known as the "Levirate Law," Deuteronomy 25:5-10), it was expected that when a man dies childless, his next oldest brother would marry his widow, thereby to raise up a male descendant to carry on the deceased man's family name and to succeed to the rights of the firstborn. Although Onan's sin of contraception (wasting his seed) was prompted by the selfish desire to retain the prerogatives of the firstborn for himself, the text makes it clear that God punished him for the immorality of the act.[5] Because Juda did not make good on his promise to give Sela (next in line to Onan) to Thamar in order to raise issue to Her, she plays the role of a harlot with her own father-in-law by posing as a Chanaanite temple-prostitute. This shows the great yearning of women of that culture for children, and also Juda's weakness in committing this inexcusable sin of impurity. Because the older twin born of this union, Phares, was an an-

---

[5] The law was designed to keep the family property within the clan among relatives who dwelt together in the same place. *La Sainte Bible de Jerusalem*, p. 46, ft. d, concludes that Onan's punishment covered both the selfishness and the contraception.

cestor of David and Christ, Thamar's name has been preserved in the messianic genealogy along with Rahab, Ruth and Bethsabee ("the former wife of Urias").

Psalm 77: History Employed to Teach a Lesson

Here is another psalm which belongs to the loosely styled class of "didactic" or "Wisdom Psalms." As we saw in Chapter VIII, Psalm 1 contained a meditation on the contrast between the lot of the just and that of the unjust man. Psalm 77 is a detailed review of Jewish history from the time of the Exodus to David. The Temple is portrayed as still standing; hence, we assume that this poem is certainly pre-Exilic, probably composed near the beginning of the wisdom movement. The reader is asked to meditate on the many instances of Yahweh's goodness to Israel; how the people prospered when they obeyed His precepts, and suffered when they defected from the Law (of Moses). Our analysis includes only those sections of the psalm which pertain to the historical material covered thus far.

vv. 1-8: The sacred author sets forth his purpose: to put down for later generations the mighty benefactions of Yahweh in favor of the Jews (note how they are designated simply as "Jacob" and "Israel" in v. 5) in order to inspire confidence in Him and fidelity to His commands, and that they might "not be like their fathers, a generation wayward and rebellious" (v. 8).

32-39: Having recounted the wonderful deeds of God during the Exodus, the psalmist takes up the "party line" faithfully: man's heart is ungrateful and prone to sin. Yahweh is called the "Rock" in v. 35, a favorite Hebrew title to express His Providence. Verse 39 is a classic, reminiscent of Genesis 2:7.

65-72: The psalm ends on a happy note, picturing Yahweh as "a Champion overcome with wine" awakening from slumber. Note finally the theme of divine election: this time it falls on Juda and his descendant, David, rather than on the more distinguished Joseph, whose exploits will be taken up in the next chapter.

Suggested Readings

Anderson, *Understanding the Old Testament*, pp. 173-180. A penetrating analysis of the patriarchs from Abraham to Joseph; his exegesis, however, is a bit extreme in places, e.g., in the last paragraph on p. 175.
Hunt, *The Book of Genesis, Part 2*, pp. 5-17.
Vawter, *A Path Through Genesis*, pp. 181-238; 247-252.

Chapter XI

Joseph In Egypt: Providence and "Prophecy"

READINGS: *Genesis 37; 39–50; Wisdom 10; Psalms 104, 105. (Note: Genesis 49:10)*

Had the story of the patriarch Joseph not been part of an inspired book, it still would surely be a best-seller. The clear-cut, detailed portrait which the sacred author has left us of his beautiful character, with its crescendos and climaxes, effects a powerful catharsis in the reader. Its sublime moral tone rivals that of much later biblical books, such as Tobias. Not only do these pages reflect true literary genius; they also present a reliable picture of Egypt about the middle of the second millennium before Christ. Like other dates of this era, much is still conjecture; however, if we place Joseph's entrance into Egypt about 1700 B.C., we find that biblical events harmonize nicely with Egyptian history. This would make him rise to power under the Semitic (and friendly) Hyksos rulers who invaded Egypt about 1710 B.C. and moved the capital from Thebes in the south to Avaris in the north. This agrees with the implication of Genesis 46 and 47 that the Jews settled near the Pharao when they moved into the section of Gesen in the north of Egypt.[1]

Joseph's Affliction and His Virtue

(Genesis 37, 39, 40)

Not all was peace and harmony among the members of the chosen family of Jacob, as we learn from Chapter 37. The fact that the twelve boys were born of four different mothers created factions among them. Joseph first gets into trouble by tattling on four of his brothers, who had committed some evil deed. Nor did it help matters any that he was the favorite of his father, having been born of the beloved Rachel. Joseph manifests a childlike simplicity, limpid and thoroughly guileless. His imprudence in relating the dreams presaging his future grandeur stems actually from his naiveté. He seems to have had no

---

[1] Anderson, *Op. cit.*, has two very helpful historical correlations on pp. 29-30.

suspicion of his brothers' evil designs. Note that it is Ruben, the first-born, and Juda, who eventually took over Ruben's prerogatives, who try to befriend their young brother. Their efforts are in vain and Joseph is sold into slavery. The ruse of the bloody tunic convinces Jacob that Joseph is dead. In his extreme grief, he speaks of joining his son "in the nether world" (Sheol).

In resisting the attempted seduction by Phutiphar's wife, Joseph reveals a heroism which is head and shoulders above the average patriarch. His quick rise to a position of authority in prison seems to mark a pattern reminiscent of a hero from a Horatio Alger, Jr. story; he is "bound to rise." Chapter 40 (and most of 41) are from the Elohist tradition, which delights in dreams. They usually represent an attempt to avoid portraying God in a too human form; He is made to communicate with men remotely. At any rate, it is through divine enlightenment that Joseph is able to interpret the dreams of his fellow prisoners: this, in turn, provides him with an entree to Pharao's house.

Joseph's Triumph, God's Providence

(Genesis 41–47)

The details of Pharao's dreams stand out so clearly that he demands an interpretation from his magicians and wise men. Divination, including the interpretation of dreams, was a recognized art in Egypt. Pharao's men were put on the spot by their inability to explain his dreams, and Joseph's entrance thus precipitates a showdown between his God and those of the land, similar to the contest later on between Moses and the Egyptian magicians in connection with the Ten Plagues. Joseph's immediate appointment as prime minister is another sign of divine assistance, even though it was not the first time that a foreigner became a vizier in Egypt. In accordance with local custom, the thirty-year old Second Man of the country is further exalted through an honorable marriage with the daughter of one of the priestly caste. Aseneth bears him two sons, Manasse and Ephraim. Events turn out precisely as he had foretold: seven years of plenty, during which vast quantities of grain were stored under Joseph's prudent supervision, then a drastic famine covering the whole Middle East. The saying became proverbial, "Go to Joseph." Egypt became the granary for the whole area.

Joseph's harshness to his brothers recorded in Chapter 42 in no way compromises his virtue. Indeed, it furnishes the clue to his true role in the providence of God. His accusation that they are spies and his order to put their money back in the mouth of their grain sacks was Joseph's method of purifying them and making these sons of Jacob worthy of the great mission Yahweh had in store for them. In other words, Joseph begins to emerge not merely as the economic deliverer of the Middle East, but even more as the spiritual "redeemer" of the Chosen People.[2] Under duress, his brothers gain a fresh insight into their heinous betrayal of him and are inspired to feel compunction for the deed. His warnings and later favoritism of Benjamin teach them a lesson in fraternal charity; they can lavish on their youngest brother the love which they had enviously denied Joseph. From verse 23 we learn that the Egyptians spoke a different language from the Hebrews.

It is Juda who finally persuades Jacob to permit Benjamin to make the trip to Egypt for the second round of grain. A semi-climax is reached in 43:30 when Joseph's emotions nearly betray his secret. The suspense must have been almost unbearable for the brothers when they noted that they were seated "in the order of age, from the oldest to the youngest" (v. 33). The plot nears the denouement in Chapter 44 with the discovery of Joseph's silver cup in Benjamin's sack. Never were the brothers nearer despair. The unabashed manifestation of Joseph to the eleven in 45:3 makes hot tears well up in the readers' eyes, and again at the meeting between Joseph and his father in the following chapter. Joseph's magnanimity matches his providential role as he reassures his brothers, "God sent me before you to save life" (45:5). The genealogist is careful to note in Chapter 46 that the number of Israelites entering Egypt was sixty-six, bringing the total there to the round number of seventy.

By telling the Pharao that their occupation is shepherding upon advice from Joseph, the brothers are assured of segregation from the pagan Egyptians. Thus begins the informal education and hardening of God's Chosen People in a friendly, civilized atmosphere far superior to that provided by the hostile Chanaanites.[3] Joseph's seemingly harsh economic policy (47:21) was doubtless in accord with contemporary political science. Throughout his rise to power he has been portrayed as the "efficiency expert" of Egypt; the climax is reached when the people become completely dependent upon the Pharao. Thus, Joseph uses his tremendous power for the common good and to cement the Pharao's authority, when he might well have unseated him by a coup d'etat.

Israel's Oracles: A Look to the Future
(Genesis 48–50)

To do honor to Joseph, savior of Egypt and of his own family, Jacob adopts his two boys, Manasse and Ephraim. In this way, Joseph's posterity would get a double share in Jacob's inheritance. But in the

---

[2] Other parallels to Christ: he was innocent, and sold for a few pieces of silver.
[3] Note God's promise in 46:3, "there I will make you a great people."

actual conferring of the blessing, the nearly blind patriarch reverses the order, giving preference to the younger Ephraim. This may be due to a later editor's "hindsight" to explain Ephraim's subsequent superiority or it may be a true prediction of what actually was to take place. This remark holds true also for the "blessings" (cf. v. 28) bestowed by Jacob on the twelve brothers in Chapter 49. The tradition from which they are taken seems surely older than David; yet, there is definite evidence that these final words of Israel have been touched up by another hand who had seen them partially fulfilled (e.g., Zabulon's blessing, v. 13).

Ruben is cut off from the position of firstborn because of his crime of incest (Gen. 35:22). Simeon and Levi (second and third in order of birth) are by-passed because of their violent treatment of the Sichemites (Gen. 34:25). Juda is granted the rights of the firstborn as far as carrying on the family name is concerned; indeed, his tribe will enjoy authority over the others. This pre-eminence will continue until the promised Messia claims it, and his authority will be expanded to other nations: so the traditional interpretation of verse 10.[4] Note the designation of Yahweh as Israel's "Shepherd" in 48:15 (cf. Psalm 22), and as both "Rock" and "Shepherd" in 49:24. Jacob's command in 49:29 occasions the funeral procession in Chapter 50. Just as Joseph's loyalty to the Pharao had been unwavering, so is his magnanimity towards his brothers. He had been able to play God to both, yet he had usurped neither divine honors nor royal supremacy: " . . . can I take the place of God? You intended evil against me, but God intended it for good, to do as he has done today, namely, to save the lives of many people. Therefore do not fear. I will provide for you and your dependents" (vv. 19-20). Like Jacob, Joseph commands his bones be taken back to Chanaan. The Book of Genesis ends with the death of Joseph; the story will be resumed with the birth of Moses.

Two characters stand out in this section of Genesis: the venerable Jacob — more and more evidently the chosen vessel of Yahweh as the story progresses; and his heroic son, Joseph, the "Man of the Hour." Fr. Gaston Brillet's evaluation provides the best conclusion to the religious meaning of Joseph:

> Here is a man who is magnificent in wise conduct, patiently courageous in work and suffering, magnanimous before injustice, wickedness and ingratitude, always guided by a prudent, limpid and unfaltering faith. No other young man, in fact, no other man in the whole Bible is his peer. . . . Once trials begin in his life they never cease: the treachery and cruelty of his brothers, the heavy physical and moral suffering of slavery, the seduction of a

---

[4] It is now recognized that these oracles have been touched up by the Yahwist-Priestly editors. This is particularly true of v. 10.

woman, the imprisonment and forgetfulness of those whom he had helped. Then a still more searching trial: success, royal favor, power and riches. Last of all: his criminal brothers are placed completely at his mercy.

During all these years, we cannot detect in him any infidelity in his response to the demands of a delicate and vigilant conscience, never a devious act, not even a thought of revenge, or of just retribution, or of calculated self-interest. Toward his masters, toward his odious temptress, toward his companions in misfortune who so lamentably repay his nobility by their forgetfulness, he conducts himself with unfailing firmness and an always equable simplicity.[5]

Psalms 104 and 105: History Used to Lament and to Praise

Like Psalm 77, these are among the great historical psalms. One of them uses the history of the Chosen People as the basis of a national lamentation over their sins and consequent misfortunes; the other uses that history as an occasion of praising Yahweh. Read the first 24 verses of Psalm 104, and all of Psalm 105, then decide which is the "Psalm of Lament" (cf. Chapter 7), and which is the "Hymn" (cf. Chapter 6).

Suggested Readings

Hunt, *The Book of Genesis, Part 2,* pp. 17-25.
Sullivan, *God's Word and Work,* pp. 3-13. This is a book of applied meditations on the Bible. The pages referred to cover the Book of Genesis.
Vawter, *A Path Through Genesis,* pp. 241-246; 252-308.

---

[5] Fr. Gaston Brillet, *Meditations on the Old Testament,* Vol. I: *The Narratives* (Desclee, 1959), pp. 39-40.

Chapter XII

The Call of Moses: A New Revelation

READINGS: *Exodus 1–6; Acts 7:17–43; Psalm 46 (Note: Exodus 3:14, 4:22, 6:3)*

From the viewpoint of the Jews, Exodus is the most important book of the Bible. It describes the central event of their history as a nation: the marvelous intervention of God to extricate them from pagan Egypt and to make of them the People of God. Had it not been for this striking prodigy, Genesis and the other books of the Old Testament would not have been written. In fact, by way of stressing the importance of the Exodus, many modern authors of biblical manuals now begin their treatises with the book named after this event. Thus, Genesis becomes virtually a "flashback" on world history to explain the historical setting of the Exodus, evolving as it does from the story of the patriarchs. Genesis also provides a reason for the detailed prescriptions of the Mosaic Law in outlining the pattern of sin which developed in the wake of the Fall of our First Parents. Even though Genesis seems to be the logical (as well as psychological) place to begin from the Christian viewpoint, the Book of Exodus nevertheless remains critically significant for our faith also — as our exegesis will demonstrate.

Until the last few decades the accepted date of the Exodus was about 1450 B.C. This figure was arrived at by starting with the notation given in III Kings 6:1; 480 years from the fourth year of Solomon's reign (= 968 B.C.) would place the Exodus about 1448 B.C. But can we rely on the historicity of these biblical numbers? It seems definitely that we cannot; they are more schematic than historical.[1] Here is a

---

[1] Cf. Orchard, A *Catholic Commentary on Holy Scripture*, col. 268a, where Fr. K. Smith, S.J., exposes the artificial nature of III Kings 6:1 and suggests that the figure 480 may be a gloss. For the detailed reckoning behind the 1448 date, see Dyson and Jones, *Op. cit.*, pp. 18-19. The artificiality of these patriarchal ages can be seen clearly in the case of Jacob's age of 130 at the time of his entry into Egypt, Genesis 47:9. If we assume from Genesis 26:34 ff. that Jacob was also about 40 when he married Lia, then we must conclude from Genesis 31:41, 41:46, and 45:11 that he was only about 100 years old when he went into Egypt. Cf. Murphy, *The Book of Exodus*, Part 1, pp. 9, 15.

case, indeed, where we are permitted to use the data of solid scientific research to throw light on vague Scriptural texts. The research of archeologists pointing to the relocation of the royal Egyptian residence from Thebes in the south to the Delta in the north at the time of the Hyksos invasion and again about 1300 B.C.; the mention of the "supply cities of Phithom and Rameses" in Exodus 1:11; the fact that the returning Hebrews found iron weapons in Chanaan during the conquest of this land: all of these factors lend solid support to dating the Exodus much later than the traditional date. It seems best to put it between 1290-1250 B.C.

The Exodus represents not only a religious epic; it also represents a literary milestone. For it was with Moses, the great Prophet and Lawgiver, that Sacred Scripture began to take its shape. Yet, while we accredit Moses with starting the process of recording Divine Tradition and providing the basic outline of the first five books (this is what is meant by "substantial authorship"), we recognize that many other hands contributed to the final composition of the Old Testament. What the modern reader tends to forget is that the multitude of themes gathered together into the harmonious religious epic contained in these forty-six books once existed only on the tongues and in the memories of men. It was only the genius of an unknown number of editors, over a long period of literary endeavor, and under divine inspiration, that the frequently isolated fragments of this fresh chapter of divine communication were woven together. Because the peculiar differences of three of the four literary traditions of the Pentateuch show up so clearly in the Book of Exodus, we shall include some identification and description of them (i.e., J, E, and P) in our treatise.

Every civilization has its own traditions: the Hebrews were no exception. They possessed their genealogies, poems, folk stories, favorite heroes, etc., reaching back into the dim past. The memories of the ancients were much better trained than ours: they could reproduce episodes word' for word handed down from time immemorial. We can imagine the Hebrew community, later on after the Exodus, in the desert, pitching tent in the wilderness, and gathering around the campfire at night to reminisce. Those venerable elders with a special knack for story-telling would begin the account: how the patriarch Abraham had brought his family from the midst of pagan ancestors into the Land of Promise. The narrator would emphasize that Abraham was quite different from his relatives; whereas they brought with them the traditional household gods, Father Abraham worshipped the one true God, Yahweh. Tears would well up in the eyes of his listeners as the local spell-binder described the hand of Abraham poised in heroic obedience over the heart of his only son, Isaac. Other equally gifted bards would push back the origins of the Hebrews to a descendant of Noe, the blessed Sem. Still another tradition would be volunteered, showing how Noe was related to the father of the human race, Adam. Here we have the skeleton of the YAHWIST TRADITION (also known as "J"): primitive, archaic, colorful, epic, concrete and anthropomorphic —linking up the story of creation with the Mosaic era. This tradition bears the stamp of Southern Palestine (later the Kingdom of Juda). It puts special emphasis on the free choice of Yahweh and on His gratuitous promises—regardless of birth. Thus, it stresses Jacob over Esau, Juda over Ruben. The primitive account of creation, the symbolism of Eden, the Fall and the Deluge, the Tower of Babel: all of these deeply theological themes are reported by the Yahwist, so-called because the later title, "Yahweh," has been substituted for *God.*

Northern Palestine would give its recollection of the beginnings of salvation history a slightly different twist, especially after the secession of the ten tribes during the reign of Roboam, when Chanaanite practices were degrading Jewish worship. This influence helps to explain the sober, anti-anthropomorphic trend of the ELOHIST TRADITION (because the name used for God is usually *Elohim,* rather than *Yahweh;* hence called the "E" tradition). The Elohist goes back only as far as Abraham, and takes particular delight in glorifying Moses as the greatest figure in the Pentateuch.

The PRIESTLY TRADITION, finally, represents the viewpoint of the liturgical assembly at Jerusalem (i.e., in the South: Juda). Reflecting, as we have already noted, great depth of meditation, this strain is almost theological in its preciseness (e.g., the story of the six days). Legal in character, the "P" Tradition loves to reproduce genealogies. It manifests the mature mentality of the Jewish people.

Crisis in Egypt: Oppression of the Jews

We can easily understand, from what has just been said, why it is the Priestly tradition from which the first five verses of Exodus are taken. They give us to understand that only seventy souls made up what was to become, under the mighty hand of Yahweh, a large nation. It is the Yahwist who gives us in vv. 6-14 the first inkling of trouble in the vivid account of Pharao's cruelty (cf. vv. 13-14)[2] towards these aliens. Note the dramatic dialogue found here and also in the Elohist tradition; this is *not* the word-for-word record of a court reporter! The Yahwist concludes with the reduction of the Hebrews to forced labor; in 1:15-2:10, the "E" tradition continues with the decree of Pharao to the midwives to kill all male Hebrew infants, and when this doesn't

---

[2] Some exegetes trace these two verses to "P."

work, the decree to all of his subjects to throw Hebrew males into the Nile River to drown. Moses is saved by a clever ruse, and seems clearly to have been brought up in the royal palace (Acts 7:22). Note that "J" assigns the killing of the Egyptian as the reason for Moses' flight into Madian; the motion picture, "The Ten Commandments," emphasized the discovery of his Semitic ancestry as a key factor, in view of Exodus 1:8 (which seems to refer to the expulsion of the friendly Hyksos kings, probably Semites, at an earlier period. See also Heb. 11:24-25). No doubt both of these considerations influenced Pharao to turn against the erstwhile "Prince of Egypt" (though we need not go as far as the motion picture does in portraying him as a candidate for the hand of Nefretiri, hereditary Princess of Egypt, through whom succession to the throne was secured). At any rate, Moses seems to have given up whatever hopes he might have had of using his position at the Egyptian court to rescue his fellow Hebrews from their deplorable lot (cf. Acts 7:25, 35) after "they" had "disowned" him. Settled in the occupation of his ancestors and married to a daughter of a Madianite priest (whom the Yawhist calls Raguel), Moses has apparently let his ideals and his countrymen disappear into the background.

The Call of Moses

(Exodus 3–6)

In Chapter 3, the Yahwist and Elohist traditions are joined together (= JE), with certain "E" terms (such as *Jethro* for *Raguel*, *Horeb* for *Sinai*) betraying the presence of the latter. After arresting the attention of Moses via the phenomenon of the burning bush, Yahweh-Elohim identifies Himself as "the God of Abraham, the God of Isaac, the God of Jacob," and commissions Moses to deliver the Hebrews from Egypt. In response to Moses' request for His credentials, God makes a startling revelation. He tells Moses His name. The word which Exodus 3:14 gives us is: YHWH, third person singular of the Hebrew word "to be" (without the vowels, which were pronounced but not written in Hebrew). Various explanations of this term have been offered:[3]

1. "He Who is": — i.e., Existence itself; Self-existent Being (This interpretation is popular with philosophers).
2. "He causes to happen" — perhaps, "Watch and see what I shall do!" "let My actions be the answer to your question."
3. "I am Who I am": — i.e., "It's none of your business Who I am."

---

[3] Cf. Anderson, *Op. cit.*, pp. 33-34; Dyson and Jones, *Op. cit.*, p. 23; *Theology Digest*, VII (Autumn, 1959), pp. 174-176 (which supports interpretation #3.) The application of the burning bush to the Virgin Mary is a liturgical accommodation.

Probably both 1 and 3 represent extremes, the truth lying more toward the middle alternative; scholars still dispute the interpretation. The Jews never pronounced this sacred word, but used the term "Adonai" (Lord) in its place. In the Middle Ages — long after Hebrew had become a dead language — the vowels of this latter term were combined with YHWH in an attempt to reconstruct the sacred name; the result was the erroneous "Jehovah."

In response to his objection, Moses receives two more credentials to support his claims: the power to change his staff into a serpent, and to make his hand leprous (Chap. 4). Because of Moses' lack of confidence in himself, God gives him his brother Aaron as spokesman. A new era is presaged in 4:22 with the stated adoption of Israel (descendants of Jacob) by Yahweh. The incident in verses 24-26 is evidently a means of connecting the rite of circumcision with the Mosaic tradition. Upon their arrival in Egypt, Moses and Aaron win the confidence of the Hebrews by means of the signs God gave them.

According to our reckoning, the Pharao before whom they appeared in Chapter 5 may well have been Rameses II. The "Pharao of the Oppression" would have been either Rameses I (as pictured in "The Ten Commandments") or Seti I; the death of this tyrant is recorded in Exodus 2:23. Instead of allowing the Hebrews to make a three-day pilgrimage into the desert to offer sacrifice to Yahweh as Moses had requested, Pharao made their servitude even more unbearable by withdrawing their supply of straw. The two brothers are chagrined, and their kinsmen quickly lose confidence in them.

Chapter 6 represents a second account of the call of Moses — this time from the Priestly tradition. More condensed and matter-of-fact, this source gives us the precious assurance (6:3) that the name "Yahweh" is a Mosaic revelation, a true landmark in divine communication. God had manifested the title "El Shaddai" ("God Almighty") to Abraham (Gen. 17:1), but the revelation of Yahweh is even more intimate. God renews His promise to deliver the Hebrews from Pharao through the agency of Moses. True to form, the Priestly editors furnish the genealogy of their own line of Levi — later on to be given the exclusive right to the sacred ministry. The fact that Moses and Aaron are only the third generation from Levi leads us to suspect that the sojourn in Egypt — the "Silent Period" of Scripture — may have been much less than 430 years, even if we grant that some names have been omitted.[4] At the end of the chapter, Moses is again told to appear before Pharao as he continues to protest his lack of forensic aptitude.

---

[4] In Galatians 3:16-17, St. Paul seems to include in these 430 years the time that Abraham, Isaac and Jacob spent in Chanaan before entering Egypt.

The Meaning of the Revelation

In a sense, the manifestation of the proper name, Yahweh, to Moses was a favor closely rivaling the Exodus itself. We human beings do not reveal our intimate secrets (e.g., our nicknames) to any but our closest friends. Hence, Exodus 3:14 represents a distinct advance in divine-human relationships as Yahweh prepared his Chosen Ones for the New Covenant He was about to establish. Moreover, in the Semitic culture, the name of a thing was the embodiment of that thing's nature, giving the knower of its name a certain influence or even power over the thing. After the revelation of the divine name in Exodus, then, the Hebrews came to consider that they had a special claim on Yahweh, unique among the nations of the earth. This revelation was truly a fitting prelude to their rescue from Egyptian slavery.

Psalm 46: Yahweh is the King of the Whole Earth!

This short poem introduces us to another category of psalms: Yahweh's Kingship (or Enthronement). Portraying Yahweh's dominion over all the earth, such psalms were often used in processions (e.g., the transfer of the Ark of the Covenant). Possessing a characteristic universalism, these hymns of praise usually end with an invitation to all nations to acclaim Yahweh's kingship. Psalm 46 matches the sentiments of these first chapters of Exodus wherein the God Who is about to save the Jews from Pharao's might is revealed as the same God worshipped by Abraham, Isaac and Jacob. Psalms 92, 96 and 98 are other examples of this category.

vv. 1-5: An invitation to praise Yahweh, pictured as subduing the nations of the earth only after a struggle.

6-10: After the victory, Yahweh assumes His rightful place as universal Monarch amidst great rejoicing among both Jews and Gentiles.

Suggested Readings

Anderson, *Understanding the Old Testament*, pp. 29-37.
Bouyer, *The Meaning of Sacred Scripture*, Chapter 2.
Dyson and Jones, *The Kingdom of Promise*, pp. 20-26.
Martin, *A Guide to Old Testament History*, p. 30. Date of the Exodus.
Moriarty, *Foreword to the Old Testament Books*, pp. 6-11. A brief survey of the four traditions.
Murphy, *The Book of Exodus*, Part I (No. 4 of the Pamphlet Bible Series of the Paulist Press) pp. 5-16.

Chapter XIII

Yahweh Versus Pharao: The "Passover"

READINGS: *Exodus 7–13; Romans 9; Ezechiel 16:1–14; Psalm 113; Hasseveldt, pp. 75–83 (Note: Exodus 7:12; 8:14–15; 12:27, 40)*

Preparations for the Showdown

The Priestly editors now give their account of Aaron's call to be spokesman for Moses. He had been referred to as the "mouth" of Moses by the "JE" tradition in Exodus 4:16; here he is called a "prophet."[1] Quite understandably, the Priestly tradition emphasizes the role of the first High Priest of the Levitical line, Aaron. Thus, "P" passages in this section (e.g., 7:10, 7:19) speak of *Aaron's* rod as the agency whereby the miracles were wrought; but "E" passages (e.g., 7:15, 9:23) attribute the prodigies to *Moses'* staff. The ages of the two brothers are given as eighty and eighty-three (i.e., twice forty in the case of Moses); surely this is an approximation, as it is hard to imagine an eighty-year-old man "roughing it" across the Red Sea and the desert.

"Yet I will make Pharao so obstinate that . . . he will not listen to you" (7:3-4). Here we have a splendid example of the concrete manner in which the Hebrews formulated the most profound theological truths. This quotation shows their awareness of the universal causality of Yahweh — even to the point of His moving man's free will. (We would soften the concept by saying that God withdrew His grace.) Yet a little later, the sacred text has Pharao admit his "sin" in the affair (9:27, 10:17). So there is clearly a recognition that Pharao was responsible for his acts — and therefore free — at the same time that Yahweh is seen to be the cause of his actions. Instead of fighting the mystery and trying to solve the paradox in a tidy "reconciliation" as we logically-minded Westerners tend to do, the Oriental mind simply accepted the two horns of the dilemma and let it go at that. St. Paul, a Semite to the core, proceeds in this same vein to offer a higher synthesis rather than a solution: God's mysterious election of some and His "reprobation" of others reveals His power and glory through the delicate blending of justice and mercy (Rom. 9).

---

[1] Cf. "Prophecy" on page 28.

The "Finger of God"

The preliminary sign given to Pharao through Moses and Aaron, viz., the changing of Aaron's staff into a snake, failed to move him because "the magicians of Egypt did likewise by their magic arts" (7:11). The explanation of this "magic" may lie merely in legerdemain, or (more likely) in diabolical influence. The latter seems to be evidently implied in Wisdom 17:7 and 18:13. These two chapters will be analyzed, along with other references to the Plagues in Wisdom, in the next section (Chap. XIV). Like the rest of the material with which we are dealing, the Ten Plagues are very skillfully used to teach a lesson. The lesson will become clearer if we lay them out and examine them.

Before we do this, it should be noted that the first nine Plagues are natural phenomena in themselves; the supernatural element lies in their intensity, and in the control which Moses and Aaron exercised over them as agents of Yahweh. The ancients did not make the clean cut distinction which we do between the natural and the supernatural; they tended to stress the continuity between the two orders. For them, the "signs" and "wonders" (their equivalents for "miracles") wrought by God did not demand a suspension of the laws of nature, even though such was often the case. A sign was simply the manifestation of the divine will, and could be perceived by any person who possessed the right disposition. Hence, the Egyptian magicians and people were convinced by the ninth Plague, but Pharao was not (cf. Ex. 11:3).[2]

PLAGUE	TRADI-TION	EXPLANATION	SIGNIFICANCE
1. The Nile is "changed into blood"	J, E, P	Each year the Nile becomes red with silt as it overflows its banks, but it is not undrinkable nor lethal to fish life.	The sacred author's declaration that the magicians were able to duplicate these first two plagues sets the stage for the contest: Pharao and the gods of Egypt (Ex. 12:12) versus the one, true God, Yahweh, Whose agents are Moses and Aaron.
2. Frogs	J, P	This time Pharao agrees to let the Hebrews go, then changes his mind; the pattern is fixed.	
3. Gnats (=Mosquitoes?)	P	By means of Aaron's staff, "the dust of the earth was turned into gnats"; no termination is recorded for this Plague.	The failure of the magicians to produce this Plague evokes from them the admission "This is the finger of God" (8:15).

[2] See the fine treatment of this topic by Anderson, *Op. cit.*, Chap. 2, pp. 43-44.

4. Flies	J	Note the similarity of this J Plague to the third, a P item. [3] When Moses refuses to offer sacrifice in Egypt, Pharao agrees to let them go, then retracts.	Exodus 8:18 notes the immunity of the Israelites; not even this sign is sufficient to change Pharao's heart.
5. Pestilence (Murrain)	J	Apparently not all the Egyptian livestock died (cf. 9:25). No termination is mentioned.	The distinction between Hebrew and Egyptian property continues to the end.
6. Boils	P	A "double handful of soot" is used to produce this Plague; ulcers afflict man and beast.	This time even the magicians are affected—an even clearer sign of Yahweh's power.
7. Hail	J, E	"Some of Pharao's servants" are won over before the Plague strikes, but not Pharao himself.	Pharao admits his sin when the Plague strikes, but recants again when Moses arrests it.
8. Locusts (Grasshoppers)	J	At the urging of his servants, Pharao agrees to let just the men go, but Moses refuses. It is the wind which brings and removes this Plague; J is not as dramatic as E and P items.	Again Pharao admits his fault, and again he recants as soon as the Plague is ended; "the Lord made Pharao obstinate" (10:20).
9. Darkness	J, E	The three days of darkness were probably the result of a severe sand storm; it moved Pharao to let all but the Hebrew livestock depart, but this was unsatisfactory.	Pharao's obstinacy reaches a climax: after the darkness, he forbade Moses to appear before him again. In so doing, Pharao acted against the sentiments of his people.

The Tenth Plague and the Passover Celebration

The various accounts of the first nine Plagues are worked together with such literary artistry that they blend into a harmonious whole. Gradually a crescendo is reached: the power of Yahweh manifested through Moses and Aaron undermines the morale of the Egyptian people, leaving Pharao virtually alone in his obstinacy. Just how much historical nucleus underlies the encrustations of subsequent elaboration

---

[3] It seems possible that the third and fourth Plagues, and also the fifth and sixth, are actually identical, leaving a total of eight Plagues instead of ten. Compare the account in Exodus with the poetic description in Psalm 104:25-45.

and interpretation is difficult to determine. The discriminating reader will have to make his own judgment in this matter. To see an apparent identity between the third and fourth Plagues is one thing; to deny the Providential deliverance of the Hebrew slaves from Egypt is quite another. God certainly did (and still does) intervene in history, but to exactly what extent His interventions counteract the laws of nature is not easy to pinpoint. To deny completely any element of the supernatural in the events leading up to and including the Exodus from Egypt is to fall into deism.

It took the death of the first-born of man and beast, including Pharao's oldest son, to convince the King of Egypt that Yahweh meant business. This was the tenth and most fearful of the Plagues. In fact, we are told that he summoned Moses and Aaron in the middle of the night to order them to depart, "and you will be doing me a favor" (12:32). In the meantime, the Hebrews were not idle during that memorable night. In accordance with Yahweh's instructions, they celebrated the first Passover ceremony. The details were very explicit: the sacrificial lamb had to be a one-year-old male without any defect; it was to be slaughtered on that very evening, and some of its blood sprinkled on the doorpost of the family residence. Then it was to be roasted and consumed with unleavened bread and bitter herbs. The ordinances contained in 12:43-49 are evidently a later enactment, forbidding the breaking of any bones of the lamb (or kid: cf. 12:5), and excluding all uncircumcised from the sacrificial meal.

Further instructions required the Israelites to eat the Passover meal "with your loins girt, sandals on your feet and your staff in hand . . . like those who are in flight" (12:11). They are enjoined to abstain from all leaven (yeast) for seven days, and to make a point of going through with these same ceremonies each year for the future. All of these injunctions were designed in imitation of their actual departure from Egypt: a hasty, nocturnal journey for which they were ill-prepared (cf. 12:42). The first meaning of the term "Passover" (similar in Hebrew to the verb meaning "to pass over") is indicated in 12:27. A further token of gratitude is exacted from the Israelites by Yahweh in commemoration of the sparing of their first-born in the wake of the tenth Plague: they are thenceforth to consecrate all of their first-born, "both of man and of beast" (13:2) to God, since such belong to Him in a special manner. First-born animals were to be sacrificed; but first-born boys (and also asses, since they were valuable animals) were to be "redeemed," i.e., bought back from Yahweh, since human sacrifice was forbidden. Finally, the month in which the Exodus took place (from mid-March to mid-April) was to be put first on their calendar. (Later, this came to be known as the month of Nisan.)

Yahweh Versus Pharao: The "Passover"

The Israelites Depart

We are told that the Israelites "despoiled" the Egyptians of their silver, gold and clothing (12:35-36) as Yahweh had promised Moses (3:21-22); the justice of this can be seen easily if we credit it to "back wages" for their slavery. The departing population figure, 600,000, would be more significant if the last cipher were lopped off: the three million persons implied are unthinkable, especially wandering through a desert. The validity of the 430 years as the length of time spent in Egypt has been discussed in the last chapter. The "mixed ancestry" mentioned in verse 38 indicates that the Israelites had intermarried with the Egyptians to some degree. As they left with Joseph's bones, we are given the reason why they did not take the shorter sea-coast route (13:17). The end of Chapter 13 gives us a precious detail:

> The Lord preceded them, in the daytime by means of a column of cloud to show them the way, and at night by means of a column of fire to give them a light. Thus they could travel both day and night. Neither the column of cloud by day nor the column of fire by night ever left its place in front of the people.

This constant presence of Yahweh during the desert sojourn was to constitute a landmark in the memory of Israel's sages, a striking token of His intimacy with His elect. The cloud would thenceforth always symbolize the "glory of Yahweh," which the prophet Moses alone was permitted to view (cf. Ex. 24:15-18).

The Meaning of the Passover Celebration

This religious ceremony performed for the first time on the vigil of their deliverance from Pharao set a liturgical pattern for all time. The careful reader will note that what they were directed to do by Yahweh was actually a dry run or rehearsal of what He, Yahweh, was going to accomplish in their behalf on the following day. The Mosaic Covenant had already been initiated; Yahweh had adopted the Jacobites as His own (Ex. 4:22), their supernatural existence had been assured.[4] But to realize the fruits of divine election, they had to get out of Egypt — that land of diabolical intrigue — and become an independent nation. Nothing short of the omnipotence of Yahweh could accomplish this feat. And Yahweh was willing to stretch out the right arm of His power under certain conditions. The principal condition was that every single family of this people participate in a religious ceremony in which they would imitate in symbolic fashion the manner in which He planned to execute their deliverance. Indeed, this anticipatory imitation was a *conditio sine qua non* of their salvation from slavery.

---

[4] Read Ezech. 16:1-14. Cf. also Bouyer, *Op. cit.*, Chap. 3.

But just as their new birth had not been accomplished without a tremendous battle, with Yahweh fighting on their side, so would their continued existence as His people make special demands on them. Not only would it be necessary to redeem every first-born and to observe other prescriptions of the Mosaic Law about to be revealed, but in addition, the Israelites were asked to renew the liturgical rite of the Passover each recurring year at the same time. Granted that this rite had no intrinsic efficacy to accomplish the event that it signified, nevertheless its performance was an indispensable condition of remaining in Yahweh's favor. It remained for Christ, the true Paschal Lamb, to fulfill this Old Testament type and inject a dynamic efficaciousness into it by transforming the Passover into the first Mass. In this, He was simply following the pattern: rehearsing the bloody business of Calvary on its vigil by way of symbolic imitation of what He was to do on the morrow.

Psalm 113: Hymn of the Exodus

(Compare with Psalm 134)

Apparently post-Exilic, this hymn originally was probably two separate psalms. Serving as a kind of corollary for Psalm 112, it is one of the finest pieces in the Psalter with its smooth, dramatic tempo, vividness and imagination. It is used in the Divine Office as the fifth psalm of Sunday Vespers.

vv. 1-8: Proof that the Jews always looked back to the Exodus as the central point of their history as a people.

9-11: Words of praise to Yahweh, the only true God. This second part of the psalm (different in tone) was apparently sung antiphonally (by alternate groups).

12-16: The inefficacy of pagan idols (including the gods of Egypt).

17-26: A reminder that Yahweh blesses those who trust in Him. The "House of Israel" is the Jewish laity; "the House of Aaron," the priests; "those who fear the Lord," Gentile converts to Judaism.

Suggested Readings

Anderson, *Understanding the Old Testament*, pp. 38-44.
Bouyer, *The Meaning of Sacred Scripture*, Chap. 3.
Hasseveldt, *The Church a Divine Mystery*, pp. 75-83.
Murphy, *The Book of Exodus, Part 1*, pp. 16-24.

Chapter XIV

Theophany and Theocracy: The Decalogue

READINGS: *Exodus 14–20; Numbers 11:31–34; Wisdom 11; 13–19; Psalm 135. (Note: Exodus 16:15, 23; 17:7, 14; 19:6, 12)*

The Miraculous Crossing

Yahweh did not permit the Hebrews to take the short route to Chanaan along the seacoast (Ex. 13:17); rather, He sent them south toward the Sinai Peninsula, whither He had ordered them to repair in order to offer sacrifice (3:12). The first four verses of Chapter 14 imply a deliberate detour from an easy crossing at the shallow marshes above the Bitter Lakes at Etham to a rougher crossing below these Lakes in order to provide a better set-up for the great miracle about to take place (see map of the Exodus). The sudden appearance of the hardened, obstinate Pharao produces consternation and grumbling among the Israelites. After reassuring them, Moses says that all they have to do is to trust in Yahweh and "keep still" (14:14). Note that the Yahwist Tradition attributes the dry crossing to "a strong east wind" (v. 21), while the Priestly Tradition speaks of a "wall" of water "to their right and to their left," (v. 22). We should not conclude that all the Egyptians perished; here is another case of a "restricted universal."[1] (Cf. Deluge story).

The Canticle of Moses (Chapter 15), featuring the tambourine and the dancing of Mariam (called here a "prophetess") and the other Hebrew women, is one of the most ancient biblical texts which we possess. The refrain, "Sing to the Lord, for he is gloriously triumphant; horse and chariot he has cast into the sea" (vv. 1 and 21) sounds like the account of an eyewitness. Verses 13-17 are not prophetic; they were added in retrospect by a later (inspired) editor. Like a notable portion of the Pentateuch, this piece is in the genre of liturgical chant, embellishing the historical details into epic proportions. After this initial elation, there followed the inevitable let-down and discouragement as they entered the desert of Sur. The wonders of Yahweh which

---

[1] Strictly speaking, the body of water they crossed was the *Reed* Sea (now the Gulf of Suez), not the *Red* Sea (the main stream to the south).

had inspired a sublime faith (14:31) were soon forgotten; however, they had not forgotten how to murmur. As Moses quiets their grumbling by turning the bitter waters of Mara into a potable drink with a piece of wood, he warns the people that God is permitting these hardships to "put them to the test" (15:25). Note the symbolic numbers in verse 27 in reference to the oasis at Elim.

Quail, Manna, Water: The Law of Sabbath

God's Providence did not desert His People, in spite of their murmurings. No doubt the quail were in the process of migrating; a number of them would be flying low out of exhaustion, and could be easily caught. Still, there is certainly a providential element involved in the timing and the quantity of the fowl, and even this mark of divine care is turned by some of the Jews into an occasion of sin. The manna has a more intriguing explanation. Though described as "bread from heaven" (16:4), it seems to be fairly well established that this substance is actually a resinous substance exuded by the tamarisk tree when it is pierced by a certain type of plant insect. It forms into little white balls and falls to the ground during the night; if allowed to remain there after 8:30 or so in the morning, the ants consume it. All of the biblical details have been verified (cf. vv. 14, 20, 31 of Chap. 16).[2] According to the popular etymology of Scripture, this food derived its name from the question which the Jews asked when they first beheld it, "What is this?"=*manhu*. The physical composition is not the most important element; however, what should be noted is the fact that this miraculously multiplied food was a remote preparation for the acceptance of the doctrine of the Eucharist by the Jews of Christ's era (cf. John 6:32, 49-52).

The manna incident provides the Priestly editor with an occasion to lay down the first explicit law of Sabbath observance. The people are to collect enough of the substance on Friday to take care of their Saturday needs, so that they will not have to perform this chore on the Sabbath. This regulation seems to be an anachronism, as it seems more probable that it was given with other Sabbath laws later; the directive of Moses in verses 33-34 is surely anticipated in the text. Two figurative names are assigned to the encampment at Raphidim because of the renewed murmuring of the Jews for water: *Massa* and *Meriba*. The power of prayer, and also of the peculiar efficacy of Moses' intercession, are illustrated in the first military encounter recorded; the aboriginal Amalecites are routed under the leadership of Josue. Note 17:14 — the first reference to the composition of any (inspired?) document.

---

[2] See the account in Keller, *The Bible as History*, pp. 117-122.

Origin of the Judges

We know that Chapter 18 is principally an "E" passage because the name used for Moses' father-in-law is Jethro. This priest of Madian, apparently won over to the side of Yahweh (v. 11), offers a holocaust to Him, whereupon Moses, Aaron and the elders join him in a sacrificial meal. Jethro leaves some good advice with his son-in-law before departing; it is at his suggestion that minor officials, known as Judges, are (later) appointed over the people to relieve Moses of the intolerable burden of hearing every grievance in person. From this episode, it would appear that Moses had been temporarily separated from his wife and children.

Arrival at Sinai: The Great Theophany

(Exodus 19–20)

To prepare the people for the solemn revelation of the terms of the Covenant, God surrounds the events at Mount Sinai with the "Great Theophany" (manifestation of God). Up to this point, the columns of cloud and fire had been leading them by day and by night through the desert; now lightning, thunder, trumpet blasts, fire and smoke collaborate in a mighty demonstration to show forth the divine presence.[3] The people are warned not to touch the sacred mountain, under pain of death. Yahweh is about to take them unto Himself, formally and definitively, and to make them "a kingdom of priests, a holy nation." Just what this implies and entails will become clearer as we examine the Mosaic law in subsequent chapters.

Without any further ado, God delivered the Decalogue to Moses, alone in His presence. In these ten succinct commands rests the heart of the Mosaic Covenant, around which all of the other precepts were to be centered. All except two of these provisions represent what we designate as "natural law," as opposed to "positive law." The first of these two is what most Jews and Protestants regard as a separate commandment, viz., verses 4-5, prescribing imageless worship.[4] All representations—including those of Yahweh Himself—were strictly forbidden: here was an abrupt departure from paganism. The other positive law is the Third Commandment: it is not evident from reason that every seventh day (rather than sixth, eighth, etc.) should be a day of special worship.[5] The Decalogue forms the first and basic division

---

[3] Compare this description with Psalm 17:8-16.

[4] But they consider v. 17 as a single precept, and thus arrive at a total of ten.

[5] . . . It has been claimed by some (e.g., A. M. Henry, O.P., in the *Theological Library* [Fides, 1958], Vol. I, p. 123) that the Sabbath regulation originated only during the Babylonian Captivity. But Cf. *A Catholic Commentary on Holy Scripture*, col. 172k.

of the threefold class of precepts revealed by Yahweh in the Pentateuch: they are moral precepts; the other two classes are the judicial (or civil) precepts, and the ceremonial precepts. Note the implied linking of innocence and longevity in verses 5-6 and 12. The chapter ends with a plea from the people that Moses speak for Yahweh for fear that they would die were He to speak to them in person, and a ceremonial precept forbidding the use of cut stone in the building of altars for sacrifices.

The Language of the Decalogue

The Old Testament books, as they were finally edited and completed shortly before the Christian era, have been preserved in three different languages: Aramaic, Hebrew, and Greek. In which of these languages were the Ten Commandments revealed to Moses? The answer is that Yahweh probably inscribed them in none of these three, but rather in one of the many dialects of western Semitic, pre-Chanaanite. To illustrate this point, we shall have to trace the history of the three languages mentioned above.

Aramaic: This would have been the language of Abraham as he migrated from Ur of the Chaldees (Babylonia) to Haran and then to Canaan about 1850 B.C.[6] In fact, Aramaic was the gift of the Aramean Tribes, of which Abraham was a part, to the area which they infiltrated: the whole Fertile Crescent. And it remained the common, commercial idiom of the Near East for centuries. During the subsequent patriarchal period before the Egyptian sojourn, this dialect was only slightly influenced by that of the Chanaanites among whom Abraham, Isaac and Jacob lived. Hence, we may designate the language which the Hebrews took with them into Egypt as "pre-Canaanite." It should be noted here that, though Egypt had an advanced civilization in other respects, they were infants with regard to the development of language. In fact, their hieroglyphics represent only the first of three stages:

IDEOGRAPHS: Ideas expressed through pictorial *images:* Egyptian hieroglyphics.

SYLLABIC WRITING: Ideas expressed by cuneiform *syllables:* Assyria, Persia, etc.

ALPHABETICAL WRITING: Use of letters — Consonants only: Hebrews; vowels added: Phoenicians, Greeks, Latins.
(c. 1500 B.C.)

Examples of Aramaic in the text of Sacred Scripture are: Genesis 31:47; I Esdras 4:8 to 6:18, 7:12-26; Daniel 2:4b-7; Jeremia 10-11; probably

---

[6] Cf. Robert and Tricot, *A Guide to the Bible,* Vol. I, pp. 131-143, and Charlier, *Op. cit.,* pp. 46-49. Ours is also the conclusion of Mr. DeMille in "The Ten Commandments."

the Book of Tobias; the original Gospel of St. Matthew. This is not, for the most part, the Aramaic of the patriarchs, but that of the post-Exilic Jews.

Hebrew. This seems to have been the language of the Canaanites, fundamentally; it was gradually modified and adopted by the Jews after their conquest of the land beginning with Josue. As noted above, it is one of the western Semitic dialects, and includes strains of Aramaic and Arabic. Indeed, Hebrew resembles Aramaic in much the same manner that Italian and Spanish resemble French. Nearly the whole of the Old Testament is in Hebrew, which gradually yielded to Aramaic in the three centuries following the Babylonian Captivity (587 B.C.).

Greek. An Indo-European language (along with Latin and the Romance, Germanic and Slav languages) which ultimately became the universal language after the conquest of the world by Alexander the Great (336-323 B.C.). Wisdom and II Machabees, plus all of the New Testament except First Matthew, were composed in popular Greek (known as the *koine*). Christ and the Apostles spoke both Aramaic and Greek.

The Significance of the Decalogue

The promulgation of the Ten Commandments on Mount Sinai represents a definitive step in the restoration of divine-human relationships; it is a milestone in the history of communication. We shall attempt to summarize briefly its principal meaning.

—Mount Sinai was not only, nor even primarily, the deliverance of a code of laws, but the formal meeting between Yahweh and His Chosen People. He accepts them, this is their formal adoption, but they must respond by agreeing to be governed by His will in all things. In other words, Israel — miraculously rescued from the slavery of the Pharaos by Yahweh's outstretched arm — has now become a true theocracy (from *Theos, God,* and *kratia,* rule). Human beings (e.g., Moses and the Judges) were to be merely His representatives.

—The Decalogue, then, is simply the expression of Yahweh's will — the pattern according to which He wishes His people to express their gratitude to Him.

—Therefore, it is clear that the Commandments were to be more than just a moral code, and that of themselves (apart from the will of God) they had no intrinsic power to justify a person. As Yahweh had already told Abraham, justification came only through faith: the Mosaic Law in no wise becomes a substitute.

117

—Because man is a creature composed of body and soul, certain external observances, legal and liturgical, were prescribed under obligation. The Jews actually had no conception of a religion *purely* "in spirit and in truth" — i.e., entirely interior: they saw this as contrary to human nature. Moreover, they were acutely conscious that man is a social animal — hence, religion is a community affair, and salvation is to be sought within the community. As we shall see, such concepts as the relationship between God and the individual soul, personal retribution in the next world, etc., developed only much later in Jewish religious history.[7]

A Midrashic Approach to the Exodus

(Wisdom 11; 16-19)

A portion of the Book of Wisdom was assigned in connection with the patriarchs (page 96), namely, the description of their exploits in the first half of the tenth chapter of what may well have been the last book of the Old Testament to be composed. In the second half of this chapter, Wisdom — personified throughout the book — reflects on the glories of the Exodus, Her greatest triumph. The treatment here is less historical than the Book of Exodus; it is in the genre known as *Midrash;* an imaginative, devotional development of a text or theme by Jewish scribes during the 1500 years after the Babylonian Exile. It is non-legal (i.e., doctrinal or *haggadic,* to use the Hebrew term), interpretative, and mixed with folklore. It is aimed more toward the edification of the reader than toward his enlightenment. Only loosely historical, this genre contains certain poetic liberties and a studied artificiality. It may be compared to the fourteen Stations of the Cross in Christian piety.[8]

Unlike most Midrash, however, that which we find in the Book of Wisdom is inspired, since we are dealing here with a canonical work. It proceeds by way of contrasting the success of the Jews (aided by Wisdom) against the humiliation of the Egyptians during the Plagues and the Exodus. Although Chapter 15 is not part of the contrast, it should be read for its insight on predestination (cf. v. 7 with Rom. 9:21, and vv. 14-17 with Ps. 113B:4-8).

---

[7] Bouyer, *Op. cit.,* pp. 22-24, and McKenzie, *Op. cit.,* pp. 124-125, cover this analysis very well. Fr. Bouyer sees the divine Word operative behind the Law.

[8] Cf. R. E. Murphy, *Seven Books of Wisdom* (Milwaukee, Wis.: Bruce, 1960) pp. 130-134.

TEXT	HEBREW SUCCESS	EGYPTIAN FAILURE	PLAGUE
1. Wisdom 11:2–14	Water from the rock (Ex. 17:6)	Nile made impotable	1.
2. Wisdom 11:15–16 16:1–4	Quail for meat (Ex. 16:13)	Frogs, gnats, flies, pestilence, locusts	2, 3, 4, 5, 8.
3. Wisdom 16:5–15	The bronze serpent which saved Jews from saraphs (Num. 21:8)	No remedy for plague of flies and locusts	4, 8.
4. Wisdom 16:16–29	Manna for bread (Ex. 16:14–15)	Hail, lightning, etc.	7.
5. Wisdom 17:1–18:4	Pillar of fire (Ex. 13:21)	Darkness for three days	9.

(Note Wis. 17:7, 14 for diabolical element; 18:13 speaks of sorceries)

6. Wisdom 18:5 18:21, 12	Rescue of Moses (Ex. 2) Checking of a punishment by Aaron (Num. 17:9–15)	Egyptians drowned Death of firstborn	10.

(Be sure to note poetic description of death of firstborn in 18:14–15)

7. Wisdom 19:1–5	Hebrew crossing of Red Sea	Drowning of Egyptians	

The remainder of Chapter 19 of Wisdom summarizes the theme of these chapters: the Exodus was, indeed, a "new creation" wrought by God — a landmark in salvation history whose importance can hardly be overestimated. In verses 13-17, the midrashic element is clearly seen; even the wretched Sodomites, who refused to receive hospitably the two angels sent by Yahweh just before their destruction, are favorably compared to the Egyptians, who enslaved the descendants of Joseph whom they had previously received as a friend. "For every way, O Lord! you magnified and glorified your people; unfailing, you stood by them in every time and circumstance" (v. 22).

The True Nature of Idolatry

(Wisdom 13–15)

The same pious first-century Alexandrian Jew who celebrates Yahweh's vindication of His power during the Exodus also gives us some penetrating reflections on the folly of idolatry. What is the precise nature of this vice so frequently denounced in the Bible? The sacred author analyzes it as an abuse of creatures. These should lead men to

God (13:1), but the idolater uses creatures to lead men away from God by making a substitute for Him. In fact, idolatry "is the reason and source and extremity of all evil" (14:27) — including lies and perjury. In Chapter 15, the sacred author notes the root of the malice of idolatry: it is a reversal of the Creator-creature relationship. In making idols for himself, man is really playing the role of God: he becomes the Creator, God becomes the creature. This is likewise St. Paul's conclusion in Romans 1:20-23, where he declares that idolaters "have changed the glory of the incorruptible God for an image made like to corruptible man."

Psalm 135: A Song of Thanksgiving

(Cf. Psalm 134:8–14)

A number of the poems of the Psalter are classed as "psalms of thanksgiving" — rendering thanks to Yahweh on either an individual or a national scale. Psalm 135 is perhaps the best specimen of the latter type: it is known as the "Great Hallel," and was sung on the last day of the Passover celebration. Its arrangement indicates that it was designed to be sung alternately between a soloist (first half of each verse) and a choir (second half of the verse). Our litanies are fashioned after this type of liturgical prayer.

v. 1-3: A precise attribute of Yahweh is singled out for the overall theme of thanksgiving: His loving-kindness (in English it takes two words to do justice to the Hebrew term *Hesed*).

4-9: God's universal benefits are enumerated, viz., creation.

10-22: Yahweh's special care for Israel supplies a special reason for thanks: the Passover and the triumphal journey into Chanaan.

23-26: The concept of the divine conservation of creatures provides a final reason for thanking Yahweh.

Suggested Readings

Anderson, *Understanding the Old Testament*, pp. 44-59.
McKenzie, *The Two-Edged Sword*, Chap. 7.
Murphy, *The Book of Exodus*, Part I (Pamphlet Bible Series), pp. 24-31; Part II, pp. 5-10.

Chapter XV

The Mosaic Covenant: The Ark and the Presence

READINGS: *Exodus 21–25; 32–34; 40; Galatians 3, 4; Psalm 18 (Note: Exodus 21:24; 22:28; 24:8)*

Although the Decalogue constitutes the nucleus of the Mosaic Law, it is only one of several collections belonging to the Sinaitic Covenant. Like any legal code, it developed in the course of time as new situations required new precepts. The Pentateuch (known among the Jews simply as the Torah or Law) was ultimately fixed in its final form after the Babylonian Captivity, and comprises five basic collections:[1]

I. *The Decalogue* (Ex. 20). This chapter is from the JE source, as is also the Book of the Covenant.

II. *The Book of the Covenant* or Code of the Alliance (Ex. 21-23), enacted for primitive Hebrew society in the desert and early nomadic life in Chanaan.

III. *The Ritual Decalogue* (Ex. 34) is perhaps the Yahwist account of the Covenant; it lists the principal liturgical feasts in terms proper to the agricultural society of the Tribal Confederacy and early Kingdom.

IV. *The Law of Holiness* (Lev. 17-26), a ritual formulation of the Mosaic Law codified in the seventh and even sixth century B.C. in terms of the Priestly interests of the Temple at Jerusalem — i.e., in the Southern Kingdom.

V. *The Deuteronomic Code* (Deut. 12-26), a repetition of the previous laws in terms of the later Northern Kingdom (social distinctions, commerce, etc.), codified about the middle of the seventh century B.C.

All of these collections, it should be noted, are Mosaic in content and spirit; however, they were written down in their final form at different times and places, and thus reflect different emphases and modifications. The last two codes will be discussed in connection with the biblical book in which they are contained.

---

[1] See McEleney, *The Law Given Through Moses* (Pamphlet Bible Series, No. 1).

One more basic distinction must be made before we can proceed to a consideration of the particular laws in Exodus; viz., the various types of law which we find in the Pentateuch. Traditionally, there is a threefold division into moral, judicial (or civil), and ceremonial precepts already alluded to in the previous chapter. To understand this division, it must be remembered that all laws represent a pattern of activity imposed on the various levels of creation from a variety of sources and with unequal stability and binding force. Since man is a cosmos all by himself, he is bound by a great number of laws, depending on whether he is considered as pertaining to the mineral, plant, animal, human, or divine level of society:

Mineral. Composed of matter, man is subject to the law of place through gravity.

Plant. As a living organism, man is subject to the law of self-preservation whereby every part of his being tends to work for the good of the whole, and likewise for the good of the species, through the vital functions of nourishment, growth, and reproduction.

Animal. Possessing sensation, appetite, and locomotion, man is inclined by an intrinsic law to
- eat proper food;
- use sex for reproduction;
- care for (educate) offspring;
- protect offspring.

The Decalogue considers man as Yahweh's covenant partner, not merely as a rational animal. Keeping these laws was to be his way of expressing loyalty to his Lord. But we also recognize today that the Decalogue embodied much of the contemporary common law of the Middle East, itself based largely on the Natural Law. Thus, we may classify all but the Third Commandment as "moral" precepts— i.e., imprinted on man's conscience. The prohibition of *all* images in Exodus 20:4-6 (for Jews and most Protestants the *Second*, but for Catholics and Lutherans, part of the *First* Commandment) poses a problem. For Israelites surrounded by pagans images were a proximate occasion of sin, but not for us. The analytical chart on the next page may prove helpful.

Division and Purpose of the Laws

It should be noted, in conclusion, that the *moral precepts* are those laws which are known to the majority of men through their consciences, either as immediate conclusions or corollaries of the primary precepts of morality — i.e., the natural law. Examples are Exodus 20:2-17; 22:18-23. The *ceremonial precepts* are those enactments of positive law (i.e., not manifested by conscience, but promulgated by a human

THE NATURAL LAW: MORAL PRECEPTS

PRIMARY PRECEPTS	IMMEDIATE CONCLUSIONS	COROLLARIES	POSITIVE LAW { CEREMONIAL / JUDICIAL
Self-evident to all men	to nearly all men	the majority of men	not self-evident, but promulgated by the divine or a human lawgiver. (For the distinctions among moral, ceremonial and judicial precepts, see the *Summa Theologica* of Saint Thomas, IaIIae, Q. 99, Art. 3, ad 2, and Art. 4, ad 3).
I. OBEY REASON—shun ignorance and mistakes; observe, judge, act = PRUDENCE	1. Avoid inconsideration, inconstancy, and 2. Learn from the past, avoid negligence.		
II. CONTROL APPETITES—avoid excesses in pleasure, which is a by-product, not an end, of human activity = TEMPERANCE	1. No gluttony, drunkenness, regurgitation. 2. No contraception, Gen. 38:10; bestiality, Ex. 22:18; sodomy, Lev. 18:22; fornication, Ex. 22:15.	(N. B.: REFERENCES ARE TO EXODUS UNLESS OTHERWISE STATED)	
—avoid excesses in the face of evil: if necessary, endure; if not, attack for sake of good = FORTITUDE	1. Avoid cowardice, pettiness and vanity. 2. Protect rights without excess violence.		
III. PAY DEBT TO GOD—Man's first debt is to His Creator = religious justice or RELIGION	THE DECALOGUE 1st COMMANDMENT: "You shall not have strange gods besides me . . . You shall not carve idols in the shape of anything in the sky . . ." 2nd COMM.: "You shall not take the name of the Lord . . . in vain"	No sorcery (22:17); No communication in pagan rites (22:19); No images of Yahweh (cf. Deut. 4:15-19; in modern civilization, images are no longer a temptation)	**CEREMONIAL** — 3rd COMMANDMENT: THE SABBATH OBSERVANCE. Circumcision, redemption of first-born; Sacrifices (20:24); Feasts (23:14-17); "Kosher" laws and purification rites; Name not pronounced.
IV. GIVE NEIGHBOR HIS DUE—pay debts, avoid damage to others, share the goods of the earth = JUSTICE	4th COMM.: "Honor parents." 5th COMM.: "You shall not kill." 6th COMM.: "You shall not commit adultery." 7th COMM.: "You shall not steal." 8th COMM.: "You shall not bear false witness." 9th COMM.: "You shall not covet neighbor's wife." 10th COMM.: "You shall not covet (his goods)."	"Eye for eye" (21:24) Treat slaves well Help even enemy (23:5) Respect all wives (21) Restitution (22); No usury (22:24) No bribes (23:8) Cf. Ex. 23:1-3 Cf. Gen. 2:24 Return borrowed objects (22)	**JUDICIAL** — Death for child who strikes parent (21:15) Death for kidnapper; Free slaves every six years (21:2); Levirate Law (Deut. 25:5) Five-fold restitution (21:37). Bill of divorce permitted (Deut. 24:1)

or divine lawmaker) dealing with the worship of God. Examples are Exodus 20:22-26; 22:28-29; 23:10-18. The *judicial precepts* are those positive laws dealing with matters of social justice,[2] for example, Exodus 21; 22:1-17; 23:1-9. The rewards and punishments mentioned in Exodus 23:20-31 are all in the material order, it is true; but it must be remembered that the Mosaic Law was a transitional line of communication between God and men to prepare the latter typologically for the spiritual benefits of the messianic era. It was a teaching device for sincere Jews, aimed at leading them up from external observances obeyed largely out of fear to interior worship based on love. Its prescriptions could not confer grace of themselves; but they helped to repress vice and disease, and thereby to keep alive faith. At this point one should read Galatians 3-4, recalling Hasseveldt, pp. 75-81.

Ratification of the Covenant

Exodus 24:4 assures us that the Pentateuch was in the process of formation. A solemn moment is reached in verse 8 with the ratification of the Covenant. After reading the Book of the Covenant to the assembled people, Moses seals it with blood, according to ancient custom. Verses 9-11 describe the sacrificial meal celebrated by the priests and elders. He alone remained at the top of the mountain for "forty days and forty nights" (v. 18); this seems to be the Priestly editors' way of linking up the material in chapters 25-31, dealing with the Tent and the Ark, with Mount Sinai.[3] God was preparing for the solemn moment when Christ was to take the chalice at the Last Supper and say, "This cup is the new covenant in my blood, which shall be shed for you" (Luke 22:20).

The "Dwelling" (Meeting Tent or Tabernacle) and the Ark: Yahweh "Localized"

By reading Chapters 25 and 40 the reader can gain a fairly complete idea of what principal pieces of furniture went into the construction of the Meeting Tent, and its role as the throne of Yahweh. The preservation of the stone tablets on which the Decalogue was written, the golden urn of manna and Aaron's rod: these pale into insignificance when compared with the symbolism of Yahweh's invisible but dynamic presence between the two cherubim (human-headed, winged lions, in all probability). Here Yahweh "pitched His tent" among men and communicated with His Chosen Ones. The *Shekinah* or earthly presence of Yahweh, attested to by the cloud over the Tent, was to pro-

---

[2] This traditional division differs somewhat from that given by Murphy, *The Book of Exodus*, Part 2, pp. 10-11.

[3] Cf. *Ibid.*, p. 15.

vide one of the main fibers of later Hebrew mysticism (cf. Ex. 25:22; 40:34-38; Ps. 98:1; Num. 7:89; 10:35-36; Bouyer, *The Meaning of Sacred Scripture*, Chap. 10).

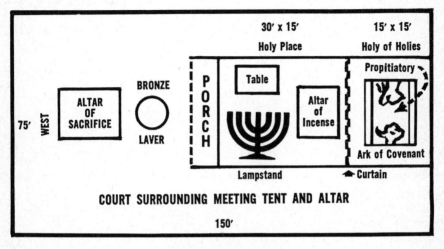

The Golden Calf

The speed with which the people who have so recently witnessed the marvels of Yahweh in their behalf now turn to idolatry seems almost incredible to the modern reader; yet, many of the later prophets would no doubt have remarked, "What would you have expected from this fickle group of murmurers?" Moses' delay at this time was a severe test for their patience; moreover, the whole incident reveals their innate need to express worship outwardly. Like the proverbial Irish wake, not only prayers but also a celebration accompanied Jewish peace offerings (cf. Ex. 32:6); such diversion — denied them until Moses should return — was a welcome interlude to the monotony of the arid desert. The gold for the statue was what the Jews had taken from the Egyptians upon their departure. Whether the calf actually was intended to represent Yahweh, His "pedestal,"[4] or an alien god, is not nearly as significant as we Westerners would like to think. For a primitive people such as the Jews, living in a sea of universal paganism, any kind of image constituted a proximate occasion of sin; hence Yahweh had forbidden all graven images. Moses' behavior in 32:11-13 is indicative of his magnificent stature: here was his golden opportunity to be a second Noe, a new Abraham. The story of the quick response of the Levites in slaying the guilty (those whom the gold-powdered water made ill) is perhaps a Priestly insertion to explain Yahweh's choice of

---

[4] Cf. W. F. Albright, *From the Stone Age to Christianity* (New York: Doubleday Anchor Books, 1957), pp. 299-302.

their tribe as custodians of worship. Exactly when or how 32:34 was fulfilled is not clear.

The Meeting Tent described in Exodus 33:7-11 seems to refer to Moses' own dwelling, not the Tabernacle where the Ark was housed. Such statements as Exodus 33:11 and Deuteronomy 34:10 must be interpreted in the light of Exodus 33:20: " . . . no man sees me and still lives." It is most unlikely that Moses enjoyed the Beatific Vision on these occasions. Nevertheless, Moses was unique among the prophets, as Exodus 34:33-35 indicates. In this connection, St. Paul's use of the event to make a comparison between the Old and New Testaments in II Corinthians 3:7-10 should be read carefully.

The renewal of the broken Covenant in Chapter 34, with Yahweh providing a new set of tablets to replace those smashed by Moses, provides the sacred author with an opportunity to work in another account of the ceremonial precepts in what has come to be known as the "Ritual Decalogue" referred to at the beginning of this chapter. Once again Moses is portrayed as the faithful Scribe, recording the words of Yahweh.

Psalm 18: Reflections on the Law

Although beginning as a hymn, this majestic poem focuses the meditation of the reader on the Torah; hence, it is to be classified as a wisdom psalm. Truly, here lies the answer to the atheist as well as abundant food for prayer. The psalm seems to consist of two distinct parts, the division falling between verses 7 and 8. Note in verse 5: "He has pitched a tent there. . . ."

vv. 1-7: The beauties of nature provide a stream of praise to Yahweh without speaking a single word or making any sound.

8-11: The perfection of the Mosaic Law is set alongside the wonders of nature for comparison; the implication is that the Law is an even greater wonder.

12-15: Mindful of his failings, the psalmist renews his resolution to observe the Law, and asks Yahweh to help him make a worthy meditation.

Suggested Readings

Aquinas, Summa Theologica, Ia IIae, Q. 94.
Moriarty, Introducing the Old Testament, pp. 19-43.
McEleney, The Law Given Through Moses (Pamphlet Bible Series of Paulist Press, No. 1).
Murphy, The Book of Exodus, Part 2, pp. 11-23.
Oesterley, W. O. E., and Robinson, T. H., An Introduction to the Books of the Old Testament (Meridian LA 23, 1958), pp. 34-38. Traces the four Mosaic traditions verse by verse. This is a standard Protestant work.
Sullivan, God's Word and Work, pp. 24-32.

The Law of Holiness: Leviticus and Liturgy

READINGS: *Leviticus 1–4, 8, 10–13:8, 17, 19, 23; Hebrews 9; I Corinthians 10; Psalms 19–20. (Note: Leviticus 11:44; 16:20–22; 17:11–12; 19:18)*

The Book of Leviticus might well be described as the "Priest's Ritual," somewhat after the model of our modern "Roman Ritual." History stands still at Mt. Sinai until the thread is resumed in the Book of Numbers. Codified probably a short time before the Babylonian Exile, Leviticus is the ceremonial of the Levites serving the Temple in Jerusalem. This is not to deny the book's Mosaic origin; rather, we are simply affirming the presence of many post-Mosaic additions in the final compilation. Leviticus itself is a combination of other collections of laws, e.g., Chapters 1-7; 8-10; 11-15; 17-26. These laws, which spell out the precepts in Exodus, are integrated by an over-all theme: the kind of behavior which is required of the people whom God has made His own. To put it another way, Leviticus is a detailed description of the meaning of holiness. Among other things, holiness demands: 1) imitation of Yahweh; 2) participation of the laity in liturgical (public) worship; 3) a dedicated clergy, set apart from the laity; 4) respect and love for one's neighbor; 5) bodily cleanliness, and 6) scrupulous avoidance of occasions of sin in the form of unclean persons and things.

Various Types of Sacrifice

The book opens with a description of the different kinds of sacrifice prescribed for specific occasions. The law provided for both animal and vegetable (cereal) sacrifices; in the case of the former, the actual immolation (slaughtering) of the animal was ordinarily performed by the person making the sacrifice, after first bringing it to the entrance of the Meeting Tent and laying his hand on its head in the presence of the priest by way of imploring Yahweh's acceptance of his sacrifice. It was also the task of the offerer to bleed, skin, divide and clean the carcass, whereupon the priest splashed the blood on the side of the altar and burned the animal, in whole or in part, according to the type of sacrifice being made:

TYPE	PURPOSE	PROCEDURE
1. Holocaust (Cows, sheep, goats, doves)	Adoration: to symbolize man's complete submission to God; also, sometimes used to expiate sin.	The whole animal had to be burned; nothing was saved for consumption by either priest or offerer.
2. Cereal oblation (Flour soaked in oil or made into edible cakes and accompanied by incense)	Usually an accompaniment of animal sacrifices, which it gradually replaced to some degree in the form of "first fruits" (thanksgiving).	Part of the cereal offering was burned on the altar and part was left for the priest. No layman was ever allowed to share in eating it. Had to be salted.
3. Peace offering (Always an animal)	Thanksgiving to Yahweh for favors received, or in fulfillment of a vow. Joyful sign of harmony.	Part was burned, and the rest was served as food for a sacred banquet consumed by the offerer and his guests.
4. Sin offering (Animal)	To expiate faults against the law committed out of human frailty or ignorance, not out of malice, and thus to effect "at-one-ment" [1]	Required a holocaust, except in the case of "guilt" offerings. Less serious faults were expiated by washing the body or one's clothes.

The Ordination of Priests
(Leviticus 8, 10)

The Jewish (Levitical) priesthood begins with Aaron, the first high priest. His descendants were given exclusive control of this office; the non-Aaronic descendants of Levi were given the lesser tasks concerning worship, such as carrying the Tabernacle from place to place in the desert, etc. Many features of Christian ordination ritual stem from Jewish practices, as is evident from Chapter 8; e.g., the use of such vestments as the tunic (alb), sash (cincture), and miter. The "Urim" and the "Thummim" (v. 8) are mysterious objects; kept in a burse-like compartment over the priest's chest, they seem to have been a form of dice with which to determine Yahweh's decision in certain matters. The blood sprinkled on the right ear, thumb and toe of the ordinand signified that "the ear must be attentive to the com-

---

[1] Chapter 5 offers examples of expiable "sins"; the more serious, malicious sins were punishable by excommunication (exclusion from community) or by death.

mands of God, the hand ready to do His will, the foot prepared to walk in His ways." The reference to the "waving" of the offerings before the Lord here (v. 27) and elsewhere signified that the object was being given to God (forward motion), Who in turn was giving it back to the offerer (backward motion).

To emphasize the sanctity demanded of priests, the account of the sacrilegious use of unauthorized fire by Aaron's two oldest sons, Nadab and Abiu (who had just been ordained), and their consequent destruction by fire from heaven, is inserted in the text at this point (Chap. 10).[2] Aaron and his two surviving sons were forbidden to mourn over their death by Moses. On this occasion the portion of sacrifices other than holocausts which belong to the offering priest is indicated: the breast, leg, and fatty portions of animals, and the unburnt portions of cereal offerings.

The Law of Kashruth: Clean Versus Unclean Animals; Childbirth and Leprosy (11–13)

The dietary laws of the Jews are well-known even to Gentiles. Chapter 11 of Leviticus outlines the categories of unclean (forbidden) animals, birds and fishes. A clean animal must possess two characteristics: it must have a cleft hoof and chew the cud. Fish must have both fins and scales. The distinction between clean and unclean birds is not so clear, though, in general, birds which feed on carrion are considered unclean. Many of these distinctions antedate the Mosaic Law: God simply goes along with contemporary notions, in many cases. A threefold basis for them can be detected: the "unclean" creatures are actually those which are less digestible, or which cause a natural aversion in man, or with which there was perhaps a superstitious association. The Mosaic Law, however, rose above purely hygienic reasons, and proposed the boycotting of these items more on religious grounds: you must be pure before you approach Yahweh (i.e., go to the Meeting Tent to pray or offer sacrifice). In other words, the Jews were expected to learn the need of moral cleanliness from these external associations: "For I, the Lord, am your God; and you shall make and keep yourselves holy, because I am holy" (v. 44; cf. Matt. 5:48).

It must be very carefully noted that a transgression of the laws contained in these three chapters does not imply that a sin in our sense of the word has been committed; a Jew who stumbled over the dead body of an animal in the dark would be unclean in the technical sense, though he had not even performed a human act in the process. This is obvious in the case of childbirth; surely there is nothing sinful in

---

[2] In Lev. 9:24 an account of heavenly fire coming down to consume the holocaust offered on the octave day of the ordination ceremony is recorded.

this natural function, yet the mother was "unclean" for forty days after the birth of a boy, and eighty days after the birth of a girl.[3] Thus, she was forbidden to approach the Meeting Tent (and later on, to enter the Temple) until her purification period was over and she had made a sin offering. In lesser infractions, such as those described in Chapter 11, the washing of one's body and/or clothes was sufficient; but in cases where the uncleanness lasted for a long period, purification was accomplished only by a sin offering. The term "leprosy" in Chapter 13 covers a great variety of skin diseases short of the dreaded Hansen's disease known to us. Note the precautions required of a leper in verse 45. One of the features of legal defilement of any kind was that any person who touched an unclean (*tref*) thing was unclean and had to wash himself and his clothing, and remained unclean until evening (Chap. 15). Persons permanently unclean had to dwell outside the camp; they were excommunicated.[4]

The "Law of Holiness"

This is the title given to Chapters 17-26 of Leviticus because of the exalted standards of cleanliness it imposes upon the Jews in consideration of Yahweh's presence among them. Blood is most sacred, not because its loss brings on death, but because it is the "seat of life" (17: 11). Hence, all slaughtering of animals—even for use in the home—took on a sacrificial character, and had to be performed at the entrance of the Meeting Tent (17:3-4 — though Deut. 12:21 removes this obligation in view of the later settled condition of life in Chanaan). Animal sacrifices were not meant to be a substitute for the life of the offerer; rather, the death of the beast was looked upon as a symbol of the complete surrender of the mind and heart of the offerer to Yahweh. Leviticus 19:18 reaches a peak in Old Testament religion: the law of love of neighbor, ranking second only to love of God (Deut. 6:5). Many of the precepts in this chapter represent legislation of a much later date (e.g., v. 29).

The three principal Jewish "holy days," on which adult males were obliged to make a pilgrimage to Jerusalem after the Temple had been built, are listed in Chapter 23:

1) *The Passover or Pasch.* Beginning on the fourteenth day of Nisan, the first month of the ecclesiastical year (just after the spring equinox), it commemorated the sparing of the firstborn Jewish male and the crossing of the Red Sea. Unleavened bread had to be used during the whole octave of the feast.

---

[3] The birth of a girl was thought to require a longer maternal recuperation time.

[4] In recent years, there has been a revival of Kosher laws: cf. *Time,* February 20, 1956, p. 54.

2) *Pentecost* (Feast of Weeks). Seven weeks (fifty days) after the Passover, to celebrate the grain harvest and, later on, the giving of the Law on Mt. Sinai.

3) *Tabernacles* (Booths). Feast celebrating the fall fruit and grape harvest; a time of joyful thanksgiving, during which the people lived in booths in commemoration of the forty years passed in the desert. This feast occurred in the seventh month after the Pasch; this was the first month (Tishri) of the civil year, with the following order of events: a) first day of Tishri is *Rosh Hashanah* or New Year's Day (about the tenth of September); tenth day of Tishri: Day of Atonement, on which every Jew fasts until sundown, and the high priest used to enter the Holy of Holies (for scapegoat ceremony, cf. Lev. 16:20-22); fifteenth to twenty-first Tishri: Feast of Tabernacles with its octave. The Book of Ecclesiastes was read at this time.

A careful reading of Hebrews 9 and I Corinthians 10 (esp. vv. 1-11) throws a new light on these Old Testament ceremonies; they were types of the Christian sacramental system. The student should now be in a position to link up the following ceremonies with individual sacraments: animal sacrifices, especially the Paschal Lamb; circumcision and the crossing of the Red Sea; the anointing of priests; purification of a legal defilement; various laws regarding sex; the Propitiatory.

Royal Psalms 19 and 20: Prayer and Sacrifice

These two psalms introduce the type known as "royal psalms" or prayers for the king. Psalm 19 is a plea for the king's success as he rides into battle; a holocaust was offered between verses 6 and 7. Though thanking Yahweh for the victory, Psalm 20 is also classed as a royal psalm.

Suggested Readings

Brillet, *Meditations on the Old Testament*, Vol I: The Narrative, pp. 47-59.
Stuhlmueller, *The Book of Leviticus* (Pamphlet Bible Series No. 6), pp. 5-17.
Sullivan, *God's Word and Work*, pp. 24-32.
Vann, *The Paradise Tree*, Chap. 3.

Chapter XVII

The Wilderness: Temptation and Test

READINGS: *Numbers 6, 10–14, 16–17, 20–25; Hebrews 3–4; Psalm 94.
(Note: Numbers 1:46, 6:23–26, 7:89, 10:35, 24:17, 31:16).*

The Hebrew text calls this book "In the Wilderness"; the title "Numbers" comes from the Septuagint, and is so named because of the census which it contains. Numbers takes up where Exodus left off, in the second year of encampment at Mt. Sinai. In 1:46, the sacred author gives us the result of the general census: 603,550 men of war. Though this agrees in substance with Exodus 12:37 and Numbers 26:51, we cannot take it at face value; otherwise, we would have a total population of about 3,000,000 souls. One plausible explanation is that the Hebrew word which has been translated "thousand" (*Eleph*), should be translated "clan" (i.e., part of a tribe) in this context. Thus, the last two ciphers would be removed from the total, leaving about 6,000 warriors, or 30,000 total population. If one prefers not to alter the figure, the large number can be explained as a strategic exaggeration to magnify the power of Yahweh in feeding so vast a group in the arid desert. A few words on the symbolism of biblical numbers would seem to be in order in treating this book.

Biblical Numerology

In general, odd numbers were considered as indicating perfection, since they are indivisible units. Even numbers possess a variety of meanings. A brief summary of the symbolism behind the more significant numbers is given on the following page.[1]

From these considerations it is clear that the early Hebrew use of numbers was often purely arbitrary; we should not be astonished at such assertions as: Moses' age of eighty when he was commanded to lead the Hebrews out of Egypt (the sacred author is simply dividing his life into three periods, each forty years); the life span of 120 years assigned to man in Genesis 6:3 (40 × 3); nor especially the ages of

---

[1] Cf. B. M. Ashley, *The Arts of Learning and Communication* (Dubuque, 1958), pp. 303-305.

ODD NUMBERS	EVEN NUMBERS
1: Stands for God, perfect unity	2: War and opposition; also, friendship and love; marriage; confirmation by witnesses
3: (In the New Testament) God as the Trinity	
5: Summary of obligations: 5 Books of the Law; 10 (5 x 2) Commandments	4: Number of corners in a square; hence the solid earth; building; city; elements
7: The perfect number, probably because ancients knew only 7 moving heavenly bodies: Sun, Moon, Mars, Mercury, Jupiter, Saturn, Venus (one week)	6: Evil, imperfection: the number of the working days in a week (purely natural order); 666 in Apocalypse is Antichrist
9: (3 x 3) Emphatic 3: Kyrie Eleison	8: (7 plus 1)—Eternity; 8 Beatitudes
11: Sum total of time to the present; the eleventh hour	10: Equals 5 x 2: the Decalogue
50: Actually, 7 x 7 plus 1: fulfillment; has more the character of an odd than an even number. Jubilee year	12: A nation: 4 (a city) x 3 (blessed by God) hence, 12 Tribes, 12 Apostles (New Israel). Also the ages of the world (because 12 hours in a day)
39, 99, etc.; lacking completion	14: (7 x 2)—Messianic number (David =14)
	40: (10 x 4)—One generation; used to signify an extended but uncertain period of time: cannot be taken literally before David

the patriarchs in Genesis 5; here it seems as though a cipher has been added to what would otherwise be a reasonable figure, just as apparently two ciphers have been added to the census figures in Numbers 1 and 3.

The Role of the Levites

It is obvious that these first ten chapters of Numbers are from the Priestly tradition. A special census of their Tribe is recorded in Chapter 3, yielding a total of 22,000 males. These are accepted by Yahweh as the price of the redemption of the firstborn males of all the other Tribes: in other words, He considered the precept He had laid down in Exodus 13:13 to be retroactive. To redeem the 273 "supernumeraries," a price of five shekels was prescribed; this money went to the Levites. Only the priests (i.e., Aaronites) were allowed to touch the Ark and the sacred vessels; the other Levites were assigned the task of carrying the various articles from one encampment to the next.

After a lengthy description of an ordeal to be undergone by suspected adulteresses in Chapter 5, the "Nazarite Vow" is taken up in the following chapter. By consecrating his or her hair to the Lord and refraining from cutting it, a Nazarite was "set apart" or vowed to God for a specified time or for life. This will explain why Samson's strength left him when Dalila had his head shaved. John the Baptist seems to have been numbered among these "monks" of the Old Testament. Chapter

6 concludes with the beautiful formula of priestly blessing,[2] known to many Christians under the title of the "Blessing of St. Francis." When the Dwelling had been set up and consecrated, God spoke to Moses from the Propitiatory (7:89), but His message has been lost. Yahweh directed the stages of their journey by lifting the Cloud when they were to depart from a given site, and halting it when they were to encamp (9:17-18), with Moses pronouncing the official signal according to the formula in 10:35-36 (and partially enshrined in Ps. 67:2).

Murmurings and Punishment: 38 More Years of Wandering

No sooner had the Israelites set out from Sinai in the second year after their arrival (10:11) than some of them became discontent with the diet of manna. Upon Moses' plea to be relieved of leading such a rebellious people, God directed him to appoint seventy elders to aid in governing them. The spirit of prophecy which came over these chosen souls (including the two stragglers) was probably little more than a prudent zeal and competency in settling disputes. The sacred author portrays the gift of the quail as an answer to their murmuring, and provides a detail omitted from Exodus: the plague whereby the greedy were punished. At this juncture, Mariam (the instigator) and Aaron manifested their envy of Moses' exclusive intimacy with Yahweh ("face to face" in 12:8 is again being used metaphorically). The "meekness" of Moses, reflecting his progress in heroic virtue over the years, is a far cry from the mighty Prince of Egypt; yet it must not be interpreted as softness. Again his magnanimity is shown in obtaining Mariam's cure of leprosy through prayer.

A much more serious murmur broke out among the Israelites in the wake of the pessimistic report of ten of the twelve scouts sent ahead to reconnoiter the Promised Land. For urging the people to turn back to Egypt for fear of the "giants" (oversized aborigines), the ten false scouts were struck down by Yahweh (14:37), and the whole population was condemned to spend thirty-eight more years in the desert. This drastic penalty was to insure that all murmurers who were twenty years or older would die out before the entrance into Chanaan. Only Josue and Caleb, the two "good scouts" were exempt from the punishment. The unregenerate obstinacy of this people is illustrated in 14:44. Numbers 14:22-23 and 28-30 explain Psalm 94:10-11.

The two rebellions related in Chapters 16-17 may be summarized as follows: 1) Core and 250 of his fellow Levites demanded a share in the priestly privileges of Aaronites (16:10), and were consumed by heavenly fire as they swung their censers along with Aaron in the

---

[2] Used, for example, to bless pilgrims to Jerusalem; cf. Psalm 133.

"showdown" arranged by Moses. 2) Dathan and Abiram were laymen, descendants of Jacob's firstborn son, Ruben; they spurned the authority of Moses and were swallowed up by a sudden rift in the earth, together with their families. 3) The "whole Israelite community" blamed Moses for the death of the guilty parties; to punish their murmuring, God sent another plague, which was checked by Aaron's quick action of running among them while swinging his censer—but only after 14,700 of them had died. It was on this occasion that Aaron's staff—later to be placed in the Ark with the Decalogue—blossomed into ripe almonds, thus vindicating the authority of the Levites and, in particular, of Moses and Aaron.

Chapter 20 is one of the saddest in the Old Testament. After Mariam's death, the people again grumbled for lack of water; the Lord ordered Moses to strike a rock with his staff. After upbraiding the rebels, Moses struck the rock twice and water came forth in abundance. Where did the sin of Moses and Aaron lie? It lay in their failure to "show forth the sanctity" of God: instead of making the occasion "a joyful manifestation of God's effortless control of nature, they had turned it into a scene of bitter denunciation."[3] The death of Aaron is also recorded in this chapter. In Chapter 21 God sends poisonous snakes to punish the chronic murmuring of His people for food and water. The incident is significant because the brazen serpent which Moses fashioned at Yahweh's command to heal those who would look upon it was referred to by Christ as a type of the salvific value of His crucifixion (John 3:14). Here is an example of a "graven image" not only permitted, but commanded, by Yahweh.

Balaam's Messianic Utterance

The Israelite victory over Sehon, King of the Amorrites, and Og, King of Basan (21:14ff.; cf. also Ps. 135:19-20) so frightened Balac, King of Moab, that he summoned a soothsayer all the way from the district around Haran to curse this threatening horde. Although, Balaam was certainly a pagan, the sacred author portrays him as the instrument of Yahweh, compelled to pronounce a blessing over the Jews rather than a curse. This illustrates forcefully the tremendous respect which the ancients had for the spoken word: granted that it was uttered by the "right" person under the proper circumstances, it would infallibly produce its effect, so they thought. The talking of the ass is a fictional detail deliberately inserted by the sacred author; it shows how not only pagan soothsayers, but even dumb beasts, are guided by the inexorable power of Yahweh to work out His designs. All four attempts of Balaam result in prophetic blessings on the

---

[3] Cf. Moriarty, *The Book of Numbers*, Part 1, p. 19.

Israelites; in fact, the last (24:17) has been traditionally held to be messianic. It points to some distinguished Jew ("star") who shall rise to a position of authority and defeat the Moabites and Edomites. If our Confraternity translation is correct, the passage may be referred to Christ in the spiritual sense, as David is a recognized type of the Messia.[4] Numbers 31:8 recounts the slaying of Balaam by the Jews. In 2 Peter 2:15 and Jude 11, it is implied that his sin was one of avarice over the fee he was to receive from Balac; however, Numbers 31:16 reveals a different crime: that of instigating the sacrilegious participation of the Jews in the pagan rites surrounding Baal-Phogor (25:1ff.). It was on this occasion that Aaron's grandson Phinees distinguished himself for his zeal in slaying one of the guilty ones and his consort.

Psalm 94 and the Meaning of the Wilderness

(Cf. Hebrews 3 and 4 for commentary)

In this cosmological hymn which daily begins the Divine Office and which ends in a reflective mood, the real issue at stake in the wilderness is brought into clear focus: God intended those forty years as a testing of His people to confirm them in virtue, but they turned the tables on Him and committed the crime of "temptation of God." This theme will be examined in the next chapter through the Deuteronomic Tradition.

Suggested Readings

Ashley, *The Arts of Learning and Communication,* pp. 303-305.
Guillet, *Themes of the Bible,* Chap. 1.
Moriarty, *The Book of Numbers,* Parts 1 and 2 (Pamphlet Bible Series, No. 7 and No. 8).
Sullivan, *God's Word and Work,* pp. 33-40.

---

[4] However, Prof. Albright translates the passage differently: "When the stars of Jacob shall prevail, and the tribes of Israel shall rise."

Chapter XVIII

The Deuteronomic Tradition: A Theology of History

READINGS: *Deuteronomy 1–12, 17–19, 34; Psalm 90. (Note: Deuter-onomy 6:4–5, 17:14–20, 18:15, 24:1, 25:5–10, 28:64)*

The title of this last book of the Torah or Pentateuch means "other" or "second" law; actually, it is not a new law, but rather a repetition and an enlargement of the precepts contained in Exodus, Leviticus and Numbers. Thus, although it provides a handy framework with which to summarize what has gone before, it simultaneously raises a problem: why this extensive duplication of material? The answer consists in the realization that we have here another (fourth and final) basic Mosaic Tradition with its own distinct emphases and lesson: the so-called "Deuteronomic Code." Notice that virtually the whole book is in quotation marks: it is a highly oratorical exposition of the Law in an historical setting, placed on the lips of THE lawgiver, Moses.[1] Re-calling all that Yahweh has done for them, Moses vehemently urges them to be faithful to the Covenant which He has made with them in singling them out in a most special manner from among the other na-tions of the earth. He appeals to their sense of gratitude, citing the many instances of God's loving care over them. In a very special way, Deuteronomy is to be classed as a "Theology of History."

Historical Review

The first four chapters (probably a post-Exilic addition) constitute a brief review of the events during the forty years in the desert. Of special note is the immunity granted to the Edomites (descendants of Esau) and the Moabites and Ammonites (descendants of Lot) by Yahweh against slaughter by the Israelites (Chapter 2). In Chapter 4 the theology is evident in verses 15-20, which should be carefully underlined. The importance of imageless worship is stressed here, as the fashioning of ANY figure would be an occasion of sin to God's chosen ones. The reason for the 400-year sojourn in Egypt is hinted at in the word "foundry" (v. 20): this was their education! Verses 32-40

---

[1] Cf. Orchard, *A Catholic Commentary on Holy Scripture*, col. 210c.

should likewise be marked for special study; they epitomize Deuteronomic history, and draw the conclusion reached at this point: your first
obligation under the Covenant is to avoid idolatry.

Down through the centuries Jews have prided themselves on the
title of "Sons of the Covenant" (B'nai Berith). God had made a Covenant with Noe, and a second one with Abraham; but THE Covenant
is the one made with Moses and his contemporaries. And the heart of
that Covenant is the Decalogue, repeated in Chapter 5 of Deuteronomy
—almost word for word as in Exodus 20, except that the two acts of
coveting are more clearly distinguished in Deuteronomy. Like the
northern Elohist editor, the Deuteronomist designates the mountain
on which Moses received the Decalogue as "Horeb." This and similar
instances are clues to the origin of this tradition.

The Shema, Heart of the Decalogue

Each day faithful Jews still recite a prayer made up of Deuteronomy
6:4-9, 11:13-21, and Numbers 15:37-41. Even before the birth of Christ,
it was clearly realized by them that the love of God was supposed to
be the heart of the Decalogue, just as the latter is the heart of the other
precepts. This prayer is known as the *Shema*, from the opening word,
"Hear!" in Deuteronomy 6:4, which expresses Jewish monotheism.
Christ quoted verse 5 as the "First Commandment" and Leviticus
19:18 (q. v.) as the "Second" in Matthew 22:37-40.

This whole-hearted devotion to Yahweh was to include not only a
prohibition against idolatry, but also an abrupt separatism from all
other peoples: the Jews are to "doom" their enemies to destruction,[2]
being particularly careful to avoid any intermarriage with pagans
(7:1-4), and to remove all danger to idolatry by tearing down their
altars and smashing their sacred pillars.

> For you are a people sacred to the Lord, your God; he has chosen
> you from all the nations on the face of the earth to be a people
> peculiarly his own. It was not because you are the largest of all
> nations that the Lord set his heart on you and chose you, for you
> are really the smallest of all nations. It was because the Lord loved
> you and because of his fidelity to the oath he had sworn to your
> fathers, that he brought you out with his strong hand from the place
> of slavery, and ransomed you from the hand of Pharao, king of
> Egypt. (7:6-8)

Chapter 8 analyzes the forty years in the wilderness in terms of a
prolonged test to "find out whether or not it was your intention to
keep his commandments" (v. 2). The next verse contains the punch
line, quoted by Our Lord in reply to the first temptation to which
the Devil subjected Him during His forty days fast (Matt. 4:4)—

> He therefore let you be afflicted with hunger, and then fed you
> with manna, a food unknown to you and your fathers, in order to

---

[2] The practice of *herem* will be considered in the next chapter.

show you that *not by bread alone does man live, but by every word that comes forth from the mouth of the Lord.* The clothing did not fall from you in tatters, nor did your feet swell these forty years. So you must realize that the Lord, your God, disciplines you even as a man disciplines his son. (8:3-5)

This is just about as close as the Old Testament gets to the concept of man's elevation to the supernatural order; it seems almost as if one is reading the Sermon on the Mount, especially Matthew 6:31-34. These words are the very antithesis of secularism. The Mosaic exhortation proceeds to warn against sins opposed to the two special prohibitions. The Chosen People are not to let their separation turn into a self-suffi- cient righteousness (later known as Pharisaism), as 9:4-6 forcefully declares; nor are they to offend against monotheism by any form of idolatry, such as the graphic incident of the Golden Calf (9:7-21). The implication of their behavior on that occasion and subsequently is the same as the implication of Psalm 94: they have been failing the test (cf. 9:24). Indeed, they have been tempting Yahweh by their lack of confidence in demanding water and food constantly. It is now time to reform, to "circumcise your hearts, therefore, and be no longer stiff- necked" (10:16). Yahweh demands that they return to the spirit of the Decalogue, which is love, by refusing bribes and befriending the orphan, the widow and the alien (vv. 17-18).

The Deuteronomic Code

The moralizing tone of these phrases introduces the "Deuteronomic Code" (Chap. 12-26)—the fourth Mosaic tradition which went into the construction of the Torah. Beginning with the law centralizing wor- ship around a single sanctuary (which was probably "Sichem" in the original tradition), this "D" tradition represents the reaction of the northern Levites to the idolatrous practices of the schismatic Kingdom of Israel. It is a recasting of the Book of the Covenant to provide a

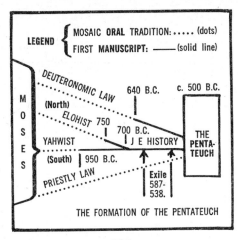

THE FORMATION OF THE PENTATEUCH

139

basis for the reform that these Levites were attempting to effect. Brought to Jerusalem some time before 621 B. C., it furnished fuel for Josia's reform in that year.

Outline of the Torah

Besides the law of unity of sanctuary, other later enactments appear in Deuteronomy. The following schema includes the basic core of Pentateuchal laws, plus key Deuteronomic additions, according to the traditional divisions:

[handwritten marginal note:] add not. upon in drawing of Deuteronomy

THE PENTATEUCH or WRITTEN TORAH
****

Genesis
Exodus
Leviticus
Numbers
Deuteronomy

CEREMONIAL PRECEPTS
—worship

Circumcision: redemption of the first-born (Ex. 13:2).

Religious feasts: Sabbath, Pasch, Pentecost, Tabernacles.

Sacrifices: Holocausts; cereal, sin, and peace offerings.

Tithes and first-fruits.

Legal purity: avoidance of uncleanliness associated with_____ Purpose: 1) moral purity; 2) hygiene.

> Sex: childbirth, menstruation.
> Food: meat, fish, blood.
> Disease: leprosy; corpses.
> Contact with Gentiles.

Purification rites: Those who contracted a legal impurity (not necessarily a sin) were ostracized from the community and public worship until they had bathed and washed their clothes, or made a sin offering in specified cases.

JUDICIAL PRECEPTS
—social justice

PRINCIPLE was Law of Talion: "An eye for an eye" by way of mitigating the violent vindictiveness of pagan practices.

Trial before at least 2 witnesses; "cities of refuge" set up.

No usury (interest) from Jews (Ex. 22:24); kindness to aliens.

Remission of debts every 7 years (Deut. 15:1).

Rights of first-born son not to be transferred (Deut. 21:15).

MORAL PRECEPTS
—natural law

DECALOGUE—sparked by Deut. 6:4–5 and Leviticus 19:18.

Matrimony was qualified by toleration of polygamy (cf. Deut. 21:15); divorce (Deut. 24:1); and the Levirate Law (Deut. 25:5).

The "Unwritten" Torah

As is the case with every legal document, new interpretations and applications of the Torah were made and handed down by the rabbis; the first codification of this "Tradition of the Ancients" was the *Mishna* (which accurately reflects Jewish mentality of the first century A.D.), followed by the *Gemara:*

N B 1

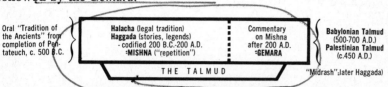

| Oral "Tradition of the Ancients" from completion of Pentateuch, c. 500 B.C. | Halacha (legal tradition) Haggada (stories, legends) - codified 200 B.C.-200 A.D. =MISHNA ("repetition") | Commentary on Mishna after 200 A.D. =GEMARA | Babylonian Talmud (500-700 A.D.) Palestinian Talmud (c.450 A.D.) |

THE TALMUD   "Midrash":later Haggada)

THE POLITICO-CULTURAL SITUATION AND THE DEVELOPMENT OF BIBLICAL LITERATURE:

| 1250-1150: Nomadic life; Sinai and MOSAIC SOURCES OF TORAH | 1150-1000: Judges; Tribal Confederacy to Davidic Dynasty. YAHWIST (SOUTH) | 1000-721: First Temple, then Divided Monarchy. ELOHIST (NORTH) | 721-538: Two Captivities; Synagogue; DEUTERONOMY (NO.) | 538-323: 2nd Temple & Esdras' CANON. PRIESTLY (SO.) | 323-63: Hellenism vs. JUDAISM Egypt & the SEPTUAGINT |

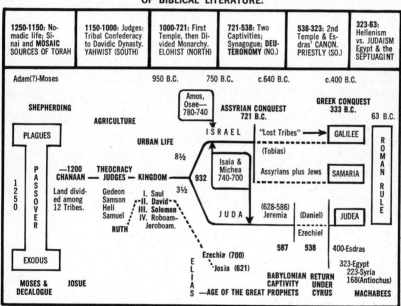

A Look at the Future: Apocalyptic Literature;
A Messianic Utterance: Moses' Death

Unmistakable evidence of the later composition of Deuteronomy is contained in Deuteronomy 17 ff. The qualifications of the king (17:14-20) are hindsights: verse 17 is a dead giveaway for Solomon. The Northern origin of the tradition is betrayed in 20:6-8 where equal access is accorded *all* Levites to *the* Sanctuary (Jerusalem). The fifth messianic prophecy to be considered is contained in 18:15; though envisioning a group rather than an individual, it was applied to Christ by the Apostles (cf. John 1:21, 6:14; Acts 3:22 and 7:37). Cities of refuge are set up to take care of such accidental cases of homicide as mentioned in 19:5. Verse 15 specifies the minimum number of witnesses in a lawsuit. The Israelite's "Credo" is given in 26:5-10, pronounced on the occasion of the payment of first fruits. Chapter 28 is largely apocalyptic (cf. v. 64 with 4:28, and review "Apocalypse" on page 28). A Covenant-renewal ceremony is prescribed for every seventh year in 31:10 ff.; this rite seems to have been without parallel in the Southern Kingdom before the Exile. The blessings of Moses in Chapter 33 are quite different, in most cases, from those of Jacob in Genesis 49. Obviously a later addition, Chapter 34 describes the death of him "whom the Lord knew face to face" (v. 10) and who "had no equal" (v. 11) in the Old Testament (cf. St. Jude's Epistle, v. 9).

Down through the centuries the Jews would look upon the forty years in the wilderness as the "ideal" era in their history. Though it was a period of severe trial and often of failure, the later prophets were to hold it up nostalgically before their contemporaries as the time of their greatest intimacy with Yahweh, the perfect theocracy. Each subsequent reform movement would be proposed as a return to the desert, a New Exodus:

> Therefore, behold I will allure her, and will lead her into the wilderness; and I will speak to her heart. And I will give her vinedressers out of the same place, and the valley of Achor for an opening of hope; and she shall sing there according to the days of her youth, and according to the days of her coming up out of the land of Egypt. (Os. 2:14-15; cf. Isa. 43; Jer. 2:2-6; Ps. 76)

The three big feasts of the year—Passover, Pentecost and Tabernacles—which were originally the thanks offerings of an agrarian people, became solemn memorials of the Exodus, the revelation at Horeb, and the trek through the wilderness, respectively. Thus, they tried to capture those blessed moments of their divine espousal and subsequent honeymoon and turn them into "a permanent act of God." But they were only types of the authentic Exodus wrought by Christ, as Scripture assures us in I Corinthians 10, Hebrews, etc. In the righthand column below, authentic antitypes are indicated by an asterisk:

TYPE IN OLD TESTAMENT	CHRIST AND HIS CHURCH ANTITYPES AND CHRISTIAN SYMBOLS	
1. Moses, Josue (and Jews)	The New Israel, leading us to true Promised Land, Heaven	Christians*
2. Egypt, Jericho	Flight into Egypt	House of Satan
3. The EXODUS	His passing to the Father	Our spiritual Odyssey
4. Red Sea; Circumcision; Jordan	Passion and death	Baptism*

TYPE IN OLD TESTAMENT	CHRIST AND HIS CHURCH ANTITYPES AND CHRISTIAN SYMBOLS	
5. Mount Sinai	Mount of the Beatitudes Sermon on the Mount	Pentecost
6. The Wilderness	40 days' fast in the desert	Temptations, trials
7. The Fire and the Cloud	Beatific Vision which He	Holy Spirit
8. Eden, Sabbath, Promised Land	enjoyed continuously	Heaven, eternity*
9. Ark of the Covenant	The Divine Word	The Gospel
10. The Propitiatory	Physical presence	The Real Presence*
11. Animal sacrifices, Paschal Lamb	Crucifixion	The Mass*
12. Anointing of priests, kings	Christ's baptism	Confirmation
13. Purification of legal defilement		Penance
14. Concept of legal purity	God's absolute holiness	Christian perfection
15. Bloody doorposts	Crucifixion	Sign of the Cross
16. Ashes of the Red Heifer (Num. 19)	Crucifixion	Holy Water
17. Day of Atonement	Crucifixion	Good Friday
18. Water from rock, Manna, Unleavened bread	His body	The Holy Eucharist*

The Hebrew Concept of Authorship

As in the case of Oriental literary genres, so also in regard to the very notion of authorship we must be prepared to enlarge our viewpoint. Our modern "Hellenistic" outlook is a *literary* concept; the Semitic outlook was a *psychological* one. In ancient times there was no such thing as the publication of a book. The only sure way to preserve one's ideas was to diffuse them throughout the community; this "collective memory" was the best depository. But what remained of the original author? His initiative, his inspiration, and in the case of Scripture, the original divine commission and guidance. In a word, authorship was equivalent to authority. There was no issuing of copyrights; whatever literary endeavors produced became the property of the community, for the result was not a book but an anthology. In the case of the Pentateuch, Moses fulfilled the modern role of editor with this difference: his jurisdiction was exercised only at the beginning of the literary activity. His initial impetus, however, was sufficient to imbue subsequent accretions with his spirit. Later on it became customary for the great prophets to commit their oracles to a nucleus of faithful disciples who would preserve and disseminate them (cf. Isa. 8:16ff.).[3]

---

[3] Moriarty, *Introducing the Old Testament*, pp. 83-84, quotes R. A. F. MacKenzie on this topic. See also Anderson, *Op. cit.*, pp. 256-267. These remarks on authorship also apply to the New Testament.

143

God's Kingdom in the Old Testament

Psalm 90: God's Unfailing Protection of Those Who
Put Their Trust in Him

(Cf. Psalm 89)

Like Psalm 22, this is a Psalm of Confidence. It reflects perfectly the Deuteronomic spirit: "For what nation is there that has gods so close to it as the Lord, our God, is to us whenever we call upon him?" (Deut. 4:7). Here again we see the Psalter rising almost to the heights of the divine immanence expressed in the New Testament; e.g., Romans 8:28: "Now we know that for those who love God all things work together unto good, for those who, according to his purpose, are saints through his call." Although a servant of Yahweh will continue to be surrounded by evil and will have to face many dangers, none of these will harm him. We do not know when or in what national or personal crisis (if any) this psalm was composed. It is arranged to be sung antiphonally by different choirs or voices, and is addressed to any God-fearing Jew.

vv. 1-2: The psalmist instructs his hearer (the trusting Israelite) to express his confidence in Yahweh by means of the formula given in verse 2.

3-13: In these verses the psalmist enumerates different types of evil which a faithful soul will overcome through Yahweh's protection. Verse 11, quoted by Satan to Christ when he tempted Him to jump off the Temple, expresses an early Old Testament belief in guardian angels.

14-16: Yahweh confirms the claims made by the psalmist, adding a promise of longevity and "salvation."

Suggested Readings

Anderson, *Understanding the Old Testament*, pp. 154–182; 225–227; 71; 305–322; 379-393. These pages deal with the Yahwist tradition, the Elohist tradition, the Deuteronomic Code and the Priestly tradition, respectively.

Brillet, *Meditations on the Old Testament*, Vol. I: *The Narratives*, pp. 41-46; 60-65.

Danielou, *The Bible and the Liturgy*, Chap. 5

————————————————, *From Shadows to Reality*, Book 4. These two works of Danielou's treat of typology in the Old Testament.

Glanzman, *The Book of Deuteronomy*, Parts 1 and 2 (Pamphlet Bible Series No. 9 and No. 10).

Goldin, *The Living Talmud: The Wisdom of the Fathers*, pp. 13-26. There is also a recording by the same title, put out by Mentor Books.

McEleney, *The Law Given Through Moses* (Pamphlet Bible Series No. 1). Treats the Four Traditions.

Robert and Tricot, *Guide to the Bible*, Vol. II, pp. 247-248. Discusses the Tahmud.

Sullivan, *God's Word and Work*, pp. 41-50. Treats the typology in the Old Testament.

Chapter XIX

Josue and Ruth: *Herem* and the Role of the Gentiles

READINGS: *Josue 1–3, 6–8, 22, 24; Ruth 1–4; Wisdom 12; Psalms 86, 108 (Note: Josue 6:17; 10:13; 18:1, 7; 22:29; 24:2; Ruth 2:4; 4:17; Wisdom 12:10)*

The Book of Josue begins at the point where Deuteronomy left off, with the Israelites drawn up on the eastern bank of the Jordan across from Jericho, ready to storm that ill-fated city. As one begins reading the first chapter, he is inclined to agree, perhaps, with certain exegetes who maintain that Josue is the sixth book of a "Hexateuch"—i.e., that it is simply a continuation of the four Mosaic traditions. The vibrant theme of the Deuteronomic editors rings in his ears as he reads the magic success formula contained in the Lord's words to Josue in verses 5-8:

> No one can withstand you while you live. I will be with you as I was with Moses: I will not leave you nor forsake you. Be firm and steadfast, so that you may give this people possession of the land which I swore to their fathers I would give them. Above all, be firm and steadfast, taking care to observe the entire Law which my servant Moses enjoined on you. Do not swerve from it either to the right or the left, that you may succeed wherever you go. Keep this Book of the Law on your lips. (Cf. also Jos. 23:10 ff.)

However, subsequent chapters soon reveal to the careful reader that Josue is a complex book with its own distinct sources, and that the "Deuteronomic ring" results from the fact that those editors gave the book its final form.[1] Hence, Josue continues the theology of history theme; in fact, this theme runs through Judges and the four Books of Kings. Thereupon a new editor enters the scene. He is the Chronicler; his editorship extends to I-II Paralipomenon and I-II Esdras. His interpretation of history is even more penetrating than the Deuteronomic editors as he tries to view all events from the divine perspective — especially the permanence of the Davidic dynasty. Most of the "historical" books can be put into three categories:

---

[1] Cf. Joseph De Vault, *The Book of Josue*, pp. 5 ff.

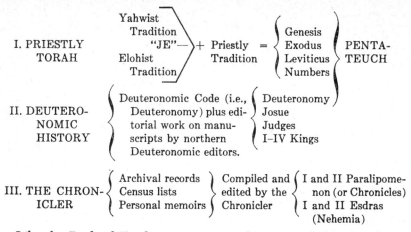

Like the Book of Exodus, some parts of Josue probably date back to the period in question. Scholars are fairly well agreed today that most of this book found its way into writing between the years 1000 and 600 B. C. Moses himself had commissioned Josue (also written "Jesus" and "Osee"; the word means "Savior") during the sojourn in the desert (Num. 27:22-23). His first step is to send ahead two spies to reconnoiter the land surrounding Jericho. Through the aid of a pagan prostitute, Rahab, their mission is successful. It is evident from the words of this convert-to-Yahweh in Josue 2:9 that a sense of doom has settled over the Chanaanites. With the Ark of the Covenant carried by Levites at the head of the procession, the Jordan River behaves much as the Red Sea did during the Exodus; perhaps a miraculous landslide dammed up the water. Chapter 4 betrays the continued presence of a multiplicity of traditions; most of the details recounted in Chapter 3 are repeated. We learn in Chapter 5 that the rite of circumcision had been neglected in the desert; the term "for the second time" in verse 2 is a euphemism.

Capture of Jericho

The fall of Jericho seems to be a foregone conclusion. The magic formula laid down by Yahweh (people with Ark marching around the city for six successive days) is followed, and Jericho falls on the seventh day after the seventh encirclement. The fact that Yahweh may have used an earthquake as a secondary cause in no way detracts from the supernatural element present. In accordance with the terms of the "Lord's ban" (6:17), every man, woman and beast is slaughtered and all the booty is destroyed. By way of exception, Rahab and her family are spared in fulfillment of the spies' oath to her. Here we have a fore-shadowing of the role of the Gentiles in God's economy of salvation. Not only is this reformed prostitute praised by New Testament authors (cf. Jas. 2:25; Heb. 11:31) for her faith and piety, but she actually enters into the family tree of Christ through her marriage to Salmon (cf. Matt. 1:5).

The Problem of Herem

The destruction of innocent people by the Israelites at the command of Yahweh creates a genuine biblical problem. This practice is known as *herem.* Originally the word meant the setting aside of something from profane use — also called "dooming." As adopted by the Jews, it meant the slaughtering of all living creatures and the dedication of inanimate goods to worship or else to destruction. Because of the repugnance of this practice to the modern mind, some exegetes attempt to explain it on the grounds that Yahweh did not actually order this procedure; rather, it was imputed to Him by the primitive Israelite community (cf. Deut. 20:16-17; Jos. 8:2), who attributed whatever was done by the Chosen People to Yahweh Himself, bypassing secondary causes.[2] I believe, however, that the older explanation is more consistent with the concept of biblical inspiration, viz., that Yahweh DID command the elimination of these pagans, for the reason given in Deuteronomy 20:18; they would be a proximate occasion of sin to the Israelites if they remained alive and among them. Certainly this command would be within God's province, as He possesses absolute dominion over life and death (cf. the case of Isaac), and His Providence is able to harmonize the scales of justice in the next life.[3] Scripture makes it clear that such casualties among the Chanaanites were used by Yahweh to punish them for their sins—e. g., Deuteronomy 9:4. Hence, while I feel that the undeveloped state of morality among the Israelites may well explain why this policy was followed by Yahweh, there seems to be no sufficient reason to disclaim divine responsibility in the matter.

A Digression: Psalm 108—An Imprecatory Psalm of Lament

In basically the same manner we can analyze that type of psalm known as "imprecatory" or "maledictory"; e. g., Psalms 34, 68, 108. In addition to the explanation given above for the practice of *herem,* the following points must be kept in mind to provide an understanding of the presence of what amounts almost to curses in these inspired poems:

a) We must remember that Semitic people tend toward a concrete frame of mind; hence they found it difficult to distinguish between the sin and the sinner—as even we speculative-minded Westerners often do.

---

[2] Cf. De Vault, *Op cit.*, p. 15.
[3] This is basically R. A. F. MacKenzie's approach in: Orchard, *A Catholic Commentary on Holy Scripture*, col. 211g.

b) The psalmist—like Josue—did not speak as a private person, but rather as a representative of Yahweh and under His inspiration. His cause was Yahweh's cause.

c) Hence, the vindication of God's justice was always primary, not the extermination or punishment of human beings.

d) In the case of the Psalms, especially, hyperbole and other poetic licenses are often present. Many times the dire threats of evil are predictions, not wishes: the Psalmist was enabled to see what was actually going to happen—unpleasant though it was.[4]

Imprecatory psalms do not constitute a special class by themselves; they are a division of Psalms of Lament, discussed on page 53. We shall consider Psalm 108, the date and author of which are unknown. Consult the footnotes in the Confraternity Version of the Bible.[5]

vv. 1-5: This is a statement of the psalmist's appeal to Yahweh for help against what seems to be a group of foes.

6-15: Here begins the special request of the psalmist, who singles out a specific individual for punishment because of the latter's malice toward him. The list of woes heaped upon the head of this enemy are merciless, and some scholars believe that this section may represent a quotation of the foe rather than of the psalmist himself. Verses 18-21 resume his request.

16-17: The psalmist interrupts his request to present his complaint against his enemy; verses 22-25 are a continuation of the complaint.

26-31: Returning to the theme of his appeal, the psalmist ends on a note of confidence.

The Hai Incident: Violation of the Ban

If compliance with the will of Yahweh spells success, failure to do it His way brings failure. This principle is amply illustrated in the capture of the city of Hai. When the Israelites fail to conquer this next outpost and are roundly defeated, they "consult the Lord" at the Meeting Tent. Under His direction (Urim and Thummin?) the cause of the set-back is uncovered: an Israelite named Achan has violated the ban by holding out some booty. The anger of the Lord relents only after the guilty individual, together with his family and livestock, has been stoned (the ordinary method of execution among the Jews). After that the capture of Hai was easy. Josue 8:31 describes the care with which Josue follows the prescriptions of the Torah. The end of the chapter notes the fulfillment of Deuteronomy 11:29. The deception of the Jews by the Gabaonites in Chapter 9 is a notable example of "failure to consult the

---

[4] Cf. Callan, *The New Psalter*, pp. 108; 389-395.

[5] *The Holy Bible*, Confraternity Version (New York: Benziger Bros., 1961).

Lord." In the battle occasioned by the siege of Gabaon, the footnote in the Confraternity Version gives an up-to-date explanation of the famous "arresting of the sun" by Josue: it is more likely that the sunlight was obscured than that it was prolonged.

The Division of Palestine Among the Twelve Tribes

Chapters 13-17 contain a tedious account of the portioning out of Chanaan to the various tribes. Ruben and Gad presented the least problem; they had already received their "heritage" east of the Jordan. Manasse had received part of a share in the same area, with more to come on the west side; hence the term "half-tribe of Manasse" (13:7). This tribe, together with Juda and Ephraim, were the first to draw lots for their official handout; they seem to have forced the issue with Josue (cf. 14:12 and 17:14). After noting the location of the Ark of the Covenant at Silo (v. 1), Chapter 18 hints at the reason why the other seven tribes had failed to receive any land (v. 3). This rebuke seems finally to have stirred them into action. Nor are we to conclude from the optimistic picture painted in the first twelve chapters that the conquest of Chanaan is now an accomplished fact; Judges 1 assures us to the contrary. In the meantime, certain cities were designated for residence by the Levites (Chap. 21).

The apparently effortless seizure of the central hilly section of Palestine poses a first-class problem. When and how did the Israelites conquer this important territory, later known as Samaria? There is no record, for example, of any struggle for the city of Sichem where Josue held the covenant-renewal ceremony in Chapter 24. Modern exegetes propose an intriguing solution: this area may have been occupied by kinsmen of the Jews — descendants of Abraham, Isaac, or even Jacob — who never went down into Egypt and managed to ride out the famine.[6] At the same time, the Israelites did not by any means drive out, much less kill, all of the Chanaanite population living in the territories which they did conquer (cf. 15:63, 16:10, 17:13). Yahweh was tolerant, but still His people would have to pay for their neglect in this matter.

The Near-Schism Over the Rival Altar: Unity of Sanctuary

That the law of unity of sanctuary (Deut. 12) was taken seriously at this time, in spite of rather frequent sacrifices in unofficial ("high") places, is evident from the striking episode narrated in Chapter 22.

---

[6] B. W. Anderson discusses this line of thought in *Understanding the Old Testament,* pp. 84-90, suggesting that perhaps these friendly kinsmen were incorporated into the Israelite community on the occasion of the covenant-renewal. Cf. also pp. 56-57.

When the two and one-half Eastern tribes were dismissed with the euphemistic statement in verse 4, they proceeded to set up a large altar on their side of the Jordan, visible to the other nine and one-half Tribes. Now, for the Israelites any sort of religious schism was bound to produce political schism as well: they were a close-knit theocracy. Thus, we can understand the consternation of the majority who worshipped at the central sanctuary of Silo, and their readiness to go to war over the incident. The story has a happy ending, however, when the minority group justifies their action on the grounds that their altar is to serve merely as a model of the one at Silo, not as a rival place of worship.

The Covenant-Renewal at Sichem

Another noteworthy contribution of contemporary biblical scholarship has been the discovery of ancient treaties in use among Semitic peoples, particularly the Hittites. What interests us here is the suzerainty treaty customary between lord and vassal — matched almost to the letter in the ceremony described in Chapter 24. This important episode may have been the formation of the Tribal Confederacy; at any rate, it seems to have set a pattern of religious renewal for posterity. At the command of the aging Josue, the twelve Tribes gathered at Sichem to pledge their allegiance to Yahweh. The ritual consisted of the following steps, paralleling Hittite custom:

1) The naming of the sovereign to whom fealty is being pledged: Yahweh (v. 2).
2) A reminder of all of His benefactions to His Chosen People — especially the Exodus (2-13).
3) A statement of the "vassal's" obligations: in this case, a rejection of the false gods of Thare and of the Amorrites, etc., in favor of Yahweh's service (14-15).
4) Declaration by the vassals of their firm decision to abide by their part of the agreement (16-18; 21).
5) A warning of the sanctions to be imposed in case of failure to live up to all of their obligations (19-20).
6) A recording and depositing of the deed (25-26).
7) Calling of witnesses: in this case, the people themselves (22) and the stone (26-27).

Later on the Greeks were to coin a word for this primarily religious tribal union around a central shrine, imposing on the tribes involved the obligation of defending the shrine and supporting it: *amphictyony*. It can be seen already that the Tribal Confederacy of Josue, though loosely organized politically, constituted a religious totalitarianism. The whole Israelite community and each individual within it were directly answerable to Yahweh for their deeds. Their lives, their fortunes, their destiny, and now even their government were incorporated into the field of worship. Here is another milestone in the divine economy of salvation at the theocratic level.

The Book of Ruth: Great-Grandmother of David

We have seen in connection with the practice of *herem* that non-Jewish peoples (Gentiles) played a distinctly subordinate role to the Israelites. In fact, we may even be inclined to conclude that Yahweh was indifferent to the salvation of the Gentiles unless we recall Exodus 22:20 and parallel texts. A careful reading of Deuteronomy 20:10-18 reveals that only the Chanaanites (since they would constitute a proximate occasion of idolatry to the Jews) were to be "doomed"; pagans in distant areas were not to be put to death unless they resisted the Israelite army. The story of Ruth (which we are considering prior to Judges, the period during which the events actually took place) helps to fill in the positive aspect of the ambivalent role of the Gentiles. The account is simply told and is not hard to follow. By presenting a picture of a Moabite (pagan) widow who enters into not only the Jewish community, but — like Rahab — into the messianic line, this story insinuates that Gentiles are not therefore to be written off the list of predestined souls. The precise relationship of Ruth to David through her Levirate marriage to Booz can be seen in the genealogy on page 90. St. Matthew makes a special point of including pagan women in his genealogy (1:1-6). Unfortunately, the author of the Book of Ruth is unknown; modern scholars prefer a post-Exilic date.

God's Mercy Towards the Chanaanites
(Wisdom 12)

We have already tapped the precious insights contained in the Book of Wisdom, Chapters 11 and 13-19. Another such insight is furnished us regarding the personal fate of the doomed Chanaanites. The universalist viewpoint of the inspired Jewish author assures us that even these pagans were the object of God's mercy: "condemning them bit by bit, you gave them space for repentance" (12:10). At the same time, we are assured that the Chosen People — partners in a bilateral treaty with Yahweh — are subject to more severe punishments for their violations of the Covenant:

> For these were enemies of your servants, doomed to death; yet, while you punished them with such solicitude and pleading, granting time and opportunity to abandon wickedness, with what exactitude you judged your sons, to whose fathers you gave the sworn covenant of goodly promises! (12:20-21)

Psalm 86: Sion, Mother of All Peoples

The theme of Ruth is not an isolated instance in the Old Testament; even the Psalms clearly reflect the inclusion of Gentiles in salvation history. Technically, Psalm 86 is a "Song of Sion" — a poem glorifying Jerusalem; putting it into one of our standard categories is difficult, but it seems to fit best with Psalms of Yahweh's Kingship (cf. p. 106). Reflecting the author's inspired insight into the non-temporal destiny of Judaism following the Exile and destruction of the Temple, this psalm pictures Sion (Jerusalem) as the spiritual mother of all peoples (cf. Psalm 116).

Suggested Readings

Anderson, *Understanding the Old Testament,* pp. 56-57; 72; 78-91; 434-435.
De Vault, *The Book of Josue* (Pamphlet Bible Series, No. 11).
Moriarty, *Introducing the Old Testament,* pp. 44-57.
Sullivan, *God's Word and Work,* pp. 51-61.

Chapter XX

Period of the Judges:
From Deliverer to Prophet

READINGS: *Judges 2–8, 11–13, 16; I Kings 1, 2 (Canticle of Anna),*
3–4, 8–9 (Note: Judges 2:11–19; 8:23; 21:25; I Kings 8:7)

The First Twelve Judges, Othoniel to Samson

(Book of Judges)

The obscurity of authorship and date characteristic of Josue carries over into the Book of Judges, which shows unmistakable evidence of double editorship. Judges 1:1-2:5 were added on by the second editor, together with the last four chapters, in order to show the unsettled conditions of the land. These passages clearly indicate that Josue 11:23 is another case of restricted universality and that many more battles remained to be fought for possession of Chanaan. The original author's preface is contained in 2:6-9. Almost identical with Josue 24:28-31, these verses mark the continuation of Deuteronomic history. Some portions of this section are no doubt firsthand accounts—such as the Canticle of Debora in Chapter 5; other portions were written during the period of the kings. Even the preface and appendix of the second editor are probably pre-Exilic, though this conclusion is not certain.

The Book of Judges presents us with a picture of the dark days of the Tribal Confederacy. The pattern is clearly laid out in 2:10-19: *sin* (lapsing into idolatry); *punishment* (as Yahweh permits his people to fall into the hands of their enemies); *repentance;* then *deliverance* (as Yahweh raises up a strong-arm man to lead them in a successful rebellion). Twelve of these charismatic leaders through whom Yahweh intervened in favor of His people at strategic moments of history are described in the Book of Judges: Othoniel, Aod, Samgar, Debora-Barac, Gedeon, Thola, Jair, Jephte, Abesan, Elon, Abdon, Samson. The last two judges, Heli and Samuel, are described in the First Book of Kings. Usually little more than local military captains aided by divine power, they were seldom judges in the strict sense of dispensers of justice in common lawsuits. As each judge died, there would be a relapse into idolatry and the cycle would be repeated.

The first judge, Othoniel, was of the Tribe of Juda, and he delivered the Israelites from the obligation of paying tribute to the King of Aram. Aod, the next judge, resorted to trickery to eliminate Eglon, King of Moab. The only significance to be attached to his left-handedness seems to lie in the fact that this factor furthered his plan, since the average man would not be expected to carry a dagger on his right thigh. The hero of Chapter 4 is actually Debora, the fourth judge, though Barac shares some of the honor. Debora was a genuine "judge," dispensing justice from under a palm tree. Through her inspiration and Barac's military leadership, Israel was liberated from the Chanaanite king, Jabin, and his general, Sisara. Another woman, Jahel, figures in the account because of her astute execution of the fleeing Sisara with a tent peg. Presumed by him to be neutral in the conflict, she opts in favor of the Israelite cause.

Although Debora's Canticle in Chapter 5 is a repetition of the events of the previous chapter, it deserves notice as one of the oldest extant pieces of Semitic poetry, along with the Canticle of Moses (Ex. 15) and that of Anna (I Kgs. 2). It sounds very much like a victory march and has the earmarks of an eyewitness account. The Confraternity Version explains the few difficult passages. Verse 8 is explained not only by the military laxity of the Israelites, but also by the fact that at this period the Philistines held a monopoly on iron (cf. Jgs. 1:19; I Kgs. 13:19-22).

Gedeon, the fifth judge, had become skeptical of divine assistance in the wake of Madianite incursions, which had reduced southern Palestine almost to starvation. It took three signs on the part of the angelic visitor to convince him that Yahweh's call had fallen upon him. His subsequent defeat of the Madianites in Chapter 7 is a pointed exemplification of the Deuteronomic theme: when you do it God's way, the odds against you are unimportant. Deliberately cutting down the Jewish fighting men to 300 by choosing only those who lapped up water with their hands rather than by putting their mouths into the stream, Yahweh illustrated unmistakably the true source of Israelite success. The story also reveals the loose organization of the Tribal Confederacy.

In 8:22-23 Gedeon rises to truly noble heights in his rejection of kingship in favor of the theocracy. Yet, in the very next paragraph he gets himself into trouble. The ephod that he manufactured from the gold was probably similar to the Urim and the Thummin; no doubt Gedeon made it in good faith, and Yahweh would seemingly have tolerated it if the Israelites had not shown it idolatrous worship. But "it caused the ruin of Gedeon and his family" (v. 27). Again we have an example of how proximate to sin was the manufacture of any graven image or device by the Israelites. As a sequel to Gedeon's story, we are presented in Chapter 9 with an attempt by one of his lowborn sons, Abimelech, to make himself king—and thereby turn the theocracy into a monarchy. The coup was finally thwarted by his youngest brother, who alone had escaped Abimelech's fratricidal purge. One of the interesting features of this account is the fable of the trees (9:7ff.). The whole story illustrates how widespread polygamy was during the period. Gedeon, a decent man, had fathered seventy sons.

The controversial figure of Jephte next steals our attention. His sad family background had made him a juvenile delinquent, marauding the countryside with his gang. Yet, when the Galaadites were oppressed by the Ammonites, they called upon him to lead them in battle. Jephte's simple but crude moral sense manifests itself in a rash vow: he promises the Lord a human sacrifice (the first person who shall meet him upon his return) if he is successful. His word given, he considered it irrevocable—even though it is his only daughter who joyously comes out to salute him after the victory. Her request to mourn her virginity in a mountain seclusion underscores the Semitic concept of the essential role of woman in society. The Shibboleth incident in Chapter 12 indicates not only the existence of different dialects in Israel, but also the sensitiveness of the Ephraimites (Josue's tribe; cf. also 8:1-3).

The story of Samson covers four chapters. Two of them are highly legendary. This does not mean that they are untrue; here imagination is added to fact to illustrate a point: Samson's great strength, as well as his fatal weakness for women and his otherwise impetuous character. His strength lay in his Nazarite vow, made in accordance with the instructions of the angel who had announced his forthcoming birth to his mother (cf. Num. 6). The pivotal factor in the observance of the vow was to let one's hair grow. Although he should have learned from his divorced wife's betrayal of confidence that Philistine women were not to be trusted, he foolishly reveals his vow to his nagging Philistine paramour, Dalila. She arranges a haircut for him while he sleeps and his strength departs, leaving him a victim of his enemies' vengeance. Though man defects, Yahweh remains faithful, sometimes even to stupid, blundering souls such as Samson. His hair having grown back, he is endowed with the final burst of strength needed to pull down the crowded temple in which his buffoonery had been entertaining the Philistines. And so the Strong Man died a hero, killing more of the enemy "at his death than he had killed during his lifetime" (16:30).

Two unflattering episodes close the Book of Judges by way of the second editor's appendix. The idolatry practiced by the Tribe of Dan is exposed, along with their ruthless violence against Micha and the citizens of Lais (cf. Gen. 49:17 and Deut. 33:22). In the other episode, the Benjaminites are nearly wiped out by the other eleven tribes for repeating the crime of sodomy. The last verse of the Book of Judges sums up the tenor of the times: "In those days there was no king in Israel; everyone did what he thought best."

Heli and Samuel, The Last Two Judges
(I Kings 1-9)

The story of the Judges overflows into the First Book of Kings, as does also the Deuteronomic history (cf. p. 146). Scholars today agree that the four Books of Kings contain much contemporary material, although the final editing took place some time between the split in the Kingdom and the Exile of 587. With the founding of the Kingdom under Saul and especially after David's accession to the throne, new sources became available to the sacred authors in the form of archival records and census lists. Historic events are recorded with much greater precision, numbers become more reliable—though we must ever beware of Hebrew statistics! A familiar scene greets us as we begin I Kings: a childless woman, Anna, wife of Elcana, praying for a cure of her sterility. Her prayer at the site of the Ark in Silo in the presence of the priest and judge, Heli, is heard by Yahweh and a son is born to her. Named Samuel, the boy is deposited in the "temple" (priestly quarters in the precinct of the Ark) in fulfillment of Anna's vow to make him a Nazarite.

The Tribal Confederacy is evidently at low ebb, and the Philistines are on the rampage again. The Deuteronomist editor offers a reason (2:12ff.): the two sons of Heli, Ophni and Phinees, are profaning the priesthood by their irregular conduct, and their father fails to correct them efficaciously (3:13). Yahweh's plans now center around the youthful Samuel, a promising lad, who responds immediately to His call. Being a descendant of Levi (but not of Aaron: cf. I Par. 6:33-38), he was qualified to "minister before the face of the Lord" (2:17-18) to Whom he was as pleasing as the wicked sons of Heli were odious. Punishment for his over-indulgence toward Ophni and Phinees is meted out to the aging judge in Chapter 5 in the form of a triple tragedy: the loss of the Ark to the Philistines after the Israelites had taken it into battle with them; the death of his evil sons as they attend the Ark; and the subsequent death of Heli himself when he hears the bad news about the Ark.

Although the Ark brought no comfort to the Israelites in the decisive Philistine victory which apparently resulted in the destruction of Silo, it brought a peck of trouble to their enemies. Probably the crime of the Israelites was a brazen reliance on the material presence of the Ark without due reverence and change of heart; at any rate, the Philistines returned the sacred treasure which had boomeranged on them and had brought seven months of terror. The "slaughter" of the seventy Beth-samites (the figure 50,000 is probably a gloss) is attributed to their irreverent staring at the Ark.[1] It was then decided to send the Ark to the town of Cariathiarim to the private home of the Levite Abinadab, where it remained neglected for twenty years. Samuel's exhortations to the people on this occasion produced a genuine reform, and the Isra-elites were able to rout the Philistines with the aid of a miraculous thunder (7:10).

Samuel and Prophecy in Israel

From the account of Samuel's deeds thus far it is evident that he was superior to all previous judges. He has become judge of the whole of Israel permanently, not just in a single crisis, a prerogative which no one had enjoyed until the time of Heli. He moved about the three cities of Bethel, Galgal and Masphath not only judging, but also offering sac-rifice—a privilege exercised during this era by mere Levites, at least in the absence of an Aaronite.[2] Samuel thus emerges as the greatest spiritual leader of Israel since the time of Moses. The truth is that Samuel was more than a judge; he was a prophet, and he lived at a time when prophecy became a prominent institution in the land. There had been isolated prophets: Moses, Aaron, Debora, and the unnamed "man of God" in I Kings 2:27; but now we begin to read about "com-panies" and "schools" of prophets (cf. 10:10). In fact, we are even told by one tradition that the term "prophet" replaced the older designation "seer" at this period (9:9).

A prophet is basically "one who speaks for another," not necessarily one who foretells the future. It is in this sense that Aaron was Moses' "prophet" (Ex. 7:1). A prophet did not have to be a Levite, nor did his office qualify him to offer sacrifice; all he needed was a commission from God plus a divine communication intended for others (e. g., Isa. 6). This communication could be given in the form of 1) an *external* vision (Moses and the burning bush); 2) an *internal, imaginative* vi-sion (Amos 6-8), including dreams; 3) an *internal, intellectual* vision

---

[1] Both the Septuagint and the Smith-Goodspeed English edition, *The Com-plete Bible* (University of Chicago Press, 1931) give a different reason: "The sons of Jeconiah, however, did not rejoice with the men of Bethshemesh, when they looked upon the ark of the Lord. Therefore he smote among them seventy men ... " (cf. Num. 4:20).

[2] The Micha episode in Judges 17-18 illustrates the practice of the Levitical clan at this period. With regard to unity of sanctuary, apparently Deut. 12:8-9, not 12:10-11, was still applicable.

(II Cor. 12:2), which often involves a trance. Sometimes a trance came over the "sons" (associates) of the prophets, so that they spoke and acted enthusiastically under divine impulse. The royal charter of prophecy is Deuteronomy 18:9-22, where it is foretold that one of the marks of the promised Messia will be his prophetic character (v. 15). The principal task of the prophet was to condemn evil customs (idolatry, social injustice, etc.) by urging a return to the spirit of the law, to warn men of the consequences of their wickedness, and occasionally to predict the future—especially the messianic age. As God's spokesmen, they ranked above even priests and kings—as we shall see in the case of Saul vs. Samuel. It was the latter's privilege to anoint two kings. That the Jews themselves understood the role of the prophet as an interpreter of the mind of Yahweh is manifest from the traditional division of the Hebrew Bible. Note the listing of Josue, Judges, I-II Samuel and I-II Kings under the category of "Prophets," and, on the other hand, Ruth, Daniel and I-II Chronicles (Paralipomenon) as "Writings":

I. THE LAW (Torah)	II. THE PROPHETS (Nebi'im)		III. THE WRITINGS (Kethubim)	
Genesis	Former Prophets	Joshua	Psalms	
Exodus		Judges	Job	
Leviticus		I–II Samuel	Proverbs	
Numbers		I–II Kings	Festal Scrolls	Ruth—Pentecost
Deuteronomy				Song of Songs—Pasch
	Latter Prophets	Isaiah		Ecclesiastes—Tabernacles
		Jeremiah		Lamentations—Mourning
		Ezekiel		Day
		The Twelve		Esther—Purim
		Minor	Daniel	
		Prophets	Ezra—Nehemiah	
			I–II Chronicles	

Samuel's greatest feat, however, was precipitated by the people's request for a king in Chapter 8. Having unified the Tribes in their common offensive against the Philistines, his final contribution to the Confederacy was the skillful transition from charismatic leadership to kingship—especially in view of Yahweh's complaint in 8:7. But this will be taken up in the next chapter.

The Canticle of Anna (I Kings 2)—The "Magnificat of the Old Testament"

(Cf. Luke 1:46)

Note the striking similarity between Anna's prayer of thanksgiving for the birth of Samuel and the Blessed Virgin Mary's *Magnificat*, especially verses 1, 4, 5, 7, 8.

Suggested Readings

Anderson, *Understanding the Old Testament,* pp. 92-121.
Bouyer, *The Meaning of Sacred Scripture,* Chap. 4.
Dyson and Jones, *The Kingdom of Promise,* pp. 31-48. Excellent for prophecy.
King, *The Book of Judges* (Pamphlet Bible Series, No. 12).

Saul vs. David: Kingship in Israel

READINGS: *I Kings 10, 12, 15–16, 18, 28, 31; II Kings 3, 6–7, 11–12, 15, 22 (= Ps. 17); Psalms 15, 23, 50, 100, 109, 131. (Note: I Kings 10:8; 15:22; II Kings 7:12–13; Psalm 131:11–12, 17)*

At the end of the last chapter it was noted how Samuel's attitude toward a monarchy seemed to undergo a change in I Kings 9 as he enthusiastically went about the task of discovering Yahweh's choice for the position of king. The same zeal is manifested in the first half of Chapter 10 as he secretly anoints Saul. A casting of lots confirms God's previous choice, and the already-anointed sovereign has to be brought out from hiding, for he was a reserved and simple individual. Samuel proclaims the worth of the man whom God has chosen, and the majority of the populace joyfully accept him as their king (but see v. 27 and its sequel in 11:12-13). All is rejoicing as Saul rallies the fighting men of Israel in a decisive victory over the Ammonites. But Chapter 12 reverts to the rejection-of-Yahweh theme, and ends with another solemn renewal of the Covenant similar to Exodus 24 and 34, Deuteronomy 27 and Josue 24.

Biblical scholars point out that there are two different sources involved here: one pro-monarchical (Benjaminite?): 9:1-10:16, 11; the other (Deuteronomical) anti-monarchical: 7, 8, 10:17-27, 12. But the truth transcends this material consideration, valid as it probably is. As happens in many instances, the inspired incorporation of more than one version of an incident into the sacred text permits the Divine Author to convey the ambivalent character of a delicate situation. The request for a king was just such an instance: it was a rejection of Yahweh insofar as it adulterated the theocracy by bringing an intermediary between God and His people; yet, it was not only a political necessity, but also part of God's over-all plan in the progress of salvation history. Samuel's inspired hesitation and sourness at the demand for a king even after he had already compromised to the extent of making his own (unworthy) sons hereditary judges indicates the pejorative aspects of royalty. The people's "crime" is revealed in 8:20: they desire to have a king "like the nations" (Gentiles), for whom kingship represented an incarnation of the rule of the gods. All too often pagan sovereigns assumed divine prerogatives; compare 8:11-19 with Deuteronomy 17:14.

Saul's False Idea of Kingship

(I Kings)

For a time Saul seemed to justify the people's hopes. He was tall, rugged and handsome, capable of rallying his countrymen and leading them in battle. The Spirit of Yahweh had made him a "changed man" (10:6). Nature, however, had endowed him with a melancholic disposition; moreover, he was impetuous and self-willed. His first crime of offering a holocaust when he, neither a priest nor a Levite, had been expressly told by Samuel to wait for his arrival at Galgal, might have been forgiven (cf. 10:8 and 13:9, 13). But when he repeated his disobedience in failing to kill Agag and to destroy the choice booty under the pretext of using it for sacrifices, Yahweh's decree was final: his dynasty would end with himself (15:20-23). He had sinned against the theocracy; by refusing to be obedient to Yahweh's will as relayed to him by the prophet, Samuel, Saul had snatched at absolute monarchy after the fashion of the pagans. Like Adam and Eve and the builders of Babel—and like Moses who deflected an opportunity of manifesting Yahweh's power into a venting of his own irritation at the waters of Meriba—Israel's first King tried to make her glory the product of merely human endeavor in refusing to serve as Yahweh's instrument.

After the sad parting of Samuel from Saul (cf. 15:35), the prophet anoints David secretly as Saul's successor. Again it is Yahweh Who makes the choice—not hereditary genes (16:7). Later events were to prove that David's character matched the comely appearance of this youngest son of Isai (Jesse) and great-grandson of Ruth. Ironically, when Saul seeks someone to soothe his melancholic spirit by playing the harp in his presence, the choice falls on David! Saul's ailment has the earmarks of both a nervous breakdown and diabolical possession. The well-known feat of the slaying of the ten-foot Philistine champion, Goliath (a descendant of the Enacim of Num. 13:22?) illustrates David's profound faith (17:47), but the episode also alienates him from Saul (cf. 18:7-8). From that time on David was forced to roam about Palestine as a fugitive from the king's anger.

David's maneuvers in escaping from Saul were not without adventure. His hospitable reception by the priests of the line of Heli at Nobe occasions their slaughter by Saul—with the sole exception of Abiathar, who aligns himself with David. After saving the city of Ceila from the

Philistines, David and his men are forced to flee because of their beneficiaries' ingratitude. The Philistine King of Geth, Achis (Abimelech) refuses to receive him upon hearing of his former exploits against his countrymen, and David feigns madness in order to escape from him. The fugitive's one consolation during these trying days is the friendship of Jonathan, who visits him and again promises loyalty, even though he is aware that David is to supplant him on the throne of Israel. On two occasions the king-elect spares the life of him whom he recognizes as the "Lord's anointed," and each time Saul's gratitude is extremely short-lived. On one of his adventures, David acquires another wife, Abigail, widow of the hostile Nabal. Seeking refuge a second time among the Philistines, David is well received by Achis and is incorporated into his army, together with his followers. Providentially, he is saved from having to fight against Saul and his own people when the other Philistine princes refuse to let him join with them in the showdown with Saul.

In the meantime, Samuel has died. As the battle waxes furiously against the Israelites, Saul's morale—never too firm since his estrangement from the great prophet—cracks completely. Unable to obtain a response from Yahweh "by dreams, nor by priests, nor by prophets" (28:6), Saul is reduced to consulting one of the few mediums who had escaped his purge made in conformity with Exodus 22:17. His disguise is effective until the seance begins and this Witch of Endor realizes that it is the king who sits before her. By divine permission, the spirit of Samuel is "brought up" at the request of Saul; but instead of encouragement, the wretched king receives a dark prognostication: Samuel foretells the fateful events of the morrow. And so it comes about. The Philistines not only routed the Jews, but slew two sons of Saul, who falls on his own sword in despair, being mortally wounded by the enemy.

David, The Ideal King

(II Kings)

The Deuteronomic history continues uninterruptedly with the story of Israel's second King. At this point it would be well to note the correlation which exists between the four Books of Kings and the two Books of Paralipomenon. The latter books, as indicated in the previous chapter, represent a different tradition: that of the Chronicler. Nevertheless, these two books parallel events in the Four Books of Kings quite closely, and offer even more penetrating theological interpretations of the events recounted. Stressing heavily the Davidic dynasty, I and II Paralipomenon tend to omit episodes unfavorable thereto—e.g.,

David's sin of adultery. The following table will illustrate the correlation referred to, and give a few examples of the Chronicler's "insights":

		Chronicler's interpretations:
I KINGS: The reign of Saul II KINGS: The reign of David	I PARALIPOMENON	Two sins of Saul (10:13) Reason behind Oza's death (15:2, 13) The sinful census (21:1)
III KINGS: The reign of Solomon IV KINGS: Fall of Israel and Juda	II PARALIPOMENON	Reason for Sesac's invasion (12:2) Asa's sins (16:7–10; 12) Josia's untimely death (35:21–22)

Instead of rejoicing over the death of his bitter enemy and persecutor, David mourns sincerely over the untimely end of Saul and Jonathan. His greatness of soul is again manifested in his order that the Amalecite messenger be put to death when he claims (falsely, it turns out) to have struck the fatal blow against "the Lord's anointed." The poem composed by David on this occasion (1:18-27) illustrates his exquisite literary ability and reaffirms his undying love for Jonathan. Chapter 3 gives a picture of David's complex marital status (vv. 2-5) and summarizes the political condition of Israel after Saul's death. Only Juda has rallied to the side of David; the other eleven tribes cast their lot with the house of Saul in the person of his spineless heir, Isboseth. The schism lasts for seven and one-half years until finally Abner, who had been Saul's general and was the real power behind Isboseth, changes his loyalty. Smarting under a rebuke from the latter and observing David's growing popularity, Abner makes a pact with the King of Juda—only to be struck down treacherously by the violent Joab, David's nephew and commander of his army. Shortly after this, Isboseth is likewise murdered. Once more David manifests his political astuteness in mourning their deaths, executing Isboseth's killers, and demanding back his wife Michol, "the daughter of Saul" (3:13). He is now anointed king of all Israel.

Let us turn at this point to another phase of King David's career: that of psalmist. Of the 150 psalms in the Psalter, seventy-three are attributed to David in the Massoretic text, and fourteen more are attributed to him in the Septuagint. This ascription of the lion's share to the Poet-King agrees with constant Judeo-Christian tradition; moreover, the Biblical Commission has declared not only that this tradition cannot be prudently denied, but also that it would be imprudent to deny the Davidic authorship of certain individual psalms cited under his name in the Old or New Testaments (e. g., 2, 15, 17, 31, 68, 109; cf. *A Catholic Commentary on Holy Scripture*, col. 49a-f). Not only does Scripture refer to him as "the excellent psalmist of Israel" (2 Kgs. 23:1), but we may even work out a fairly complete biography of him from those psalms attributed to him. Apparently he began to compose these poems while he was quite young; several are assigned to the period of his persecution by Saul: Psalm 58 (while hiding in his own house), Psalm 51 (with the priests at Nobe), Psalm 55 (while seeking refuge with the King of Geth), Psalm 53 (among the Ziphites), and Psalms 56 and 141 (hiding from Saul in a cave). Other psalms give us glimpses of his later life, which we shall follow in conjunction with those psalms assigned in this chapter.

Psalm 100. At the outset, David set forth his "platform" of administration, if we may rely on the title of Psalm 100, ascribed to him. His resolutions reflect the policy of an ideal monarch: he intends to set a good example by a spotless life (vv. 1-2); he will shun all unjust and deceitful men (vv. 3-5); his ministers will be selected from the tried and the true (v. 6); he will purge the kingdom of all evil men (vv. 7-8). Had David only followed this program perfectly in treating all rebels with a firmer hand, his reign would have been much more peaceful (e. g., Joab, Absalom).

Psalm 23. David's first concern after subduing the Philistines is to transfer the Ark of the Covenant, neglected for twenty years in the house of Abinadab, to Jerusalem. Having captured this city from the Jebusites, he had decided to make it his extra-tribal capital. But the actual transfer of the Ark is interrupted by the formidable death of Oza. Although a Levite, this unhappy man had dared to touch the Ark as it began to fall off the ox-cart during the journey. For usurping a privilege reserved to Aaronites, he was struck dead by Yahweh— though we are not to assume that he therefore went to hell. Israel had entered upon a new era in which Yahweh was determined to vindicate His incomparable holiness and uniqueness over the pagan gods of all other nations. Any attempt—even the sincere gesture of an Oza—at undue familiarity would be severely punished until the Jews learned the fundamental lesson of God's transcendence. The sudden death of Oza, then, is a grim reminder that those who would approach Yahweh intimately must do so on HIS terms, not their own.[1] A more careful ceremony was worked out for the occasion, the Ark reposing meanwhile in the home of another Levite, Obededom (cf. 6:11). It appears that Psalm 23 was composed for this occasion, and its whole tenor points to Davidic authorship. This religious song is, like Psalm 14, an example of a Hebrew introit hymn: one choir would chant the ques-

---

[1] Cf. Num. 4:15, 19-20; also, I Par. 15:2, 13 for a deeper insight in the matter.

tions in verses 3, 8 and 10 regarding the qualifications required of those "seeking the face of Yahweh," and another choir would respond (cf. Micheas 6:6-8).[2] One can readily understand after a careful perusal of this striking psalm why it is used in the Catholic pre-ordination rite of tonsure whereby a young man passes from the ranks of the laity into the clerical state. This is a Psalm of Yahweh's Enthronement (Kingship) while Psalm 100 is classed as a Royal Psalm.

Psalm 131. In response to David's desire to build a temple in which to house the Ark properly, God sends word through the prophet Nathan that this accomplishment is to be reserved for his son. As we are told later in III Kings 5:3 and I Paralipomenon 22:8-9, David had spent too much time in fighting wars and shedding blood: building the temple would be the work of a more peaceful man. Instead, God reverses the tables and promises to build David a "house"—that is, a dynasty— which would last forever (II Kgs. 7:11-13). Psalm 131:11-12 contains this same promise in a dramatic setting; verse 17 is messianic (note explanatory footnotes in the Confraternity Version). This psalm has elements of two categories; it is both a Royal Psalm and a Psalm of Yahweh's Enthronement. The implications of this divine choice of the Davidic dynasty will be considered in the next chapter in conjunction with Solomon; it is a dominant theme.

Psalm 109. By the time of David, the immunity of the Moabites, Edomites and Ammonites indicated in Deuteronomy 2 had run its course; it was his lot to fulfill Numbers 24:17-19 in what may be termed the Syro-Ammonite War (II Kgs. 8; cf. Ps. 59:1-2). As king and conqueror, David united in himself two important characteristics of the Messia-to-come; it was the second which, perhaps more than any other, established him in the minds of the Jews as the perfect messianic type. To these two titles, Psalm 109 (a Royal and most important messianic psalm) adds a third; that of priest "according to the order of Melchisedec" (v. 5). David was not a priest, since he was not a Levite; hence, the Messia will rather resemble Melchisedec, the ancient king and non-Levitical priest of Jerusalem. As this psalm is very old, the reference to Melchisedec probably was inserted in order to provide a link between David and the ancient Jebusite city (Jerusalem) via one of the latter's

---

[2] Note that the qualifications of a sincere worshipper are all in the interior moral order; later prophets will contrast them against the mechanistic reliance on external rites characteristic of the pre-Exilic periods in Israel and Juda. The lofty sentiments prescribed in this and other psalms are worthy to be transferred from the non-sacramental presence of Yahweh between the cherubim of the propitiatory to the Eucharistic liturgy. David's ceremonial dancing on this occasion resulted, incidentally, in a permanent rift between himself and his wife Michol, "the daughter of Saul" (II Kings 6:16-23. Her story can be traced in I Kings 18:20-28; 19:11-17; 25:44; II Kings 3:13-14; 21:8, footnote. Blood ties often proved stronger than the marriage bond).

former kings. Although the notion of royal priesthood seems to be included, Jewish leaders tended to overlook that feature and to concentrate on the material symbols contained in verses 5-7 of the psalm. Among the ancients, kings were viewed as sons of God by special adoption and sat at His right hand (vv. 1-3; cf. Ps. 2 and 71). Christ was later to use this passage against the Pharisees (cf. Confraternity Version footnotes).

Psalm 50. David's sin of adultery (II Kgs. 11-12) is one of the few scars on his beautiful character. Even that sin can be charged to human frailty; in a pagan monarch, it would have gone virtually unnoticed. But David's treatment of Urias, Bethsabee's husband, makes the whole episode shameful. After failing to get Urias reunited with his wife and thus to appear responsible for her pregnancy, David yields to the expediency of securing his death by having him put in the front lines against the Philistines and then abandoned in that vulnerable position by his own army. Nathan's parable stirs the King to repentance, and he faces up to his punishment manfully. In his mysterious Providence, Yahweh does not demand that David give up Bethsabee, but rather that he lose his adulterine child. Their second son is named Solomon. Psalm 50 represents his prayer of repentance. Classified as a Psalm of Lament, it is the fourth of the seven Penitential Psalms, and is extensively used in the Christian liturgy (e.g., v. 9, "Asperges me"; the Divine Office daily begins with v. 17). Original sin seems to be hinted at in verse 7; verse 16 may well refer to the murder of Urias. This psalm has all of the elements of a perfect act of contrition.

Psalm 17. The remaining chapters of II Kings deals with the later years of David's hectic reign. His soft-heartedness toward the crime of his firstborn son, Amnon, and later toward another son, Absalom, who had murdered Amnon, almost cost him his kingdom. Pardoned and permitted to return to Jerusalem, Absalom gathered together a band of ruffians and led a revolt against his father, forcing David to flee for his life. There are some indications that Psalms 3, 60 and 62 were written during this troubled period. The revolt finally collapses, and Joab cannot resist the temptation to slay the helpless royal rebel as he hangs by his hair from the low branches of a tree. Though deposed by David for this act of disobedience, Joab's instinctive loyalty prompts him to seize control of the army in putting down another revolt by Seba, who had stirred up the northern tribes against the King. After another victorious skirmish with the Philistines, David finds his domain at peace. In a profound expression of thanksgiving to Yahweh, he pours out his soul in a poem which is a Psalm of Thanksgiving and also a Royal Psalm. It is the seventeenth psalm of the Psalter and is reproduced almost word for word in II Kings 22. Such duplication is found elsewhere among the psalms: Psalm 13 = Psalm 52; Psalm 69 = Psalm 39:14-18; Psalm 107 is taken from parts of Psalms 56 and 59; Psalm 104:1-15 is like I Paralipomenon 16:8-22; while Psalm 95 is like verses 23-33 of the same.

Psalm 15. Almost certainly to be attributed to David, this Psalm of Confidence (used in the rite of tonsure) expresses the psalmist's loyalty to Yahweh while others are apostatizing. He takes refuge in the thought that God is his "inheritance," and ecstatically declares: "You will not abandon my soul to the nether world, nor will you suffer your faithful one to undergo corruption. You will show me the path to life, fullness of joys in your presence, the delights at your right hand forever" (vv. 10-11). Does this mean that the psalmist understood the doctrines of the resurrection of the body and Beatific Vision? This conclusion does not follow necessarily, even though the psalm is apparently messianic. Here is a case of compenetration, wherein the sacred author's description cannot be entirely verified of himself (as also in the case of the "order of Melchisedec" in Psalm 109), and the fulfillment of which exceeded his limited viewpoint. The footnote on 15:10 in the Confraternity Version explains the antitype.

One final blotch appears on David's record toward the end of his life: he took a census. Exodus 31:12 reflects an ancient Hebrew belief that census-taking smacks of sacrilege, and is justified only when a temple-tax is simultaneously levied. We are told in II Paralipomenon 21:1 that Satan ("adversary," though here perhaps the devil) was behind the suggestion. David's choice of punishment (II Kgs. 24:13-15) was three days of pestilence over the land, which killed "70,000" people. The last verse of the book can be explained in either of two ways: David offered the holocausts by divine dispensation (since he was not a Levite); or he did it through the instrumentality of the Levites, as he had done during the ceremony of the transfer of the Ark in 6:17-18, which is clarified in I Paralipomenon 15:26 and 16:1.[3] In spite of his imperfections, David remained loyal to Yahweh, never once falling into the sin of idolatry. His harrowing experiences in escaping from Saul served only to purge and mature his character rather than to embitter him. His magnanimity toward even his enemies won him the support of the populace, though at times he permitted this trait to degenerate into softness. His biggest troubles began on the day on which he committed adultery, as Nathan had predicted (12:10-11). But his repentance was sincere, and the Lord did not abandon him. Whereas Saul usurped theocratic power and remained stubborn to the

---

[3] Cf. Orchard, *A Catholic Commentary on Holy Scripture*, col. 264e. Or, as we have noted in connection with Psalm 109, David may be exercising his royal priestly power.

bitter end, David was content to be the humble servant of Yahweh, finding his greatest delight in dancing before the Ark of the Covenant and composing hymns of praise to Him Who is "faithful toward the faithful" (cf. Ps. 17:26).

The Psalter

(Cf. Page 54)

In addition to what has already been laid down regarding the Psalms, a few brief notes on the composition of the Psalter are in order. The work of composing and collecting the psalms required centuries; the collection was fixed at 150 by the year 167 B.C., though the majority were produced between the time of David and the Exile. Those psalms which refer to the king are presumably pre-Exilic, whereas those which extol the Law are probably post-Exilic. Most of the psalms begin with an inscription, which usually attributes authorship; e.g., Psalm 89 to Moses, Psalm 71 and 126 to Solomon, etc. As we have previously noted, more than half of the psalms are attributed to David. However, modern scholarship has shown that these inscriptions are not completely reliable; this point should be kept in mind with reference to their citation on these pages. Due to a difference in traditions regarding the point at which these sacred poems should be divided (the books of the Bible were not separated into chapters and verses until the Middle Ages), an unfortunate discrepancy exists between the numbering of the Psalms in Catholic and Protestant Bibles, as follows:

Hebrew/							
Protestant:	1–8	9–10	11–113	114–115	116	117–146	147	148–150
Greek/							
Vulgate:	1–8	9	10–112	113	114–115	116–145	146–147	148–150

The Jews divided up the Psalter into five books, no doubt in imitation of the Pentateuch; this division is largely arbitrary, for research has proven that at least half a dozen groups of psalms have been brought together in the Psalter. Rather than burden the reader with these details, we shall summarize the seven categories previously discussed. This division is based on the brilliant pioneering of Hermann Gunkel, who concentrated principally on the literary form of the psalms, and used the original life-setting and later liturgical use of these poems in the work of their classification. As with any literary division, ambiguities create difficulties; hence, the listing of those psalms treated in this text under the various categories is not meant to be a rigid determination.

CLASSIFICATION AND DESCRIPTION	PSALMS:
I. HYMNS: The motif of this type is always primarily that of praise although some authors include psalms of national thanksgiving under this category. In common with other categories, we find a standard structure: 1) A summons; 2) Motive of psalmist; 3) His expression.	8, 28, 94, 103, 104, 113.
II. PSALMS OF LAMENT: This is the largest class of psalms; most are individual laments, though Psalms 105 and 136 are national. Note that not only expiation, but also petition (against enemies, for salvation, etc.) is included here. Psalms 6, 31, 37, 50, 101, 129, 142 are the seven Penitential Psalms. Psalm 108 is imprecatory.	21, 41–42, 50, 105, 108, 129, 136.
III. WISDOM PSALMS: This class comprises didactic poems: those which indicate the way of the blessed, warn the sinner, reflect on the Law or the problem of evil, etc.	1, 18, 49, 72, 77, 118, 126, 138.
IV. PSALMS OF CONFIDENCE: Even though the psalmist may begin his poem with a lament, if trust in Yahweh predominates, we put it in this class. These psalms may be the aspirations of either an individual or a group.	15, 22, 90
V. PSALMS OF YAHWEH'S KINGSHIP (OR ENTHRONEMENT): Picturing Yahweh as enthroned in heaven or on the Ark, or as King of the universe or of Israel, this class includes the Songs of Sion (45, 75, 83, 86, 131, etc.).	23, 46, 86, 131.
VI. PSALMS OF THANKSGIVING: Expressions of thanks on the part of an individual or a group upon obtaining a request in some need or distress. Such psalms were often accompanied by a communion banquet in the Temple.	17, 102, 135, 146, 147.
VII. ROYAL PSALMS: These psalms are so named because they are about or for the king, specifically the Davidic dynasty. Many are messianic (cf. remarks on Psalm 109).	(17), 19, 20, 44, 71, 100, 109, 131.
PILGRIM or GRADUAL PSALMS, 119–133, are those sung by pilgrims going to Jerusalem, and are not a separate type. [4]	(126, 131).

Suggested Readings

Anderson, *Understanding the Old Testament*, pp. 122-143.
Callan, *The New Psalter*, passim.
Dyson and Jones, *The Kingdom of Promise*, pp. 59-65.
Gelin, *The Religion of Israel*, Vol. 65: *Twentieth Century Encyclopedia of Religion*, Chap. 4.
King, P. J., *The Book of Psalms*, Parts 1 and 2 (Pamphlet Bible Series Nos. 43, 44).
Moriarty, *Introducing the Old Testament*, pp. 58-88.
Murphy, *Seven Books of Wisdom*, Chap. 3. An excellent treatment of the Psalms.
North, R., *The Book of Psalms*, Parts 3 and 4 (Pamphlet Bible Series Nos. 45, 46).
Weiser, Artur, *The Psalms* (Old Testament Library: 1962), 841 pp. An excellent source by a Protestant author for the system of classification used by Gunkel.

---

[4] To these categories some scholars have added the "Oath of Exculpation" (e.g., Psalm 138) — also called "Negative Confession." Fr. North speaks of a "Loyalty Oath" genre (e.g., Psalms 14, 23, 117) in *The Book of Psalms* (Pamphlet Bible Series No. 46), p. 33.

Chapter XXII

Solomon's Fall From Wisdom Into Idolatry: Israel vs. Juda

READINGS: *III Kings 1, 3, 6, 9, 11–12, 15; Wisdom 6–9; Proverbs 1, 3, 4, 6, 10, 22, 25, 31; Psalms 44, 126. (Note III Kings 3:3; Proverbs 1:7)*

Evidence suggests that the last two books of Kings were written during the Babylonian Captivity. Jeremia was thought to be their author by later Jews, as his style agrees closely with the Deuteronomic history of these books; however, he would have been nearly 100 years old at the earliest possible date of composition, 561 B.C.[1] Like I and II Kings, they are not merely a "catalogue of historical events but a demonstration of God's fidelity to His promise."[2] The messianic line, as we have seen, was narrowed down from Abraham's to Jacob's to Juda's offspring; I-II Kings show how Yahweh accomplished this feat, with Saul as His foil and Samuel His instrument. The contest between fidelity and infidelity continues in III-IV Kings as the instability of the northern dynasty is contrasted with the permanence of the southern (Davidic) dynasty. Every detail is fitted into this continuing Deuteronomic theme.

The first few verses of III Kings describing the ambiguous role of David's young concubine, Abisag, indicate that his declining health has reached the bedridden stage. His oldest surviving son, Adonias, takes advantage of the situation by trying to seize the kingdom, as Absalom had done. Now, Solomon, son of Bethsabee, was David's favorite; II Paralipomenon 28:5 informs us that God Himself had selected him to succeed his father. Adonias apparently realizes this (cf. III Kgs. 2:15), but decides to risk all on his prerogative as the older son. Again David's indulgent attitude toward his children has brought him trouble (1:6). This time, however, the aged king acts in

---

[1] See Orchard, *A Catholic Commentary on Holy Scripture*, col. 266b. Plurality of authorship, however, is implied in passages such as III Kings 11:41.

[2] Dyson and Jones, *Op. cit.*, pp. 58-59.

time to prevent a crisis. By the strategem of having Sadoc publicly anoint Solomon as king, David makes the coup collapse as Adonias' partisans desert him.

Solomon's Early Reign

Solomon's reign begins auspiciously, even as the seeds of his future defection are being sown. Carrying out the instructions of his father, he purges the kingdom of possible trouble-makers: Joab and Semei, who had sided with Adonias, are put to death; Abiathar is banished for the same defection and replaced by Sadoc, insuring the fulfillment of I Kings 2:32 regarding the transfer of the priesthood from the line of Heli. Adonias was either still aspiring to the kingship or else very stupid in asking for his father's concubine in marriage; at any rate, Solomon shows a firmness which David lacked in having that possible usurper slain.

The third chapter begins with an account of Solomon's political marriage with Pharao's daughter. Mixed marriages were later to bring about Solomon's downfall; there is a remote suggestion of compromise even in this union provided by II Paralipomenon 8:11. A more ominous note is sounded in III Kings 3:3, where we are told that Solomon "sacrificed in the high places"; i.e., centers of worship (whether of Yahweh or of a pagan god) apart from the "central sanctuary." The choice of Gabaon is explained by the fact that the Tabernacle, separated from the Ark ever since the destruction of Silo by the Philistines, was there. Its presence raised that city to the dignity of a shrine; in fact, the Tabernacle had eclipsed the Ark as a religious rallying-point, as can be seen from a consideration of the various locations of each.

LOCATION OF THE TABERNACLE:	LOCATION OF THE ARK:
At Galgal under Josue (Jos. 4:19; 10:6) . . . With the Tabernacle	
At Silo under the Judges (Jos. 18:1) . . . . . With the Tabernacle (I Kgs. 4:3)	
At Nobe under Saul (I Kgs. 21:7) . . . . . . At Cariathiarim (I Kgs. 7:2)	
At Gabaon under David (I Par. 16:37, 39) . At Jerusalem, in a temporary tabernacle	
At Jerusalem, in a storeroom of the Temple (III Kings 8:4) . . . . In the Holy of Holies of the Temple [3]	

Yahweh tolerated this dual site of worship, at least until the Temple was built. Yet, the suggestion of the Deuteronomic editor is unmistakable: this sacrifice of Solomon lacks perfection, even though we

---

[3] Cf. Orchard, *A Catholic Commentary on Holy Scripture*, col. 265 h, k, for duality of worship; see also articles on the Ark and the Tabernacle in *The Catholic Biblical Encyclopedia*, (*Old Testament*).

are told that "he loved the Lord." Nor must it be concluded that this is an irrelevant detail; for, as was noted in connection with Josue 22, plurality of places of worship among the Jews was always a potent source of idolatry and political schism.

Solomon and the Concept of Wisdom
(III Kings 3–4; Wisdom 6–9)

Another important theme is contained in this same third chapter: God's gift of wisdom to Solomon (III Kgs. 3:6-14). A famous example of Solomon's keen insight into human nature is furnished in the story of the two harlots in the latter half of the chapter. The following chapter, in describing the organization of the kingdom, assures us that "the wisdom of Solomon surpassed the wisdom of all the Orientals and of the Egyptians" (4:30). Although these verses undoubtedly represent some hyperbole, they contain such a basis in fact that we are moved to ask, "Just what is this wisdom which the ancients appraised so highly?"

The value of human wisdom had long been recognized among pagan nations. For them it was the art of managing one's life well, including a studied skill for winning friends and influencing people. At the highest level, it was understood to be the ability to govern men. In this latter sense, wisdom was looked upon as a collective enterprise — the result of pooling all the resources of the wise men of past and present toward the smooth running of the state. Schools of wisdom flourished at the royal courts. The prophet Daniel received a three-year training course in such a school in Babylon (Dan. 1:3-5). But this concept, like that of kingship, could never be nakedly taken over and adopted by the People of God and applied to the Israelite government without qualification. True wisdom, as the Saul-David struggle clearly demonstrated of true kingship, consists in the supernatural habit of submitting in all things to the will of Yahweh. Joseph had been a shining exemplar of such wisdom in both his personal and public life in Egypt. Like Moses,' his wisdom vastly transcended that of the native soothsayers.

As Solomon began his reign under the aegis of this same gift, "all good things together came . . . in her company" (Wisd. 7:11). The sapiential author of these lines has just enunciated the principle that all authority comes from God; he then makes Solomon proceed to warn the kings of the earth against abusing their power (Chap. 6). The personification of wisdom in Chapter 7 (see especially 7:26) will be treated later, along with Proverbs 8. It suffices to note here that Pseudo-

Solomon is not teaching the doctrine of the Blessed Trinity, but simply identifying wisdom as an attribute to God rather than of man. In Chapter 8 wisdom is portrayed as a bride who teaches, among other treasures, "moderation and prudence, justice and fortitude" (8:7). Here the influence of later Greek philosophers is evident. The identification of wisdom with immortality is clearly stated in Wisdom 8:17-21, as also in 6:17-21, through the middle-term of innocence; the final editors of the Pentateuch incorporated this concept in the genealogy of Genesis 5, as has been already noted. Chapter 9 of the Book of Wisdom reproduces in beautiful midrashic terms the prayer of Solomon for wisdom of III Kings 3. While these inspired reflections from the Book of Wisdom are not those of the real Solomon, nevertheless it is the latter who firmly established the claim of the relatively small state of Israel to what had previously been the exclusive possession of such large states as Egypt and Mesopotamia.

It is difficult to determine with any precision which sacred writings were actually composed by Solomon. In III Kings 4:32 he is credited with the writing of 3,000 parables and 1,005 poems. It must be remembered, however, that many later authors and compilers appended the name of this famous wise man par excellence to their works, in line with the Semitic concept of authorship (cf. p. 143). Just as the name of Moses lends greater authority to legal material and the name of David lends dignity to the Psalms, so the name of Solomon enhances the value of Wisdom Literature. Even two of the psalms are attributed to Solomon; of these, Psalm 126 (a wisdom poem written after the return from the Babylonian Exile as the Jews were beginning the work of restoration) reflects the essence of Hebrew wisdom: "Unless the Lord build the house, they labor in vain who build it; unless the Lord guard the city, in vain does the guard keep vigil."

The Book of Proverbs: The Fear of the Lord is the Begining of Wisdom

From the standpoint of final editorship, this work should logically be considered in Chapter XXVIII with other wisdom books; it is generally regarded as post-Exilic (fifth century?). From what has been said above, however, there seems to be adequate justification for including it here, especially since Parts II and V are explicitly attributed to Solomon, the attribution having foundation in fact. Parts III and IV, as well as VI, VII and VIII are admittedly borrowings from pagan wisdom assimilated by the inspired editor. The latter apparently added Part I (Chap. 1-9) as an introduction to the whole work. Most of the verses fulfill the connotation of the Hebrew term *Mishle* (pointed sayings or proverbs), which is its Hebrew title. The assigned chapters give a cross-sampling of the book; a brief commentary on these chapters follows:

Chapter 1. The purpose of the book is manifested: to instruct the inexperienced in good conduct; hence, we have here a moral treatise rather than a dogmatic theology. Verse 7 underscores the reorientation of secular knowledge within the Hebrew theocratic state. The same phrase is repeated in 9:10. Note how wisdom is personified.

Chapters 3 and 4. Besides reiterating the urgency of finding wisdom, these chapters contain a fundamental theme: the Deuteronomic principle of the Two Ways (3:33-35 and 4:10 ff.). The way of the wise man is that of virtue — as described in this book; it will lead to happiness and prosperity. The other way is that of the foolish man (note that foolish, not ignorant, is opposed to wise); it is the way of evil, and will lead to misfortune. Thus, Proverbs extends the principle of national reward and punishment enshrined in Deuteronomy 11:10 ff. to the individual. These rewards for fidelity to God and punishments for infidelity are temporal and material as they also are in Deuteronomy; not even five centuries after Solomon when Proverbs was probably edited had the revelation of other-worldly retribution developed, although individual responsibility had superseded purely collective retribution. Moreover, Proverbs 3:9 contains virtually the only reference to sacrifice and other ritual obligations stressed in the historical books. We are dealing with a literary genre quite different from the Books of Kings!

Chapter 6. Several recurrent themes are contained in these typical *Mishle:* industry (vv. 6-11); the value of submitting to parental discipline (vv. 20-23); warning against fornication and adultery (vv. 24 ff.; note the natural basis of the arguments offered).

Chapter 10. Here begins the first Solomonic collection. One is pleasantly surprised to find verse 12 in the Old Testament. The doctrine of the Two Ways recurs in verses 15 ff.

Chapters 22 and 31. The first 16 verses of Chapter 22 are exceptionally pungent flashes. With verse 17 begin thirty proverbs adapted from the savings of the Egyptian wise man, Amen-em-ope; the name is omitted from the Douay-Rheims Version. Agur (30:1) and Lamuel (31:1) were probably Arabian sages, from whom the sacred author has borrowed proverbs. The well-known epistle for the Mass of a married woman comes from Proverbs 31:10 ff.

Chapter 25. The second collection attributed to Solomon, gathered together in the reign of King Ezechia (v. 1), begins in this chapter. Christ cited verse 7, and St. Paul quoted verses 21-22. There are a great number of gems among these homely aphorisms, particularly in

Chapter 26 where the sacred author is merciless in his reprobation of the fool. The Book of Proverbs has placed pagan wisdom within the context of revealed religion, it is true; the message of the book is incomplete, however, because the rewards and sanctions do not yet transcend the temporal order.

The Temple of Solomon
(III Kings 6 ff.)

What David failed to accomplish, his son now brings to successful fruition. Using materials gathered by his father, Solomon constructs the first Temple in the capital city of Jerusalem.[4] It was a magnificent structure of dressed stone, with the interior finished in cedar and cypress wood. The general plan of the Tabernacle was followed, except that the dimensions were approximately doubled (cf. p. 125 and III Kgs. 6). In solemn pomp the Ark of the Covenant is carried into the Temple and placed in the Holy of Holies (8:4-11; see footnote on v. 9). Again, we may suppose, the stately strains of Psalms 23 ring out as the mighty procession of Levites with the Ark and Solomon with his retinue in all his glory wend their way toward the Temple enclosure. At the entrance they are forced to halt; the iron gates are closed. Then, in accordance with pre-arranged liturgical protocol, a choir accompanying the Ark begins the singing of verse 7 to the music of harps and timbrels:

Lift up, O gates, your lintels; reach up, you ancient portals,
   that the king of glory may come in!

From behind the gates comes the chanted response from a second choir:

Who is this king of glory?

To which the first choir before the gate answers solemnly:

Yahweh, strong and mighty, Yahweh, mighty in battle.
Lift up, O gates, your lintels; reach up, you ancient portals,
   that the king of glory may come in!

Slowly the heavy iron gates swing open, and the procession continues on its way.[5] Surely the dedication of the Temple and the installation of the Ark represent the climax of King Solomon's career. We should understand 8:5 in the sense that it was through the priests and Levites that the sacrifices were offered.

---

[4] We have already discussed the chronology suggested in 6:1 on page 101, footnote.

[5] See J. W. Flight, *The Drama of Ancient Israel* (Boston, Mass.: The Beacon Press, 1949) Chap. 21 and also p. 191.

Renewal of the Promise of the Perpetuity of the Davidic Dynasty

After the Ark had been safely installed, Solomon offers a long prayer to Yahweh, reminding Him of His promise to David. In 8:27, we see a remarkable awareness on the part of the sacred author of God's transcendence. The Lord deigns to answer his prayer in a second vision in which the permanence of the Davidic dynasty is again affirmed (9:4-5). It should be noted here that, although the permanence of the Davidic line is an absolute promise (being part of the messianic utterances), the continuance of that line on the throne of Israel is conditioned: "if thou wilt walk before me, as thy father walked, in simplicity of heart, and in uprightness . . ." In evaluating this oracle in the light of the subsequent fortunes of the dynasty, we must keep this clause in mind. Neither Solomon nor his successors fulfilled the condition; hence, the ominous alternative in verses 6-9 was realized in the dethronement of Sedecia at the time of the Babylonian Captivity. The line itself, however, was destined to continue through Jechonia (but without royal sovereignty) until the time of Christ.

Solomon's Defection

Corruptio optimi pessima goes the aphorism — and so it was with Solomon. The wisest of men fell from the heights of glory to the basest of crimes: idolatry. We need not take his marital statistics in 11:3 in the proper literal sense; one thousand wives would have been more of a burden than a consolation. Solomon fell victim to the grandeur of his vast commercial empire and to the luxury of his oriental court. His industrialization of Palestine had taken its toll not only in manpower (5:13-16), but also in religious orientation. Modern archeologists have dug up his incredible copper and iron mines at Asiongaber on the Gulf of Akabah (9:26) and his stable at Megiddo (cf. 4:26 and 10:26-29). His palace took twice as long to build as the Temple (compare 6:38 with 7:1), and we are told that "all the vessels, out of which king Solomon drank, were of gold. . . . There was no silver, nor was any account made of it in the days of Solomon" (10:21). Phoenician architects and materials had been employed in the construction of his buildings, including the Temple (which betrayed this pagan influence).[6] In the perennial battle between faith and culture in Israel, Solomon had succumbed to the latter. It was his mixed marriages which proved, above all other factors, to be his downfall by ensnaring him in idolatry (11:4-5). He had forgotton the principle of "separatism," although he had once acknowledged it (8:53).

---

[6] Cf. Anderson, *Op cit.*, pp. 143-153, especially pp. 146-147; also, Keller, *The Bible As History*, pp. 191 ff.

Upon his death, the fate of the kingdom was already sealed: secession of the northern tribes. As Ahias had predicted (11:31-32), this territory — actually only eight and one-half tribes, since Juda, Benjamin, Simeon and part of Dan remained under the Davidic dynasty — went into schism when Solomon's heir, Roboam, imprudently announced that he would continue the heavy taxation and other harsh policies of his father. Banding together under Jeroboam, formerly an official of Solomon's administration, they formed the "Kingdom of Israel," while the remaining three and one-half tribes were known as the "Kingdom of Juda" under Roboam. Though the latter was minded to attempt to reunite the kingdom by force, Yahweh forbade him, declaring "this thing is from me" (12:24). It had not been His intention that Israel become an empire like other nations; her pride and glory were meant to rest in being Yahweh's adopted son, "a kingdom of priests, a holy nation" (Ex. 19:6). Faith, not wealth, was to be the measure of her greatness.

The Divided Kingdom

Almost from the outset of his reign, Jeroboam turned away from the Lord in building two "high places," one at Bethel in central Palestine, the other in the far north, where the people could worship Yahweh in the form of a golden calf and thus not be tempted toward reunion with Juda by having to journey to Jerusalem. As one would expect, these shrines soon became centers of idolatry.[7] Moreover, "there was war between Roboam and Jeroboam always" (15:6); in fact, if we turn to II Paralipomenon 13, we note that there was an all-out battle between Abiam, Roboam's successor, and Jeroboam. The outstanding victory won by Abiam (whom III Kgs. 15:3 dismisses as an evil man whose only saving grace is the fact that he is a descendant of David, v. 4) ending with the death of Jeroboam, is an example of the Chronicler's trait of stressing whatever enhances the Davidic dynasty. Of all the Kings of Israel, Scripture has almost nothing good to say; IV Kings 10:30 is a rare exception. Archeology has shown that Amri, sixth king of Israel, was an admirable administrator; among other things, he built an almost impregnable capital at Samaria, crushed the Moabites, made an alliance with Juda, kept the Syrians at bay, and fathered a powerful dynasty (Achab, Ochozia, Joram). Yet, III Kings 16:25, representing the Deuteronomic viewpoint of history, portrays him as an evil man "above all that were before him" because "he walked in all the way of Jeroboam" (v. 26). In fact, verses 25-30 are stereotyped phrases covering the various changes of rule in the Northern Kingdom, just as

---

[7] See Osee 8:4-6, 11 and footnote on the latter in the Confraternity Version for the religious implications of political schism.

PROPHET	KINGS OF ISRAEL	KINGS OF JUDA — BEFORE ISRAEL'S FALL	KINGS OF JUDA — AFTER ISRAEL'S FALL	PROPHET
	Jeroboam I 931–910 B.C.	Roboam 931–913	EZECHIA 716–687	ISAIA and Emmanuel Prophecy
	Nadab 910–909	Abia(m) 913–911	Manasses 687–642	Nahum
	Baasa 909–886	Asa 911–870	Amon 642–640	Sophonia
	Ela 886–885			Habacuc
	Zambri (7 days)			JEREMIA
	Amri 885–874			
ELIAS—	Achab 874–853	Josaphat 870–848	JOSIA 640–609	
	Ochozia 853–852			
ELISEUS—	Joram 852–841	Joram 848–841	Joachaz (3 months)	
	Jehu 841–814	Ochozia 841	Joakim 609–598	
	Joachaz 814–798	Athalia 841–835	*Joachin (3 months)	
	Joas 798–783	Joas 835–796	Sedecia 598–587	EZECHIEL
AMOS	Jeroboam II 783–743	Amasia 796–781	FALL OF JERUSALEM, 587 B.C.	
OSEE	Zacharia 743	Azaria (Ozia) 781–740		
	Sellum (one month)			
	Manahem 743–738		*The Davidic dynasty continued through Joachin (Jechonia) in Babylon.	
	Phaceia 738–737	Joatham 740–736		
ISAIA	Phacee 737–732			
MICHEA	Osee 732–724	Achaz 736–716		
	FALL OF SAMARIA: 721			

178

15:8-14 are typical of the eight decent kings of the Southern Kingdom.

It must not be assumed, however, that most of the kings of Juda were model sovereigns. Out of a total of twenty, six are given qualified praise by the Deuteronomist, and only two are ranked as "perfect" (cf. also Sir. 49:4, which includes *David*): *Ezechia* and *Josia*. To obtain this rating, it was necessary that they destroy not only pagan shrines and altars, but also the "high places" erected to Yahweh's cult. In the preceding table of the kings of Israel and Juda, the "fair" kings are italicized; the two "perfect" kings are also in capitals.[8]

The Deuteronomist verdict is unmistakable: kingship as a whole in both the Northern and Southern Kingdoms has been a failure; moreover, I and II Paralipomenon (the work of the Chronicler) agree in this matter with III and IV Kings. God's agents, mere creatures subject to human frailty because they refused to rely completely on Him, had betrayed Him and led His people into sin. His justice will compel Him to deal severely with both kingdoms. Indeed, it is quite reasonable to suppose that, were it not for the great prophets whom He raised up, there would not have been a remnant to survive.

Psalm 44: Solomon's Nuptial Ode

This Royal Psalm, similar in theme to the Canticle of Canticles, may well have been composed for Solomon's wedding. After a brief introduction, the beauty and strength of the king as he rides into battle are described (vv. 3-10), then the charms of the queen (Pharao's daughter? — vv. 11-16). In the messianic sense, the bridegroom is Christ, and the bride is God's People under first the Old, then the New, Testament.

Suggested Readings

Anderson, *Understanding the Old Testament*, pp. 143-153; 190-222.
Dyson and Jones, *The Kingdom of Promise*, pp. 52-59.
Forestell, *The Book of Proverbs* (Pamphlet Bible Series, No. 37).
Keller, *The Bible As History*, pp. 191-244.
McKenzie, *The Two-Edged Sword*, Chap. 8.
Murphy, *Seven Books of Wisdom*, pp. 8-27 (Proverbs); 143-156 (nature of wisdom).

---

[8] These dates follow closely those in *La Sainte Bible de Jerusalem*, p. 1642 ff.

Chapter XXIII

Elias, Amos, Osee: A New Theophany and the Golden Age of Prophecy

READINGS: *III Kings 17–19; IV Kings 1, 2, 5; Amos 3, 5, 7–9; Osee 1–4, 6, 8, 11; Canticles 2, 6; Psalms 49, 102. (Note: Amos 3:2; 5:18; 9:7–15; Osee 2 [all]; 6 [all]; 11:1, 9; III Kings 19:11–13; IV Kings 2:11)*

In addition to the remarks made in Chapter XX regarding prophecy in Israel, a few more points should be noted. Most of the writings of the prophets which have come down to us are in poetry rather than in prose. Logically, then, poetic license abounds; we find in them not only allegory, parable, symbol, etc., but quite often the message is contained in strange dramatic actions (i.e., Yahweh's order that Isaia go about naked in Isa. 20:2). In regard to predictions of the future, it is important to remember that the time element is meant to be obscure, since it is always subordinated to the central idea. Often we get the impression that what is described as future is going to follow very soon, when in reality it will not take place for centuries (e.g., Isa. 7:14). Many descriptions are "without perspective like the landscape drawing of a child or like a view of distant mountains"[1]—usually because of the compenetration of the type and antitype (as in the case of Psalm 15). The ultimate criterion for dating most predictions in the Old Testament lies in their actual fulfillment in the New Testament!

Elias and Eliseus: A New Theophany

(III Kings 17–19; IV Kings 1, 2, 5)

The exploits of a remarkable pair of prophets serve to lighten the monotonous relapses of the kings of Israel and Juda during the ninth century B.C. Making a sudden and unannounced appearance from nowhere before Achab, sixth king of Israel, Elias tells this man described as doing "evil in the sight of the Lord above all that were

---

[1] Dyson and Jones, *Op cit.,* p. 44. This whole chapter is most helpful. *Compenetration* is discussed in *A Catholic Commentary on Holy Scripture,* cols 417f-418d.

before him" (III Kgs. 16:31) that there will be no more rain or dew on the land. Then the prophet quietly disappears and takes up his abode with a destitute widow. The first of his prodigies is the miraculous replenishment of her cruse of oil and pot of meal, followed by the resuscitation of her dead son.

The eighteenth chapter contains the story of the dramatic showdown between Yahweh and Baal. Jezabel, Achab's pagan wife, was determined to replace the worship of Yahweh with that of the Syrian Baal in the Kingdom of Israel. To this end she had imported large numbers of her foreign priests to minister to him. The spineless Achab supported her idolatry; yet, when Elias calls for a contest between the two deities on top of Mt. Carmel, the king agrees. The conversion of Achab and the people who witnessed Yahweh's striking intervention was only temporary; there could be no permanent reform until Jezabel was gotten out of the way. Although predicted by Elias, the queen's wretched end comes only several years later under the founder of a new dynasty, Jehu, the bloody king anointed by the prophet's successor. In the meantime, Elias is forced to flee from the irate Jezabel. God directs him back to the cradle of Israel's adoption, Mt. Sinai, and there favors him with a vision of Himself such as Moses had experienced. But there is a notable difference in this new Shekinah: whereas previous theophanies had taken the form of violent natural phenomena (thunder, lightning, clouds, fire), Yahweh now by-passes such media. He is not to be associated with nature as are pagan gods; He transcends nature: He is more ethereal than even the "gentle air" (19:12). Exegetes offer many interesting interpretations of this event, and not all are in agreement. In the light of subsequent developments, however, it seems reasonable to conclude that this unpretentious manifestation symbolizes the approaching end of mighty sensible theophanies. Such violent interventions as the fire from heaven, followed by Elias' bloody purge of the 450 prophets of Baal, must yield to the subtler influence of prophecy. The reference to the 7,000 Israelite men "whose knees have not been bowed before Baal" in III Kings 19:18 is the first suggestion of a "remnant."

Anointed by Elias after his vision, Eliseus becomes the faithful disciple of that master. In IV Kings 1:8 we get a precious description of the latter, reminding us of the New Testament description of John the Baptist. After the unhappy death of Ochozia of Israel from his fall out of the upper chamber of his palace, it seems that Elias' work is done. In the presence of Eliseus, he is taken up bodily into "heaven" by a whirlwind (2:11), and Eliseus succeeds to his office with double his spirit. The orgy of miracles continues, including the raising of the dead to life (Chap. 4). The cleansing of a Gentile leper, Naaman, was later to provide Christ with a telling example of the hardness of the

Chosen People even at this early date (Luke 4:27). The orgy finally ends with the resuscitation accomplished by the bones of Eliseus (13:21). We have been prepared for the golden age of prophecy.

Amos, Denouncer of Social Injustice
(The Book of Amos)

From excavations carried out at Megiddo and Samaria we know that the reign of Jeroboam II was an exceptionally prosperous one, stemming largely from Phoenician trade. The social evils which accrued in the wake of this prosperity are clearly depicted in the Book of Amos, one of the "literary" prophets (as opposed to those who have left no record of their preaching, such as Elias and Eliseus). Chapter 5 classifies the main disorders: 1) idolatry at the shrines of Bethel and Galgal; 2) oppression of the poor through collectivization of farms (v. 11); 3) bribery (v. 12); 4) formalism in religion (vv. 21-26; be sure to read footnotes in the Confraternity Version). To prick men's consciences and thus to stir up a reform in the Kingdom of Israel, Yahweh sent a Judean shepherd named Amos to preach against these evils. He was not one of the "professional" prophets who lived in companies; these had been somewhat discredited prior to this time (cf. III Kgs. 22: Micheas vs. the 400 court prophets). The rustic crudeness of his language betrays the rural simplicity of this man of God.

Amos' Message: The Justice of God

Throughout the book Amos is preoccupied with the "Day of the Lord" (cf. footnote on 5:18). In the mind of the average Jew, this phrase had come to designate the final intervention of Yahweh in human history and the eschatological events leading up to the inauguration of the messianic era. Although admitting that the Israelites are truly the Chosen People of God, his interpretation of this choice runs directly contrary to the view of his contemporaries: "You alone have I favored, more than all the families of the earth; *therefore I will punish you for all your crimes*" (3:2). The typical Jew had come to look upon God's choice of his people at the time of the Exodus as an absolute privilege; the Mosaic Covenant was conceived as a unilateral contract binding God to the Israelites. Amos reminds them that the Covenant is a two-way agreement placing serious obligations upon its beneficiaries, and that they will pay a heavy price for infidelity to it. In fact, he declares that Yahweh will demand a stricter reckoning of them than of the pagan Gentiles because the Chosen People have not lived up to their part of the Covenant:

> Woe to those who yearn for the day of the Lord! What will this day of the Lord mean for you? Darkness and not light! As if a man were to flee from a lion, and a bear should meet him; or as if on entering his house he were to rest his hand against the wall, and a snake should bite him. (5:18-19)

In other words, the Day of the Lord is going to boomerang on the Jews, insists Amos. The Israelites are not as unique as they think they are; Gentiles share in the possession of the Promised Land along with them:

> Are you not like the Ethiopians to me, O men of Israel, says the Lord? Did I not bring the Israelites from the land of Egypt as I brought the Philistines from Caphtor and the Arameans from Kir? (9:7)

As the story of Jona was to illustrate later on, God has not abandoned the Gentiles; they have a definite place in salvation, even though this place is not clearly revealed.[2] It is the burden of the Book of Amos to shatter the narrow nationalism so characteristic of the popular messianic view which had developed by the middle of the eighth century B.C. when Amos began his mission. According to this view, the advent of the Messia would inevitably result in judgment and punishment for all non-Jews; they would either be exterminated or else become slaves of the triumphant Jews in an earthly Israelite paradise. The absolute demands of Yahweh's justice, says Amos, will compel Him to "exile you beyond Damascus" (5:27). This passage refers to the captivity of the Northern Kingdom by the Assyrians in 721 B.C.

In order to lend dramatic force to the prophet's words, Yahweh presents Amos with five striking visions depicting the catastrophe which threatens this sinful kingdom (Chap. 7-9). God first portrays His justice under the form of a plague of locusts, then as a devouring fire. On each of these occasions Amos is able to persuade Him to spare Israel, because "he is so small." But after the third vision, that of the plummet, Yahweh is implacable: "I will forgive them no longer" (7:8).[3] At this point Amos is rebuked by the priest of Bethel (cf. III Kgs. 12:31), Amasia, for "conspiring" against Jeroboam II and the Kingdom of Israel and told to go home. But Amos proceeds to relate the last two visions manifesting Yahweh's justice, i.e., the basket of ripe fruit (representing that the time is ripe for Israel's punishment and followed by a catalogue of her crimes, 8:4-6), and the vision of the Lord destroying their house of worship (9:1).

---

[2] Cf. Chapter XXVI, this text.
[3] The Douay Version erroneously translates this term as a "mason's trowel." A plummet or plumb line is a weighted cord used by masons to check vertical planes.

Dire and drastic as the words of Amos sound, they do not shut out all hope. If the subjects of Jeroboam II will hearken and "hate evil and do good . . . then it may be that the Lord, the God of hosts, will have pity on the remnant of Joseph" (5:15). Here we have a term which will be used with increasing frequency by the prophets: the "remnant" designates that fraction of the Jewish nation which will survive the "purges" to which Yahweh will allow His people to be subjected as punishment for their sins; more specifically, it refers to the survivors of the Assyrian and (especially) the Babylonian Captivities. Amos returns to this concept at the end of his prophecy:

> But I will not destroy the house of Jacob completely, says the Lord . . . on that day I will raise up the fallen hut of David; I will wall up its branches, raise up its ruins, and rebuild it as in the days of old, that they may conquer what is left of Edom and all the nations that shall bear my name. . . . (9:8, 11-12)

In this passage the prophet teaches not only the fact of a remnant, but also that it will include Gentiles. This is the inspired interpretation of St. James in the Acts of the Apostles (Acts 15:15 ff). *Here is the first Old Testament hint that the "Day of the Lord" will not be the sudden, decisive judgment on the world which most Jews were expecting, but rather an extended period of time for conversion and repentance.* The remaining verses of the Book of Amos (9:13-15) are typical of the many prophetic descriptions of the messianic era couched in earthly, material terms. Many features should have been interpreted figuratively, but the Israelites never managed to break very far beyond their proper literal sense.

Psalm 49: Condemnation of Formalism in Religion

(Cf. Amos 5:21-27)

This forthright, hard-hitting Wisdom Psalm pinpoints a favorite theme of Amos: a purely mechanistic and hypocritical approach to the worship of Yahweh. The Israelites, like their pagan neighbors, were attempting to obtain Yahweh's blessing through bribery by offering Him the external rites prescribed under the Law, but at the same time denying Him the one thing He wants: their wills. The psalm clearly teaches that religion and morality cannot be separated; external worship may not be divorced from the two great commandments contained in Deuteronomy 6:5 and Leviticus 19:18.

vv. 1-6: The setting of the psalm — the Day of the Lord with Yahweh appearing on Sion.

7-15: Condemnation of the "formalists," whose unworthy dispositions do not match their elaborate holocausts.

184

16-21: Castigation of those hypocrites who pay lip-service to the Law and continue to sin with impunity.

22-23: A warning that those whose hearts are far from the true spirit of sacrifice will find their worship boomeranging on them.

Osee's Experience with His Unfaithful Wife, Gomer

With tender-hearted Osee we begin the study of a trilogy of prophets who were specially prepared for their mission by tailored personal experiences. In the case of Osee, a contemporary of Amos, his relationship with his wife is made to serve as a model of the relationship between Yahweh and Israel. By his patient disciplining of the unworthy and adulterous Gomer (climaxing in her rehabilitation), Osee is prepared to preach Yahweh's merciful punishment of the Northern Kingdom in order to make it repent and return to Him. Presupposing a careful study of the footnotes in the Confraternity Version on the part of the student, we can indicate this analogy carried out in the first three chapters as follows:[4]

OSEE—GOMER	CHAPTER	YAHWEH—ISRAEL
Providentially married to a woman named Gomer, Osee discovers her adultery.	I	Yahweh takes cognizance of the infidelity ("harlotry") of the Northern Kingdom.
Osee uncompromisingly denounces her infidelity and sets her out on a program of disciplined rehabilitation. (Note delicate transition in vv. 16–17.)	II	Yahweh denounces Israel's idolatry and threatens to lead her back to the "desert," scene of the Covenant. This was the "honeymoon" between God and Israel.
After a long period of testing, Osee succeeds in wooing back Gomer from her lovers and reuniting her to himself.	III	In His mercy, Yahweh decrees a devastating punishment for Israel (the Assyrian Captivity) to win her back to Him.

Osee's Message: The Mercy of God

Lest Amos' description of Yahweh's justice paralyze those Jews who, reading the handwriting on the wall, might be inclined to take it seriously, Osee is raised up by God to counterbalance (without in any way diminishing) this concept of justice by means of the reciprocal attribute of mercy. God will not rely on justice alone; in the final analysis, it will be His transforming love which will redeem the Jews from their evil ways. Seen in this light, even the terrible punishment of 721 is an act of mercy—a needed discipline making the Northern

---

[4] Cf. footnotes, Confraternity Version of the Bible.

Kingdom worthy of Yahweh's love. The beautiful image of the nuptial union between God and the New Israel in 2:21 represents a new theme in Old Testament theology; in the New Testament it will blossom into a symbol of the union between Christ and His Church. It finds its ultimate expression in the Old Testament in the Canticle of Canticles. Chapter 4 of Osee hints at this nuptial image in condemning Israel of a "want of knowledge" (i. e., experienced intimacy) of Yahweh. Unfortunately, her sporadic repentances will be too short-lived to stay God's decree (6:1-7).[5] Indeed, they have been on the wrong path ever since the schism of the Northern Tribes (8:4); they sealed their fate by the building of high places (8:11-13). Yet, Yahweh's love is seen in Chapter 11 to be a creative force, capable of building on destruction (11:1 ff.); "for I am God and not man, the Holy One present among you: I will not let the flames consume you" (11:9).

The Canticle of Canticles: A Parable of Marital Fidelity

We are told that the Jewish rabbis had serious misgivings about the admission of this book into their canon because of its purely natural tone; it seems that the traditional view that Solomon had written it finally gained its acceptance. While modern Catholic scholars deny its Solomonic origin and place its composition after the Exile (fifth to third centuries B.C.), they agree with the Church that it is worthy of the canon. What we have here is a series of love songs placed on the lips of a bride and groom, and strung together rather loosely. Some exegetes have seen in Canticles a triangle situation in which Solomon and a humble shepherd are vying for the love of the same girl. This view is not generally accepted, however. The tenor of the poem can be illustrated as a series of mutual romantic eulogies between two lovers, who evidently are married. In line with Osee's insertion of the marriage bond into divine revelation as a type of Yahweh's love for the Jews, we can see why later inspired editors saw fit to include it in the canon. It seems best to treat it as a parabolic allegory (i. e., a parable with allegorical features) depicting the divine love: in the literal sense, for the Jews; in the spiritual sense, for the Christian Church.

Psalm 102: Thank Yahweh for His Loving Kindness

Characterized by its tender piety, this Psalm of Thanksgiving is an expression of gratitude to Yahweh for His enduring mercy. The same word used in Osee 2:21 for mercy is employed generously throughout the psalm: *hesed.* After a careful reading of this magnificent poem, we can perhaps appreciate why this term is better translated "kindness"

---

[5] This passage provides the first lesson for the liturgical service of Good Friday.

here (vv. 4, 8, 11, 17).[6] This psalm as a whole underscores a concept already taught in Osee: the sins of Israel—especially idolatry—are not merely transgressions of the rules of the Covenant; they represent infidelity, a breaking of faith with Yahweh, the violation of a person-to-person relationship.

Suggested Readings

Anderson, *Understanding the Old Testament*, pp. 222-251.
Bouyer, *The Meaning of Sacred Scripture*, Chap. 5 (Amos), 6 (Osee), and 14 (Elias).
McKenzie, *The Two-Edged Sword*, Chap. 9.
Moriarty, *Introducing the Old Testament*, pp. 103-119.
Murphy, *Seven Books of Wisdom*, Chap. 5; and *Pamphlet Bible Series* No. 38, pp. 51 ff. (Canticles).
Sullivan, *God's Word and Work*, pp. 90-100 (especially pp. 99-100).

---

[6] Cf. Jacques Guillet, *Themes of the Bible* (Notre Dame, Ind.: Fides, 1960) pp. 76-80.

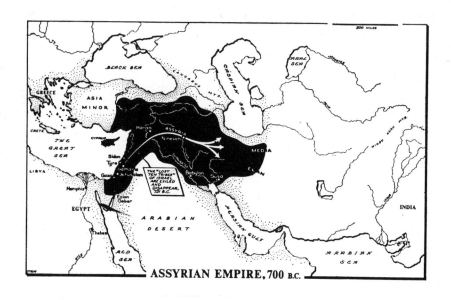

ASSYRIAN EMPIRE, 700 B.C.

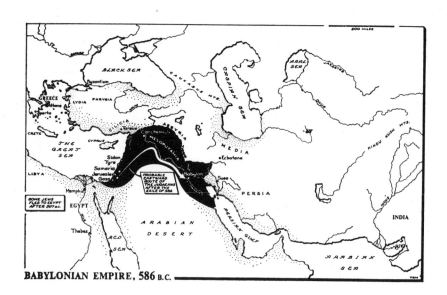

BABYLONIAN EMPIRE, 586 B.C.

Chapter XXIV

First Isaia: God's Transcendence and the Davidic Dynasty

READINGS: *IV Kings 16–20; Isaia 1–12; Michea 6; Nahum 3; Habacuc 1; Sophonia 1; Psalm 138. (Note: Isaia 2:11; 6 [all]; 7:14; 8:6–8; 9:5–6; 11:1–2; 35:5–6; Michea 5:1)*

The lordly prophet Isaia succeeds Amos (not the same man as Isaia's father) and Osee as troubler of Israel and Juda. This cultured gentleman preached to both kingdoms, though his special concern was for the Kingdom of Juda and the Davidic dynasty. He began to preach "in the year that King Ozia died" (6:1), and continued his mission under the three subsequent kings of Juda (1:1, cf. p. 178 for historical orientation). Isaia recapitulates the themes of justice and mercy found in Amos and Osee into a higher synthesis: Yahweh's justice is swept up into the loftier concept of His holiness; His mercy will concentrate on the preservation of a remnant of Juda, from which the Messia ("Emmanuel") is to come. Although these themes are more complex, and the oracles scattered in even more haphazard fashion than in most of the other prophets, we shall be able to unravel the main threads with the key furnished us by biblical scholarship. But first a word about the authorship of the book.

As the introduction to the Confraternity Version indicates, the Book of Isaia is actually "three" books, according to our modern notion of authorship. Isaia himself composed most of the first portion, Chapters 1–39, addressed to his contemporaries, c. 740-700. Chapters 40-55 were written by "Deutero-Isaia," a faithful disciple of the school of Isaia, to the Jews of the Babylonian Captivity, 587-538. Finally, Chapters 55-66 were written by a later disciple to the Jews of Judea after their return from captivity in 538 B.C. It must be carefully noted, however, that this triple division of the book in no way impairs the Isaian authorship of the whole book, any more than later additions impair the Mosaic authorship of the Pentateuch (cf. p. 143.); in both cases, the spirit of the original writer pervades the whole work.

189

Isaia's Preparation: The Theme of Holiness:
Yahweh Alone Is To Be Trusted

It is best to begin the reading of this prophecy with Chapter 6, the vocation of Isaia. Like Osee, he is prepared for his mission by an overwhelming personal experience: a vision of Yahweh surrounded by six chanting Seraphim. So terrifying is the presence of the Lord that these angels cover themselves with their wings as they fly about singing what has become the *Sanctus* of the Mass. One of them touches a red hot coal to the lips of the prophet in the course of the vision to make him worthy to preach the word of God. This experience obviously has left an indelible impression on the mind of Isaia; his book is saturated with the concept of Yahweh's tremendous holiness—His unique preeminence over creatures, from whom He differs not only in degree but also in kind. Man is holy only insofar as he resembles (very faintly, to be sure) the holiness of God. Hence, a more potent term to express this quality of Yahweh is transcendence; it forcefully denotes His *excelling otherness*. This quality is the main thread of the Book of Isaia. Like the theme of justice in Amos, it will demand that "Sion . . . be redeemed by judgment, and her repentant ones by justice" (1:27). But it goes further; Yahweh's holiness requires that He be vindicated in all of the affairs of men. Basically, this means that rational creatures must be put in their place whenever they get out of line:

> The haughty eyes of man will be lowered, the arrogance of men will be abased, and the Lord alone will be exalted on that day. (2:11)

"That day" to which Isaia refers is the "Day of the Lord," familiar to us from Amos. At Yahweh's visitation, all of the puny plans of men will be put to nought as His designs emerge victorious (8:9-10). Hence, Isaia insists, God's chosen ones must trust in Him alone, and avoid all alliances with foreign powers.

The Hardness and Impenitence of the Jews
Demand That Both Kingdoms Be Punished

The sixth chapter of Isaia is more than an introduction; it is the key to the whole book. Verses 9 and 10 graphically depict the advanced state of moral decay in Israel. Osee has already intimated the degree of their impenitence, "Their deeds do not allow them to return to their God; for the spirit of harlotry is in them, and they do not recognize the Lord" (Os. 5:4); Isaia now seems to say that both kingdoms are doomed. Chapter 1 is a litany of their crimes: formalism in religion (vv. 11-15); injustice (vv. 17 ff.); idolatry (v. 29). In Chapter 5 occurs the famous poetic description of Israel under the figure of the Lord's vineyard; it is about to be trampled because it has produced nothing but wild grapes. Yet even in Isaia, the door is not entirely closed to repentance (1:19-20); there will certainly be a remnant, which is the topic of Chapter 4:2-6. This passage together with Chapter 5 provide the scriptural portion for the third lesson of the restored Easter vigil liturgy. Chapter 6 speaks of captivity and deportation, but does not specify who will be the parties involved (vv. 11-12; Isaia has been using the term "Israel" to designate both kingdoms; he uses the term "Ephraim" usually when he wants to indicate the Northern Kingdom). The last verse of this chapter returns to the concept of the remnant; the following diagram is offered to explain the pivotal terms. (The last word, "trunk," is better translated "stump.")

In this passage, the "tree" ("terebinth or an oak") represents the Jewish people; those who will survive the captivity physically are the "trunk"—also known as the "remnant"; those among the remnant who remain humble and pious followers of Yahweh are the "stump," designated by later Hebrew writers as the *Anawim*. The term "shoot" occurs in 11:1, to be explained in the next section.

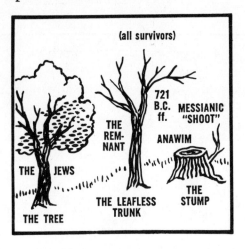

The Permanence of the Davidic Dynasty: Emmanuel Will Be the Sign

(Isaia 7–12)

Throughout his book Isaia is obsessed with the concept of the permanence of the line of David (II Kgs. 7:13). This dynasty is represented, of course, by the kings of Juda, of which Isaia is primarily interested in Achaz and Ezechia. The scene of Chapter 7 is set for us in IV Kings 16. Shortly after ascending the throne of Juda, the weak Achaz finds himself threatened by a league between Rasin, King of Syria ("Aram"), and Phacee, King of Israel (i. e., the Northern Kingdom). These monarchs are planning to dethrone him because he refuses, out of fear, to make an alliance with them against powerful Assyria. At the critical moment, Isaia appears on the scene to warn Achaz not to make any alliances: he has only to trust in Yahweh, Who will destroy those two kingdoms (7:8-9). Putting on his prophetic spectacles (but unable to focus them very sharply,) Isaia offers Achaz a "sign" of their destruction. Although Achaz' disbelief causes him to refuse the sign, Isaia gives it to him anyhow: peering into the future (always vague and indeterminate in such prophecies), the prophet sees, coming from Achaz' (Davidic) line, a child born of an unmarried woman (7:14).[1] The messianic character of this child is indicated by the name given to him, "Emmanuel." The point is clear: the future birth of Emmanuel presupposes the survival of the Davidic line; hence, the credibility of Isaia's assurance regarding the fall of Syria and Israel and the salvation of Juda.

But again we have to ask the question: Did the prophet receive a direct revelation of the Messia, and is he therefore describing *Christ exclusively* in the literal sense of his words, and independently of any type? This solution is possible, and has long been popular with certain exegetes.[2] Yet, it seems to violate a generic Old Testament principle whereby salvation-history is portrayed typically, with the fulfillment coming only in the New Testament. To have Christ appear on the stage in person at this juncture would seem to be premature. Moreover, Isaia does seem to have in mind some contemporary event in the two verses immediately following, 7:15-16. Our conclusion, then, is that the prophet envisages a composite picture: some human type (probably Achaz' son, Ezechia) mixed with descriptive phrases verified only in Christ, the Emmanuel to come. Once more the problem is solved by an appeal to compenetration; or, if the reader prefers, the fuller sense of Scripture.

The theme of Isaia 7:14 is continued in 9:5-6, where additional messianic characteristics are delineated. The Church sees here, in the fuller sense, the divinity of Christ. In 10:33-34 and 11:1 we are confronted with the holy "shoot" sprouting from the Davidic stump. The gifts of the spirit (*ruah*) of Yahweh are imputed to the *shoot* in 11:2 (see Confraternity Version footnote for the derivation of the Gifts of the Holy Spirit). Verses 6-9 are a Utopian model of the messianic age; they appear in marked contrast to the more spiritualized concept contained in Isaia 2:2-4. In retrospect, we can see more clearly why Isaia offered the Emmanuel prophecy as a "sign" of Juda's predicted deliverance. There

---

[1] The Hebrew word used here (*'almah*) is not the technical word for virgin.
[2] E.g., E. Power in Orchard, *A Catholic Commentary on Holy Scripture*, cols. 426a-1.

was still in his mind, as in that of his contemporaries, the tendency to identify Juda's military triumph with the notion of judgment, i.e., to lump both events together under the heading of the "Day of the Lord."[3] At the same time, however, Isaia does much to counteract the popular conception of "that day" as a sudden, definitive intervention settling human affairs once and for all. Amos began this corrective therapy (as noted in the previous chapter); unfortunately, it proved unsuccessful. So confident is Isaia of the certitude of the events which he is foretelling that he gives his new-born son a name symbolic of the Assyrian destruction of the kingdoms of Syria and Israel: Maher-shalal-hash-baz ("quick spoils, speedy plunder"). The wretched Achaz, however, is not convinced; he makes an alliance with the Assyrians against his enemies. God's judgment comes quickly via Isaia:

> Because this people has rejected the waters of Siloe that flow gently [divine help], and melts with fear before the loftiness of Rasin and Romelia's son, therefore the Lord raises against them the waters of the River, great and mighty [the king of Assyria and all his power]. It shall rise above all its channels, and overflow all its banks; it shall pass into Juda, and flood it all throughout: up to the neck it shall reach. . . . (8:7-8)

Israel Falls to Assyria

(IV Kings 17–20)

And so it happened. When Phacee's successor on the throne of Israel refused to pay tribute to Salmanasar, King of Assyria, the latter marched into Samaria and laid siege to it. He died in the course of the battle, but his successor, Sargon II, took the city after three months. In accordance with their harsh policy, the Assyrians carried away (according to Sargon's annals) 27,290 leading Israelites into Persian cities (IV Kgs. 17:6), thereby fulfilling Amos 5:27 and Osee 9:3. Worse still, the Assyrians imported foreign colonists to prevent the remaining Jews from ever rising to power again (17:24; note how vv. 25-28 reflect the pagan concept of territorial deities). This mixture of Gentile blood in the veins of the descendants of those Jews who escaped deportation and intermarried with the colonists was later to stigmatize them as "Samaritans."

Turning now to the Kingdom of Juda, we find that Achaz has died and Ezechia has succeeded to the throne of David. He is one of the three "perfect" kings of Juda who destroyed all of the high places; Sennacherib (the new Assyrian king) alleges that this act has turned Yahweh against him and that Juda is therefore doomed! On the advice of Isaia, Ezechia puts all of his trust in Yahweh, Who has doomed the

---

[3] From his perspective, Isaia could not see that Emmanuel would arrive only centuries later; Yahweh kept the timing of these events out of focus.

Assyrians. The actual outcome is described in the "Historical Appendix"
of Isaia, Chapters 36-39, generally considered today to have been ex-
cerpted from IV Kings 18-20. Yahweh intervened to destroy Sennacherib's army (via the bubonic plague?) and thus to spare Juda and
the Davidic dynasty (cf. Isa. 37:33-38; IV Kgs. 19:32-37; II Par. 32:21;
and Tob. 1:21-24). This near-destruction of Jerusalem, with Sennacherib reaching "up to the neck," occurred in 701 B.C. It has been im-
mortalized in Lord Byron's "The Destruction of Sennacherib," and
perhaps also in Psalm 75, especially verses 6-10. Assyria has been playing the role of God's "rod of anger," as Isaia declares in Chapter 10.
With the fall of Ninive in 612, Babylon will succeed to that role for the
humbling of Juda in 587 B.C.—an event to which Isaia seldom alludes
very clearly, obsessed as he was with the permanence of the Davidic
dynasty. His contemporary, Michea, proved less bashful, stating that
"Sion shall be like a plowed field, and Jerusalem reduced to rubble,
and the mount of the temple to a forest ridge" (Mich. 3:12).

It should be simply noted in passing that Chapters 13-14 are either
the work of a later disciple, or else the original object of the oracle has
been changed from Assyria to Babylon. Furthermore, the term *Anawim*
(included in the diagram earlier in this chapter), which is characteristic
of later prophecies, is found in 14:30 in a religious sense for the first
time. Here it is translated "poor," but implying trust in Yahweh. In
Sophonia 2:3 it is rendered "humble," signifying those "who have ob-
served His law." The term will find its fulfillment in the first beatitude,
where Christ "canonizes" those who are "poor in spirit."[4] Chapters
24-27 are known as the "Apocalypse of Isaia" (cf. definition on p. 28),
and are the work of one of the prophet's disciples, it seems. In 24:19
the restoration of the Jews is compared to the resurrection of corpses.
Finally, Chapter 35 seems to belong with Second Isaia, as it is largely
a Utopian model. However, Christ chose to fulfill verse 35 literally
(cf. Matt. 11:5).

Michea and the Birthplace of the "Child"

(Michea 5:1)

We shall simply note in passing the work of a contemporary of Isaia,
the prophet Michea. Like Isaia, he preached against both the Kingdom
of Israel and the Kingdom of Juda. He witnessed the devastation of the
Northern Kingdom and predicted the fall of Jerusalem (3:12), which
he seems to have thought was going to take place in his own lifetime.
This event did not actually take place for another century and a half;
apparently Michea's preaching produced such abundant fruits during

---

[4] Cf. Crowley, *The Books of Lamentations, Baruch, Sophonia, Nahum* and
Habacuc, p. 8. See also p. 12, where Fr. Crowley sees an interesting comparison
between Soph. 3:14-17 and the Annunciation scene of the New Testament.

Ezechia's reform that God's anger was allayed.[5] In many of his phrases, Michea seems to be paraphrasing other prophets, e.g., Isaia 2:1-4= Michea 4:1-3. In the first verse of Chapter 5, however, he makes a significant contribution to messianic literature in connecting the ancestral city of David (Bethlehem) with the advent of the "ruler" (cf. St. Matthew's understanding of this passage in Matt. 2:4-6). The well-known "Reproaches" of the Good Friday liturgy are based on Michea 6:3-4. We have already cited 6:6-8 in conjunction with Psalm 23 (see p. 165).

Nahum, Habacuc, Sophonia: Prophets of Doom

We shall take only a passing look at these three pre-Exilic minor prophets. Nahum, a contemporary of Jeremia, addressed his words of vengeance against Assyria, the cruelest of Israel's enemies (cf. Confraternity introduction to the book). The fulfillment of his prediction of the fall of Ninive, its capital, occurred at the hands of the Babylonians in 612 B.C. Habacuc saw Babylon (Chaldea) as successor to Assyria as God's scourge against the Jews. In answer to the prophet's question as to why He permits this unjust aggression (1:13), God replies that the just man will survive by faith (2:4). Scripture expands this concept in Hebrews 10:38 to include justification by faith in the New Testament.[6] The Day of the Lord is the theme of Sophonia, who preached early in the reign of King Josia. He predicted the fall and the restoration of Juda. The sequence of the Requiem Mass, *Dies Irae*, is modeled on Sophonia 1.

Psalm 138: The Divine Transcendence

The psalmist here agrees with the Isaian concept of the transcendence of God. In this Wisdom poem, we have one of the most precious bits of theology on the divine attributes in the Old Testament. Beginning with Yahweh's omniscience, which embraces man's secret thoughts (vv. 2-6), the psalmist takes up His ubiquity (vv. 7-12), then omnipotence (vv. 13-18). This last attribute seems to be the key to the others in mind of the author (note v. 15); truly the psalmist was no mean theologian. He must have written during the Wisdom period.

Suggested Readings

Anderson, *Understanding the Old Testament*, Chap. 9.
Bouyer, *The Meaning of Sacred Scripture*, Chap. 7.
Crowley, *The Books of Lamentations, Baruch, Sophonia, Nahum, and Habacuc* (Pamphlet Bible Series, No. 29).
Huesman, *The Book of Isaia*, Part I (Pamphlet Bible Series, No. 26).
McKenzie, *The Two-Edged Sword*, Chap. 10.
Moriarty, *Introducing the Old Testament*, pp. 120-137.

---

[5] Cf. Jer. 26:17-19; also Strange, *The Books of Amos, Osee* and *Michea*, p. 74.
[6] Understood in the light of St. James' Epistle; Cf. Chapter IX.

Jeremia: Exile and the Intimacy of God

READINGS: *IV Kings 21–25; Jeremia 1, 16, 20, 25, 27, 31, 36, 43;*
  Lamentations 1, 3; Baruch 3; Abdia; Hebrews 8; Psalm 136.
  (Note: IV Kings 22:8; Jeremia 16:1–9; 22:30; 23:5–6; 31:31–34)

In IV Kings 19, we left King Ezechia victorious over the Assyrians as
a result of Yahweh's intervention in the destruction of their army. The
fifteen years added on to his life at the prayer of Isaia (IV Kgs. 20:5-6),
however, proved to be a liability. In a moment of vanity, he displayed
all of his wealth and hidden treasures before the gaping eyes of the
two Babylonian emissaries (cf. II Par. 32:25, 31). Although Babylon
was just beginning to become a world threat, Isaia predicted that this
rash act would result in the capture and deportation of Juda (IV Kgs.
20:17). And in the following chapters, we are given more information:
it is in conjunction with the thorough rottenness of Ezechia's son and
successor, Manasses, that this prediction is to be fulfilled (cf. 23:26 and
Jer. 15:4. These kings of Juda are listed on p. 178).

In 640 B.C. the third and last "perfect" king of Juda came to power:
Josia, a sincere and zealous man, determined to purify the worship of
God. To this end he ordered the Temple to be repaired. An act of God
intervened to intensify his reform: during the repairs, the High Priest
Helcias discovered the "book of the Law"—generally conceded to be
the Book of Deuteronomy. As we have seen (p. 139) this section of
the Pentateuch represents the understanding of the Mosaic Covenant
on the part of the northern Levites of the seventh century B. C. It had
been brought to Jerusalem and hidden in the Temple, apparently just
a short time before its discovery. In a moving scene Josia "rent his garments" when he heard the words of the book, and realized how far the
people had drifted away from its decrees. Chapter 23 describes a typical
covenant-renewal ceremony and the drastic reform which followed it
and which Jeremia backed.

The cryptic account of Josia's death in 23:29 requires an explanation.
The once dreaded Assyrian Empire, engaged in mortal combat with
Babylonia, was on its last legs. Its capital, Ninive, had fallen in 612 —
fulfilling the prophecy of Nahum. Unwilling to see Babylonia gain

supremacy in Asia, Pharao Necho (609-593 B.C.) decided to go to Assyria's rescue. As his army wended its way up to the coastal plain from Egypt, past Megiddo, King Josia decided that this was the moment to prevent the Egyptians from getting another foothold in Palestine and Syria. Casting his lot with Babylonia, he attempted to intercept the Pharao with an army at Megiddo. Here is the Chronicler's interpretation of their meeting:

> But he (Necho) sent messengers to him, saying: "What have I to do with thee, O King of Juda? I come not against thee this day, but I fight against another house, to which God hath commanded me to go in haste. Forbear to do against God, who is with me, lest he kill thee." Josia would not return, but prepared to fight against him, and hearkened not to the words of Necho from the mouth of God, but went to fight in the field of Megiddo. And there he was wounded by the archers. And he said to his servants, "Carry me out of the battle, for I am grievously wounded." . . . And he died, and was buried in the monument of his fathers. And all Juda and Jerusalem mourned for him, particularly Jeremia: whose lamentations for Josia all the singing men and singing women repeat unto this day. (II Par. 35:21-25.)

The "mouth of God" may have been Pharao's own pagan oracles.[1]

Failure of the Deuteronomic Reform

Although we do not know what became of these lamentations of Jeremia over the death of his patron, we do know that the reform which he had so ardently supported did not outlive the death of Josia. The political reasons will be described in the next paragraph; here we shall take up the religious aspect. The whole tenor of the Book of Deuteronomy — on which the reform was based — points toward the basic need of a genuine love of God on the part of His people. The blessings which the Law held out to its observers were obviously, then, to be a reward for this intimate relationship with Yahweh. The Jews had developed what Dr. Anderson refers to as a "bargain counter religion"; they behaved as though the Deuteronomic formula spelled out in Deuteronomy 28 was a sort of magic success talisman operating automatically on a unilateral basis in their favor. Obedience to the letter of the Law became an infallible thermometer of the blessings due them. The destruction of the high places by Josia and his insistence on the centralization of worship in Jerusalem gave rise to a false sense of security in having Yahweh "localized" in their midst. But worst of all was the unbending nationalism which surged up once again in the early days of the reform as the might of Assyria collapsed.[2]

---

[1] Cf. Orchard, *A Catholic Commentary on Holy Scriptures*, col. 287aa. There was, however, an unwritten law against foreign alliance; cf. Os. 7:11; Isa. 30, 31.

[2] Cf. Anderson, *Understanding the Old Testament*, pp. 317-322.

With the victory of Nabuchodonosor at Carchemish in 605 B.C. the whole political picture changed. There was no reason for Juda to rejoice. Both Egypt and Assyria were finished, at least for the time being, but the new world-empire of Babylon brought no relief; rather, it exacted just as heavy a tribute from its vassal states. Whereas the Egyptian Pharao Necho had deposed Joachaz in favor of Joakim on the throne of Juda, Nabuchodonosor just as autocratically replaced Joakim with his son, Joachin (usually called Jechonia). It was during the reign of the father, Joakim, that the prophecies of Jeremia began to take written form. The reaction of that semi-despot to the warnings of the prophet are vividly described in Jeremia 36. For burning the scroll and ignoring its message, Jeremia predicts of Joakim: "No descendant of his shall succeed to David's throne" (Jer. 36:30). It was just a few years later that the haughty king refused to pay his tribute to Nabuchodonosor and was sent to Babylon in the first deportation (c. 598 B.C.; cf. II Par. 36:6). His son, Jechonia, lasted only three months on the throne of David; this was an adequate fulfillment of Jeremia's oracle. In Babylon, Jechonia's Davidic stock was recognized and honored by Evilmerodach (IV Kgs. 25:27-30). Though lacking a throne, he carried on the messianic line.

Back in Jerusalem, Sedecia, uncle of Jechonia, had been placed on the throne. He was for a while a faithful puppet of Babylon. This vacillating Davidic stump was wont to consult Jeremia secretly for fear of his courtiers, but lacked the courage to abide by the prophet's oracles (cf. II Par. 36:12). In the face of Jeremia's stern advice to surrender to the Chaldeans (Babylonians), the pathetic monarch revolted against Nabuchodonosor and was promptly besieged on all sides. Captured while trying to escape from the city, he was forced to witness the execution of his sons, whereupon his own eyes were gouged out. He perished in a Babylonian prison. Yahweh had had enough; He abandoned His people to the slaughter and pillaging of their capital, including the destruction of Solomon's Temple. We shall turn to the Book of Lamentations for a description of that event.

The Book of Lamentations

(Chapters 1, 3)

Sometimes joined to the Book of Jeremia (thus cutting the total number of Old Testament books to forty-five), Lamentations has been traditionally ascribed to that prophet by both Jewish and Christian sources. If we recall the Jewish concept of authorship, however, we shall realize that the work may well be an anthology. It seems to be an eye-witness account of the terrible atrocities which accompanied the sack of Jerusalem — including the description of starving mothers cooking the flesh of their own children (4:10). Certain verses (e.g., 1:12 and 2:13) have been accommodated to the Blessed Virgin Mary's sorrow on Calvary. Chapters 1, 2 and 4 (all funeral dirges) serve as the readings for Tenebrae (Matins and Lauds for the last three days of Holy Week). On these solemn days the Church seizes upon the inspired verses of Lamentations as the most effective way to express her grief at the sufferings of Christ.[3] The marriage symbolism initiated by Osee is present in this book: in the very first verse Jerusalem is depicted as "widowed." The third chapter runs in a different vein from the other three. The author (who sounds like Deutero-Isaia) identifies the sufferings of Jerusalem with his own and calls for a public confession of guilt:

> Let us search and examine our ways that we may return to the Lord! Let us reach out our hearts toward God in heaven! We have sinned and rebelled; you have not forgiven us. (Vv. 40-42; this is classed as a personal lament.)

Jeremia's Preparation and Theme

Can it be that Jeremia was the author of the quotation above, and that his principal preparation was his own complete conversion to Yahweh, with the persecution of his countrymen serving as the "dark night" of his soul? We can only conjecture; it does seem appropriate, especially since this notion of a "complete conversion" was the very message he was preaching to the Jews.[4] At any rate, Jeremia began his career shortly after the reform of the pious King Josia had gotten under way. Just as in Isaia we have a second Amos, so in Jeremia we have a second Osee. To enhance the concept of God's mercy, Jeremia adds the note of personal intimacy with God which will be an integral factor in the new messianic Covenant which he forecasts. He goes so far as to predict that eventually the Ark of the Covenant will no longer be the center of Jewish worship (3:16); truly a daring statement to hurl in the faces of his contemporaries! In fact, it was Jeremia and his companions who, according to the tradition recorded in II Machabees 2:5-7, were responsible for the loss of the Ark in the side of a mountain.

The genius of Jeremia was to interpret the meaning of the fall of Jerusalem for his contemporaries in the face of the bitterest persecution. Although unable to convince them, he declared unequivocally that the wickedness of the Jews had reached such a pitch that their only hope was *to surrender their capital into the hands of the Baby-*

---

[3] See Louis Bouyer, *The Paschal Mystery*, (Chicago, Ill.: Henry Regnery Co., 1950) esp. Chap. 1.

[4] Dr. Anderson suggests this interpretation in the light of Jeremia's "confessions" and especially Jer. 15:19, *Op. cit.*, p. 342; note literary analysis on p. 327.

lonian besiegers whom God had raised up as His avenger of their injustices. The hardness and impenitence of God's people have finally closed the door to any chance of military victory: Yahweh's mercy can be manifested only through captivity and exile. Once again His wayward children must be led into the wilderness of suffering. Jeremia's language is picturesque: the Jews can no more do good than can "the Ethiopian change his skin, the leopard his spots" (13:23); "the sins of Juda are written with an iron stylus, engraved with a diamond point upon the tablets of their hearts" (17:1). Eight key chapters have been selected for analysis; they give us a clear picture both of the prophet and his message. The Confraternity introduction is helpful.

Chapter 1. "The word of the Lord came to me thus" (v. 4): note the power implied in the concept of the word of God. It is urgent; once Yahweh speaks, His prophets are constrained to publish the message regardless of the consequences to themselves. Modern scholars find insufficient evidence in verse 5 to support the view that Jeremia was cleansed of·original sin in his mother's womb. The last three verses refer to Jeremia's preparation for his mission: this theme is elaborated in Chapter 16. Note in 2:2-6 another instance of the glamorous portrayal of the forty years in the desert.

Chapter 16. To harden Jeremia against all human respect, Yahweh forbids him to marry or to participate in any social gathering. The Babylonian Captivity is predicted as a punishment which will end in restoration, a New Exodus (vv. 13-15). The messianic era to follow will witness the conversion of the Gentiles (v. 19) and a renewed intimacy (knowledge) between Yahweh and His elect (v. 21; cf. p. 185 on Os. 4).

Chapter 20. Along with Chapters 12, 15 and 18, this is an example of Jeremia's numerous "confessions," furnishing precious insights to his life and character. For insisting that Jerusalem must fall and the Jews treated "like clay in the hand of the potter" (cf. 18:6 ff.; this symbol was copied by St. Paul in Romans 9:19-24), the prophet is put in the stocks by the priest-custodian of the Temple (20:2). This "dark night" of the soul elicits a poignant outcry from Jeremia (20:7 ff.; cf. vv. 15-18 with parallel passages in the Book of Job, which was written later). Note the Confraternity footnotes on 22:30 and 23:1-8, and the term "shoot" in 23:5.[5]

Chapter 25. Here occurs the famous prophecy of the seventy years of exile; if dated from the first deportation in 598 B.C., it is reasonably accurate. Also foretold is the destruction of Babylon (Sesach) and

---

[5] Ellis, *Op. cit.*, pp. 336-337, gives arguments for seeing in this verse reference to a "New David"—i.e., an individual descendant of this line but without royal power. For him, then, the text becomes the first prediction of a personal (as opposed to a dynastic) Messia.

other pagan foes of Israel. These oracles are expanded in Chapters 46-51. In 49:7-22, Jeremia pours out his vengeance on Edom, for reasons which are supplied by the BOOK OF ABDIA, verses 10-14. This fiercely nationalistic and shortest book of the Old Testament describes the ultimate triumph of good over evil in terms of the occupation of this ancient rival by her foes.

Chapter 27. A clear statement of Jeremia's message regarding the proper behavior of the Jews during the siege of Jerusalem. One of the many symbolic acts performed by the prophet was the wearing of a yoke around his neck to illustrate the need of submission to Babylonia. One of the false prophets, Anania, broke this yoke (28:10-11).

Chapter 31. God's mercy will eventually cause the restoration of both Israel (Chap. 30) and Juda (31:23 ff.); His "age-old love" will prevail (31:3). The most important passage in the book is the description of the "New Covenant" in 31:31-34. Although Jeremia no doubt associated it in his own mind with the return of the Judean exiles, its fuller sense certainly points to the New Testament, a term derived from this passage (see assigned commentary in Heb. 8). Jeremia here promises a unique intimacy between God and His people not hitherto realized in the Hebrew concept of collective salvation. He counters Isaia's vision of Yahweh's transcendence with his own vision of God's immanence: the messianic era will mean a personal relationship between God and the individual worshiper. To this concept is added the note of personal responsibility for sin in place of collective guilt (31:29-30; cf. Ezech. 18).

Chapter 36. The literary history of Jeremia; Baruch's role as his secretary.

Chapter 43. The non-descript remnant (the "bad figs" of Chap. 24) which escaped deportation to Babylon now decide to disobey Jeremia's warning and flee into Egypt, forcibly taking the prophet with them. Tradition affirms that he was murdered there after predicting that Nabuchodonosor would catch up with them. (He did in 568.)

The Book of Baruch

Because the earliest known form of this book was in Greek, we can reasonably suspect that it is actually a retrospective view of earlier times. Moreover, 3:9-38 is a typical wisdom passage characteristic of the wisdom movement which came into bloom three centuries before Christ. This third chapter assigns the Babylonian Captivity to "forsaking the fountain of wisdom"—i.e., disobedience to the Law: the kind of practical knowledge to which Osee referred in Osee 4:1-6. Note Baruch 3:38.

Psalm 136: Lament Over the Babylonian Captivity

This exotic, plaintive poem may have been composed during the Exile or perhaps shortly afterward. Verses 1-3 recount the Babylonians' request to sing to them; verses 4-6 gives the Jews' reply; the final three verses are an imprecation (cf. Chap. XIX) against Babylonia and Edom.

Suggested Readings

Anderson, *Understanding the Old Testament*, Chap. 11.

Bouyer, *The Meaning of Sacred Scripture*, Chap. 8.

Crowley, *The Books of Lamentations, Baruch, Sophonia, Nahum, and Habacuc* (Pamphlet Bible Series No. 29).

Flanagan, *The Book of Jeremia*, Parts 1 and 2 (Pamphlet Bible Series No. 27 and No. 28).

Guillet, *Themes of the Bible*, pp. 71-76.

Moriarty, *Introducing the Old Testament*, pp. 138-156.

Stuhlmueller, *The Books of Aggai, Zacharia, Malachia, Jona, Joel, Abdia* (Pamphlet Bible Series No. 33).

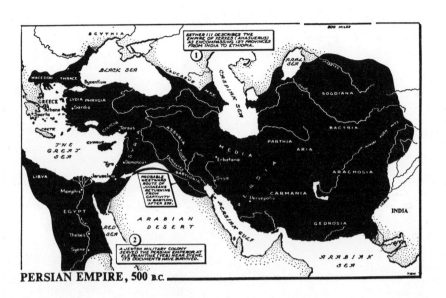

PERSIAN EMPIRE, 500 B.C.

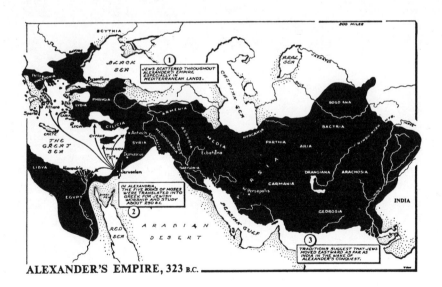

ALEXANDER'S EMPIRE, 323 B.C.

Chapter XXVI

Ezechiel and Second Isaia: The New Israel and the Suffering Servant

READINGS: *Ezechiel 10, 11, 18, 20, 37, 43, 44; Isaia 40–45, 53, 58, 65; Jona: Hebrews 7; Psalm 21. (Note: Ezechiel 11:19–20; 18:4; Isaia 40 [all]; 53 [all]; 55:9–11; 65:17–25; Jona 4:11)*

Two of the most important writers of the Old Testament collaborate to give us a picture of the Israel of the future — a picture which, unfortunately, their contemporaries viewed through rose-colored glasses. Both of these "authors" lived and prophesied during the Exile in Babylon. The first, Ezechiel, was a contemporary of Jeremia, on whom his dependence is evident. The other, Deutero-(Second) Isaia, was a disciple of the original Isaia as explained on p. 189. Each of these seers brings out vividly the universalist mission of Israel in addition to his own proper theme.

Ezechiel The Priest

Like Jeremia, Ezechiel was of the priestly class, although it is not known if or when he exercised this profession. He is nevertheless the man of worship par excellence; it is in terms of this medium that he analyzes Israel's destiny, past, present and future. Like Jeremia also, he denounced the idolatrous practices of his contemporaries on the eve of the Exile. So far had this vicious propensity progressed that a genuine syncretism or amalgamation of Mosaic and pagan rites characterized Jewish worship. Whereas Jeremia declared that Yahweh would establish a new covenant "in their hearts," Ezechiel develops the theology of messianic times one degree further; this new covenant, he insists, will demand that Yahweh give them not only the covenant, but also a new heart in which to receive it!

This concept actually harks back to the transcendence theme of Isaia: man's state as creature demands that salvation be a superhuman, divine work in him — a new creation. Ezechiel reasserts the Isaian-Jeremian justice theme according to which the door left open by Amos has now been closed so that exile looms up as a necessary punishment. In fact, he goes one step further in declaring that the Temple itself must be destroyed. The shades of Osee make their appearance in Ezechiel in several magnificent marriage analogies, especially Ezechiel 16:1-14, already considered in conjunction with Chapter XIII. To Ezechiel must be credited a vital spiritualization of religion in a new higher synthesis, in which both the letter and spirit of the Law are stressed. Unlike Jeremia, Ezechiel was not persecuted; rather, the contrary seems to have been true; people found him entertaining. Yahweh is even moved to complain about the prophet's popularity; listening to Ezechiel became the latest fad:

> As for you, son of man [a title frequently predicated of Ezechiel in this book], your countrymen are talking about you along the walls and in the doorways of houses . . . For them you are only a ballad singer, with a pleasant voice and a clever touch. They listen to your words, but they will not obey them. (33:30, 32)

One reason for this attraction of the people to Ezechiel lies in the unusual symbolism contained in both his life and his preaching. He is, for example, forbidden to mourn over the death of his beloved wife in order to impress upon the Jews the horror of the approaching destruction of Jerusalem (24:15 ff).

Ezechiel departs from a standard position of his predecessors in his refusal to look upon the forty years in the desert as a time of idyllic fidelity to the Covenant on the part of Israel; he maintains that such fidelity never existed (cf. Chap. 20). Finally, among his many contributions to the development of dogma is his clearcut statement on personal responsibility for one's sins. As in the case of Jeremia, we shall proceed by analyzing key chapters.

Chapter 10. Having been carried off to Babylon in the first deportation of 598 B.C. along with King Jechonia, Ezechiel feels "the hand of the Lord" (1:3) upon him and begins to preach to his fellow captives. The mysterious, transcendent vision of the four winged creatures is repeated here from Chapter 1; it reminds us of the vision of Isaia. Each of the winged creatures has four faces resembling that of a man, a lion, an ox and an eagle. This symbolism has been accommodated to the four Evangelists of the New Testament. Yahweh is vaguely described as sitting on a throne above the four creatures (cf. 1:26). The withdrawal of the glory of the Lord from the Temple and its settling on a mountain east of Jerusalem (10:18-19 and 11:22) is all-important: Ezechiel thus conveys the theme of the "de-localization" of Yahweh. Forced to depart because of the abominations which the Jews themselves were perpetrating in the Temple (8:6 ff.), Yahweh leaves its physical precincts in order to take up His abode in the hearts of the faithful remnant who have gone into exile.

Chapter 11. In continuation of this theme, Ezechiel is spirited off to the east gate of the Temple and given to understand that the faithful remnant — the Anawin of later Jewish terminology — are not those who will remain in the city, but those who have gone into exile to Babylon. Though Yahweh seems to them to be far away, He gives them this beautiful assurance:

> I will give them a new heart and put a new spirit within them;
> I will remove the stony heart from their bodies, and replace it with
> a natural heart, so that they will live according to my statutes, and
> observe and carry out my ordinances; thus they shall be my people
> and I will be their God. (Vv. 19-20)

Like the New Covenant of Jeremia 31:31, this passage is scarcely a stone's throw from the New Testament.

Chapter 18. In unmistakable terms Ezechiel hammers home another pet theme: the ancient notion of collective guilt must give way to that of personal responsibility! The children's teeth shall no longer be set on edge because of the sins of the father.

Chapter 20. The portrayal of the desert wandering as a "honeymoon" between Yahweh and His people under the theocracy finds no echo in Ezechiel; he shows, in fact, that Israel has been a recalcitrant daughter all of her life — even in the wilderness. Yet Yahweh refuses to be thwarted by His rebellious children, declaring: *"I swear I will be king over you!"* (v. 33). But He will be able to accept them only after they have once again been purified by the desert of Babylonia. Here is Osee's theme of redemptive punishment (as exemplified in his treatment of Gomer) being applied to the Babylonian Captivity. The people themselves will eventually become Yahweh's first-fruit offering (vv. 40-41).

Chapter 37. The vision of the dry bones in this chapter does not represent the resurrection of the body, but is a symbol forecasting the restoration of the Exiles. The prophecy of the two sticks representing the union of Israel and Juda under one monarch is idealistic; it was never realized perfectly on the political level but rather spiritually through the Messia and His kingdom as embodied in the Anawin.

Chapter 43. The apocalyptic account of Gog and Magog representing the cosmic forces of evil in Chapters 38-39 have been passed over, as reference will be made to them in the final chapter. Here in Chapter 43 the Lord is pictured as returning to the Temple once again and taking up His abode there. But it will be a different mode of presence, as in the days of the perfect theocracy when the sacred was not profaned by the secular power (cf. vv. 8-9); and it will endure forever, as Ezechiel states in verse 7 and symbolizes by the closed east gate in 44:1. We know from the Gospel of St. John that Christ replaced the Temple with His body (John 2:19) and furnished the true water of grace (Ezech. 47:1-12, the vision of water flowing from the Temple and forming the background for the paschal "Vidi Aquam"). The New Testament fulfillment reaches its climax in the Apocalypse of St. John, where there is no Temple, light, or lamp: these are supplied by the divine essence (Apoc. 21:22 and 22:5). Both sacred authors complete the cycle of salvation history by the symbol of an idealistic Utopian return to Paradise.

Chapter 44. Ezechiel capitalizes on still another unique Semitic literary genre: the *Utopian model.* This is an idealistic portrayal of an existing institution which, in God's eternal plan of salvation, is actually going to be replaced by a new institution sometime in the future. Beginning in Chapter 40, the prophet lays down a precise blueprint for the new Temple to be built after the restoration. In Chapter 44 he specifies the Levitical descendants of Sadoc as the only acceptable line to continue the formal rites and sacrifices of the new age. This chapter and other similar passages regarding the New Israel in messianic times represent the inspired manner of describing in figurative language a future which is deliberately left obscure and out of focus by God.[1] For a study in depth, turn now and re-read Hebrews 7, which has already been studied in the context of Chapter IX (Abraham's Faith). This chapter in the Epistle takes on a new clarity in the wake of Ezechiel's Utopian description of the Levitical priesthood. It is the author's genius to show the replacement of that institution by the Christian priesthood.

In the prophet Ezechiel we have a practical, down-to-earth architect spelling out the new rules of the game for his dejected contemporaries. Although they did not heed his words before the fall of Jerusalem, we know that his ideals prevailed more, perhaps, than those of any other prophet in the setting up of the new community following Cyrus's decree of liberation in 538 B.C.[2]

Second Isaia and the Book of Consolations

With Chapters 40-55 of the Book of Isaia we begin what is today generally known as Second Isaia (cf. introduction to this book in the Confraternity Version). These words of consolation to the Babylonian exiles were written, it seems, between the years 550-540 B.C. — over a century after the death of First Isaia. We have here a case where the disciple has outstripped the master: the poetry of Deutero-Isaia is unsurpassed in the Old Testament. The scene has changed completely from the charged atmosphere in which the original Isaia preached to

---

[1] Cf. Jer. 33:14-18 and footnote in Confraternity Version; also, the "New Jerusalem" in Isa. 65, 66.

[2] See Stuhlmueller, *The Books of Aggai, Zaccharia, Malachia, Jona, Joel and Abdia*, p. 8.

a proud, stiff-necked people, with the sad result that he was obliged to "bind up" his oracles secretly among his followers (cf. Isa. 8:11-20). Here we find the disciple of Isaia addressing a contrite, humbled and discouraged remnant of Babylon. Their capital and Temple have been destroyed and they are languishing on foreign soil among pagans. But suddenly a joyful note of hope is sounded in their midst: Jerusalem's "service" is at an end (40:2).

The Confraternity Version finally does justice to 40:3; it is not the *voice* which is "in the desert," but the *preparation for the Lord's coming* by means of the suffering endured by the exiles. Malachia 3:1 is needed to make the correlation with Mark 1:2 along with this verse in Isaia! The continuity of the two Isaias is illustrated in 40:6-8: Yahweh's transcendence is brought out in the contrast between flesh, which is transitory like grass, and the word of God, which stands forever. Verses 9-11 have found their way into Handel's *Messiah;* verses 12 ff. inspired Romans 11:34. The redemption of Israel from Babylon is described in terms of a "new creation" (vv. 22 ff.) — similar to the Wisdom terminology cited on p. 119. Chapter 41 pictures Yahweh calling the Gentiles into council to vindicate His special direction of Israel's destiny in the face of the pagans' boasting.

In Chapter 42 we are introduced to the first four "Servant Songs." Still full of mystery for the biblical exegete, these passages portray a persecuted, rejected figure. The solution which seems to be best in accord with the whole context is that which sees the "Servant" as an individual with a corporate personality representing the nation — specifically, the remnant. The passages are: 42:1-4; 49:1-7; 50:4-11; and 52:13-53:12. This ideal sufferer finds typical fulfillment in Christ, Who endured His sufferings vicariously for the sins of the world.

Chapter 43 depicts the restoration once again as a new Exodus (cf. vv. 2, 16-19; also Chap. 51). The Israelites are called the Lord's "witnesses" and "servants" in verse 10. Chapter 44 renews the transcendence theme with an attack on pagan idols — a prominent theme throughout the book (note v. 6). The end of the chapter begins the portrayal of Cyrus as the "Lord's Anointed"; this theme is carried over into Chapter 45. It is interesting to note that whereas the "Cyrus Cylinder" alleges that the Persian king was the agent of *his* god, Marduk, the inspired words of Scripture give the true theology of history.

The Suffering Servant of Yahweh

(Isaia 53)

So closely does the description of the Servant in the last three verses of Chapter 52 and all of Chapter 53 match the actual sufferings of Christ that we have here extensive compenetration. We see the be-

ginning of a new concept in Old Testament pedagogy: the notion of
vicarious satisfaction. The final verse of this fourth Servant Song tells
us that the victim will also be a victor through His sufferings. Nor
should we be disturbed at the use of the term *servant* in a corporate
sense; this is in complete accord with ancient Semitic literary practice.
As the world was to learn later, no individual save Christ could re-
capitulate in his person all of the qualities of the perfect redemptive
sufferer. Deutero-Isaia ends in Chapter 55 with what is tantamount to
a definition of Yahweh's transcendence (vv. 8-9) followed by an exalted
statement of the efficacy of His word (vv. 10-11).

Third Isaia and the Universalism of the New Irael (Isaia 55–66)

The final two chapters of Isaia return to the teaching that Israel is
to be the light of salvation to the whole world in unmistakable language.
The theme of the New Jerusalem to which all nations shall stream—
begun in Chapter 2—is reiterated. In 65:17-25 we have another
Utopian model of the New Jerusalem. The Jews consistently refused
to recognize the replacement of this institution by the Church of Christ
and made, instead, the glowing restoration of their capital an end in
itself by insisting on a proper literal interpretation of these texts. For
this reason they were unable as a people to fulfill their destiny toward
the other nations of the world.

The Book of Jona: The Call of the Gentiles

That a segment of the Jewish populace did appreciate this exalted
destiny of the nation, however, is forcefully illustrated by the Book of
Jona, fifth among the minor prophets. Directed by God to preach to
the Assyrians of Ninive, Jona takes a boat trip in the opposite direction
to escape this unpalatable assignment. Note that when a devastating
storm arises, the pagans pray while Jona sleeps: in spite of his bad
example, they are converted to Yahweh. After surviving the impossible ordeal in the belly of the fish, Jona is persuaded to fulfill Yahweh's
commission. At his preaching, the Ninivites are suddenly converted —
from the king down to the humblest peasant — and all do the most
extraordinary penances. Never did a prophet have such remarkable
success even among his own people. Not even Pentecost produced so
rich a harvest of souls. Nor is there any evidence of such a miraculous
conversion in the annals of Assyria. The pouting of Jona at the failure
of God to make good the destruction of Nineve, and then over the
withering of the ivy, borders on the ludicrous. All of these considerations lead to the conclusion that Jona is a satire and not historical. As
we stated previously (p. 33), *ideal* existence is sufficient to justify the
spiritual meaning attached to Jona by Christ (cf. Matt. 12:39 ff.). The

lesson is clear: if the ivy was so indispensable to Jona, surely Gentile peoples are not to be considered as "expendible"! They, too, have a place in Yahweh's plan of salvation. This book was written by an unknown author after the Exile, when it was popular to clothe moral lessons in an historical garb (e.g., Tobias, Daniel), and when Jewish nationalism was dangerously prejudicing them against all Gentiles.

Psalm 21: Another Glimpse of the Suffering Servant

From every angle except that of authorship this Psalm of Lament fits into the atmosphere of Isaia 53. Consistent with our line of exegesis thus far, we do not feel that even the uncanny similarities of this poem with the passion of Christ warrant a direct messianic correlation. Again we see here a portrait of the ideal sufferer — perhaps the psalmist himself. The meaning of Christ's fourth word from the cross is illuminated by the fact that He was quoting verse 2 of this psalm, just as His last word is a quotation of Psalm 30:6. Verses 23-27 begin an enumeration of the effects of sufferer's ordeal (gratitude), verses 28-30, the conversion of the Gentiles, and verses 31-32, the final exaltation of the sufferer himself. What constituted his particular crisis we do not know.

Suggested Readings

Anderson, *Understanding the Old Testament,* pp. 359-381; Chap. 13.
Bouyer, *The Meaning of Sacred Scripture,* Chap. 9.
Guillet, *Themes of the Bible,* pp. 55-71.
Huesman, *The Book of Isaia,* Part 2 (Pamphlet Bible Series No. 32).
Siegman, *The Book of Ezechiel,* Parts 1 and 2 (Pamphlet Bible Series No. 30 and
    No. 31).

Chapter XXVII

Esdras and Nehemia: The Canonical Torah and The Shaping of Judaism

READINGS: *I Esdras 1, 3–6; II Esdras 2, 4, 8, 9, 13; Joel; Malachia: Zacharia 3, 4, 6, 9, 12, 13; Psalms 146–147. (Note: II Esdras 8:5–8; 9:38; 13:26; Zacharia 6:9–15; Malachia 1:11; 3:23)*

In the last chapter we left the deportees languishing in Babylon, but repentant and hopeful of deliverance in the wake of the promised restoration of Deutero-Isaia. That promise blossomed rather suddenly. In 539 B.C. Cyrus the Great, the Persian military genius who had conquered the Medes a few years before, took Babylon without a struggle. The new emperor proved to be one of the most enlightened monarchs of history. In keeping with his colonial policy, he permitted the first contingent of Israelite exiles to return to their homeland in 538 B.C.

The biblical account of this phase of salvation history is contained in the second half of the Chronicler's work, the two Books of Esdras. Drawing heavily on the memoirs of Esdras and Nehemia, this compiler fills in precious details and gives us penetrating interpretations of historical events from the time of the return until the probable date of his editorship, about 400 B.C., or shortly thereafter.[1] He furnishes us with two versions of Cyrus' decree of restoration: the Hebrew text appears in I Esdras 1:2-4; the Aramaic text appears a little later in 6:3-5. Putting together the statistics contained in 2:64-65, we arrive at a total of 50,000 returning exiles: this, however, represents the population of rehabilitated Juda a century later. In fact, the population at the close of the sixth century has been estimated at only about 20,000.[2] This is a far cry from the mighty kingdom of David and Solomon!

---

[1] As we have noted on pp. 146 and 163 this same individual also edited I and II Par., as evidenced by the identity of II Par. 36:22-23 with I Esd. 1:1-3.

[2] We learn from Esd. 7:5 that it was actually Nehemia who took the census in the year 445 B.C.; the totals in I Esd. 2:64-65 and II Esd. 7:66-67 are virtually identical. Cf. Stuhlmueller, *The Books of Aggai, Zaccharia, Malachia, Jona, Joel and Abdia,* p. 9, and the authoritative article by W. F. Albright, "The Biblical Period," in *The Jews: Their History, Culture and Religion,* ed. by L. Finkelstein (New York: Harper and Brothers, 1949) p. 49. The post-Exilic term "Jew" is from "Juda."

Away from their beloved Temple and without sacrifice during the captivity, the Jews had had time to reflect in Babylon on the meaning of the catastrophe which had overtaken them. Had Yahweh abandoned His Chosen People? In other words, had they failed the final, definitive test of fidelity and now been cast off forever? And even though some were now returned to their homeland after a generation and a half, had not the glory departed from Israel? The Chronicler seems to have set out with fixed purpose to give reassuring answers to such questions as these. What the Yahwist writer (whose work — joined to that of the Elohist — was even now being finally edited by the Priestly group) had accomplished centuries earlier by way of uniting the ante-diluvian patriarchs with Abraham, the Chronicler accomplished by way of showing the continuity of post-Exilic Juda with the Davidic kingdom. The chapters assigned in I and II Esdras should be read in the order in which they are treated below.

Zorobabel and the Second Temple

(Esdras 1–6; Aggai; Zacharia)

The prophets of the Exile insisted on two things: the permanence of the Davidic dynasty, and the renovation of worship. Reading between the lines, the student of Sacred Scripture can detect that the latter theme is the more important one, and that the former gradually recedes into the background.[3] We can well understand the enthusiasm of the returning exiles when a Davidic prince, Zorobabel (grandson of Jechonia) was appointed governor of Juda after Sassabassar, the first governor and likewise a descendant of David (cf. I Esd. 5:14 and Agg. 1:1; scholars no longer seem inclined to identify Sassabassar and Zorobabel). His first task, carried out in conjunction with Josue the high priest, was to build an altar for sacrifices. Then they proceeded to the rebuilding of the Temple. At this point they were confronted by a formidable obstacle. The Samaritans, whose help Zorobabel had spurned because of their mixed blood, set up an organized program of sabotage which postponed the completion of the project until 515 B.C.[4]

Post-Exilic Prophecy: Aggai and Zacharia

During the enforced interruption of the building of the Temple, the remnant grew apathetic toward that project and toward religion in

---

[3] Contrast Ezech. 34:23 with 43:7-9 and 45:7-12, where the "prince" is definitely played down, and separation between church and state hinted; contrast Jer. 23:5 and 22:30.

[4] Cf. I Esd. 4:1-5, 24; note that vv. 6-23 are a digression in which the Chronicler cites three other (later) instances in which their enemies had recourse to the Persian court in order to interfere with the Jews.

general. The first two of the half-dozen post-Exilic prophets took this situation as the occasion of their preaching, which began in 520 B.C. In Aggai 1:9-11 we learn that Yahweh sent a drought on the land to punish the inhabitants' excessive care over temporal concerns while the Lord's house remained unfinished. His preaching was successful, and work on the Temple was vigorously resumed (1:14-15). The last verse of this short book reflects the messianic hope prevalent among the remnant; this same theme of the Davidic line is found in Aggai's contemporary, Zacharia.

Like Isaia, the prophecy of Zacharia has a double authorship, Second Zacharia beginning with Chapter 9. In First Zacharia, the prophet presents eight bizarre visions designed to bolster the morale of his countrymen. In 3:8 Zacharia sees the high priest, Josue, associated with the Davidic prince ("Shoot" — i.e., Zorobabel; cf. also 4:14). Chapter 4 is a veiled prediction of the successful rebuilding of the Temple "by my spirit" (4:6) in the face of difficulties (the "great mountain" of 4:7). Chapter 6 reaches a climax in the description of the crowning of Zorobabel by the prophet (6:11). Just what happened to Zorobabel after the completion of the Temple is not known; perhaps the Persian king deposed him, fearing that the rising Jewish nationalism would result in revolt. Later on, when the high priest had emerged as the dominant figure in Juda, a redactor substituted the name Josue for that of Zorobabel! His disappearance dampened hope in the resurgence of a Davidic ruler.

Second Zacharia represents a literary genre known as apocalypse, defined on p. 28 as one of the unique Semitic forms. It will be considered in detail in connection with the Book of Daniel in Chapter XXX. The scene of action has shifted drastically: here the "word" (divine judgment) seems to refer to the Greek conquest, thus dating this section of the prophecy two centuries later — i.e., about 320 B.C. or later. No dates are given, and the prophet himself seems to have receded into the background: as in the case of II Isaia, these chapters are the work of a disciple (or school). No more mention is made of either "prince" or "priest"; rather, there is reference to a "king" and "savior" (9:9 — cited in John 12:15 in regard to Christ's triumphal entrance into Jerusalem). This representative of the House of David, however, will not come as a conquerer, but "riding on an ass"; apparently he will meet a tragic end like King Josia (12:10-14; cf. John 19:34, 37). But his death will result in "a fountain to purify from sin and uncleanness" (13:1). Some of these verses, especially those referring to the false shepherds, are obscure. The battle for Jerusalem in the final chapter may be seen as the battle of the Messia ("Jerusalem") against the powers of evil. Zacharia is one of the Old Testament books most frequently quoted in the New Testament because of its extensive messianic allusions.

Nehemia and the Walls of Jerusalem

(II Esdras 1–7; 11–13)

Skipping the first half of the fifth century, the Chronicler resumes his narrative with the stories of Esdras and Nehemia. Following the trend of modern biblical scholars, we shall put the arrival of Nehemia in Jerusalem before that of Esdras.[5] We must go to II Esdras for this story. The "twentieth year of Artaxerxes the king" in 2:1 refers to Artaxerxes I (465-424); this gives us a date universally accepted by commentators: 445 B.C. Having heard that the morale of his Jewish kinsmen in Palestine is very low, and that Jerusalem has been left exposed to its enemies because of a lack of defensive ramparts, Nehemia obtains permission from Artaxerxes (whose cupbearer he was) to return to Jerusalem in order to rebuild its walls. Chapter 4 documents the trials which he faced in completing the project in the wake of opposition from one Sanaballat and other influential Samaritans. Turning to Chapter 11, we find Nehemia selecting by lot the ten percent who were to populate the City.

The Chronicler manifests his concern over the Temple liturgy in the prominent place he gives to the Levites (rivaling even that accorded to the "sons of Aaron") in Chapter 12. David is portrayed as the great churchman and organizer of the chant (12:35, 44-45). In the final chapter of the book, we find Nehemia correcting the decadent morals of the returned exiles. Five abuses are singled out as targets of the Wall-Builder's fury: (1) admission into the "church of God" of Ammonites and Moabites, forbidden in Deuteronomy 23:4; (2) the use of rooms in the Temple as a commercial center by Tobias the Samaritan through the connivance of Eliasib the high priest; (3) nonpayment of tithes to the Levites; (4) performance of servile work on the Sabbath; (5) mixed marriages, which "brought even him [Solomon] to sin" (13:26).

Esdras and the Torah: The Rise of Judaism

(I Esdras 7–10; II Esdras 8–10)

Backtracking to I Esdras, we find that Nehemia was assisted in his reform by a priest named Esdras, "a ready scribe in the law of Moses" (7:6),[6] and armed with a decree from Artaxerxes to restore the observance of the Mosaic Law (7:13-26). The decree betrays the superstitious self-interest of the king and his territorial concept of deity (v. 23). When he arrived in Jerusalem (428 B.C.?), Esdras found the deplor-

---

[5] Cf. Stuhlmueller, *Loc. cit.*, and Albright, *Op. cit.*, p. 53, who place his arrival at 427 and 428 B.C., respectively. For the older view, cf. Orchard, *A Catholic Commentary on Holy Scripture*, col. 289 i-q.

[6] Beginning with Esdras, the term "scribe" signifies *interpreter of the Law.*

able outrages outlined above. He rent his garments and prayed God for forgiveness; then he arranged for a public confession of guilt (Chap. 9-10). Concentrating on the correction of mixed marriages, he compelled all offenders to put away their foreign wives (10:19). The narrative continues in II Esdras 8, where we find the Levites designated to read "the book of the law of Moses" (v. 1) to the people after all had "adored God with their faces to the ground" (cf. vv. 6-8). This ceremony led to a general repentance, followed in Chapter 9 by a typical covenant-renewal (v. 38; cf. p. 150).

It seems that the answers to the questions posed at the beginning of this chapter have at last been found by this zealous scribe, Esdras — whom Jewish tradition identifies as the Chronicler.[7] No, Yahweh had not abandoned His people: he was just reorientating them. He had never meant that their principal goal should consist in Israel's becoming a world empire; rather, their true greatness lay in their function as a worshipping community. Such is the Chronicler's inspired conclusion from the history of Israel. Therefore idolatry — described by the prophets as infidelity ("harlotry") to Yahweh — is the gravest of crimes. But how were this and other sins, such as those enumerated in II Esdras 13 — often committed out of ignorance — to be avoided in the future?

The Chronicler's reasoned conclusion as to how purity of worship and perfect obedience to the will of God could be insured is through a detailed understanding of the Mosaic Law on the part of learned scribes, who in turn would promulgate its tenets to the people. The Chronicler had come to look upon the Law as the official constitution of Juda — similar to the great pagan codes of civil law. Moreover, Esdras lived at a strategic moment in the literary development of the Old Testament. The Priestly editors had just finished the work of putting the Pentateuch into its final form by amalgamating the principal Mosaic traditions. This unified Torah would provide the ideal instrument to set forth as the Jewish "constitution," and " . . . it seems highly probable that it was Ezra who introduced the complete Pentateuch into normative Jewish use and who is largely responsible for the way in which its archaic practices were adjusted to actual ritual usage in the Temple."[8] We must not conclude, however, that emphasis at this period was exclusively on the Torah; not only had the "Former Prophets" (Josue-IV Kings) been "published," but editions of most of the pre-Exilic prophets must also have been available, as shown in the chart on page 53. Nor should we blame Esdras for the excessive legalism which gradually encrusted Judaism. In his era, legal reform was most urgent because of the wanton disregard of the Torah by the returned exiles. It constitutes a betrayal to brand Esdras as standing

---

[7] So also Prof. Albright; Cf. *Op. cit.*, p. 64, note 138.

[8] Albright, *Op. cit.*, p. 54.

for the letter of the law in contrast to the prophets, on the grounds that they stand for its spirit; in fact, Esdras was greatly influenced by the work of a prophet, Ezechiel.

Other Post-Exilic Prophets

We have already analyzed the universalist theme of Jona and noted the narrowness of Abdia. Only two prophets remain to be considered: Malachia and Joel. Like Adbia, JOEL lends fuel to nationalism, though his optimism and apocalyptic tone soften the blow considerably. A devastating plague of locusts about 400 B.C. is the occasion for the proclamation of a fast by Joel. He calls for a complete change of heart: "Rend your hearts, not your garments" — this is part of the selection which makes up the Epistle for Ash Wednesday (2:12-19). Then the prophet turns to the subject of the Day of the Lord, borrowing terminology from Sophonia and Michea. Chapter 3 (the end of Chap. 2 in the Douay-Rheims Version), quoted by St. Peter in his Pentecost sermon, has truly universalist overtones. But then Joel, reversing the imagery of Isaia 2:4, calls for drastic vengeance on Juda's enemies in the last chapter.

MALACHIA preceded Joel by about 50 years. Arriving in Palestine shortly before Nehemia, he courageously upbraids his countrymen for their sins, particularly sacrilege and mixed marriages. He makes a strong condemnation of divorce (2:15-16), presaging its final elimination in the New Testament. Though Malachia employs a Utopian mold in 3:3, his vision transcends the Old Testament sacrifices in the famous messianic text, 1:11. Conceding the Jews have been chosen (1:3), Malachia displays the universalism of Amos (3:2) and Isaia (3:19). "My messenger" in 3:1 ("Malachia") was fulfilled in John the Baptist; the last verse of the book reflects the popular view that Elias would precede the Messia in person.

Psalms 146–147: Exiles Give Thanks!

These are treated as a single psalm in the Hebrew. Psalm 146 expresses the joy of the returned exiles to Yahweh, the true Builder. Psalm 147 may well have been composed for the dedication of the walls rebuilt by Nehemia.

Suggested Readings

Anderson, *Understanding the Old Testament*, Chap. 14.
Dyson and Jones, *The Kingdom of Promise*, Chap. 7.
Moriarty, *Introducing the Old Testament*, pp. 189-201.
Stuhlmueller, *The Books of Aggai, Zacharia, Malachia, Jona, Joel, Abdia* (Pamphlet Bible Series No. 33).

Chapter XXVIII

From Persian to Greek Domination: Wisdom Circumcised

READINGS: *Esther 3, 9; Job 1–3, 8–10, 28, 38, 40, 42; Ecclesiastes 1–3; Sirach: Prologue; 1–3; 6–7; 24; 34–35; 39–41, 44–51; I Machabees 1; Psalm 118. (Note: Ecclesiastes 7:29, 12:13–14; Proverbs 8; Job 28; Sirach 15:14–17; 24; Wisdom 7:26; I Corinthians 1:17–2:16).*

We now enter upon the Silent Period of Jewish history. Between II Esdras and I Machabees, over two centuries elapse without any inspired chronicle. The reason is not difficult to find; for what did the post-Exilic national life of the Chosen People have to offer by way of providing a medium for religious history? Though not oppressive, life was drab under the benign paternalism of the Persian kings. Once again the citizens of Juda found themselves a theocratic community, but the day of divine interventions on their behalf seemed past. What insight we do get into Israel's national life is afforded by those inspired books considered by the Jews themselves to be of lesser quality than the Torah or the Prophets, and designated the Writings (cf. p. 158). The so-called Sapiential or Wisdom Books fall within this class, as well as the Book of Esther, which we shall consider now.

Esther and the Jews of the Diaspora

The scene of this historical novel is laid in the Persian court of Assuerus (Xerxes I, 486-465). The King chooses a Jewess named Esther to fill the place of Queen Vasthi, who has refused to exhibit her beauty at a royal banquet. Niece of a wealthy Jew named Mardochai, Queen Esther is able to use her position to save her countrymen of the Persian Diaspora (i.e., colonies of Jews living outside of Palestine) from the wholesale slaughter plotted against them by the king's favorite minister, Aman. Through Esther's daring intervention, he is hanged on the gibbet which he had prepared for Mardochai after the latter refused to bend his knee to him. The feast of Purim (Esth. 9:26 and II Mach. 15:37) is established to commemorate the murderous revenge obtained by the Jews over their assailants, as described in Chapter 9.

217

In fact, some experts maintain that this book was written to justify the feast!

The probable date of authorship of this book is c. 350 B.C., though some scholars place it during the Machabean period. Fictional details which lead us to classify it as edifying history are exemplified in Aman's descent from Agag (3:1; this makes the whole story a counterpart of the struggle between the Amalecites and the Benjaminite King Saul; cf. I Kgs. 15:8); the colossal bribe of $18,000,000 which Aman offered to Xerxes; the amusing royal decree mentioned in 1:22, etc. The book is valuable in furnishing us with a picture of the way of life of Jewish colonies of the Diaspora. Like the followers of Esdras and Nehemia, they too observed the Mosaic Law with strict literalness, particularly with respect to the dietary laws and separatism from their pagan neighbors. It is this latter quality especially which seems to have made them unpopular (cf. 3:8). The Book of Esther reflects the trend toward a narrow nationalism at this period. The reader will note that the last seven chapters (i.e., from 10:4 to the end) represent excerpts; they are those portions of the work contained in the Greek version but not in the Hebrew text. For this reason, the Jews and Protestants do not accept them as canonical — although they contain the only explicit references to God.

The Wisdom Movement

The beginning of the Wisdom Movement among the Jews was noted in Chapter XXII in connection with King Solomon, the wise man par excellence. We saw how books written much later were attributed to him to enhance their authority. Although Solomon undoubtedly produced some writings, viz., parts of the Book of Proverbs, the Wisdom Movement did not come into its own until after the Exile. It was during this historical vacuum that the inspired writers of the period turned to wisdom literature as the "modern" medium of communicating salvation history. In order to qualify, this medium had to be loosed from its pagan moorings, just as the concept of kingship had been. The Book of Proverbs represents the circumcision of wisdom, canonizing as it does the Deuteronomic principle of the Two Ways as now applied to the individual. The Canticle of Canticles — likewise attributed to Solomon — was understood by later Jews to symbolize the love of Yahweh for His people, as we have seen in the chapter on Osee.

The Skepticism of Ecclesiastes
(Cf. Psalm 38)

The pat answers of Proverbs could not forever satisfy the minds of penetrating Israelites, particularly after they had been exposed to the wisdom of the Greeks. The Book of Ecclesiastes, almost anti-intellectual in tone, marks a sharp reaction against the doctrine that observance of the Torah automatically guarantees material happiness. The author, a God-fearing Jew who wrote about 250 B.C., adopts a technique of strategic pessimism. Mindful of the fact that the just sometimes do suffer in this life while the wicked prosper, and that the fate of the wise man is the same as that of the fool at death, he counsels a perfect detachment from the pleasures of life — even in the pursuit of wisdom. The absence of any satisfactory reward or sanction in this life compels Coholeth (the "Preacher") to place his entire hope in God, Whose ways are a mystery: "Fear God and keep His commandments, for this is man's all; because God will bring to judgment every work, with all its hidden qualities, whether good or bad" (12:13-14).

Job the Mystic

(Cf. Psalms 36 and 72)

Although earlier in composition than Ecclesiastes, the Book of Job (c. 500 B.C.?) goes one step further in giving a solution to the mystery of life. To understand the message of the book, it is necessary to realize that the first two chapters and the epilogue are in prose, while the body of the work is in poetry. Thus, the author begins by reproducing the traditional Deuteronomic solution of life's ups and downs, then counters this solution with his own ideas in the poetic portion. The "real" Job is not at all the patient sufferer envisaged by the popular mind; rather, he curses the day on which he was born (Chap. 3) and manifests a spirit of rebellion (Chap. 8-10). Like the author of Ecclesiastes, the author of Job departs from the moralistic Covenant theme whereby goodness is to be assessed in the light of temporal prosperity. In fact, he does not even find sufficient satisfaction in the theory that suffering serves as a purifying element in the case of the innocent: this too is insufficient compensation. Like Ecclesiastes, the author of Job admits that life is a mystery buried in the divine transcendence and its trials insoluble on this earth. But the book's greatest contribution consists in showing that *human suffering — when accepted on faith as coming from the hands of God — makes the sufferer a friend of God.* Did not Jeremia, too, discover and preach this doctrine of experience-of-God-through-suffering? Lying between the themes of Psalms 36 and 72 in dogmatic development, the theme of the Book of Job is a powerful refutation of all ready-made formulae attempting to explain human suffering. Job's repentance marks the turning point of the book; the answer is contained in a few short verses, 42:1-6. His encounter with the Lord has not quite enabled him to arrive at the Machabean concept of redemptive suffering, but Job now understands that man and his petty crises are but a small and insignificant part of God's universal plan of salvation. When isolated from this over-all plan, individual suffering is incomprehensible; it takes on meaning only in the context of the vast scheme of the Infinite. Both Job and Ecclesiastes offer us an existential solution to the mystery of life. It remains for St. Paul to give us the essentialist solution: "But the sensual man does not perceive the things that are of the Spirit of God, for it is foolishness to him. . . . But the spiritual man judges all things" (I Cor. 2:14-15).

Alexander the Great: The Greek Conquest
(I Machabees 1)

Only one obstacle stood on the horizon of continued Persian domination of the whole Western and Middle Eastern world: a group of small Greek city-states at the other end of civilization. As early as 490 B.C. Darius I had attempted to bring this outpost of resistance under control, but had been repulsed at the battle of the Marathon. Other encounters followed with the same result. The final blow was struck against Persia by a youth in his early twenties, Alexander the Great, in 331 B.C. at Arbela. Shortly afterwards, Darius III was murdered by one of his own men, and his Empire fell to Alexander. After 200 years of glory, the mighty, benevolent Persian dynasty finally collapsed.

A few words must be said concerning Alexander's background. The son of Philip of Macedon, who had succeeded in uniting the proud and independent Greek cities before his untimely assassination, the young Emperor had the advantage of being educated at the flowering of Greek philosophy under the tutelage of the peerless genius, Aristotle (384-322). Founder of the Peripatetic School, Aristotle had been trained in the Academy of Plato (427-347), who, in turn, had been a disciple of Socrates (469-399). It is little wonder, then, that Alexander's military ambitions were matched by his desire to extend the sway of Greek learning and culture throughout the Empire. In fact, whereas the Persians left little cultural impact on the provincial satrapies, the influence of Greece has endured to our own day.

Alexander's world conquest is briefly reviewed by the author of I Machabees in the first chapter. When he died at Babylon at the age of 33, his domains were plunged into civil war by the fight among his generals for succession.[1] After forty years of bloodshed, the Empire was divided among three of them who took the dynastic titles of Antigonus, Antiochus and Ptolemy. Palestine was parceled out to the Egyptian sphere of influence under the Ptolemies. This arrangement continued for over a century; under it the Jews managed to hold their own, since their overlords were content to live and let live. The tide

---

[1] Alexander is reputed to have answered the query, "To whom are you leaving your Kingdom?" with the reply, "To the strongest."

turned abruptly, however, when Antiochus III brought a 25-year feud to a successful climax by defeating Ptolemy V and seizing Palestine. His successors were intrepid apostles of Greek culture, imposing it by force on all of their territories. We shall save the story of Antiochus IV and his attempt to suppress Judaism for the next chapter. It is sufficient to note here that the impact of Hellenism was soon felt by the Jewish sages and was reflected in their writings.

Sirach, Cosmopolitan Sage of Jerusalem: Wisdom, The Guide of the Patriarchs

Greek influence can be clearly detected in the inspired work traditionally known as Ecclesiasticus, but now designated Sirach in the Confraternity Version. Beginning the reading of the book with 50:27-29, we learn the name of its author; Jesus-ben-Sira, or just plain Sirach. Turning next to Chapter 39, we discover that Sirach was a Wisdom teacher in Jerusalem. One of his principal contributions to the Wisdom Movement is the firm identification of wisdom with the observance of the Torah (cf. 39:1 and 1:23-24). Another theme appearing in Chapter 39 is a rather detailed notion of divine Providence — prominent throughout the book. If we turn now to the Prologue, we learn that the version which has come down to us is a Greek translation done by the grandson of the author in 132 B.C., in Egypt. The sequence of events enables us to date Sirach at approximately 180 B.C. Thus, it is a late book, as the precious division of Scripture into "the Law, the Prophets, and the rest of the books" indicates. We are near the close of the Old Testament canon. Because of its late date and Greek language, the Jews omitted it from among the Writings; however, discoveries in 1896 and again in 1931 have turned up about two-thirds of the Hebrew text. These have been used in the Confraternity Version to give as perfect a version as possible.

The Book of Sirach is best described as an anthology, probably representing a transcript of lectures delivered by Sirach in his school. There is very little order to the ideas expressed. In many places, the book sounds like little more than a cosmopolitan treatise on etiquette, but it is actually much more. The author begins in the first chapter to exalt wisdom by personifying it as a creature of God. "The beginning of wisdom is fear of the Lord," repeats Sirach, borrowing his words from Proverbs 1:7 (cf. also Ps. 110:10). The second chapter begins the theme of divine Providence and sounds like a sequel to the Book of Job. The third chapter is a beautiful encomium of filial piety and the virtues of humility and studiousness (3:22). Chapter 4 might well be termed the "Anawim manifesto": here the true nobility of the pious poor is acknowledged. This chapter should be compared with 34:18-36 and Chapter 35 where genuine religion is clearly distinguished from a mechanistic reliance on ritualism. Two favorite themes occur in Chapter 6: carefulness of speech and the virtue of friendship. The following chapter begins with a series of miscellaneous aphorisms, then turns to the obligations of parents. St. Paul seems to have been familiar with 7:34. The last verse is a favorite of modern missionaries. Skipping over to Chapter 40, we feel a distinct let-down: Sirach seems to have stolen a leaf from the pessimism of Ecclesiastes; Chapter 41 reflects the latter's impoverished view of future life.

The real meat of the book lies in the biographical praise of the patriarchs in Chapters 44-50. We can detect in these chapters the influence of the Chronicler's work; e.g., the praise of Aaron in 45:6ff. — even at the expense of David (v. 25)! By Sirach's day, King Solomon appears in a much more realistic light (cf. 47:19-24). Malachia 3:23 finds a reflection in Sirach 48:10. The only three "good" kings of Juda are listed in 49:4; Job appears in verse 9, and the "Twelve Prophets" (i.e., the Minor Prophets) in verse 10. The fiftieth chapter is a beautiful tribute to the High Priest, Simon (219-196 B.C.), and shows forcefully the liturgical orientation which followed in the wake of Esdras. The high priest has indeed replaced the king; Juda has become a worshipping community in fact. The author seems to have been a forerunner of the Sadducees; at any rate, he had not been through the purifying ordeal of Antiochus' persecution.

The Personification of Wisdom

We have saved Sirach 24 for special consideration, for the book reaches a climax here in the personification of wisdom. The author seems to have in mind the Shekinah in verse 5 ("pillar of cloud") and verse 10 ("in the holy tent"; cf. p. 124). Verse 22 again affirms the identification of wisdom with the Mosaic Law — though usually it is identified with Yahweh Himself; Jewish monotheism hindered the Scribes from forming a trinitarian concept. This chapter should be diligently compared with Proverbs 8, Baruch 3, Job 28, Wisdom 7:26; these chapters provide the Old Testament transition to the Prologue of St. John's Gospel. Finally, compare them with I Corinthians 1:17-2:16.

Wisdom in the Psalms: 118

Should the Wisdom Literature leave some doubt in the reader's mind with reference to the legalistic orientation of pre-Christian Judaism, Psalm 118 removes it. This longest of the Psalms is divided into 22 sections corresponding to the letters of the Hebrew alphabet. As the Confraternity note indicates, a synonym for the Law occurs in each of the 176 verses (with one exception). As there are only eight of these synonyms, repetition is the order of the day. But the lesson is clear: the Torah is one of God's greatest creations, and shows man an infallible route of salvation.

Suggested Readings

Anderson, *Understanding the Old Testament,* Chap. 15.
Bouyer, *The Meaning of Sacred Scripture,* Chap. 12 (Job), 11, 13 (Jewish wisdom).
Heinisch-Heidt, *History of the Old Testament,* pp. 397-407.
McKenzie, *The Two-Edged Sword,* Chap. 12.
Moriarty, *Introducing the Old Testament,* pp. 202-226 (Job and Eccles.).
Murphy, *Seven Books of Wisdom.*
Pamphlet Bible Series, Nos. 35-38; 40, 41.

Chapter XXIX

Tobias and Machabees:
From Hasidim to Pharisees

READINGS: *Tobias 1–14; I Machabees 2; II Machabees 2, 6–7, 10, 12; Psalms 41:42. (Note: Tobias 3:16–22; 8:3–9; 12:11–13; I Machabees 2:42; II Machabees 2:5–7, 24; 6:12–16; 7:9; 28; 10:8; 12:43–46).*

The Book of Tobias: The Heights of Hebrew Piety

Besides Esther, there are two other edifying histories interspersed with the later Wisdom Literature: Tobias and Judith. Judith is being saved for the next chapter; Tobias fits in here as a doctrinal sequel to the Book of Job. The late composition of Tobias is not as much of an asset to its exegesis and its dating as one might think. In general, Catholics tend to date it about a century earlier than Protestants; that is, during the fourth or third centuries B.C. It is placed by both Jews and Protestants among the Apocrypha — i.e., wholesome religious reading, but not inspired. The author is unknown; the story is older than its appearance in manuscript form.

In the Tobias story, the paths of two pious Jews cross in such a way as to benefit both parties. Tobias the Elder (*Tobit* in the Hebrew text) is a God-fearing Israelite who lives in Ninive with his wife and only son, Tobias. They have been deported there in the wake of the Assyrian Captivity of 721 B.C., but fearlessly continue to observe the Mosaic Law to the letter. The virtuous Tobit, blinded by a seemingly chance event (which the Lord has permitted to test his patience) sends the young Tobias to a distant city to collect a debt. The youth selects a companion for the journey, discovering only later that it is the Archangel Raphael who has been providentially designated as the family trouble-shooter. Besides Tobit's blindness, another problem comes to light in the home of a certain Sara, a relative of Tobias, and in whose home he and Raphael have sought lodging. The girl's seven husbands have all been slain successively by a demon, yet Raphael counsels Tobias to ask her hand in marriage! He agrees to do this after the angel has revealed to him the secret formula: 1) this marriage is in accord-

224

ance with the Mosaic Law (Num. 36:6), which requires heiresses to marry within their own clan in order to keep landed property within tribal boundaries, and Tobias is apparently Sara's only relative (cf. 6:12); 2) the demon cannot harm you if you practice continence for the first three nights. The formula is successful, and Raphael goes off to collect the debt while Tobias celebrates his nuptials. Then the three return to Ninive with the entrails of a fish killed by Tobias in accordance with the angel's instructions. Besides having purged away the demon which plagued Sara, the fish also cures Tobit's blindness.

Fictional elements are apparent in the fish and demon stories, and also in the reference to *Achior* and *Nabath* (Ahikar and Nadan or Nasbas) in 11:20 — a clear case of borrowing from a pagan tale, that of the Assyrian folk story of an uncle and nephew, who have found their way into the inspired text as relatives of Tobias.[1] The wagging of the dog's tail in 11:9 is cited frequently as an example of obiter dicta in Sacred Scripture. But the main fruit of the book is, of course, the religious teaching: the existence of demons and of guardian angels,[2] the divine attributes, particularly Providence; the value of good works such as prayer, almsgiving, fasting, and burial of the dead (on which much stress is placed). The exalted concept of matrimony found in Tobias is worthy of the New Testament (cf. 6:17-22 and 8:4-10). But the principal message of the book is the enlightened insight it gives into the role of adversity in human affairs. What Job (mentioned in 2:12 as a model of patience) was forced to swallow on sheer faith is now docilely accepted by Tobit when Raphael declares it to him: "And because thou wast acceptable to God, it was necessary that temptation should prove thee" (12:13, 13:2; Sara has already accepted this principle in 3:21).

The Book of Tobias shows us Judaism in its most brilliant light. Probably composed as an antidote to the threat of Hellenism, the story of this ideal family illustrates the high calibre of piety which a scrupulous observance of the Mosaic Law was capable of nourishing. Tobias is an exemplar of that class of persons already referred to in the Old Testament as the Anawim (Isa. 14:30-32; Soph. 2:3; see p. 190). Although the sacred author makes it clear that such pious, humble, faithful souls are definitely in the minority (e.g., in 1:5), the story shows that the religious heritage of Esdras-Nehemia was by no means sterile nor purely legalistic. We shall see this statement further verified in the Machabean crisis.

---

[1] Note difference in treatment of this topic between Orchard, *A Catholic Commentary on Holy Scripture,* col. 301 g-h, and Edgar J. Goodspeed, *The Apocrypha* (New York: Modern Library, 1959) p. 107.

[2] Demonology was of late development among the Jews; good angels had been objects of faith from the earliest times (see p. 67).

The Two Books of Machabees: A Fight for Religious Freedom

For centuries God's Chosen People had been the battleground for a grim and often losing struggle between faith and culture. Solomon's defection was a severe setback, from which the Jews never recovered; the Babylonian Captivity was another lesson in the ravages of infidelity to Yahweh. Now, in the meagre territory of post-Exilic Juda, what seemed to be the final showdown between the two ideologies was taking shape. The story is relayed to us in the two Books of Machabees — the last of the historical books of the Old Testament, and considered apocryphal by non-Catholics. Vital statistics about these books can best be handled in a comparative chart:

I MACHABEES:		II MACHABEES:
Written in Hebrew about 100 B.C. by an unknown hand, probably in Palestine.	AUTHORSHIP	Written in Greek c. 100 B.C., perhaps by an Alexandrian Jew against Hellenistic encroachments.
Characterized by high literary quality and historical accuracy; presents Hasmonean viewpoint.	LITERARY BACK-GROUND	A condensation of the "five books of Jason" (2:24; see p. 15 for note on the inspiration of quotations). [3] Written from Pharisees' viewpoint.
Covers period 175–132 B.C.; flashback to 333 B.C.	PERIOD	Covers period c. 180–160 B.C.; flashback to 587 B.C.
To set down religious history of Machabean Period; direct style; corresponds in style to Kings.	PURPOSE AND STYLE	To interpret events theologically, and to glorify Judas Machabeus; like Chronicles.

Events from the conquest of Alexander the Great in 333 B.C. until the persecution of Antiochus IV of Syria are telescoped in I Machabees 1 (assigned with previous chapter). Determined to impose Greek culture on every portion of his Empire — which now included Palestine — Antiochus aligned himself with the Hellenistic faction there which was led by two aspirants to the high priesthood, Jason and Menelaus. As one tried to outbid the other in the king's favor, and in view of the violent disorders which resulted — including the murder of the legitimate high priest, Onias III — Antiochus decided that the best way to curb these unruly subjects would be to abolish their religion entirely. It seems that the majority of the Jews, already conditioned in favor of the pagan encroachments, "esteemed the Grecian glories for the best." Yet, turning now to the second chapter, we are presented with an inspiring picture of the "resistance movement" which

[3] The qualification given would apply also to the tradition of the loss of the Ark of the Covenant in 2:5-7.

226

exploded under the leadership of one Mathathias and his five sons after one thousand of their countrymen had been killed without defending themselves on the Sabbath. Though strict observers of the Mosaic Law, Mathathias and his followers, joined by a party of zealots known as Assideans (2:42; cf. also 7:13 and II Mach. 14:6) or *Hasidim* — the Pious Ones — fled into the mountains and organized a system of guerilla warfare. Recalling the great deeds of the patriarchs (2:51-60), they concluded that good works, even fighting on the Sabbath, must be joined to faith. This passage is a fitting complement to Hebrews 11.

Continuing the story in II Machabees, we realize how desperate the situation has become. Chapter 6 tells of the abomination of the Temple by the erection of a statue of Jupiter (whose manifestation Antiochus claimed to be; hence the epithet *Epiphanes* — "[God] manifest") and of the martyrdom of the venerable Eleazar. Osee's concept of merciful punishment is clearly reflected in verses 12-16. In fact, most of the religious teaching of Machabees is contained in this section. Chapter 7, recounting the amazing fortitude of the mother and her seven sons, contains unmistakable development of doctrine: (1) belief in the resurrection of the body and eternal life (vv. 9, 14, 36); (2) creation of the world from nothing (v. 28); (3) the purifying power of suffering (vv. 32-33). Then there is the precious text in 12:43-46 in which Judas Machabeus expressed his belief in an intermediate state of purification after death, along with the conviction that prayers and sacrifices are of help to the dead.

The prophecy of the last of the Machabee boy-martyrs (7:38) begins to attain fulfillment in Chapter 8 through the successes of Judas. The following chapter describes the miserable death of Antiochus in the grandiose, embellished style of the author of II Machabees. Chapter 10 records the purification of the Temple and the establishment of a new feast to commemorate the event: Hannukah ("dedication"; cf. v. 8). In this same chapter a striking instance of divine intervention is also recorded in verses 29-30 (cf. also 11:8). The sacred author closes his work while his hero, Judas Machabeus, is still alive; the narrative is continued in I Machabees 9 ff. After making an alliance with the Romans, who enter the historical scene at this point, Judas suffers a severe setback and is slain in battle against the forces of the Syrian king, Demetrius I. His brother Jonathan takes over the Jewish armies and after adroitly championing the cause of Alexander Balas against Demetrius I, is rewarded with the high priesthood and some civil jurisdiction to boot (I Mach. 10:20). After his treacherous assassination by the Syrian general, Tryphon, Jonathan is succeeded by the last of the Machabee brothers, Simon. With him the "Hasmonean" (apparently after their ancestral city of Hasmon) dynasty may be said to originate, for the Jews "consented that he should be their prince and high priest forever, till there should arise a faithful prophet" (14:41).

Under Simon the Jews again gained independence: "the yoke of the Gentiles was taken off from Israel" (13:41) for some eighty years. I Machabees closes with the murder of Simon by his son-in-law, Ptolemy, who hoped to take over his position. Fortunately, Simon's son John escaped the purge and succeeded his father as John Hyrcanus in 135 B.C. The following table of Syrian and Jewish leaders is presented to help the student follow the historical sequence:

SYRIAN RULERS:	JEWISH RULERS:
Antiochus III (223-187) took Palestine from Ptolemy V in 198	(References are to I Machabees)
Seleucus IV (187–175)	(Mathathias: originated resistance movement, 167 B.C.)
Antiochus IV, Epiphanes (175–163)	Judas Machabeus (166–160)
Antiochus V (163–162)	Jonathan (160–143)—named High Priest (10:20)
Demetrius I (162–150)	Simon (143–134)—High Priest and Prince
Alexander Balas (150–145)	(14:41); murdered by Ptolemy, his son-in-law
Antiochus VI (145–141), Anti-King who supplanted Demetrius II	John Hyrcanus (134–104), son of Simon } These rulers favored
Antiochus VII (138–129)	Aristobulus I (104–102), son of John } Sadducees and
Demetrius II (129–125) ********	Alexander Jannaeus (102–76), son of John; first to assume title "King" } persecuted Pharisees
Rome entered the picture in 63 B.C. in the person of Pompey, whom the two sons of Alexandra, Aristobulus II and Hyrcanus II called in to arbitrate; ⟶ Pompey favored Hyrcanus II	Alexandra, widow of Jannaeus. GOLDEN ERA OF PHARISEES (76–67)—Hyrcanus II named High Priest
	{ Aristobulus II (67–63) seized power from Hyrcanus II
	{ Hyrcanus II (63–40), High Priest; Antipater, "Governor"
	Antigonus (40–37), "King" and "High Priest," backed by Parthians, but Rome favored Antipater's son,
	HEROD THE GREAT (37–4); took kingdom from Antigonus

It was during the long reign of John Hyrcanus that the Hasidim split into two factions: one was the Pharisees ("separated ones") who resented the king's usurpation of political power and separated their loyalty from him in favor of the principle of separatism from Greek influence which characterized the Machabean revolt. Those on the other hand who backed the king and were willing to come to terms with Hellenism received the designation Sadducees—perhaps after Sadoc (whose priestly line replaced that of Abiathar) in view of the fact that many belonging to this party were priests. Though the Pharisees were politically reactionary, they were doctrinally "liberal" in admitting, besides the Torah, the oral tradition which had grown

up around it, and known as the Tradition of the Ancients. In its
later written form, it is known as the Talmud (see p. 141). Thus, the
Pharisees were able to accept dogmas developed after the Exile, such
as the resurrection of the dead; indeed the prominence of this doctrine in II Machabees suggests the Pharisaical influence behind it.
After a protracted persecution, the Pharisees came into their own
under Alexandra, and thenceforward dominated the spirit of Judaism. Clinging exclusively to the written Torah, the Sadducees rejected
the doctrine of the resurrection, the existence of angels, etc. They
had developed a worldly skepticism; their influence perished with
the Temple in 70 A.D.

Finally, we should note that the Jewish *Sanhedrin* or Supreme Council dates back from the Machabean Period. A concession granted by
the Seleucids, it consisted of seventy-one members divided as follows:
(1) the Chief Priests or sacerdotal aristocracy: the High Priest, all
ex-High Priests and a few other priestly personages (cf. Acts 4:6);
(2) the Ancients or Elders: the lay aristocracy; like the first group,
these also belonged to the Sadducean party; (3) the Scribes or Doctors
of the Law, including a good number of Pharisees. The Sanhedrin
tried both civil and religious cases: in the latter instance, it seems to
have had power to pass the death sentence (cf. Acts 6:12 ff.). Synagogues likewise date from about the same era, the oldest ones excavated
dating from the third century (Jdt. 6:21). Never intended to be a
substitute for the Temple, the synagogue was at first a room, later a
building, in which devout Jews gathered to pray on the Sabbath. No
sacrifice was ever offered in them, even after the destruction of the
Temple. The synagogue ritual consists of: recitation of the Shema
followed by a series of short prayers; Scripture reading; instruction by
a competent person; the blessing contained in Numbers 6:22 ff.

The Qumran Scrolls and the Essenes

Light has been thrown on yet another Jewish faction by the discovery in 1947 of the first of the Qumran Scrolls by a Bedouin lad in
search of his lost goats. Preserved in jars hidden in caves, those scrolls
which have been translated and identified include some ancient Hebrew manuscripts of Old Testament Books — some dating back to
c. 100 B.C. — nearly 1000 years older than the hitherto oldest Hebrew
manuscripts! Fragments of every Hebrew Old Testament Book except
Esther have been found; in addition, some of the Deuterocanonical
Books have turned up (e.g., part of Tobias). The discovery among the
Scrolls of a work called "Manual of Discipline" has led scholars to conclude that they were the property of a group of ancient "monks" —
very likely the Essenes, to which John the Baptist seems to have belonged, or a branch of that movement. In opposition to both the Phari-

sees and Sadducees, they broke off from the Hasidim — probably at the time of Alexander Jannaeus — and retired to the desert to prepare the way for the Kingdom of God. They looked for two Messias: one a kingly figure of the line of David; the other a Levitical priest. They were also expecting a messianic prophet to herald the Messias' coming. Their leader was known as the "Teacher of Righteousness," and they believed in a Gnostic division of mankind into "children of light" and "children of darkness." These terms seem to have been borrowed by St. John in the Prologue of his Gospel, and in I John 4:1-6. Their dwellings were destroyed in 68 A.D. by the Romans.

Psalms 41–42: A Jew Laments His Separation from the Temple

How much the Temple meant to the pious Jew is illustrated in the lyric refrains of these two psalms, which were probably united at one time. The author must have been a Levite accustomed to lead pilgrimages to Jerusalem, but now forcibly detained in the north of Palestine. In Psalm 41 the distressed poet clothes his affliction under the figure of raging waters — suggested, perhaps, by the torrents coming down from Mt. Hermon. In Psalm 42 (part of the prayers at the foot of the altar at Mass) he entrusts his case to Yahweh in confidence. Petition, not penitence, is the theme.

Suggested Readings

Anderson, *Understanding the Old Testament,* pp. 508-515; 530-534.
Dyson and Jones, *The Kingdom of Promise,* pp. 106-118; 121-125.
Heinisch-Heidt, *History of the Old Testament,* pp. 358-397.
Hunt, *Understanding the Bible,* Chap. 22.
Murphy, *The Dead Sea Scrolls and the Bible.*
Ricciotti, *Life of Christ,* Chap. 5, 7.
Sullivan, *God's Word and Work,* pp. 147-157.

Chapter XXX

Daniel, Judith, and Wisdom: The Everlasting Kingdom and Immortality

READINGS: *Daniel 1–3, 5, 7, 9, 12, 14; Judith 1, 5, 7–8, 10–13; Wisdom 1–5; Psalms 71, 72. (Note: Daniel 2:44; 7:10, 13, 14, 18; 9:24–27; 12:1–3; Wisdom 2:24; 4:20; 5:15; 18:4)*

Now that late Jewish history of the Machabean period has been studied in detail, one is in a position to understand the significance of the three remaining books to be considered in this chapter: Daniel, Judith and Wisdom. Although none is strictly an historical book, all three fit into the literary pattern of the second century before Christ and clearly illustrate what profound insights are furnished by this important dimension (cf. again the chart on p. 53).

Apocalypse: Unique Semitic Literary Genre

Already on page 28 we have discussed the nature of apocalyptic literature, a genre which flourished from 200 B.C.-100 A.D. It combines features of both prophetic and wisdom books and helps to fill the vacuum created by the absence of prophecy in the classical sense during the period covered by I-II Machabees and subsequently. Yahweh is in complete control of the movements of history, but instead of a limited intervention in favor of the Jewish political situation, apocalyptic writers now expand their viewpoint of the Day of the Lord to embrace a world view. No longer envisioning the messianic coming as only an intermediate, dated event, they look to the end of time and a definitive judgment. Such a universal viewpoint of salvation includes Gentiles as well as Jews in its scope, although the main burden of apocalypse seems to be a comforting of the Jewish Anawim. The concept of evil in this genre has likewise outgrown the dimensions of any particular hostile earthly kingdom. Ever since the apocalyptic visions of Gog in Ezechiel 38-39, and of the resurrection of the New Israel in Isaia 24-27, the trend to personify evil and extend its influence to supra-historical, cosmic proportions has been growing. Straining their eyes into the distant future, the sacred authors confidently proclaim the dissolution of the enemies of God at the end-time era.

The Book of Daniel: Comfort for the Victims
of Antiochus Epiphanes' Persecution

This work is the principal exemplar of apocalyptic literature in the Old Testament. Modern Catholic scholars are now in general agreement with Protestant exegetes that it was composed about 165 B.C., i.e., during the persecution of Antiochus IV of Syria described in the last chapter. The book is another "Hasidim manifesto" whose unknown author simply took older traditions stemming from the Exile era and adapted them to the crisis of his own day. Thus, we find Daniel playing a threefold role: in Chapters 1-6 (nearly all originally written in Aramaic) he is a royal counselor and interpreter of dreams; in Chapters 7-12 (in Hebrew) he is portrayed as a visionary; and in Chapters 13-14 (in Greek) he appears as a wise man. This last section, a later addition to the book, is not included in the Hebrew or Protestant Bibles.

The sacred author tips his hand in the very first chapter, where we find Daniel involved in a dietary dilemma during his three-year Chaldean training course. His fear of defiling himself with food which might have been offered to idols and thereby rendered unclean is intended to parallel the situation of the author's contemporaries in the Machabean crisis described in I Machabees 1:65. Sustained by a miracle, Daniel and his three companions survive the vegetarian ordeal with flying colors — and keep their consciences unsullied. At the end of their course they are found to be "ten times" brighter than the pagan magicians and Chaldeans ("astrologers" in this context) and are advanced to important posts in the kingdom.

In Chapter 2, Daniel is summoned into the king's presence "in the second year" of Nabuchodonosor, contrary to the implication of 1:18 regarding the completion of a three-year period of training.[1] In response, Daniel does the impossible: even before giving the correct interpretation of the king's dream, he reveals the content of the dream in accordance with Nabuchodonosor's demand. The meaning of the various parts of the monstrous statue will be treated in conjunction with Chapters 7 and 8. The third chapter depicts the famous espisode of the fiery furnace into which Daniel's three companions were thrown for refusing to worship the golden idol which Nabuchodonosor had erected.[2] This colossus would immediately remind pious Jews of the second century of the "abominable idol" set up in the Temple at Jerusalem by Antiochus (I Mach. 1:57). Verses 24-90 containing the

---

[1] Fictional embellishments are also indicated by the Persian words and customs which appear at a "Babylonian" court—e.g., "O King, live forever!"; in Chapter 4 the case of lycanthropy predicted by Daniel did not overtake Nabuchodonosor, although Nabonidus (who came later) may have suffered from this dread disease.

[2] This episode may well represent a separate story joined to the others, since Daniel is nowhere mentioned, and only the pagan names of the three are used.

beautiful prayer of the three young men for deliverance is found in the Greek Septuagint, but not in Jewish or Protestant Bibles. It is used in place of a fourth psalm in Sunday Lauds of the Divine Office and is prescribed for priests' thanksgiving after the celebration of Mass. In it all gradations of nature are systematically called upon to praise God (Who, incidentally, did deliver them from the furnace through the intermediacy of an angel, v. 49).

The handwriting on the wall in Chapter 5 is equally bizarre. *Mene, Tekel, Peres* (*Mna, shekel, parsu?*) spell out cryptically the punishment of King Belsassar (actually only crown prince, and son of Nabonidus, not Nabuchodonosor) for using profanely the sacred vessels pilfered from the Temple. Daniel alone, as it turns out, is able to decipher the code. As he predicts, "the same night" the king is slain, and "Darius the Mede" (identity unknown) succeeds to the kingdom (vv. 29 ff.). Daniel's popularity with this monarch causes him to be denounced by his rival satraps for disobeying the royal decree outlawing all prayers of petition except those addressed to Darius, and specifically framed to ensnare the prophet. Falsely convicted, he does his first stint in the lion's den as a punishment. When the famished beasts refuse to touch Daniel (who is protected by a guardian angel, v. 23), the king orders his accusers with their wives and children to be devoured by the same lions.

Chapter 7 begins a series of visions on the part of Daniel himself and is perhaps the most important chapter in the book. The four beasts actually constitute a code for contemporary Jews, closely correlated with the statue of Chapter 2 and the ram and he-goat of Chapter 8. These three chapters are summarized in the chart below:

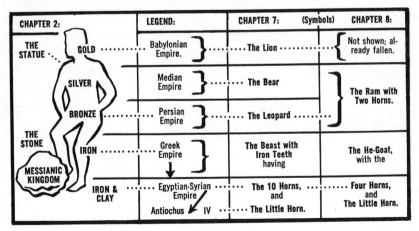

CHAPTER 2:		LEGEND:	CHAPTER 7:	(Symbols)	CHAPTER 8:
THE STATUE	GOLD	Babylonian Empire.	The Lion		Not shown; already fallen.
	SILVER	Median Empire	The Bear		The Ram with Two Horns.
	BRONZE	Persian Empire	The Leopard		
THE STONE MESSIANIC KINGDOM	IRON	Greek Empire	The Beast with Iron Teeth having		The He-Goat, with the
	IRON & CLAY	Egyptian-Syrian Empire / Antiochus IV	The 10 Horns, and The Little Horn.		Four Horns, and The Little Horn.

The climax of Chapter 7 is reached with the vision of the "son of man" receiving "an everlasting kingdom" (the Messianic Kingdom) from "the Ancient One" (God) in verses 13-14. We have to go to verse 18 for an explanation of "son of man": this is really a corporate term, standing for "the holy ones of the Most High" — the people of God who will inherit the Messianic Kingdom.[3] This is the earthly phase of the Kingdom of God which is to succeed the major worldly empires represented as beasts. The phrase "coming on the clouds of heaven" is not meant to signify a sudden or miraculous appearance but rather the unearthly origin and nature of the kingdom. We shall summarize the Old Testament teaching on the Kingdom of God at the end of this section.

The Danielic vision in Chapter 9 has occasioned the most extensive speculation through the ages, and one's interpretation of it serves as a fairly good date-line of his biblical scholarship. The passage (9:24-27) is definitely messianic; but whether it is to be taken directly or only indirectly (typologically) is disputed. The latter viewpoint is adopted by the editors of the Confraternity Version, as opposed to the Douay-Rheims Version which made the whole passage literally messianic. What we must keep in mind always is that prophecies (especially those referring to the end-time, i.e., apocalyptic) are not meant to be exact timetables of events. Thus, in taking the seventy years of Jeremia 25:11 and 29:10 and expanding them into seventy weeks of years (i.e., multiplying the whole period and its parts by seven), the author of Daniel intends to present an extended era of time, not exactly 490 years! He is telling us that the Messianic Kingdom will not come before the end of this period, though he seems to have thought it would come immediately after it. Thus, the Confraternity interpretation which terminates the 490 years with the rededication of the Temple (?) after the persecution of the Jews (typifying the persecution and death of Christ Whose presence now replaces the Temple) by Antiochus Epiphanes, seems more sound than the literal interpretation of the Douay-Rheims. To arrive mathematically at the date 30 A.D., this interpretation takes as a starting point the date of Artaxerxes' decree to Nehemia to rebuild the Temple (445 B.C., according to II Esd. 2:1) rather than the starting point of Jeremia and the Confraternity editors (587 B.C.). This necessitates identifying the term "anointed" in verses 25 and 26 with Christ, and the events in verse 27 with the destruction of the Temple by Titus in 70 A.D. A careful comparison of these two interpretations shows how wary one must be to avoid making the Scriptures a happy hunting ground (as happens when the sacred author's perspective is ignored).

---

[3] "Son of man," then, does not of itself refer directly to the Messia (cf. Psalm 8:5); but the phrase is messianic when used in its Danielic context, as in Mark 14:62.

Chapters 10 and 11 merely spell out in detail the events already symbolized in broad outline by the dreams and visions of the previous chapters. So explicit are some of the events recounted that one has the feeling the author was an eye-witness; in fact, modern exegetes suggest that 11:40 represents a transition from past to future in the author's knowledge. Notwithstanding the statement in the last verse of the chapter, Antiochus died in Persia, not Palestine. At this juncture we should note some of the important additions which the book makes to angelology. Personal guardian angels are hinted at in 3:49 and 6:23. Their vast multitude is insinuated in 3:55 and 7:10. In Chapter 8 the angel Gabriel is deputed to explain the vision of the ram and he-goat to Daniel; he performs a similar function in Chapters 9 and 10. Guardian angels of nations are taught in Chapters 10-12, with Michael being specifically designated as guardian of Israel. Finally, in Chapter 12 we have a clear-cut statement of the doctrine of personal immortality in verses 2-3. (The latter verse — a tribute to teachers — may be a reference to those who later on became known as *Hasidim*.) Further clarification and development of this vital doctrine comes in the Book of Wisdom. This theme attests to the late date of both of these books.

The last two chapters or "Appendix" of Daniel contain more martyr-legends designed to fortify the morale of the author's contemporaries. The well-known story of Susanna portrays Daniel as a wise judge. The tale of Bel and the dragon would tickle the harassed Jewish sense of humor, especially Daniel's second rescue from the lion's den — this time by the prophet Habacuc, who is borne through space by an angel.

The Kingdom of God

Probably no other biblical phrase has undergone such a deepening penetration as that of the "Kingdom of God." The Book of Daniel puts the finishing touches on the Old Testament description of this important concept, so necessary to an understanding of the Gospels. Basically, the Kingdom of God is a *state*, viz., the practical recognition or prevalence of the divine Will. In its ultimate realization, it is a state of universal submission by all creatures to their Creator. As used by the Jews and later on by the Christian community, the term was complex and rather elusive, since revelation showed that God's Kingdom admitted of two distinct stages:

The Kingdom of God on Earth

This first phase of the Kingdom was to be inaugurated by the Messia when he came; the Messianic Kingdom was to be a time of preparation for the end of the world, according to the teaching of the later prophets — especially the apocalyptic writers. Both Jew and Gentile would have access to it. The role of the Messia was to institute a spiritual revival through the preaching of penance. But he was to do more than this, as Jeremia and Second Isaia hinted: He was to aid the cause by his own vicarious suffering. Yet, as the New Israel, his lot was not to provide a substitute for suffering in behalf of the Old Israel, but rather to show them how to suffer efficaciously: was this not the lesson of the Exile and more recently of the Antiochene persecution?

It may be objected that the Book of Daniel — at the very end of the Old Testament revelation — presents rather a glorious, triumphant Messia, the "son of man" coming in the clouds of heaven. The answer is that suffering is presupposed to this glorious phase; indeed, it is the peculiar genius of the author of this book that he has combined the Jewish ordeals of 587 and 167 through his chief character Daniel into a higher synthesis, the atoning value of suffering, as expressed in Daniel 4:24 and especially 9:5 ff. Finally, we should note that the "Day of the Lord" was to be the inauguration of his mission in the midst of his Chosen People, who would provide a base of operation for his salvific activities.

The Kingdom of the World to Come

This was to be the final, heavenly phase of the Kingdom. After a certain fixed period of time — perhaps a generation, perhaps a millenium—would occur the transfer of God's Kingdom to heaven. At that time the resurrection of the dead and the general judgment are to take place, and the earthly phase come to an end.

Needless to say, there was considerable confusion among the Jews regarding these two phases of the Kingdom. The Apocalyptists (including in some measure the Essenes or Qumran community) tended to stress the second phase. On the other hand, the Sadducees were interested almost exclusively in the earthly phase of the Kingdom. The Pharisees — who dominated popular mentality — had revived the expectation of a Davidic king who would free the Jews from oppression and sin. As expressed in the apocryphal "Psalms of Solomon," this last view comes closest to the true view of the prophets — but with notable differences — as pointed out by Dyson and Jones in *The Kingdom of Promise*, p. 131 ff. In the *first* place, they envisaged the necessity of *political and even military action against their foes* (now Rome), clinging to the narrow Jewish nationalism long since outlawed by the prophets; *secondly*, the restoration of the Davidic dynasty would bring in its wake *material prosperity* as well as spiritual benefits; finally, the Messia would need some very striking credentials to distinguish him from the many false Messias who had risen up: he would *multiply "signs"* (miracles). Pharisaic insistence on a Davidic Messia, besides being solidly based on such passages as Amos 9:11, seems to have been a reaction against the hostile Hasmoneans. At the same time, they refused to resort to the open rebellion favored by "Zealots."

Psalm 71: A True View of the Kingdom of God

This magnificent Royal messianic psalm seems to mirror the key ideas of the Book of Daniel. The Messia ("King's son") will come as a judge (vv. 2-4); his kingdom will be everlasting (vv. 5-7) and universal (vv. 8-11); it will be characterized by mercy to the poor and humble (the Anawim, such as underwent the Machabean persecution rather than deny their faith) and embrace all mankind (v. 17). This picture of the ideal king cannot be fully verified of any past Davidic monarch; hence, it points to the Messia.

The Book of Judith: A God-Fearing Jewess Wins a Glorious Victory Over His Enemies

Lumping together historical periods with almost reckless abandon, an unknown author has given us a work whose literary genre is still uncertain, although it seems to be a species of edifying history. The sacred writer seems to be warning us that he intends to take drastic liberties with history when he makes Nabuchodonosor the King of Assyria rather than of Babylonia in 1:5. (The present footnote on this verse in the Douay-Rheims Version will surely not find its way into the Confraternity Version. The fact that Assyria was the classic enemy of the Jews is a much better explanation!) The setting favored by a number of modern scholars — Protestant and Catholic alike — is that of the Persian court of Artaxerxes III (359-338.)[4] But the actual composition of the work is best placed during the Machabean era, about 100 B.C. or shortly before. The name "Judith" is the feminine of Judas (a man famous among the Machabees) and means "Jewess"; hence, the heroine seems to be a type of the Machabean party or the Hasidim, and we may have here another of their manifestos. God is the master of history, and can use even women in the establishment of His reign!

While the Assyrian general Holofernes besieges the city of Bethulia (which modern scholars are having trouble locating), its citizens contemplate surrendering in five days if no help comes. At this point a rich and beauteous widow of the place comes forward to rebuke their inactivity as a sign of lack of trust in God (a flashback to I Mach. 2:41?), and undertakes to rescue the city personally. Familiar themes are struck throughout: the God of the Jews portrayed as the Lord of history (cf. Achior's speech in Chap. 5); a confession of national guilt like that in Daniel (Jdt. 7:19; see Dan. 9:16); recognition of scourges

---

[4] Cf. Tricot and Robert, *Guide to the Bible*, Vol. I, p. 302. See also Fr. Ellis' superb treatment in *The Men and Message of the Old Testament*, pp. 523 ff. He concludes that Judith is a piece of *apocalyptic midrash*.

such as Holofernes in terms of divine chastisement (8:27); the infallible efficacy of obedience to the Torah — especially to the dietary laws
(12:2), and the efficacy of the prayer of the humble (9:16). Judith's
apparent lies (e.g., 10:12) can best be explained by the *epikeia* permitted to any spy; her entrance into a proximate occasion of sin by
visiting Holofernes in his tent can be justified by the urgency of the
situation and the means Judith took to forestall any fault through prayer
and haircloth. Victory quickly ensues for the Jews once Holofernes'
decapitated head is displayed, and Judith is hailed as "the glory of
Jerusalem . . . the joy of Israel . . . the honor of our people" (15:10) —
words applied by the liturgy to the Blessed Virgin Mary. The feast
mentioned in the last verse of the book is unknown today.

The Book of Wisdom: Crisis in Alexandria; Other-Worldly, Individual Retribution

Most of this last book to be added to the Old Testament canon
(about 50 B.C.) has already been treated in previous chapters. It remains for us here merely to give a formal introduction to the work and
an analysis of the first five chapters. We noted in dealing with the Book
of Esther that many Jews remained in Persia after the restoration of
Israel. Another large colony of them fled from Palestine into Egypt
after the sack of Jerusalem in 587 B.C., as noted in Chapter 24. The
Book of Wisdom is a product of the Egyptian Diaspora, written by an
unknown Jew of Alexandria as an antidote to the peril of Greek culture.
This peril was even more acute than the Antiochene persecution in
Palestine because the very language used by the Alexandrian Jews
(Greek) breathed the atmosphere of Hellenistic culture and thought-
patterns. This association of language with culture is true of most
tongues, but particularly of Greek. The use of this language (employed
even in their Scriptures: Wisdom was composed in Greek) likewise
exposed the Jews to the fruits of the golden age of Socrates, Plato
and Aristotle. The Book of Wisdom had considerable influence on the
authors of the New Testament, especially manifest in St. Paul's Epistle
to the Romans. A division of Wisdom is given below, together with
reference to those chapters where we have previously treated certain
parts of it:

1) *Chapters 1-5.* Doctrine of Immortality (Detailed analysis below)
2) *Chapters 6-9.* Exposition and Personification of Wisdom by Pseudo-
   Solomon (See Chap. XXII) — Wisdom shown to be an attribute of
   God, not man (cf. 7:26)
3) *Chapters 10-19.* The Fruit of Wisdom in Israelite History, especially
   the Exodus
— Chapter 10: Wisdom, guide of the Patriarchs......(See Chap. XI)
— Chapters 11, 16-19: Wisdom justified in history....(See Chap. XIV)

— Chapter 12: God's Mercy on the Chanaanites.......(See Chap. XIX)
— Chapters 13-15: The folly of idolatry...................(See Chap. XIV)

It is the first five chapters which mainly concern us here, for they contain the epitome of Old Testament teaching on the doctrine of immortality. The sacred author's apologetic view is manifested in the very first chapter where he insists on the universal scope of the God of Israel (note "all-embracing" in v. 7), Who has no rival (dualism is reprobated, vv. 13-14). For the first time Scripture identifies the serpent of Genesis 3 with the devil (2:24). Chapters 3-5 are the royal charter of immortality, and are used extensively in the Divine Office for the feasts of martyrs. The judgment and punishment of the wicked is summarized in 4:20, while 5:15 points out the unending bliss of the just "with the Most High," in the company of the angels ("sons of God," v. 5). In Chapter 4, the enigma of such apparent "catastrophes" as childlessness and early death for the just (e.g., Henoch) is solved; both are compatible with virtue, which is the sole measure of a man's reward in the next life.

In Wisdom, the individual finally reaches his full stature in the Old Testament in a final development of the concept of retribution. This development witnessed roughly three stages, which we shall attempt to schematize. It must be borne in mind, however, that individual consciences down through ages were not confined to any formalized stages of development; we are simply trying to outline the doctrinal emphasis as it moved away from collectivist thinking toward a greater personalism:[5]

1) *Collective and Earthly Retribution.* At the time of Abraham and circumcision, the destiny of the individual seemed pretty well bound to the clan; then, under the Mosaic Law, individuals rose and fell with the community.

2) *Personal and Earthly.* Ezechiel spoke out forcefully in favor of personal, individual rewards and punishments; yet, Sheol was still the goal of all men, and the memory of a man's posterity seemed his best hope of immortality.

3) *Personal and Other-Worldly.* As in the case of Job, so with Israel: the greatest religious insights matured through suffering. The concept of a personal immortality with God finally ripened during and after the Machabean crisis. Inch by inch this doctrine groaned forward, particularly via the Wisdom Movement: the travails of the Anawim (Job and Tobias, etc.), then the pessimism of Ecclesiastes followed by the cosmopolitanism of Sirach, and finally the "spirituality" of Wisdom — were vital stages in the emergence of the individual personality.

---

[5] See Gelin, *Key Concepts of the Old Testament*, especially Chap. III.

Psalm 72: "With You I Shall Always Be"

It is interesting to note that while the Book of Wisdom clearly teaches personal immortality, there is no mention of the resurrection of the body as is found in II Machabees 7:9 and Daniel 12:2. Does this mean that its author had attained a knowledge of the spirituality of the human soul, capable of existing apart from the body? Down through the centuries the Jews had been accustomed to view man as an indivisible whole, avoiding all dichotomy between body and soul. It is possible, however, that this distinction did emerge in the mind of certain Alexandrian Jews who had come in contact with Greek philosophy; we don't know how extensively it influenced Hebrew mentality — especially the mind of one implicitly attempting to negate the influence. At any rate, Jewish sages did assert GOD'S spirituality: "For the spirit of the Lord fills the world, is all-embracing, and knows man's utterances . . . " (Wisd. 1:7; also Ps. 138); and by the end of the Wisdom Movement they seem to have reached an awareness of man's spirituality, at least to some degree, as the passages cited from Wisdom 1-5 indicate. Psalm 72, a Wisdom poem, corroborates this conclusion. Faced with the same problem which puzzled Job (i.e., the apparent prosperity of the wicked), the psalmist comes up with a better answer after he had "entered the sanctuary of God and considered their final destiny" (v. 17). Reassured, he confidently exclaims: "Yet with you I shall always be . . . in the end you will receive me in glory . . . my portion forever" (vv. 23-26).

Before leaving the Old Testament, we should say a final word about the important theme of the growing awareness among the Jews of their universalist mission in the divine plan of salvation — a mission which they failed to carry out, though they have left us the precious heritage of the Old Testament. The Book of Wisdom (not recognized as inspired, unfortunately, by later Jews) seems to open the door unmistakably to the Gentiles: "through (your sons, the Jews) the imperishable light of the Law was to be given to the world" (18:4). Here is one of the loftiest conclusions of profound religious intuition, which is a vital factor in the mechanics of divine revelation.

Suggested Readings

Anderson, *Understanding the Old Testament*, pp. 515-530 (Daniel); 534-537 (Canon).
Bouyer, *The Meaning of Sacred Scripture*, Chap. 15, 16.
Brown, *The Book of Daniel* (Pamphlet Bible Series No. 34).
Dyson and Jones, *The Kingdom of Promise*, pp. 95-100; 135-147; 173-176.
Gelin, *Key Concepts of the Old Testament*. The whole book is most helpful.
Heinisch-Heidt, *History of the Old Testament*, pp. 397-431.
"Introduction aux Livres de Tobie, Judith et Esther," *La Sainte Bible de Jerusalem*, pp. 493-494.
Maly, *The Book of Wisdom* (Pamphlet Bible Series No. 39).
Moriarty, *Introducing the Old Testament*, pp. 227-242.
Murphy, *The Seven Books of Wisdom*, pp. 127-156.

Appendix

On the Canon of the Old Testament

The Septuagint. The Alexandrian Jews were noteworthy for more sacred religious activity than the Book of Wisdom and the translation of Sirach into Greek. To this realm of the Diaspora we owe that version of the Old Testament books apparently used by Christ and His Apostles, the Septuagint. This translation was begun about 286 B.C. in order to provide the Greek-speaking colony with their Scriptures in a tongue they understood. The Pentateuch, according to legend, was completed in seventy days by seventy scribes, and hence called the Septuagint (seventy). The collection of books was probably not completed until well after 100 B.C. It contains forty-six books in all. The phrase "reproduction of our valuable teaching" in the Prologue of Sirach may be a reference to this version. The Christian Church, in general, adopted the Septuagint as its official version, although individual scholars had doubts about the inspiration of certain books.

The Canon of Palestine. Strangely enough, the Hebrew Bible of the Palestinian Jews lacked seven books and parts of two others found in the Septuagint. The missing books were all of comparatively late origin, and include those written in Greek and Aramaic, for the most part. We know that Esdras had not only "canonized" the Pentateuch, but also that he gathered together a number of other books with the help of Nehemia, who "made a library . . . out of the books both of the prophets and of David [probably the Psalms] and the epistles of the kings . . . " (II Mach. 2:13). This was the period of transition from Hebrew to Aramaic; probably all of the thirty-nine books in this collection (see p. 158) had been written at that time (i.e., early in the fourth century) except Ecclesiastes, Esther, Second Zacharia, Daniel and some of the Psalms. As time went on, it became necessary to make a judgment regarding the "canonicity" of the various books allegedly written by Moses, David, Solomon, etc., especially in the wake of the prolific apocalyptic literature which flourished the last two centuries before Christ. The term "canon," from the Greek *kanon* meaning rule, measure, or standard, gradually came to be understood as the official list of inspired books. Actually, the Jews seem never to have taken a formal position with regard to the Old Testament until about 90 A.D. at the "Council of Jamnia," where the thirty-nine-book Hebrew Bible was declared to be official. By that time their Temple had been destroyed by Titus and the nation dispersed. Nationalism was running high and a strong reaction against alien culture and languages — especially Greek — set in. Nostalgically Jewish leaders looked back to the pre-Alexandrian period as the golden age of prophecy (in the broad sense). Why Esther and Daniel were accepted and Tobias and I Machabees rejected, for example, is not too clear; modern Jews might argue that the religious quality of the latter is inferior. The Council of Trent settled the question definitively for Catholics by declaring all forty-six books of the Septuagint "canonical" (see p. 44, Thesis VI). The seven additional books are known as "deuterocanonical" (second list) because of the doubts attached to them in the early Church. Today, Protestants follow the Jewish canon of the Old Testament.

COMPARATIVE TABLE OF JEWISH–PROTESTANT AND CATHOLIC OLD TESTAMENTS

I. HEBREW BIBLE ("Massoretic" Text)	GENESIS* EXODUS* LEVITICUS* NUMBERS*	GENESIS* EXODUS* LEVITICUS* NUMBERS*	I. CATHOLIC BIBLE (Septuagint)
II. CRITERIA OF CANONICITY	DEUTERONOMY* Joshua† Judges†	DEUTERONOMY* JOSUE* JUDGES*	DEUTEROCANONICAL BOOKS: (called "Apocryphal" by Prot.)
1. Antiquity (pre-Machabean, with exceptions)	Ruth‡ I Samuel† II Samuel†	RUTH* I KINGS* II KINGS*	TOBIAS (Aramaic)* JUDITH (Hebrew?)* Wisdom (Greek)‡
2. Written in Hebrew or Aramaic (in Palestine?)	I Kings† II Kings† I Chronicles‡	III KINGS* IV KINGS* I PARALIPOMENON*	Sirach (Hebrew)‡ Baruch (Hebrew)† I MACHABEES*
3. Religious quality: conformity with Torah	II Chronicles‡ Ezra‡ Nehemiah‡	II PARALIPOMENON* I ESDRAS* II ESDRAS*	(Hebrew) II MACHABEES* (Greek)
	Esther (part)‡ Job‡	ESTHER* Job‡	ESTHER 10:4–16:24 Daniel 3:24–90; 13–14
III. PROTESTANT VERSIONS (which include New Testament, of course)	Psalms‡ $\begin{cases} 114\text{–}15 \\ 146\text{–}47 \end{cases}$ Proverbs‡ Ecclesiastes‡ Song of Songs‡	Psalms‡ (9 and 113 are split) Proverbs‡ Ecclesiastes‡ Canticle of Canticles‡	II. CRITERION: The authority of God as proposed through the Church.
A. King James Version —Official English version until modern times	Isaiah† Jeremiah† Lamentations‡ Ezekiel†	Isaia† Jeremia† —Lamentations Ezechiel†	
B. Revised Standard Version (1946–1952) is the modern American translation	Daniel (part)‡ Hosea† Joel†	Daniel† Osee† Joel†	III. CATHOLIC VERSIONS 1. Latin Vulgate of St. Jerome (see Thesis VI, page 44).
C. Smith–Goodspeed Bible put out by the University of Chicago is a fine translation	Amos† Obadiah† Jonah† Micah† Nahum† Habakkuk†	Amos† Abdia† Jona† Michea† Nahum† Habacuc†	2. Douay–Rheims (1609 O.T.; 1582 N.T.)—formerly the standard English Catholic version (revised by Challoner, 1752).
	Zephaniah† Haggai† Zecharia† Malachi†	Sophonia† Aggai† Zacharia† Malachia†	3. Confraternity (1946) Modern American version.
Key: *Law †Prophets ‡Writings		Key: *"Historical" †Prophetical ‡Doctrinal	

Appendix

Myth in Genesis

Modern man has been conditioned to accept the term *myth* in but one sense: the personification of natural forces and their elevation to the status of deities. When the modern poet does this very thing we take it in stride as an exercise of poetic license; but let the ancient tribal bard attempt it and we immediately cry out, "Idolatry!" It is no wonder that in our day myth has become synonymous with falsehood. What we have failed to realize until just recently is that these bards WERE poets, and were writing as such. Even more, we have forgotten the truth contained in the adage, "magic is the science of the primitive and myth is his philosophy."[1] The truth is that the term myth, at least as far back as Plato, has also signified a figure of speech in which a concrete, imaginative construct is used to convey some abstract truth. The trouble with the pagans was that eventually those later generations who were far removed from the origins of their tribal myths came to identify myth with reality. This the Jews never did: in all of their originalities (but more often in their borrowings from neighboring tribes) they were able to keep reality distinct from its packages.

Genesis and other books of Sacred Scripture contain unmistakable evidence of ancient myths. The watery abyss of Genesis 1:2 suggests the widespread pagan notion of a primeval sea monster slain by the chief of the gods and then used as the raw material of the universe.[2] In finding their way into Scripture, however, these borrowed elements are always subordinated to the pure, monotheistic purposes of the sacred author. The unscrupulous struggle among the gods for supremacy is scornfully rejected by the Priestly editors, while the Yahwist source uses the Tower of Babel legend to illustrate man's chronic rebellion against God.

Psalm 28 provides an excellent example of biblical expurgation. One of the oldest poems in the Psalter, it begins with a forceful summons to worship: "Give to the Lord, you sons of God . . . glory and praise!" The occasion is His "epiphany," described in the next section. The phrase, "sons of God" betrays the hymn's pagan origin. What we have here is a Ugaritic prayer to the storm-god worshipped in Chanaan. The Hebrew psalmist, however, sees the angels or perhaps even the holy people of God behind the phrase. He now proceeds to express his faith that the storm is not a god, but that Yahweh is God of the storm.

Verses 3-9 express the motive for this act of praise: Yahweh's vast empire of creation which He controls with a mighty hand. He makes

---

[1] Here I am indebted to Fr. McKenzie's *Two-Edged Sword*, especially pp. 50 and 85.

[2] In Chanaanite mythology, "Leviathan" (or *Rahab*: cf. Job. 3:8 and Ps. 73:13-17) is slain by Baal: the Babylonian Tiamat is slain by Marduk. See *Thomas, Documents from Old Testament Times*, pp. 3-26.

the earth shake from Mt. Lebanon and Mt. Hermon ("Sarion") in the north to Kadesh in the far south. One suspects that the phenomenon may have been not a storm but an earthquake. Yahweh's epiphany in nature reaches a climax in the lightning and the wind which "twist the oaks and strip the forests" as His voice thunders. At last (vv. 9b-11) puny man is able to rise above his awe sufficiently to express his doxology: Glory! The "temple" in the original poem was probably the whole universe for the pagan, who had come to believe the myth and to identify the storm with God. In Psalm 28, the reference seems to be to the structure in Jerusalem.

The poem ends with a generic petition to Yahweh to bless His people. What the psalmist has given us is certainly not an *essentialist* picture of God! The Psalms and other pages of the Old Testament reveal to us a race of *existentialists:* God's chosen people. For them, He is not the Self-existent Being; He is rather the GOD WHO ACTS. Other psalms expressing a similar theme are 46, 92, 96 and 98. These sacred poems illustrate how the Jews — surrounded as they were by a sea of idolatrous pagans — never completely lost sight of Yahweh's transcendence. Their cosmic perspective gave rise to a sublime mysticism on which the Fathers of the Church capitalized. Some of the fruits of this patristic development are summarized in the section which follows.

I. *The Abyss.* ("The earth was waste and void; darkness covered the abyss," Gen. 1:2.) Here is the "womb of nature," filled with water; the purely passive principle, completely open to the creative action of God; a type of the baptismal font.

II. *Water.* ("And the spirit of God was stirring above the waters," Gen. 1:2.) Raw material in the womb of nature, awaiting God's touch. An ambivalent symbol: lethal if not harnessed by God; but life-giving under His providential hand. The harnessed waters will make the garden in Genesis 2 fruitful.

III. *Creation.* God acting on the abyss; He must first separate (but not isolate) creatures from Himself, then establish a union between Himself and them (cf. firmament).

IV. *Light.* The presence of God; darkness represents His absence. In the New Testament, light will also mean God's revelation.

V. *Firmament* (see diagram on page 48). The powerful metal "dome" separating the waters above from the waters beneath the earth and firmly established in the bed-rock below. But the firmament also serves to separate creatures from God, thus establishing the necessary "otherness" or polarity between them and preparing the stage for God's activity.

244

VI. *Dry Land, Vegetation.* The harnessed waters produce the first life on earth; God's loving care uses the water to irrigate the land.

VII. *Heavenly Bodies.* The sun and stars shine with unfailing regularity in the heavens; for the pagans this spelled fatalism, determinism; but for the Jews, it was God's celestial calendar and represented the order He had established and His Law (see Psalm 18). The moon and the planets are reflected light, hence inferior. The work of the fourth day affirms the creaturehood of all heavenly bodies; they are not gods, and therefore are not to be worshipped.

VIII. *Fish.* Represent life from the depths, hence a symbol of Christ for Christians. Friday abstinence is not merely turning away from meat, but also a conversion to fish (Christ).

IX. *Animals* were blessed by God and told to reproduce; here life is considered in all its mysteriousness as the product of sexual union demanding the special intervention of God.

X. Thus, God's *Blessing* is seen as the communication of His very life. Note how the Hebrews approached the question existentially, making God *act* (i.e., bless); we tend to speak more essentially in terms of sanctifying grace.

XI. *Holy Marriage.* A union of male and female for the sacred purpose of transmitting life, God's most precious gift. Hence, marriage is to be used according to the divine Will and in perfect submission to it. Adam and Eve lacked this submission and thus developed a wrong relationship with each other, with Eve leading and her husband following. (This perversion is the root of erotism.) To punish and rectify the fault, God made Eve subject to Adam in marriage.

XII. *The Sabbath.* A break with servile labor, which represents the purely natural, godless order. Periodically man must rest in God through the observance of the Sabbath; otherwise his work will represent merely human activity (such as the Tower of Babel and the forty years of wandering in the desert. Cf. Psalm 94:11, "Therefore I swore . . . they shall not enter into my rest").

XIII. *The Recapitulation of the Universe in Christ and Mary.* In Genesis 3 Eve sank into the depths of sin, an extreme of misery, and carried Adam with her. By contrast, the New Adam has exalted the New Eve, Mary, to the extreme heights of virtue. Both Eve and Mary are pure creatures (not divine beings). Mary's greatness lay in the fact of her complete openness to grace, making her the perfect womb of God's creative activity ("I know not man").

245

Index

Aaron, 105, 107, 128, 133–135, 157, 216
Abel, 74–75
Abdia, 201
Abiam, 177
Abiathar, 161, 171, 228
Abigail, 162
Abimelech, 91, 155, 162
Abinadab, 157, 164
Abiram, 135
Abisag, 170
Abner, 163
Abraham, 82–89;
  and polygamy, 85
  and retribution, 239
  and Yahwist Trad., 102
  covenant, 85
  death, 91
  election, 84
  faith of, 85–88
  sacrifice of Isaac, 86–87
Abram changed to Abraham, 85
Absalom, 164, 166, 170
Abyss, 31, 48, 244
Accommodated sense, 35
Achab, 177, 180–181
Achan, 148
Achaz, 190, 192
Achior, 225; 237
Adam, 57 ff., 85
Adonai, 105
Adonias, 170–171
Agag, 160, 218
Agar, 85
Aggai, 212
Agur, 174
Ahias, 177
Ahikar, 225
Akabah, Gulf of, 176
Albright, William F., 106, 125, 136, 211, 214
Alexander the Great, 220
Alexander Jannaeus, 228, 230
Alexandra, 228–229
Alexandria, 31, 228, 241
  canon of, 241–242

Allegorism, 31
Allegory, 26
Alliances, Foreign, 192, 197
'Almah, 192
Amalecites, 114, 218
Aman, 217
Amasia, 183
Amen-em-Ope, 174
Ammonites, 86, 137, 155, 160, 165, 214
Ammorites, 82
Amnon, 166
Amos, 182ff., 193, 204, 236
Amphictyony, 150
Amri, 177
Analogy of Faith, 39
Anania, 201
Anawim, 191, 194, 206, 225, 237
"Anawim Manifesto," 221, 225
"Ancient One," 234
"Ancients," 229
Anderson, B. W., 40, 52, 60, 80, 82, 104, 108, 143, 149, 192, 197, 199, 240
Angels, 67, 86, 93, 225, 235, 239
  bad angels, 229, 239
Anna, 156
Annunciation, 194
Anthropomorphism, 57
Antigonus, 220, 228
Antioch, 31
Antiochus III, 221
Antiochus IV (Epiphanes), 226–227, 232
Antipater, 228
Antitype, 33ff., 142
Aod, 154
"Apocalypse of Isaia," 194, 231
"Apocalypse of Zacharia," 213
Apocalyptic genre, 28, 231
Apocrypha, 224, 226
Aramaic, 115, 241
Arameans, 183
Arbela, 220
Aristobulus, 228
Aristotle, 31, 220
Ark, 78–79

Ark of the Covenant;
at Silo, 149, 156
and Temple, 175, 199
brought to Jerusalem by David, 164–165
built, 124–125
crossing of Jordan, 146
locations of, 171
loss of, 199, 226
Artaxerxes I, 214
Artaxerxes III, 237
Ashley, B. M., 132
Asiongaber, 176
Asperges of Mass, 166, 207
Assuerus, 217
Assyria, 191, 203, 237
captivity of Israel, 183, 193–194, 203, 224
Astrue, Jean, 32
Augsburg Confession, 88
Augustine, St., 15, 31–32, 36, 91
Authorship, biblical, 143, 173, 188, 198
Autographs, 15

Baal, 181, 243
Baal–Phogor, 136
Babel, Tower of, 6, 74, 80, 243
Babylon, 193–200, 202, 203, 211
Babylonian Exile, 1, 184, 198ff.
return from, 211ff.
"Bad Figs," 201
Balaam, 135–136
Balac, 135
Ban, 148ff.
Baptism, types of, 79, 142
Barac, 154
Baruch, 10, 201, 222
Bauer, Bruno, 2
Bel, 235
Belsassar, 233
"Benedicite," The, 232–233
Benedict XV, 41
Benjamin, 98, 156, 177, 218
Benoit, Pierre, 30, 35
Bethel, 97, 157, 177, 182
Bethlehem, 194
Bethsabee, 166, 170
Bethsamites, 157
Bethulia, 237
Bible
and Church, 7
and science, 40

and Tradition, 8
criticism of, 1–6
debunking of, 1–4
definition of, 44
Bible, versions of
Confraternity, xxi, 242
Douay–Rheims, 242
Jerusalem, xxi, 94, 179, 240
King James, 242
Revised Standard, xxiii, 242
Septuagint, 241–242
Smith–Goodspeed, xxiii, 242
Vulgate, 44, 242
Biblical Commission, 39, 46, 163
Biblical Theology, 38
Bitter Lakes, 113
B'nai Berith, 138
Book of the Covnenant, 121
Booz, 151
Bouyer, Louis, 118, 125, 199, 240
Brillet, Gaston, 99–100
Bronze Age, 75
Brown, R. E., 31, 35, 240
Byron, Lord, 194

Cain, 74–75
Caleb, 134
Callan, Charles, 55, 73
Canon of Scripture, 222
Canticle of Anna, 158
Canticle of Canticles, 179, 186, 218
Canticle of Debora, 154
Canticle of Moses, 113
Cariathiarim, 157, 171
Causes of Bible, 11
efficient, 11ff.
final, 43
formal, 11, 22
material, 11, 22
Census, 132–133, 167
Cetura, 70
Chaldeans, 82, 198, 232
Chanaan, Son of Ham, 79
Chanaan, Land of, 84ff.
Chanaanites, 6, 84, 116–117, 147ff., 151, 243
Charlier, Celestin, 12, 42–43
"Chosen People," 82, 117, 212, 236
Christ, see Jesus
Chronicler, The, 144–146, 162–163, 177, 197, 211, 215, 222
Chronicle, Books of, see Paralipomenon

Church
  as Body of Christ, 6
  as a worshipping community, 215
  as Kingdom of God and the New
    Israel, 236
  formation of, 6
  and Tradition, 7
  types of, 79, 207, 209
Circumcision, 85, 146
Cities of Refuge, 141
Clement of Alexandria, St., 31
The "Cloud," 111, 134, 222
Coholeth, 219
Commandments, Ten, see Decalogue;
  the Great Commandment, 138, 184
Compenetration, 167, 180, 192
Comparative Religions, 2
Concordism, 3, 26
Confidence, Psalms of, 88, 144, 167,
  169
Core, 134
Cosmogony, Semitic, 47
Covenant
  Amos and the, 182
  at Sinai, 115
  Ezechiel and the, 205–206
  Jeremia and "New", 201
  Mosaic, 111–112, 124, 137–138
  Ratification of, 124
  Renewal of, 126, 142, 150, 160, 196,
    215
  with Abraham, 85
  with Noe, 79
Creation, 46ff., 51ff., 227, 244
  Priestly Tradition, 48–51
  Yahwist Tradition, 51ff.
"Credo," Hebrew, 142
Criticism, biblical, 1–6
Crowley, E. J., 194
Cyrus the Great, 207ff., 211
"Cyrus Cylinder," 208

Dalila, 155
Dan, Tribe of, 155, 177
Daniel, 171, 232ff.
Danielou, Jean, 144
Darius, 220
"Darius the Mede," 233
Darwin, Charles, 2
Dathan, 135
"Daughters of men," 76, 81

David
  and the Ark, 164
  and Messia, 90, 136, 151, 161, 165,
    167, 200, 213
  and Psalms, 163ff., 214, 241
  dynasty of, 145, 165, 170, 176, 188ff.
    198, 212–213, 236
  ideal king, 161, 179
  platform of, 164
Day of Atonement, 131
"Day of the Lord," 182–183, 189, 193,
  195, 216, 236
Dead Sea Scrolls, 6, 229
Debora, 154
Decalogue, 115–118, 122–124, 137
Deism, 1
Deluge, see Flood
Demetrius, 1, 227
Demonology, 67, 225
Deposits of faith, 39
Deutero-, see "Second"
Deuterocanonical books, 224, 241–242
Deuteronomic code, 121, 137–139
Deuteronomic history, 146, 177, 179
Deuteronomic principle, 145, 154, 174,
  197, 218–219
Deuteronomic reform, 140, 196–197
Deuteronomic tradition, 137, 139
Deuteronomy, 137ff., 196
De Vault, Joseph, 147
Devil, see Satan
Diaspora, 217, 241
"Dies Irae," 195
Dina, 92–93
"Divino Afflante Spiritu," 23–25
Divorce, 140, 216
Documentary hypothesis, 2
Douay–Rheims Version, 85, 174, 183,
  234
Dramatic dialogue, 27
"Dry bones," 206
Dyson, R. A., and Jones, A., 89, 101,
  170, 180, 236, 240

Eber, 80
Ecclesiastes, 61, 131, 218–219
Ecclesiasticus, see Sirach
École Biblique, 4
Eden, 58–66
Edomites, 94, 137, 165, 201, 202
Efficient cause, 11ff.
Eglon, 154

Egypt: meaning, 111, 137
El-Elyon, 84
El-Shaddai, 105
Elcana, 156
Elders, 134, 229
Eleazar, 227
Elias, 180–181, 216
Eliseus, 180–182
Ellis, Peter, xxii, xxiii, 200, 237
Elohim, 57, 66, 103
Elohist Tradition, 51, 97, 115, 212
  and Abraham, 86
  and Exodus, 102–103
Emmanuel, 192
Empires (chart), Inside Covers
Endor, witch of, 162
Ephraim (and Manasses), 93–99; 190
Epic poetry, 27
"Epiphanes," 227
Esau, 91–94
Esdras, 145–146, 211ff., 217
Essenes, 229, 236
Esther, 217–218, 238
Eucharist (in type), 114, 143
Euphrates, 59
Eve, 59ff., 68ff.
Evilmerodach, 198
Evolution, 2, 62–05
  chart, 64–65
Exile, 183–183, 194ff.
  see also Babylonian Exile
Exodus, Book of, 101ff.
Exodus from Egypt, 111–112
  date of, 101–102
  "New Exodus," 142, 200
Ezechia, 174, 179, 190ff.
Ezechiel, 107, 204ff., 216
Ezra, see Esdras
Faith, 85–88, 195
Fall, The, 67ff.
Fathers of the Church, 39
Feasts, Principal, 130, 142
Federaman, Xiel, 6
Fernandez, A., 34
Fertile Crescent, 6, 82–83
Firmament, 47–50, 244
Flight, J. W., 175
Flood, 6, 74ff.
Formalism in religion, 182ff., 189, 197
"Former Prophets," 158, 215

French Revolution, 31
Fuller sense, 32ff., 58, 67, 201
Fundamentalists, 3, 22

Gabaon, 148, 171
Gabriel, 235
Galaadites, 155
Galgal, 157, 161, 182
Galileo, 4
Gedeon, 154–155
Gelin, Albert, 55, 169, 239
Gemara, 141
Genealogies, 9, 27, 41, 74ff., 77, 90
Genesis, Book of, 46ff., 243
Genres, Semitic literary, 21ff.
  definition, 22
  list of, 27–29
  of Psalms, 169
  Pius XII and, 23–25
Gesen, 96
Geth, 162, 164
Gifts of Holy Spirit, 192
Gnosticism, 230
Gog, 206, 231
Golden Calf, 125
Goldin, Rabbi, 144
Goliath, 161
Gomer, 185
Gomorra, 6, 85
Grace, 60–61, 207
Gradual Psalms, 169
Graff, K., 2
Greek
  conquest, 203, 220
  culture, 220, 226ff., 238
  language, 117, 238, 241–242
  thought patterns, 26
Grollenberg, L., xxiv
Gunkel, Herman, 168
Guy, P. L. O., 6

Habacuc, 195, 235
Haggada, 118, 141
Hai, 148
Halacha, 141
Hallel, 120
Ham, 79–80
Handel's "Messiah," 208
"Handwriting on the wall," 233
Hannukah, 227
Haran, 82, 87
Hasidim, 227, 230, 232, 235, 237

Hasmonean, 227, 236–237
Hasseveldt, R., 81, 107
Hauret, Charles, 66–68
Hebrew, 80, 117, 241–242
Hebrew Bible, 158
Hegel, G. W. F., 2
Helcias, 196
Heli, 156
Hellenization, see Greek
Henley, William E., 1
Henoch, 76, 239
Henry, A. M., 115
Herem, 138, 147
Hermeneutics, 21ff.
Herod the Great, 228
Hesed, 120, 186
Hethites, see Hittites
"Hexateuch," 145
High places, 171, 179, 186, 197
Historico–lilterary method, 22
History, use in Scripture, 27, 40–41
Hittites, 87, 150
Holiness of God, 129, 188ff.
Holofernes, 237
Holy of Holies, 124–125, 131, 171
"Holy ones of the Most High," 234
Horeb, 104, 138
Huesman, J. E., 210
Hunt, Ignatius, 84, 92
"Humani Generis," 62, 71
Hyksos, 96, 102
Hymn, 55, 169
Hyrcanus, 228

Idolatry, 119, 125, 177, 182, 187, 189, 243
Immanence, 201ff.
Immortality, 59, 61, 69, 173, 239
Impassibility, 58, 61, 69
Imprecatory Psalms, 147
Inerrancy, biblical, 14–17, 36
Inspiration, biblical
  criteria of, 44
  false theories, 18–19
  notion of, 11ff.
Instrumental cause, 9ff.
Integrity, 59, 61, 68
"Invictus," 1
Iron, 75, 154
Isaac, 86–87, 90
Isai, 161

Isaia, 180, 188
  First Isaia, 188ff.
  Second Isaia, 207ff.
Isboseth, 163
Ismael, 86, 91
Israel:
  Kingdom of, 177, 183
    exile of, 183–186, 193–194
  Jacob's new name, 93–94

Jabel, 75
Jabin, 154
Jahel, 154
Jacob, 82, 90ff., 96–99, 101
  changed to Israel, 93
James, St., 88, 147, 195
Jamnia, Council of, 241
Japheth, 77, 79–80
Jason, 226
Jebusites, 164
Jechonia, 198, 205
Jechonia (Joachim), 198, 205
Jehovah, 105
Jehu, 181
Jephte, 155
Jeremia, 170, 198ff., 219, 236
  and III–IV Kings, 170
  "Confessions" of, 200
  "Seventy Years," 200
  "New Covenant," 201
Jericho, 146–147
Jeroboam I, 177
Jeroboam II, 182
Jerome, St., 44
Jerusalem
  and Temple, 175
  capital by David, 164
  central sanctuary, 139, 149, 171
  destruction of, 198–199
  "New Jerusalem," 207, 209, 213
  walls rebuilt, 214
Jesse, 161
Jesus Christ
  and Church, 7, 186
  Davidic descendant, 176
  "Josue," "Osee," 146
  "Son of Man," 234, 236
  typology, 192, 208, 209, 210
Jethro, 104, 115
"Jews," 211
Jezebel, 181
Joab, 163–4, 166, 171

Joachaz, 198
Joachin (Jechonia), 198, 205
Joakim, 198
Job, 35, 200, 219–220, 239
Joel, 216
John Chrysostom, St., 31
John the Evangelist, St., 114, 206, 213, 222, 230
John, son of Simon, 228
Jona, Book of, 209
Jonathan, 162–163; 227
Jordan River, 146, 150
Joseph, 96–100, 172
Josia, 174, 196ff., 213
Josue, 114, 134, 146, 212
    Book of, 145ff.
Jubal, 75
Juda, 94–98
    Kingdom of, 177, 193, 211, 222
        exile, 198ff., 206
    Tribe of, 163, 177
Judaism, 211, 214–215, 225
Judas Machabeus, 226–228
Jude, Epistle of, 136, 142
Judges, Book of, 153ff.
    role of, 115, 153
Judith, 93, 237
Justification, 85–88, 195

Kashruth, 129ff.
Keller, Werner, 6, 114
King James Bible, 192
King, Philip, 159, 169
Kingdom of God, 7–10, 230, 235ff.
Kings, Books of, 27, 146, 157ff., 163, 170, 179, 226
Kingship in Israel, 160–161, 179
    Psalms of Yahweh's, 106, 165, 169
Kir, 183
"Knowledge of God," 186, 201
Kraeling, Emil, 81

Laban, 92–93
Lagrange, M. J., 4
Lamech, 75–76
Lament, Psalms of, 73, 169
Lamentations, Book of, 198
Lamuel, 174
Languages, Semitic, 116–117
Lateran, Fourth Council of, 72
Law, 115–116
    kinds of, 121–124

Law of Holiness, 121, 130
Leakey, L. S. B., 62
Legal literature, 27–28
Leo XIII, 4, 12, 14–18, 23, 39
Leviathan, 243
Levi, 93, 99, 105, 107
Levirate marriage, 94, 140, 151
Levites, 125, 128–129, 134, 141, 149, 157, 164, 175, 207, 214–215, 230
Leviticus, Book of, 127ff.
Lia, 92–93
Liberal Protestantism, 3
Litany, 120
Liturgy
    and Exodus, 110–112
    and Old Testament, 131
    and Psalms, 54
    and Temple, 175
    Divine Office, 54, 199, 233, 239
    Holy Week, 142–143, 186, 199
    Mass, 92, 174, 189, 207, 216, 230
    Virgin Mary in, 199, 238, 245
"Localization" of Yahweh, 197, 205
Loisy, Alfred, 4
Lot, 82, 84
Love of God, 138
Love of neighbor, 130
Lucian, St., 31
Luke, St., 53, 104, 124, 158, 182, 229
Luther, Martin, 88

Machabees, 227–228, 237
Machabees, Books of, 17, 217, 220ff., 226ff., 231, 241
MacKenzie, R. A. F., 143, 147
Madianites, 90, 104, 154
Magisterium, Church's, 36, 39
"Magnificat," 158
Magog, 206
Maher-shalal-hash-baz, 193
Malachia, 216
Maly, Eugene, 240
Manasses, 98–99; 196
Manna, 114
"Manual of Discipline," 229
Marathon, 220
Mardochai, 217
Marduk, 208, 243
Mari, 6
Mariam, 113, 134–135
Mark, St., 208, 234

Marriage, concept of, 59–62, 92, 224–225, 245
  mixed, 171, 214–216
  see also Polygamy
Masphath, 157
Massa, 114
Massoretic Text, 163
Mathathias, 227–228
Matthew, St., 53, 138–139, 147, 151, 194, 195, 209
Mathusale, 76
McEleney, Neil, 121
McKenzie, John L., xxii, 68, 70, 118, 243
Medes, 211
Meeting Tent, 124–126
Megiddo, 6, 176, 197
Melanchthon, Philip, 88
Melchisedec, 84–85, 165–166
Menelaus, 226
Meriba, 114
Mesopotamia, 78, 82, 173
Messianic line, 90ff., 165, 198
Messianism
  Essenes' view, 230
  in Daniel, 184
  in prophecy, xix–xxii
  in Psalms, 165–166, 237
  individual, 198
  true vs. false, 235–237
"Methode Historique, La," 4
Michael, 235
Michea, 165, 182, 194
Michol, 93, 163, 165
Midrash, 118, 141, 173
Mishle, 173
Mishna, 141
Moabites, 86, 135–137, 151, 165, 177, 214
Modernism, 4
Monogamy, 59, 85
Monophyleticism, 72
Monotheism, 8, 138, 222, 243
Morality, Old Testament, 42, 84
Moriarty, F., 106, 135, 143, 240
Mosaic Law, 87, 95, 121ff., 214, 222
Moses, 102ff., 168
  and wisdom, 172, 222
  birth and calling, 104
  death, 142
  Pentateuch, 2, 102, 143
  sin of, 135

Murphy, R. E., xxii, 118, 223
Myths in Bible, 79, 243–244

Naaman, 181
Nabath, 225
Nabonidus, 232
Nabuschodonosor, 198, 201, 232
Nahum, 195
Nathan, 165, 166–167
Nationalism, 183, 210, 218, 236, 242
Natural Law, 115, 122–123
Nazarite Vow, 133, 155, 156
Necho, 197
Nefretiri, 104
Nehemia, 211ff., 214, 241
"New Creation," 208
"New Heart," 204–206
Ninive, 195–196, 209, 224
Nobe, 161, 164, 171
Noe, 76–79
North, Robert, 169
Numbers, Book of, 132ff.
Numerology, Book of, 132ff.
Nuptial image, 186, 199, 205

Obededom, 164
Ochozia, 181
O'Doherty, E., xxii
Oesterly, W. O. E., and Robinson, T. H., 126
Og, 135
Old Testament: literary history, 53, 215, 241–242
Onan, 94
Onias, 226
Ophni, 156
Origen, 31
Original Justice, 58ff., 72
Original Sin, 67–69, 72
Osee, 146; 185, 193, 201, 227
Othoniel, 154
Oza, 163–164
Ozia, 188

Palestine, 149
  canon of, 241–242
Pantheism, 72
Parable, 26
Paralipomenon, Books of, 145–146, 162–163, 167, 171, 177, 179, 211, 226
Parthians, 228

Index

Paschal Lamb, 110, 112, 143
"Pascendi," 4
Passover, 110–112, 130
Patriarchs, praise of, 222
Paul, St., references to: 16, 31, 44, 86–87, 91, 105, 107, 118, 120, 124, 126, 142, 144, 200, 208, 220, 222, 238
Penitential Psalms, 166, 169
Pentateuch
   authorship, 2, 102, 143
   division of laws, 122–124
   formation of, 121, 139, 215
   promulgated by Esdras, 215, 241
   traditions in, 139
Pentecost, 131, 142
"Period" Theory, 3
Persians, 203, 211ff., 232, 237
Personal responsibility, 200, 205
Peter, St., 216
Phacee, 192
Pharao, 35, 84, 97–98, 103, 197
   daughter of, 171, 179
Phares, 94
Pharisees, 228–229, 236
Philistines, 6, 155ff., 161, 166
"Philosophical Approach" to biblical criticism, 2
Philosophy, Bible and, 41
Phinees, 136, 156
Phithon, 6, 102
Phoenica, 116
Pilgrim Psalms, 169
Pillar of Fire, 111, 222
Pius X, St., 4
Pius XII, 23–25, 62, 71
Plagues, 108–110, 118–119
Plato, 220, 243
Poetry, Hebrew, 28, 148, 180, 243
Polygamy, 42, 85, 91, 176
Polygenism, 71–72
Polytheism, 84
Pompey, 179
Ponce de Leon, 59
Positive Law, 115, 122–124
Prayer in Old Testament, 54
Precepts, division of, 115–116, 122–124, 140
Pre-Chanaanite, 115
Predestination, 107
Preternatural gifts, 60–61

Priesthood in Israel, 115, 128, 213–215, 227–229.
   of Messia, 165–166
Priestly Tradition, 51–53, 57, 78, 102–105, 107–109, 113, 215
   in Genesis, 48–51, 53
"Priestly Torah," 146
Prophecies, messianic, xix
Prophecy, nature of, 28, 107, 157, 158, 180, 182
Prophets, "Former," 158, 215. "Latter," 222
Propitiatory, 124–125, 134
Protestant, canon, 241–242
Proverbs, Book of, 173–175, 218
Providence, 97ff., 221, 225
"Providentissimus Deus," 4, 12, 14–19, 23
Psalms
   authorship, 163–164
   genres, 169
   index, inside back cover
   introduction to, 54, 168
   numbering, 168
"Psalms of Solomon," 236
Psalter, see Psalms
Ptolomies, 220, 228
Purim, 217

Quail, 114
Qumran, 6, 229, 236
Quotations in Bible, 17

Rachel, 92–94
Raguel, 104
Rahab, 94, 146, 151; 243
Rameses, City of, 6, 102
Rameses II, 105
Raphael 224
Rasin, 190
Rationalism, 1–3, 32
Rebecca, 91
Red (Reed) Sea, 113, 142
Redemeptive suffering, 209, 219
Remnant, 181, 184, 190, 201, 206
Renan, Ernest, 3
"Reproaches," 195
Resurrection of body, 227, 229, 235, 239, 240
Retribution, problem of, 239
Revelation, 13, 43
Revised Standard Version, xxv, 242

Riciotti, G., 230
Ritual Decalogue, 121, 126
Robert and Tricot, 116, 237
Roboam, 177
Romans, 227–230
Rosh Hashanah, 131
Royal Psalms, 131, 165, 169, 179, 237
Ruben, 94, 97, 99, 135
Rules of interpretation
  general, 17
  particular, 35–40
Ruth, 151, 161

Sabbath, 50, 55, 114–115, 214, 227, 245
Sacraments and Bible, 43, 63
Sacrifices 127–128, 130
  "new sacrifice," 216
Sadducees, 222, 228–229
Sadoc, 171, 207, 228
Salmon, 147
Salmanasar, 193
Salvation history, 5–10
Salvation vs. justification, 88
Samaria, 177, 193
Samaritans, 193, 212–213
Samson, 133, 155
Samuel, 156–158, 160–162
Samuel, Books of, see Kings, I–II
Sanaballat, 214
Sanctuary, unity of, 139–140, 149–150, 171
Sanctus of Mass, 190
Sandmel, Samuel, 5
Sanhedrin, 229
Sapiential Books, 28, 218ff.
Sara, 82ff.; 224
Sargon II, 193
Sassabassar, 212
Satan, 67–69, 108, 239
Saul, 158, 160ff., 167, 218
Schism, 149–150, 177
Scholastics, 31
Science and Bible, 40
Scouts, Twelve, 134
Scribe, 214, 229
Second Isaia, 207ff.
Second Zacharia, 213
Sedecia, 198
Sehon, 135
Sem, 77, 79–80
Semei, 171

Semites
  language, 116
  literary genres, 21ff.
  thought patterns, 25ff.
Sennacherib, 193
Senses of Scripture, 30ff.
Septuagint, 157, 163, 241
Serpent, devil as, 67–69, 239
Serpent, brazen, 135
Servant Songs, 208–209
Seth, 76
Sheets, J. R., 32
Shekinah, 124, 181, 222
Shema, 138
Sheol, 47, 97, 239
Shepherd symbolism, 88, 99, 213
Shibboleth, 155
"Shoot," 192, 200, 213
Sichem, 93, 139, 150
Siegman, E. F., 39, 210
"Silent Period," 217
Silo, 149, 150, 156, 171
Siloe, 193
Simeon, 93, 99, 177
Simon, 222, 227–228
Simon, Richard, 32
Sinai, 104, 181
Sirach, 8, 35, 221ff., 239, 241
Sisara, 154
Smith–Goodspeed Bible, 157
Socrates, 220
Sodom, 6, 86
Sodomy, 86, 119
Solomon, 6, 35, 67, 101, 141, 166, 170ff., 214
  and wisdom, 172ff., 186, 218, 222
"Son of Man," 234ff.
Songs of Sion, 152
"Sons of God," 76, 81, 239
Sophonia, 194, 195
"Space men," 72
"Spiritus Paraclitus," 41
Steinmann, Jean, 10
Strauss, D. G., 2
Studiousness, 221
Stuhlmueller, C., vii, 7, 131, 202, 207, 211, 214
"Stump," 190
Suffering Servant, 208, 210
Sullivan, Mother K., 230
Summa Theologica, 32, 57, 61, 71
Supernatural gift, 60–61

Index

Susanna, 235
Symbols, 142–143, 244–245
Synagogues, 229
Synave, Paul, 30, 35
Syncretism, 204
Syrians, 177, 190
Syro–Ammonite War, 165

Tabernacle, 124–125, 171, 175
Tabernacles, Feast of, 131
Talmud, 141, 229
"Teacher of Righteousness," 230
Temple, 175ff., 205–207, 230
    abomination of, 205, 232
    and synagogue, 229
    destruction of, 198–199, 205, 234
    rebuilt, 212–213
Temptations of Christ, 138
Ten Commandments, see Decalogue
    motion picture, 104–105
Thamar, 94–95
Thare, 82
Thanksgiving, Psalms of, 120, 166, 169
Theandric nature of Bible, 42
Theocracy, 117, 154, 206
Theology of history, 137, 145, 212, 215, 238
Theology and Bible, 32, 41
Theophany, 115, 181
"Theoria," 32
Thomas, D. Winton, 243
Thomas Aquinas, St., 32, 61, 88
Thubalcain, 75
Tiamat, 243
Tobias, Book of, 14, 224–225, 242
Tobias the Samaritan, 214
Torah, outline of precepts, 140
    and Sadducees, 228–229
    and Sirach, 221–222
    obedience to, 215, 219, 224–225, 238
    promulgation by Esdras, 215
Tradition and Bible, 7–10, 44
Tradition of the Ancients, 141, 229
Traditions in Pentateuch, 51ff., 102–103, 215, 243
Transcendence of God, 85, 93, 164, 181, 188ff., 195, 204–205, 208, 219
Treaties, 150
Tree of Knowledge, 59, 67–68, 80
Tree of Life, 57, 59, 61
Trent, Council of, 32, 242
Tribal Confederecy, 150, 153

Tribes, Twelve, 149
"Trunk," 190
Tryphon, 227
"Two Ways," 174, 218
Typical sense, 32–35, 192
Typology, 30, 67, 71, 86, 98, 124, 131, 135, 142–143, 185, 234

Ugarit, 6
Universalism, Jewish, 151–152, 181, 183, 204, 209–210, 216, 240
Ur, 82
Urias, 166
Urim and Thummin, 128
Utopian Model, 29, 194, 207, 209, 216

Vashti, 217
Vaux, Roland de, xxv
Vawter, Bruce, xxv, 81
Vicarious satisfaction, 209, 236
Vulgate, 44

Weiser, Artur, 169
Wellhausen, Julius, 2
Wisdom literature, 28, 171ff., 217ff.
Wisdom, Book of, 118–120, 151, 172, 222, 238–239
Wisdom
    Movement, 34–35, 172, 201, 218ff.
    obedience to Torah, 215, 219, 222, 224, 238
    personified, 172, 222
    Psalms, 81, 95, 169, 173, 184, 195, 240
Wooley, Sir Leonard, 6
Wright and Fuller, xxvi
"Writings," 158, 217

Xerxes, 217

Yahwist Tradition, 57–60, 67ff., 78, 102–103, 113, 212
    and Genesis, 51ff.
    Yahwist–Elohist, 104, 107ff., 212
YHWH, 104–106
"Yom," 3

Zacharia, 212
Zealots, 237
Zinjanthropus, 63
Zorobabel, 212

Index of Psalms

PSALM	PAGE	PSALM	PAGE
1	**81**	41	**230**
2	164, 166	42	**230**
3	166	43	
4		44	**179**
5		45	169
+6	169	46	**106**, 244
7		47	
8	55, **66**, 234	48	
9		49	**184**
10		+50	**166**, 169
11		51	164
12		52	81, 167
13	17, 81, 167	53	164
14	169	54	
15	164, **167**, 180	55	164
16		56	164, 167
17	115, **166**, 168	57	
18	**126**, 245	58	164
19	**131**	59	165, 167
20	**131**	60	166
21	**210**	61	
22	**88**, 99	62	166
23	132, **164, 175**	63	
24		64	
25		65	
26		66	
27		67	134
28	55, **243**	68	147
29		69	167
30	210	70	
+31	131, 164	71	166, 168, **237**
32		72	219, **240**
33		73	243
34	147	74	
35		75	169, 194
36	219	76	142
+37	169	77	**95**
38	218	78	
39	167	79	
40		80	

+ Penitential Psalm

* Gradual or Pilgrim Psalm

Index of Psalms

PSALM	PAGE	PSALM	PAGE
81		116	152
82		117	169
83	169	118	**222**
84		*119	
85		*120	
86	**152**, 169	*121	
87		*122	
88		*123	
89	144, 168	*124	
90	67, **144**	*125	
91		*126	168, **173**
92	106, 244	*127	
93		*128	
94	134, **136**, 139	+129*	**73**, 169
95	167	*130	*
96	106, 244	*131	**165**, 169
97		*132	
98	106, 125, 244	*133	134
99	55	134	112, 120
100	**164**	135	**120**, 135
+101	169	136	169, **202**
102	**186**	137	
103	**55**, 66	138	169, **195**, 240
104	55, **100**, 167	139	
105	28, **100**, 169	140	
106		141	164
107	167	+142	169
108	**147**, 169	143	
109	84, **165**, 167	144	
110	221	145	
111		146	**216**
112	112	147	**216**
113	55, **112**, 118	148	
114		149	
115		150	

+ Penitential Psalm

* Gradual or Pilgrim Psalm

TIME CHART OF BIBLE HISTORY, Continued

Time scale (left): 400 B.C. · 350 B.C. · 300 B.C. · 250 B.C. · 200 B.C. · 150 B.C. · 100 B.C. · 50 B.C.

PALESTINE (Hebrews)

- Judah part of Fifth Persian Satrapy
- Jews under Greek rule
- Ptolemaic control 301
- Seleucid control of Palestine
- Revolt of Maccabees 167
- Judas Macca-baeus 166-160
- Jonathan 160-142
- Simon 142-134
- John Hyrcanus 134-104
- Temple of Horus
- Aristobulus I 104-103
- Alexander Jannaeus 103-76
- Alexandra 76-67
- Aristobulus II 67-63
- Pompey enters Jerusalem 63
- Hyrcanus II 63-40

EGYPT

- XXIX
- XXX
- XXXI Persians regain control
- Alexander conquers Egypt
- Ptolemy I 323-285
- Pharos lighthouse
- Ptolemy II 285-246
- Ptolemy III 246-221
- Ptolemy IV 221-203
- Battle of Raphia 217
- Ptolemy V 203-181
- Ptolemy VI 181-145
- Later Ptolemies subject to Roman domination 168-30 B.C.
- Cyrenaica given to Rome 96
- Decline of Seleucid Kingdom
- Syria annexed by Pompey 64

MESOPOTAMIA AND SYRIA

Persian control

Battle of Issus 333

Seleucus I 312-280

SELEUCID KINGDOM 312-64 B.C.

- Antiochus I 280-261
- Antiochus II 261-246
- Seleucus II 246-226
- Seleucus III 226-223
- Antiochus III (the Great) 223-187
- War with Rome 192-189
- Seleucus IV 187-175
- Antiochus IV (Epiphanes) 175-163
- Antiochus V 163-162
- Demetrius I 162-150
- Demetrius II 145-139
- Antiochus VII 138-129
- Mithridates VI of Pontus 131-63

Roman aqueduct

ROME

- Sack of Rome by Gauls c. 390
- Samnite & Latin Wars 343-290
- War with Pyrrhus 282-272
- 1st Punic War 264-241
- Sicily Roman 241
- 2nd Punic War 218-201
- Hannibal in Italy
- Spain annexed 201
- 3rd Punic War 149-146
- Corinth & Carthage destroyed 146
- Revolt of the Gracchi 133, 122
- Jugurthine (African) War 111-105
- 1st Mithridatic War 88-85
- Sulla dictator 82-79
- 3rd Mithridatic War (Lucullus & Pompey) 74-63
- Caesar's conquest of Gaul 58-51
- Civil War 49-46
- Caesar

GREECE

- Philip of Macedon 359-336
- Alexander the Great 336-323
- ALEXANDER'S EMPIRE
- Wars of the Diadochi 322-279
- Aetolian League
- Achaean League
- Celtic invasion 279
- Macedonian Wars against Rome 215-148
- Macedon falls to Rome

PHOENICIA

- Alexander takes Tyre 332
- Ptolemaic control
- Seleucid control
- Ptolemy II regains control 275
- Arsaces I est. Kdm. of Parthia 248
- Arsaces II secures independence 225
- Seleucid invasion
- Mithridates I 171-138
- Tyre independent 120.
- Sidon independent 111
- Roman rule 64

PERSIA

- Artaxerxe 358-3
- Arses 338-3
- Darius III 336-330
- Conquest Alexan
- Seleucid control
- Diodotus Bactria Kdm. 25
- Euthyde 230-1

BACTRIAN KINGDOM

- Demet conqu n. India

PARTHIAN EMPIRE

- Scythia end Bact Kdm. 139
- Mithridates (the Great) 124-88
- Tigranes of Armenia seizes western provs.
- Phraates II 70-57
- Orodes I 57-
- Defeat of Crassus 53

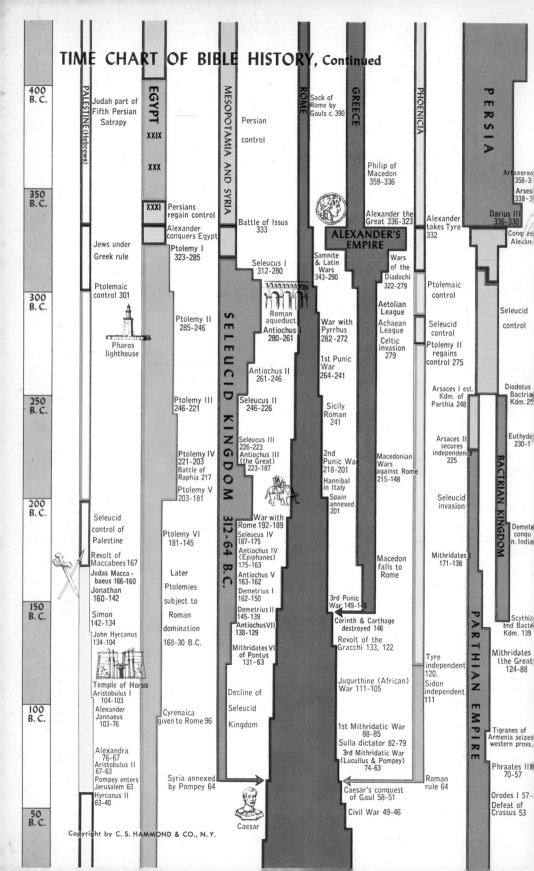